ARBITRATION ISSUES FOR THE 1980s

ARBITRATION ISSUES
FOR THE 1980s

PROCEEDINGS OF THE THIRTY-FOURTH
ANNUAL MEETING
NATIONAL ACADEMY OF ARBITRATORS

Maui, Hawaii   May 4–8, 1981

Edited by
James L. Stern
Professor of Economics
The University of Wisconsin

and

Barbara D. Dennis
Editorial Associate
The University of Wisconsin

The Bureau of National Affairs, Inc.   Washington, D.C.

Library of Congress Cataloging in Publication Data

Arbitration issues for the 1980s.

   Includes indexes.
   1. Arbitration, Industrial—Congresses. I. Stern,
James L. II. Dennis, Barbara D. III. National Academy
of Arbitrators.
HD5481.A75   331.89'143   81-20658
ISBN 0-87179-374-1   AACR2

Printed in the United States of America
International Standard Book Number: 0-87179-374-1

PREFACE

Those members and guests who made the long trek to Hawaii distinguished themselves by faithfully attending the various sessions despite the lure of the attractive surroundings of the Maui meeting place. Although total attendance was down—probably because of travel costs—the ratio of members to guests was higher than usual, and there was more time for members to chat informally with each other and with familiar guests who had attended many of our past meetings. This contributed to an "Aloha" atmosphere in which all of us relaxed and enjoyed both the formal meetings and casual conversations.

Arbitration of disputes involving nonrepresented and unorganized employees was considered at our opening session. We learned how it worked in U.S. plants as well as how the English did it. At noon we heard about the I.L.O. and the international labor scene. And, that night, for those of us who still had the strength, there was a session at which public-sector interest arbitration in Australia, Canada, and the U.S. were compared. Interest arbitration in the public sector was again the topic under discussion at another meeting later in the week.

The familiar subject of "Remedies" was covered in a double session at which we looked again at old problems and also considered a few new ones. For those arbitrators who thought that one session on remedies was sufficient, there was another meeting going on simultaneously at which trends in grievance arbitration in the federal service were considered.

We also had a double session on "How Others View Us" and heard critiques of the arbitration process from a federal judge, a state judge, and representatives of the NLRB and the EEOC. The remaining meeting was about tripartite arbitration of both rights and interests disputes.

In her Presidential Address, Eva Robins listed thirteen threats to arbitration that have been raised over the years and drew our attention particularly to the need for new arbitrators and advocates alike to understand the negotiation process and the importance of contributing to the maintenance of a sound continuing relationship.

The Editors wish to express the appreciation of the Officers and

Executive Board members of the Academy to Dan Collins, the Program Chairman, and his committee, and to Ted Tsukiyama, the Arrangements Chairman, and his committee, for the work they did in connection with what most participants considered to be an outstanding meeting. The Editors are grateful to the authors for the promptness with which they submitted their papers, enabling us to get this year's Proceedings out on time.

James L. Stern
Barbara D. Dennis

July 1981

CONTENTS

CHAPTER 1

THE PRESIDENTIAL ADDRESS: THREATS TO ARBITRATION

EVA ROBINS*

I.

Although I am about to talk of what I perceive to be threats to arbitration, a rather somber pursuit in such glorious surroundings, I should say at the outset that there also are joys for the arbitrator in the arbitration process. Incidents occur at hearings which point up that we deal with a people process. What arbitrator has not wanted to shout with laughter and pleasure because of a surprise event at a hearing!

I remember one such event and the pleasure it gave me. A grievant was asked by union counsel a sort of a throwaway question, "And you want your job back, of course?" The response came fast and clear: "Hell, no, I don't want the job or any back pay—I just want the satisfaction." And I recall my appreciation of the sensitivity of the employer's labor relations vice president who gently invited the stunned union counsel and the grievant into the hallway—to work out the elements of "satisfaction."

One more story and we get to work. I had an interest arbitration dispute involving a police unit and a state employer in which the union was offering in evidence many, many fact-finding reports and arbitration awards as comparability evidence. In the third, or whatever, day of hearing, union counsel continued with the offers, as follows: "And, as Union Exhibit 362, I offer the fact-finding report of Arbitrator A, in a case between the PBA Unit of X Township and the X Township Police Department." As I took the offered document, I noticed that it was illegible; it had been copied so many times as to be impossible to read.

I expressed mild interest in being able to read the exhibits which were received in evidence. Counsel looked them over and

---

*President, 1980–1981, National Academy of Arbitrators, New York, N.Y.

1

agreed that I was right and that the other 361 exhibits also seemed to be illegible. Counsel then resolved the dilemma. Without tongue in cheek, with total seriousness, he said, "Well, Madam Arbitrator, take them for what they're worth." And I did. It is worth noting that the case was settled and I did not need to meet the problem of determining the worth of illegible documents. But I do cherish the experience.

II.

In 1975, at our Annual Meeting held in Puerto Rico, Ben Rathbun, Associate Editor of the Bureau of National Affairs, in a talk titled "Will Success Ruin the Arbitrators,"[1] said that we appeared to be engaged in a form of worship of past presidents. He added, "I hope some future president will open his [sic] address by asserting that he had not reviewed a syllable of the past presidential papers, and that if any of his brilliant remarks happens to coincide with the papers of the past—and many of those were, and are, splendid—so be it." Ben said he thought we were pushing it a bit far—that we were perusing prior presidential papers more exhaustively than Edmund Wilson researched the Dead Sea Scrolls.

You understand that the reason I came across and reread the Rathbun paper was because I was right in the middle of perusing past presidential and other papers, but not as an exercise in hero or heroine worship. My examination came out of an attempt to find out if the subjects I wanted to cover had been talked about too much in the recent past. The trouble is, of course, that when subjects are "over-talked" and "over-revisited," they probably continue to reflect problems that have not been solved. We read past presidents' addresses out of an effort to determine what now should be brought to the attention of our members and guests. The choices are many.

In reading some of the papers presented at our meetings, it is interesting to note that since 1959—in the past 22 years—every meeting has included one or more references in the program talks (presidential addresses or others) to the threats facing labor arbitration as we have known it in the past. From 1959 on (maybe before, too—I did not go any further back), presi-

---

[1]Rathbun, *Will Success Ruin the Arbitrators,* in Arbitration—1975, Proceedings of the 28th Annual Meeting, National Academy of Arbitrators, eds. Barbara D. Dennis and Gerald G. Somers (Washington: BNA Books, 1975), 155–169, at 156.

dents or member or nonmember speakers have referred with concern to such matters as (1) the growing formalization of arbitration and what appeared to some to be a growing effort to convert arbitration into a litigation-type process; (2) what Ben Rathbun called "the dangers of undue judicial intervention in labor-management arbitration";[2] (3) the burden of outside law —EEO, NLRA, OSHA, etc.—imposed on the arbitration process with different criteria and with law enforcement or administrative obligations, rather than private dispute resolution; (4) the reduction of the labor contract's influence as the *sole* criterion in resolving a labor dispute initially arising under that contract, such reduction at least partly due to public-sector arbitration; (5) the growing incidence of grievant representation by personal counsel (with or without union counsel or representation), and personal counsel's lack of knowledge or interest in the continuing relationship between employer and union; (6) the new advocates, without knowledge of or responsibility for continuing relationships, presenting cases as one-shot litigation rather than as arbitration; (7) so-called arbitration in situations where it is *not* final and binding, where the process includes appeals procedures—a growing concern; (8) the increasing incidence of charges against unions alleging failure to represent grievants adequately or properly, and the effect on the arbitration process and on the ability of a union to function responsibly; (9) in the face of the continuing growth of arbitration, the continuing shortage of qualified, knowledgeable, professional arbitrators; (10) the quality of the training of persons who seek in arbitration their major professional careers, either as advocates or as neutrals; (11) written opinions of arbitrators in the arbitration process and, as Sam Kagel once described it, going beyond the "necessities of the case" in writing the opinion;[3] (12) the conduct of the hearing—unnecessary litigation-type conduct of advocates and/or arbitrators; and (13) the increasing cost of arbitration and the delays in arbitration.

These are only some of the areas in which experts have noted present or potential threats to the process. Obviously, I cannot today talk about all of those threats, but I ask you to join me in examining a few of them. For discussions of all of these subjects,

---

[2]*Id.*, at 168.
[3]Kagel, *Recent Supreme Court Decisions and the Arbitration Process*, in Arbitration and Public Policy, Proceedings of the 14th Annual Meeting, National Academy of Arbitrators, ed. Spencer D. Pollard (Washington: BNA Books, 1961), 1–29.

and more, I refer you to the previous issues of the *Proceedings*.
They are worth rereading.

III.

What I most want to talk about today is what arbitration was
and is now; what it has held out and now holds out to the parties,
and how they view the process; how would-be arbitrators are
"trained" or given some understanding of the process in order
to minimize an employer's or union's risk in selecting them; how
the new advocates or representatives are trained or developed;
what the Academy's responsibility is for offering training to
potential arbitrators or advocates; and what the results may be
if we allow a continuation of the effort to remove from arbitration its important characteristic as a process for the establishment of an internal, final and binding system of dispute resolution, growing out of consent.

Arbitration under a labor contract is established by the parties
as the last step of the grievance procedure, to serve their joint
needs. It may be changed by them from time to time, as changes
in their needs appear to dictate. Some changes appear to result
from the confidence or lack of confidence which employers and
unions have in the process. For example, the level within an
employer or union hierarchy at which contract interpretation
disputes are to be decided may differ from plant to plant or
even, within a plant, from department to department. The parties know what they want to achieve: In one employer/union
relationship they might well decide that it is safer to have all
contract interpretation disputes decided at the highest union
and employer level, and they will so provide; in another, equally
thoughtfully, they might have sufficient faith in the judgment
and ability of lower levels of management and union to allow
persons at those levels to make dispute resolution judgments,
and their contracts or practices will so provide. And if the dispute cannot be resolved in their grievance procedure by a full
and proper use of that procedure, they have agreed that, recognizing and accepting their failure, they will, of their own choice,
proceed to use a third party—a stranger—to decide their dispute. The confidence in that selection, too, must be total. The
parties must be confident, from the reputation of the arbitrator
or prior experience with her or him, that the one they select will
justify their designation. They must be persuaded that the final

and binding concept—that important characteristic of arbitration—will not place them at such risk as to warrant change.

The need for arbitration has grown dramatically over the past 20 or 30 years. It no longer can be handled primarily by the "old timers" who participated in the growth of the process in the late thirties or forties, even if that were a desirable option. No longer are there in sufficient numbers the arbitrators who came out of the shining experiences of War Labor Board or similar activities, who grew into the arbitration process and developed it, giving it its deserved reputation for integrity, quality, and knowledge. It was they who persuaded employers and unions to place their faith in this system and in the individuals who were part of the system. Because of what they brought to the process, it has been seen as the best means of resolution of labor/management grievances and perhaps interest disputes.

The great growth in labor arbitration has reached proportions for which we—labor, management, and arbitrators—have made inadequate preparation. Arthur Stark, in his presidential address in 1978, talked of that growth, of the strength and flexibility of the process, and of how the parties have continued to fashion processes that meet their needs.[4] There has not been a year in which grievance arbitration has not shown large growth.

Examine, if you will, some of that growth. In the Federal Mediation and Conciliation Service (FMCS), for the years 1960 compared to 1980, the following case loads have been shown:

	1960	1980	Increase
No. of requests for an arbitration panel:	2,835	29,906	27,071
No. of panels sent out:	2,993	33,327	30,334
No. of appointments made:	2,039	13,911	11,872
No. of awards issued:	1,320	8,405	7,085

All kinds of interesting questions might be looked into as to the meaning of some of those figures, but this is neither the time nor the place to examine those questions. The numbers do raise a question, though, as to the quality of the grievance procedures which, theoretically, should have been fully used and exhausted before the request for arbitration was made.

---

[4]Stark, *The Presidential Address: Theme and Adaptations,* in Truth, Lie Detectors, and Other Problems in Labor Arbitration, Proceedings of the 31st Annual Meeting, National Academy of Arbitrators, eds. James L. Stern and Barbara D. Dennis (Washington: BNA Books, 1978), 1–29.

The American Arbitration Association (AAA) keeps its figures in a different fashion. In 1951, AAA had a countrywide total of 1,403 requests for arbitration panels and, with a 30 percent settlement estimate (as their general rule of thumb), it had less than 1,000 cases that actually went to arbitration in that year. In 1960, it had 3,231 requests, and an estimated 2,262 cases arbitrated. In 1980, AAA's figures had jumped to 17,061 requests and an estimated 11,944 cases arbitrated to decision.

These figures represent only two of the major designating agencies. Other cases go to arbitrators through the National Mediation Board, state and local designating agencies, public-sector designators, ad hoc direct designation by the parties, the great impartial chairmanships, and the parties naming their own arbitrators in their contracts. As only one example of the growth of public- (or quasi-public) sector arbitration, the United States Postal Service and the several unions that represent its employees entered into the Service's arbitration processes in 1980 a countrywide total of 9,824 "regular" arbitration cases and 4,115 "expedited" cases. Many hundreds of private arrangements are made, where the parties agree on arbitration procedures tailored to meet their needs and directly name the arbitrators.

Sometimes, the need for local arbitrators has been so great that new arbitrators have been named, having no background or knowledge of collective bargaining or labor/management relations, no real knowledge of the so-called "law of the shop," and no awareness of the contribution of arbitration to the continuing relationship of the parties. Some have been fortunate; they have worked with labor/management people, or with other arbitrators who knew and could convey the labor relations philosophies of Harry Shulman, Abe Stockman, Ralph Seward, Ben Aaron, Sylvester Garrett, Harry Platt, and so many others. Those fortunate new arbitrators were able to obtain an understanding of how the giants in the practice, neutrals and practitioners, had fashioned their labor arbitration practices with an understanding of those philosophies, and some of the new arbitrators had the great value and opportunity of continuing what the War Labor Board graduates had begun.

Others were not so favored, but were able, nevertheless, to absorb through their own abilities the sense of what arbitration should be, and they went on to recognized acceptance by the labor/management community. Some have come from union or management backgrounds in which they understood the need to contribute to an ongoing labor-management relationship, and they, too, have achieved acceptance as arbitrators. Others have come from the law, but have recognized the very substantial difference between the arbitration of labor disputes and litigation, and they, too, have gained acceptance as arbitrators.

But there are some who never have had the benefit of working with parties who understood that they were not engaged in one-shot litigation, who have not been so fortunate as to have gained a clear understanding of how arbitration differs from the administration and enforcement of a law. Included in that group is a growing number of arbitrators who have gained acceptability because they are dealing with the new presenters of cases for management and unions. Their law backgrounds are much the same as those of the presenters. Together, they change the process.

We stand at a crossroad. As part of the growth in the numbers of cases and relationships, there has been a recognized need for new arbitrators. Employers and unions have needed new persons to present cases to arbitrators. Perhaps because arbitration employs some of the language of the courts—we talk of hearings, opinions, decisions, testimony, briefs, evidence—when the time came for management and unions to hire additional presenters of cases, they have tended to hire outside counsel having little understanding of the need to treat dispute resolution as part of the continuing relationship between the parties. Thus, we have the labor relations philosophy of employers and unions being developed away from the bargainers, away from the plant, and even away from the labor relations management and union officials, by persons who treat the presentation of the case to the arbitrator as a hard-fought litigation, with no holds barred. And there are then added to arbitration the delays of the legal process, and its costs. Arbitration becomes even further removed from what it set out to be, what it was, and what it still purports to be. It is removed from the consideration of effect at the workplace.

As parties, through their representatives or on their own, become increasingly formal and more litigious, as they place greater emphasis on winning and less on their obligation to the continuing relationships, there does develop on the part of some arbitrators a responsiveness to the changed demands. Some arbitrators believe that the parties, not the arbitrator, must determine how they want their hearings to be run, even though the new presenters of their cases appear to be having an unfortunate effect on their labor/management relationships at the shop.

If arbitrators adopt the more formal, litigation-type presentations, there is a loss of the kind of dispute examination which, in the past, allowed arbitrators to come up with imaginative solutions. Is it likely that the arbitrator who developed and awarded the progressive, corrective discipline concept in a plain old discharge-for-cause case would be supported in today's climate? His award might have been tossed out because he exceeded his authority. Yet the concept he developed is now accepted as sound by industry, unions, and arbitrators, and in some situations also has translated into the public sector and is a contractual commitment. It was a great contribution to labor relations.

IV.

Another development causing some concern for the process is the higher incidence of statutory or other provisions for review or appeal of arbitrators' awards, so that the arbitrator's judgment, on the merits of the dispute or on procedural grounds, may be reviewed. The final and binding nature of the process has undergone real change in the past 15 or so years in some relationships. Does this constitute a threat to the process? Obviously, I think it does. It seems to me that it was of the essence of arbitration that this process, as we knew it, was the last step of dispute resolution, to be used only if parties failed to solve their own problems in their own, properly used grievance procedure. Inroads made on the final and binding nature of grievance arbitration tend to change the process. Where appeals procedures are statutory or required by regulation, there does appear to me to be an obligation on the parties, or on those who are represented, to use it with restraint—that neither overuse nor abuse is warranted. If the parties, by their action, make of arbitration simply a step in the process of dispute resolution to yet another level of resolution, on the merits, they will be doing to arbitration what some employers and unions have done to the grievance procedures. When they lost confidence in the lower levels of supervision or management, or in the shop-

steward or business-representative levels of unions, they sometimes made of those steps simply a rubber-stamp operation; in
the alternative, some of them made it a practice to waive the
lower steps. There is indication, in some areas, that certain
attitudes—a lack of confidence because of insufficiently trained
or inexperienced arbitrators, or an unwillingness of formal-
minded presenters for employers or unions to put trust in a
somewhat informal process—may be pushing people toward
heavier use of appeals or review. These trends inevitably will
greatly increase the cost of arbitration, and its delay. The transcripts of hearings, briefs, and other expensive aspects of the
more formal process are almost automatic in many of the situations in which appeals are possible. It will be a pity if we cannot
in some way prevent the further dilution of finality.

Judicial review of arbitration awards has been talked about in
the Academy's meetings and in the labor/management community for many years. To that aspect of judicial involvement in
decision-making on the merits, there is now added the appeals
and review procedures, making a further inroad on finality.
Some of the comments made in speeches to Academy audiences
regarding judicial review appear to me to have equal applicability to the appeals procedures which are now appearing in
greater variety and numbers.

In 1967, Bernard Meltzer talked with us about judicial review.[5] Nine years later, Rolf Valtin, in his 1976 Presidential
Address, referred to the Meltzer paper and said:[6]

"Meltzer, having shown that an outright separation of arbitration
tribunals from public tribunals was not achievable, went on with an
exploration of the arbitral and judicial functions. It is difficult to
summarize so meticulous a thinker as Meltzer, but I think that the
following threefold proposition is correctly attributable to him: (1)
the trilogy is well-nigh airtight, and soundly so, in making the arbitration forum the proper one for determining arbitrability questions; (2) the trilogy is not of such airtightness, again soundly so,
when it comes to judicial review of arbitral determinations on the
merits; (3) judicial review of arbitral decisions on the merits, *if*

[5]Meltzer, *Ruminations about Ideology, Law and Labor Arbitration,* in The Arbitrator, the
NLRB, and the Courts, Proceedings of the 20th Annual Meeting, National Academy of
Arbitrators, ed. Dallas L. Jones (Washington: BNA Books, 1967), 1–20.
[6]Valtin, *The Presidential Address: Judicial Review Revisited—The Search for Accommodation
Must Continue,* in Arbitration—1976, Proceedings of the 29th Annual Meeting, National
Academy of Arbitrators, eds. Barbara D. Dennis and Gerald G. Somers (Washington:
BNA Books, 1976), 1–11, at 3.

sparingly invoked by losing parties and if exercised in limited and discreet fashion by the judiciary, constitutes the necessary and appropriate coordination." (Emphasis supplied.)

Valtin concluded that there had been little heeding of the warning signals, and he saw a more troublesome problem for the future. He described the challenge to bilateralism and referred to third-party challenges to arbitration. Rolf's concern was that the Meltzer proposal for "workable coordination" had not been developed or realized. He was asking for a measure of predictability as to the firmness of results "coming out of the arbitral sphere," and he asked if "effective collective bargaining is still to be considered a cherished national goal."[7]

Since Valtin's talk in 1976, appeal and review procedures appear to be encroaching still further on the collective bargaining process. We have no knowledge of the extent of this encroachment or the effect it has had or will have on the strength and durability of the arbitration process. I think that this is a source of a real problem for the future and that it must be examined seriously. The confidence of parties in the continued national recognition of effective collective bargaining as "a cherished national goal" may suffer yet another sharp jolt if arbitration, in a substantial portion of the labor/management community, becomes yet another level of decision-making, subjected to scrutiny on the merits by a review level.

What Meltzer warned against in 1967 and Valtin considered a growing and serious concern in 1976 are, in 1981, magnified not only by judicial review but also by appeal and review procedures built into dispute-resolution systems.

It is fair, at this point, to ask what we—employers, unions, and arbitrators—want arbitration to be. We have an obligation to examine periodically where we are and what the trends appear to be. Do we really want what some of the new presenters of cases are supplying—a litigation-type process—or have we simply fallen into it because a new element has been added to the process without much scrutiny? Is it too late to change the growing incidence of presentations by persons having highly developed killer instincts and no knowledge of the effect of their actions on the day-to-day relationships at the plant? Have we committed ourselves to a path of appeals and review? If so, is that commitment limited to the public sector, or will it spread

---

[7]*Id.,* at 11.

to the private sector in significant volume? If the answers to these and other questions show process deterioration, should we not try to reverse that deterioration?

V.

Let me now go on to another aspect of the practice of arbitration—the combined subjects of continuing education for arbitrators and the development of arbitrators. The need for new arbitrators has been apparent for some time, and to some extent new arbitrators have come along and been accepted. Whether the market will supply a sufficient number of new arbitrators to meet the need for trained and able people is conjectural. Much depends upon the training we consider to be appropriate.

The need for continuing education for established arbitrators became apparent to Academy Presidents Arthur Stark and Richard Mittenthal, in successive years, and they were successful in establishing programs for the continuing education of our members. What they did led to the establishment of seminars on subjects related to arbitration. The seminars were run by the Academy, for members only. Many members contributed to the content and preparation of the discussion guides used in the seminars. In the past year, the Board of Governors has authorized interns of Academy members to attend seminars. This year, too, we have broadened the coverage from simply seminars to whatever activities are decided upon as coming within the concept of continuing education. We have not yet explored this as fully as might have been desirable, but a start has been made. Academy regions whose members wish to engage in some activity of benefit to them are being encouraged to engage in education activities for members and the interns of members, whether through establishing a course of study or through workshops, lectures, or similar activities. We hope that this will become a continuing activity, meeting the needs of as broad a group as is possible.

We have initiated two new efforts. For the first time, at this Annual Meeting, we have prevailed upon Ralph Seward, a distinguished Charter Member, to participate in a meeting with a group of new or fairly new members, to discuss with them the history of the Academy (which probably parallels the history of the major growth of arbitration), and to tell them of some of the discussions and subjects which engaged members in the past, ever since the Academy was formed in 1947. Twenty-two new members attended (those admitted in 1978, 1979, 1980, and 1981). It is probable that something of the same kind will be done again, or the transcript of the tapes of the May 5, 1981, meeting will become a part of the material given to a new member. From what we have been told by some of the new members who attended, this was a source of understanding of the Academy and its roots, and probably has done much to add to the new members' understanding of the development of arbitration as well.

The second effort recognizes that arbitrators outside our membership also will have an interest in continuing education. We think, particularly, of new arbitrators or those who have gone through one of the training programs but who really have not had much experience and no real opportunity to talk with experienced arbitrators. Bob Coulson, President of the AAA, has given his blessing to the use of AAA facilities at an appointed time once a week, at which time a few of our members will be at the AAA to answer questions, to discuss some of the subjects of interest to arbitrators, and just to help the new arbitrators over the rough spots. This will depend upon the interest and initiative of the regional chairmen or chairwomen of the Academy and of the local AAA offices. So far, I have been told of two AAA regions in which this has been done—Boston, which previously had engaged in a similar type of activity though not necessarily for the same type of attendees, and Philadelphia. For regions which have expressed concern over the quality of training, experience, and new arbitrator exposure to an understanding of the arbitration process, this appears to me to offer an opportunity for our members to participate in the development of the skills and ethical values that we consider essential. It is readily available for those who want to use it.

What appears to continue to be a need is for new persons coming into the arbitration field to have an understanding of a common philosophy of arbitration—what it is, why it is, what it is hoped that arbitration will achieve. And this brings me to the questions I raised at the beginning of my talk—how would-be arbitrators are trained or given an understanding of the process, the Academy's responsibility for participating in training, and the substance of the available training.

For a person coming out of a background which did not include collective bargaining and labor contract administration, the training need is critical. I suggest that whether the background is law, labor economics, law enforcement, law administration, or industrial and labor relations, there is a need for the kind of knowledge that comes from a study of the writings of Shulman,[8] or the early writings of Archibald Cox,[9] or *any* of the writings of Ben Aaron.[10]

What concerns many of us is that the new arbitrators and new advocates come from backgrounds that offer no real understanding of the collective bargaining process, of the philosophy of labor relations which produced labor arbitration as its dispute-resolution mechanism, or of the philosophy of grievance arbitration. Skilled technicians are available; they have been taught the techniques. But many have not learned the essence of arbitration as the unique process it is. Shulman said in 1949,[11] and Ben Aaron referred to the statement in 1959,[12] that arbitration was a "procedure that 'can be ever consciously directed— not merely to the redress of past wrongs—but to the maintenance and improvement of the parties' present and future collaboration.' 'It's authority,' he said, 'comes not from above but from their own specific consent. They can shape it and reshape it.' "

Archibald Cox also quoted Shulman in 1959, as follows:[13]

"The parties to a collective agreement start in a going enterprise with a store of amorphous methods, attitudes, fears and problems. . . . [The contract] covers only a small part of their joint concern. It is based upon a mass of unstated assumptions and practices as to which the understanding of the parties may actually differ, and which it is wholly impractical to list in the agreement."

Cox added:

"This background not only gives meaning to words of the instrument but is itself a source of contract rights.
"The generalities, the deliberate ambiguities, the gaps, the un-

---

[8]Example: Harry Shulman, *Reason, Contract and Law in Labor Relations,* 68 Harv. L.Rev. 999, 1024 (1955).

[9]Example: Archibald Cox, *Reflections upon Labor Arbitration in the Light of the Lincoln Mills Case,* in Arbitration and the Law, Proceedings of the 12th Annual Meeting, National Academy of Arbitrators, ed. Jean T. McKelvey (Washington: BNA Books, 1959), 24–67.

[10]Example: Benjamin Aaron, *On First Looking Into the Lincoln Mills Decision,* in Arbitration and the Law, Proceedings of the 12th Annual Meeting, National Academy of Arbitrators, ed. Jean T. McKelvey (Washington: BNA Books, 1959), 1–14.

[11]Shulman, *The Role of Arbitration in the Collective Bargaining Process,* address delivered at the Institute of Industrial Relations, University of California. In Collective Bargaining and Arbitration, 19 (1949).

[12]Aaron, *supra* note 10, at 11, 12.

[13]Cox, *supra* note 9, at 37.

foreseen contingencies and the need for a rule even though the agreement is silent, all require a creativeness in contract administration which is quite unlike the attitude of one construing a deed or a promissory note or a three-hundred page corporate trust indenture. *The process of interpretation cannot be the same because the conditions which determine the character of the instruments are different."* (Emphasis supplied.)

The understanding we need for the new arbitrators we also need for the new advocates. The process will never be what once it was unless the parties recognize that their advocates—their presenters of a case to the arbitrators—must speak in the voice of the principal—of the employer or of the union—and must know and apply the arbitration philosophy of the party represented. What I believe is lacking is pointed up at the seminars and workshop meetings conducted for arbitrators by the Academy and for the parties by the American Arbitration Association and, sometimes, by the FMCS. Whatever the subject discussed, conduct of hearings, evidence, examination of witnesses, remedy, discipline and discharge, or even philosophy of labor relations or of arbitration, the earnest questions or comments of the persons attending deal primarily with *legal* questions: the admissibility of a document, the right to call a witness, the appropriate ruling on an objection. I have attended a large number of these workshops, seminars, and programs. I have waited in vain for a question from the floor or a comment that deals with the continuing relationship between the parties or with the philosophy of arbitration involved in the examples being discussed. It would be valuable if those seminars, lectures, workshops, and programs sought to show the impact of actions in the grievance procedure and in arbitration on the relationships between the parties, on shop-level problems. In my judgment, the education and training offered to advocates and arbitrators must give some understanding of how labor/management relationships are developed and nurtured, and the influence on those relationships of the quality of arbitrators' and advocates' conduct at the hearing.

I think it is for the employers and the unions, as well as for the arbitrators and those bodies offering training, to do something about revising the scope of the training for new advocates and arbitrators. It is not enough to offer training for procedure and case law; it is *required* that new advocates and new arbitrators get to know the essence of this unique process, the contribution that arbitration makes to the continuing relationship between the parties and to their continuing accommodation.

VI.

For the past seven or eight years I have had calls from many would-be arbitrators, from various parts of the country, asking for help in analyzing their backgrounds and for suggestions about how they might enter the field. There have been as few as five and as many as fourteen persons each year. I invite them to talk with me, either when I am in their part of the country or in New York. Generally, they are with me for at least one day of observation and talk. I help analyze their backgrounds and training needs and try to describe what the process is and how it developed. If there is a real interest, I try to suggest what will be needed to contribute to their understanding of the responsibility of arbitration and of the arbitrator. Where these persons do not have experience in the collective bargaining process in their backgrounds, I generally recommend that they make up for that deficiency first, preferably at a school which does not fashion the teaching of collective bargaining only for unions or only for management. I have felt that those persons must know how language finds its way into a contract—what it means when, during negotiations, at four in the morning before contract expiration, the parties leave unclear language in their agreement, saying, "Well, *we* know what it means." The point is, of course, that they do not know what it means, exactly, but they do know what their relationships are, so that they may contemplate working out problems if they arise. It never is totally clear what are the unstated commitments of their contracts. I have tried to lead these persons who seek to get into arbitration into an understanding of that kind of problem—an understanding of the Shulman/Cox references I quoted a few minutes ago.

It is in connection with that effort that Peter Seitz and I have developed a new project. Peter and I have had a tremendous amount of help, in our early days, from a number of persons. Each of us had the benefit of working with people of great heart, who spent much time and effort helping each of us to develop an understanding of collective bargaining, mediation, grievance handling, contract administration, and arbitration. They contributed to our understanding of arbitration as the final and binding dispute-resolution method of the parties' choice.

We wish to repay that great gift we received by sharing our knowledge and our intuitions with others—with the new hopefuls coming along. Peter and I will give to perhaps six persons at a time the opportunity to discuss arbitration with us, to read and talk about some of the treasured writings on the subject. The persons who will be admitted to our discussion series will have to have tried to prepare themselves for arbitration by obtaining some practical exposure to collective bargaining and the administration of the labor contract which we think is so important to an understanding of the philosophy of arbitration.

We will talk of that philosophy. We will not discuss or, to any extent, consider case law. Our interest will be in the conduct of the hearing, the analysis of the positions of the parties as submitted to the arbitrator, and what their presentations tell us about their grievance administration and their relationships at various levels within the employer and union organizations. We will talk of the opinions supporting the awards, how statements made in the hearing affect the future quality of the parties' relationships. Mostly, we will want to convey the essential, unique nature of the process that has made it so valuable an asset to the labor/management community.

The participants will not have to pay, of course, except as they may have to travel to reach us. We hope this will work, that we will be able to furnish to a few future arbitrators some of the same opportunities for learning that the apprentice arbitrators have had in the great steel and other umpireships, or that we ourselves have had from the arbitrators and others who shared with us.

VII.

I have tried to convey my sense of disquiet as to three aspects of labor arbitration: the technical and legalistic approaches to arbitration, the increase of appeal and review procedures, and the training and development of arbitrators and advocates. I think it is our responsibility, in the Academy, to bring to your attention some of the problems we have been seeing, and some of the solutions or actions we have been suggesting. The loss of arbitration as a dispute-resolution mechanism may not be the end, but if its character is changed by the technicians, or if its final and binding nature is threatened with appeals or other judicial review, or if the new arbitrators or advocates are not given adequate background or experience, we may find arbitration so changed as no longer to be able to fulfill its unique function.

In the word of our Hawaiian friends, "Mahalo."

Chapter 2

ARBITRATION OF JOB SECURITY AND OTHER EMPLOYMENT-RELATED ISSUES FOR THE UNORGANIZED WORKER

I. The British Experience With Unfair Dismissals Legislation

Bob A. Hepple*

The Background

There has been legislation in Great Britain against unfair dismissals in operation since February 1972. Before then there was little protection for the unorganized worker.

The common law relating to termination of the contract of employment is somewhat more favorable to the employee in England and Scotland than in the United States. The English and (separate) Scottish courts never adopted the doctrine that the employer may terminate the contract of employment for an indefinite period at will. Notice is required, except in cases of gross misconduct. In the absence of express agreement, the period of notice may be fixed by the "custom of the trade," or otherwise is such period as is "reasonable" in the circumstances, depending on factors such as length of service, rate, and periods of payment. At common law this could be as long as one year in the case of the editor of a newspaper, and as little as two hours to terminate at the end of a workday in the construction industry.

There is, however, at common law no protection against abusive dismissals of the kind that has recently developed in several American jurisdictions. The courts have not been willing to apply either a prima facie tort theory or an implied contract theory to protect the employee who is dismissed for refusing to

---

*Chairman of Industrial Tribunals (England and Wales); Honorary Professor of Law, University of Kent, Canterbury, England.

perform an act which is unlawful or contrary to established public policy. Nor does the common law require the employer to follow any particular form of procedural due process when dismissing an employee. In recent years some exceptions have developed to this general rule. In particular, when the person dismissed is what is known as an office holder (that is, someone holding a job involving the exercise of a public function), the rules of natural justice (that is, a fair hearing) must be complied with; and where a statute regulates the appointment and dismissal of the employee, the procedural requirements of the statute must be followed (for example, teachers, dock workers, most university teachers, etc.). Another important exception is where the contract of employment itself makes provision for a procedure to be followed, or for there to be "just cause" for the dismissal. In this respect the British courts have anticipated by some years decisions such as that in *Toussaint* v. *Blue Cross and Blue Shield of Michigan.* [1] The contractual provision may be express or it may be implied. Parliament has encouraged the express incorporation of procedural requirements since 1971 when the law first provided that every employer must present to his employees within 13 weeks of commencement of employment a written notice of any disciplinary rules and grievance procedures applicable to that employee, including an appeal procedure. Breaches of rules and procedures incorporated in the individual contract of employment in this way are construed by the courts as a breach of contract. However, the only remedy for breach is a claim for damages. The contract will be effectively terminated, even if in breach of procedure, and there is no possibility of reinstatement at common law. There is also very little taste for litigation of this kind among dismissed employees.

Although there is legislation against race and sex discrimination which parallels Title VII of the Civil Rights Act, this has been used only by those employees who, for one reason or another, do not qualify for protection under the unfair dismissal legislation (for example, because they have been employed for less than one year). The discrimination legislation is less favorable to the employee than the unfair dismissal legislation because the burden of proof to show "less favourable treatment" is on the employee, and, in general, discrimination can be shown

---

[1] 408 Mich. 579, 292 N.W.2d 880 (1980).

only if a comparison can be made with a worker of the opposite sex or another racial group, as the case may be, and this is often not possible.

Turning to the organized sector of workers, it must be noted that the degree of unionization is considerably higher in Britain than in the United States, currently being about 60 percent of the workforce. Despite this, there was little collective bargaining before the 1970s on the question of disciplinary dismissals (that is, those relating to conduct or capability). In 1963 Frederic Meyers, in *The Ownership of Jobs: A Comparative Study,* [2] found that discipline was regarded among British employers as being a managerial prerogative, and he commented: "Surprisingly to the American observer, with the exception of victimization for union activity, this attitude of British employers was generally shared by union officials." He found that wildcat strikes by groups of workers were a common method of securing reinstatement for dismissed workers. However, it needs to be added that in the public sector (employing nearly one-third of the labor force) there have for a long time been negotiated procedures relating to discipline and termination. In the public sector there were also collective agreements for redundancy (that is, economic) dismissals covering matters such as selection procedures and severance pay. But there were relatively few schemes of this kind in the private sector before 1965, and most of these were not negotiated agreements.

It is against this background that legislation in Britain must be seen. In 1963 statutory minimum periods of notice, including a guarantee of earnings during the notice period, were introduced. As extended by later legislation and now incorporated in the Employment Protection (Consolidation) Act 1978,[3] these are currently (1) one week's notice if the period of continuous employment is four weeks or more, but less than two years; (2) one week's notice for each year of employment of two years or more, but less than 12 years; (3) 12 weeks' notice if the period of employment is 12 years or more.

In 1965 the Redundancy Payments Act, now incorporated with amendments in EPCA, Part VI, gave to employees dismissed by reason of redundancy (that is, the closure of their place of work or a diminution in the requirements for employees

---

[2]Los Angeles: Institute of Industrial Relations, University of California, Los Angeles, 1964.
[3]S. 49 (EPCA).

to do a particular kind of work), the right to lump-sum compensation assessed according to age and length of continuous employment, with a minimum qualification of two years' continuous employment. Currently, the maximum payment for an employee with 20 years' employment over the age of 41 is £3,900 (about $8,970). The payments are made by the employer, who can claim a rebate (currently 41 percent) from a fund to which all employers contribute. Less than one-third of all redundant employees have been eligible in practice, and the average lump sum paid to each employee is approximately one-fifth of the median adult male annual earnings. Because of the larger payments to older workers, the main effect of the act appears to have been to increase the significance of age as a criterion for redundancy. In this sense it has facilitated movement out of the labor force, but not mobility between jobs. It cannot be classified as a "job security" measure.

Two major pressures can be detected behind the movement toward the enactment of unfair dismissals legislation which took place in the Industrial Relations Act 1971. The first was international influences: One of these was the ILO Recommendation No. 119 of 1963 and the other was the precedent of laws against unjustified termination in most of the member states of the European Economic Community which Britain was then considering joining. The second was very strong domestic pressure in the 1960s for procedural reforms in industrial relations. These reforms were the main thrust of the Donovan Royal Commission on trade unions and employers' associations (1965–1968) which was heavily influenced by the statistics that showed that each year in the period 1964–1966 on average some 276 unofficial strikes (that is, wildcat) took place over dismissals, and 203 of these arose out of dismissals other than redundancies. As late as 1967 a tripartite working party of the Ministry of Labour reported against the introduction of legislation and favored voluntary reform, one of the major arguments being that a statute would increase legalism at the place of work, a prediction that has to some extent proved true. The Donovan Commission, however, believed that it was necessary to raise standards immediately and that legislation was the only way to do this. Starting from the proposition that legislation was necessary to protect those seeking to participate in union activities, the Commission decisively moved in favor of a general right against unfair dismissal for all employees, whether organized or not.

At the stage that the legislation was introduced, the unions were still very hesitant about it. Their attitude has now changed. Len Murray, General Secretary of the Trades Union Congress (TUC), said in a speech at Birmingham in April 1980:

> "I have to accept that there is no evidence that trade union membership has declined as the result of individual employment legislation: indeed the membership of our affiliated unions has risen from just over 8,000,000 in 1965 to over 12,000,000 today.
> "And there can be no doubt that because of the law, unions are now able to offer better services in some respects to members in small and dispersed groups on whose behalf it had proved difficult to negotiate effectively. At the end of the day they can represent their members in cases before industrial tribunals and perhaps win compensation, whereas previously they could, in practice, do nothing. In short, our view is that the industrial tribunal system has been valuable insofar as it has provided workers with some protection against abuse in areas where trade union organisation is non-existent or ineffective."

In the organized sector the unions make use of the unfair dismissals legislation in some collective disputes. For example, in a wildcat strike situation the union official is now able to say to his members, "Don't strike about dismissal. We'll take it to an industrial tribunal." There does seem to have been some decline in the number of working days lost due to strikes over dismissals since the legislation was introduced and also a decline in the proportion of all strikes that are attributable to disputes over dismissal, although it would be impossible to say that the legislation, rather than a large number of other factors which have affected the strike pattern, is the cause of this change.

The major importance of the legislation, however, has been in the unorganized sector. Before considering the impact, it is necessary to say something about the content and scope of the legislation which is now embodied with amendments in EPCA 1978 Part V, as amended in 1980 by the Employment Act which restricts the application of the law in various ways, in particular as it affects short-service employees and those in undertakings with 20 or fewer employees.

The Meaning of Unfair Dismissal

Every employee, with certain exceptions, has the right not to be unfairly dismissed by his employer. The remedy is by way of complaint to an industrial tribunal. The employee must prove that he was "dismissed," which includes actual termination by the employer, expiry of a fixed-term contract without renewal, and so-called "constructive" dismissal where the employee resigns because of a significant breach of contract by the employer going to the root of the contract (for example, unilateral reduction in pay, hours, or status or job-content, failure by the employer to investigate genuine grievances, harassment, or other unjustified or intolerable treatment).

It is then for the employer to show a set of facts known to him, or it may be beliefs held by him, at the time of dismissal which was the reason for dismissal. These facts must fall within one of the following categories: (1) "the capability or qualifications of the employee for performing work of the kind that he was employed by the employer to do" ("capability" is to be assessed by reference to skill, aptitude, health, or any other physical or mental quality); (2) "the conduct of the employee"; (3) the employee was "redundant" as defined in the redundancy payments legislation; (4) "the employee could not continue to work in the position which he held without contravention (either on his part or that of his employer) of a duty or restriction imposed by or under any enactment" (for example, a driving disqualification imposed on a truck driver); (5) "some other substantial reason of a kind such as to justify the dismissal of an employee holding the position which the employee held." (Among such reasons have been held to be unreasonable refusal to agree to changes in employment terms, the temporary nature of the employment, structural reorganization, and irreconcilable conflict of personalities.)

Certain reasons render dismissal automatically unfair: trade union membership or activities, refusal to belong to a nonindependent trade union, refusal to belong to a union in certain "closed (union) shop" situations, refusal to belong to a trade union on grounds of conscience or other deeply held personal conviction, pregnancy and confinement, and selection of an employee for dismissal on grounds of redundancy in breach of an agreed procedure or customary arrangement relating to redundancy, or on grounds of trade union membership or activities.

In all other cases, where the dismissal is not automatically unfair, if the employer has shown a potentially fair reason, then the tribunal must determine whether, in the circumstances (including the size and administrative resources of the employer's undertaking), the employer acted reasonably or unreasonably in treating the potentially fair reason as a sufficient reason for dismissing the employee; and that question must be "determined in accordance with equity and the substantial merits of the case." Between 1974 and 1 October 1980 the burden of proof on this issue rested upon the employer. Under the Employment Act 1980, the pre-1974 position of the so-called "neutral burden" has been restored, but it has to be remembered that the industrial tribunal has no power to call witnesses or order production or discovery of documents on its own motion, the procedure being essentially an adversary one.

The "reasonableness" test has produced results probably not dissimilar from those under grievance arbitration in the U.S. The tribunals are reluctant to take a "second guess." The general approach is to ask, in the case of a dismissal on grounds of misconduct or incapability: (1) Was the employer's reason a genuine one? (2) Did the employer have reasonable grounds for his belief at the time of dismissal? (3) Did the employer conduct as much investigation as was reasonable in the circumstances, including giving the employee an opportunity to explain? (4) In the case of minor acts of misconduct, or alleged incapability, did the employer give the employee a reasonable opportunity to improve, for example, by administering oral and written warnings making it clear that the job was at risk if the employee did not improve? (5) Was the sanction of dismissal within the band of reasonable options open to the employer? If more than one option was reasonably open to the employer, then the dismissal will not be regarded as unfair. The tribunals give regard to agreed disciplinary procedures and also to a Code of Practice on Disciplinary Practice and Procedures in Employment issued by the Advisory, Conciliation and Arbitration Service (ACAS) which gives guidelines for disciplinary warnings and so on, prior to dismissal, but if the tribunal concludes that the employee would have been fairly dismissed even if proper procedures had been followed, the failure of procedure will not be fatal to the employer's case. In the case of redundancy dismissals, provided agreed procedures and customs have been followed regarding selection, it is rare for an employee to win on grounds of "unfair selection," although the employer is usually expected to take reasonable steps to help find alternative employment within the undertaking.

Excluded Categories

The following is a summary of those classes of employees who may not bring a complaint of unfair dismissal.

1. Employees who have been continuously employed for less than 52 weeks, unless the dismissal was for trade union participation (between 1975 and 1979 the period was 26 weeks).

2. Employees who commenced employment on or after 1 October 1980 and have been continuously employed for less than 2 years, if at no time in that period did the number of employees of the employer and any associated employer exceed 20.

3. Employees who have reached the age of 65 in the case of a man and 60 in the case of a woman, or who have reached the normal retiring age for the particular job.

4. Employees employed by their husbands or wives.

5. Registered dock workers (who have their own scheme).

6. Share fishermen.

7. Persons ordinarily working outside Great Britain.

8. Persons employed on United Kingdom registered ships wholly outside Great Britain and not ordinarily resident in Great Britain.

9. Persons employed under fixed-term contracts made before 28 February 1972, or fixed-term contracts for one year or more made after that date if they have waived their rights in writing.

10. Persons who do not present claims within three months of the date of termination, or such further period as the tribunal considers reasonable in a case where it is satisfied that it was not reasonably practicable for the complaint to be presented before the end of three months.

11. Employees dismissed "for purposes of safeguarding national security" (conclusively proved by a Minister's certificate).

Apart from these categories, an industrial tribunal may not determine whether a dismissal is fair or unfair where, at the date of dismissal, the employer was conducting a lockout or the employee was taking part in a strike or other industrial action, unless one or more employees who at any time took part in the strike or industrial action have not been dismissed, or have been offered reengagement, but the employee concerned has not been offered reengagement. The effect is to make selective dismissals subject to the legislation. In determining whether a dismissal was fair or unfair, no account may be taken of pressure by strike or industrial action put on the employer to dismiss, but in certain closed (union) shop dismissals after 8 September 1980, a contribution or full indemnity may be sought by the employer from any person (including a union who exerted pressure) in respect of an award of compensation made against the employer.

It was always hoped that the organized sector would make their own arrangements for unfair dismissals more favorable than the legislation, but providing for an appeal to an independent arbitrator. Accordingly, the legislation allows the Secretary of State to grant formal approval for the replacement of the statutory provisions by collective agreements which improve on the statutory minimum standards. However, in the 16 years since the redundancy payments legislation came into force, only three such agreements have been approved, and in the nine years of the unfair dismissals legislation, only one agreement contracting out of that legislation has been approved. The latter agreement (1979) covers members of the Electrical Electronic Telecommunications and Plumbing Union who work for employers belonging to the Electrical Contractors' Association.

Remedies

When the legislation was first introduced, tribunals could only recommend, but not order, reemployment. But the primary remedies available since 1 June 1976 are (1) reinstatement, which means that the employer must treat the employee in all respects as if he had not been dismissed, restoring his pay, pension, and other benefits to him; and (2) reengagement, which differs from reinstatement in that the employee may be reengaged in a different job from that which he formerly held, provided that the new job is comparable to his old one or is otherwise suitable. Reengagement may be by a successor or associated employer. In exercising its discretion whether to grant reinstatement or reengagement, the tribunal must consider the complainant's wishes, whether he caused or contributed to the dismissal, and whether it is practicable for the employer to comply with an order for reinstatement or reengagement. The mere fact that the employer has engaged a permanent replacement does not automatically make these remedies "impracticable." If the employee is reinstated or reengaged, but the terms of the order are not fully complied with, the tribunal must award compensation to the extent that partial noncompliance has caused the employee's loss, with a maximum award of £6,250. If the order for reinstatement or reengagement is not complied with at all, then the tribunal must award a basic and compensatory award (see below) and an additional award of compensation which will be either between 13–26 weeks' pay, or, in the case of discrimination on grounds of race, sex, or trade union activity, 26–52 weeks' pay.

If orders for reinstatement or reengagement are not made, the tribunal must award compensation under two heads: (1) *A basic award.* This is calculated in the same way as a redundancy payment, subject to a maximum award of £3,900 (that is, a maximum weekly pay limit of £130 × 20 years' continuous service × 1½ weeks' pay for each year). A deduction may be made in respect of the contribution of the employee to his own dismissal, and any redundancy or other payment received will be deducted from whatever sum is awarded. (2) *The compensatory award.* This is such amount as the tribunal considers just and equitable in all the circumstances, having regard to the loss sustained by the complainant in consequence of the dismissal, insofar as that loss is attributable to action taken by the employer. This is calculated according to principles laid down by the courts and includes benefits lost to the date of hearing and subsequently, loss of pension rights, and expenses. Reductions are made in respect of the employee's failure to mitigate his loss, the employee's contribution to his own dismissal, and any other payments received from the employer and earnings elsewhere. It will be seen that the maximum award which can be made amounts to £16,910 ($38,890), made up as follows:

Basic Award	£3,900	($ 8,970)
Compensatory Award	£6,250	($14,370)
Additional Award for failure to reinstate	£6,760	($15,550)

Statistics for 1979 (the latest available) show that 64.9 percent of all completed cases were conciliated. The proportion of conciliated cases has increased each year, and in most of these cases ACAS has been instrumental in securing a settlement or withdrawal. The statistics reveal the startling fact that only a tiny proportion of all complainants were reinstated or reengaged.

The proportion has declined since these were made the primary remedies in 1976. In 1973, 4.2 percent of those whose cases were settled before a hearing were given back their jobs. This percentage has fallen each year and was only 1.8 percent in 1979. Of those who went to a hearing, 2.3 percent were recommended to be given back their jobs in 1973. In 1977 (the first full year in which orders and not simply recommendations could be made), only 1.4 percent were reinstated or reengaged, and in 1979 this figure had declined to 0.8 percent. The median award of compensation in 1979 was just over £400 (about five weeks' net pay at the average wage). This should be compared to the national maximum award in 1979 of £14,800.

A number of reasons may be suggested for these statistics. It is generally believed, although there have been no firm statistics since 1967, that the proportion of employees reemployed after the use of agreed procedures in the organized sector is very much higher than that under the legislation. This reflects the difficulty of enforcing orders for reemployment without union support. The financial penalties for failing to comply with a tribunal order are apparently not costly enough to the employer to make reemployment the most attractive solution. It also has to be said that only a minority of employees wish to be reemployed after the unpleasant rupture of dismissal. This may have something to do with the hierarchical structure of the labor market. Those in relatively secure employment who are eligible to present a complaint under the legislation (at present, with one year or more of service) are usually able to find new employment within a relatively short period, a fact which is reflected in the apparently low level of awards by tribunals for future loss of earnings. In this situation, reinstatement is not particularly attractive. The payment of compensation as a lump sum instead of by way of periodical payments so long as the worker is unemployed is a disincentive. In 1979, in 18.7 percent of cases in which tribunals awarded compensation, only the basic award was made. As with redundancy payments, the allurement of even a small lump sum is enough to coax many employees to give up their wish to return to the job.

Handling of Complaints

The procedure for dealing with complaints of unfair dismissal is intended to be accessible, speedy, and informal. Within three months of a dismissal (a time limit that may be extended in exceptional cases), the applicant presents a simple originating application setting out particulars of the grounds on which he seeks relief to the Central Office of Industrial Tribunal who sends it to the employer. The employer must send back its notice of appearance, setting out the particulars of its defense, within 14 days (which may be extended), and 14 days' notice of hearing (which may be shortened by agreement) is then given. The average time it takes to get a case heard by a tribunal is 8 to 10 weeks from the date the complaint was presented.

The tribunal has powers to order further particulars and, on application, may order discovery, inspection and production of documents, and the attendance of witnesses. Evidence is usually taken on oath or affirmation. The tribunals are tripartite, consisting of a legally qualified chairman, drawn from a panel appointed by the Lord Chancellor in England or Secretary of State in Scotland. There are about 66 full-time and 122 part-time chairmen. Two lay members sit with the chairman and have full voting rights. They are drawn by the tribunal staff from panels nominated by the Secretary of State for Employment after consultation with the Trades Union Congress (TUC) and the Confederation of British Industry (CBI), respectively. There are about 2,200 panel members in England and Wales. They are expected to act as independent, impartial judges and do not have any connection with the parties; quite often they are drawn from an industry different from the one in which the dismissal occurred. The cases are allocated to the 16 regional offices in England and Wales, or to Scotland, depending upon where the cause of action arose. Tribunals sit in these regional centers and also in other towns.

Applicants are represented in some 60 percent and employers in some 65 percent of all cases. In 1979, about 37 percent of all applicants and 54 percent of all employers had legal representatives at the hearing. Applicants were represented by trade union officials in a further 15 percent of cases. Legal costs are not normally awarded, each party being expected to bear his or her own expenses. Exceptionally, costs may be awarded against a party who unnecessarily causes postponements or who acts frivolously or vexatiously, or otherwise unreasonably. Parties and their witnesses may be paid traveling costs and small attendance allowances out of central government funds. The average cost to the taxpayer of a day's hearing in 1980 was estimated to be about £220 ($500).

An appeal from an industrial tribunal to the Employment

Appeal Tribunal (EAT) may be made on a question of law. The EAT consists of a judge, drawn from a panel of English High Court and Scottish Court of Session judges, and there are two to four lay members (with equal voting rights) sitting with him for each hearing. There may be a further appeal, with leave, to the English Court of Appeal (three senior judges) or the Scottish Court of Session, and with further leave from there to the House of Lords. In practice, most appeals do not go beyond the EAT. In 1978–1979 there were appeals to the EAT in about 4 percent of all tribunal cases that went to hearing. Of those that went to appeal, 13.6 percent were allowed, 12.7 percent were remitted for rehearing, 42.7 percent were dismissed, and 26.5 percent were withdrawn. Fifty-six percent of all appeals were lodged by employees. Industrial tribunals are bound by decisions of the EAT and of the higher courts.

All complaints of unfair dismissal are sent to the ACAS before being scheduled for hearing for conciliation. ACAS conciliation officers have a statutory duty to try to settle the complaint without the need for a tribunal hearing. As mentioned earlier, about two-thirds of all cases are conciliated.

The number of unfair dismissal applications to tribunals increased from 5,197 in 1972, the year the legislation became operative, to 34,180 in 1978. The increase arose primarily from the reduction in the length of service qualification for applicants, first from 104 weeks to 52 weeks in September 1974, and second, from 52 weeks to 26 weeks in March 1975. The qualifying period was again raised to 52 weeks with respect to dismissals on or after 1 October 1979. This led to a reduction to 33,383 in 1979 and a further reduction to 28,876 in 1980.

Statistics relating to the industrial, occupational, and earnings characteristics of tribunal applicants are available only for the period from 1972 to 1976; they are set out in Tables 1–3. They indicate that the industries which are overrepresented in unfair dismissal applications are generally those in which the density of union membership is relatively low and collective bargaining is relatively weak, and where there is a concentration of small employers and low-paid, short-service employees. These industries include agriculture, construction, distributive trades, and miscellaneous services. Industries which are underrepresented tend to be those where density of union membership is high and where there are large employers, such as mining, quarrying, gas, electricity, water, and public administration.

TABLE 1

UNFAIR DISMISSAL APPLICATIONS
BY SELECTED INDUSTRIES AND UNION DENSITY, 1972–1976

Industry	Employees as % of Labor Force	Union Density	Percentage of All UD Applications
Agriculture, forestry, fishing	1.7	22.2 / 60.5	4.2
Mining and quarrying	1.5	96.2	0.6
Metal manufacturing and engineering	16.6	69.4	17.0
Construction	5.7	27.2	13.9
Gas, electricity, and water	1.5	92.0	0.5
Distributive trades	12.1	11.4	16.6
Insurance, banking, finance	4.9	44.8	3.2
Professional and scientific services	16.1	75.0	3.6
Entertainment		64.9	
Hotel and catering services	10.2	5.2	16.0
Public administration and defense	7.2	90.5	1.7

There are no overall statistics that enable one to say what proportion of all employees dismissed for cause present complaints. A survey of 970 manufacturing establishments with at least 50 workers, undertaken on behalf of the SSRC Industrial Relations Research Unit (Warwick University), indicated that in the years 1978 and 1979 from 2 to 3 percent of the total workforce covered by the survey had been dismissed (not including those made redundant). Of those dismissed, 9.8 percent made an application to an industrial tribunal. These figures provide some reflection of the situation, but probably underrepresent the proportion who complain in view of the predominance of

TABLE 2

OCCUPATIONAL ANALYSIS, 1972–1976

Occupational Group	Percentage of All UD Applications
Other managerial	10.2
Clerical	9.3
Selling	9.3
Catering	9.7
Processing (metal and electrical)	15.7
Painting and repetitive assembly	3.4
Construction	5.4
Transport	13.5

TABLE 3

ANALYSIS BY WORKFORCE SIZE, 1972–1976

Firm Size	Percentage of All UD Applications
Less than 20	22.0
20–49	16.5
50–99	14.0
100–499	23.4
500–999	8.2
1000 plus	15.9

Source: Department of Employment *Gazette.*

small private service establishments among unfair dismissal respondents.

Criticisms of the Law

The operation of the legislation has been subjected to considerable criticism, particularly by small employers. Among the main allegations are the following:

1. The legislation discourages recruitment, particularly in small businesses, and actually prevents the creation of jobs by employers. The only empirical evidence—a study commissioned by the Department of Employment and published in 1978 and

a study by the Department staff published in July 1979—does not support this view and indicates that only a relatively insignificant number of small employers regard the legislation as a factor inhibiting recruitment. The first of these surveys indicates that the legislation has made employers more careful about the *quality* of recruits, but not about the *numbers* employed.

2. The law is particularly burdensome to small employers who have to bear their own costs and who cannot be expected to have formal disciplinary procedures. (Over half of all complaints come from firms with less than 100 employees.) Recent research by the Warwick Industrial Relations Research Unit indicates that small firms are much less likely than large ones to have disciplinary procedures, and they do have a greater propensity than the large firms to dismiss employees. The Employment Act 1980 attempts to meet these criticisms by excluding employees with less than two years' service in firms with 20 or fewer employees, directing tribunals to have regard to the "size and administrative resources" of the employer, reintroducing the "neutral" burden of proof of reasonableness, and allowing tribunals to award costs and expenses in cases of "unreasonable" conduct by a party.

3. The tribunals have become too "legalistic." Originally, hearings lasted a few hours at the most, but in recent years the majority of cases have lasted a whole day or longer. The unions blame this primarily on the increasing use of legal representation. Undoubtedly part of the reason is the complexity of the statutes the tribunals have to apply and the many restrictions and "guidelines" imposed on them by the case law of the EAT. Recently the tribunal rules have been amended to make it clear that tribunals must avoid formality and are not bound by the rules of evidence in ordinary court proceedings. There is also a new procedure for "pre-hearing assessments" to weed out hopeless cases by advising the party concerned that an order for costs may be made if the matter proceeds.

4. The unions complain that the odds of the employee winning—1 in 4—are too low, and that the orders of reinstatement are too few and the level of compensation awarded inadequate.

Conclusions

The overall assessment of the legislation must be that it has not led to a flood of litigation. Indeed, the estimates of the caseload of the industrial tribunals have always been considerably higher than what has materialized in practice. It was originally believed on the basis of a survey of manufacturing industry that about 3 percent of employees were dismissed for cause and about 10 percent of those were likely to complain. In fact, the caseload has never exceeded just over half the estimated figure. The actual size of the caseload depends upon factors such as the length of the qualifying period of service to get the statutory rights, bearing in mind that short-service employees are more likely to be dismissed than long-service employees; the size of establishments covered, bearing in mind that about 22 percent of all complaints come from firms with 20 or fewer employees; and also the extent to which employees may have available legal and other services.

I have already indicated that trade union fears about the consequences of the legislation have not materialized and, as the quotation from Len Murray indicates, the legislation is now generally welcomed and utilized by the trade unions. The fear among employers that the legislation would lead to a weakening of discipline has not proved to be well-founded. On the contrary, the legislation appears to have given employers an opportunity to introduce disciplinary rules and procedures which have legitimated managerial decisions and, through the use of fair procedures and severance payments, facilitated some kinds of disciplinary action and also dismissals on grounds of redundancy.

Labor laws are not for export. You may find some helpful ideas in the British experience, but the essential point that needs to be made is that any statutory scheme for protecting the unorganized worker will succeed only to the extent that it is organically related to the existing culture of industrial relations. One cannot transplant an organism which will be rejected because it is alien to the system.

II. GRIEVANCE PROCEDURE AND ARBITRATION IN A NONUNION ENVIRONMENT: THE NORTHROP EXPERIENCE

LAWRENCE R. LITTRELL*

In the earliest days, just prior to World War II, Northrop Aircraft, Inc. consisted of a small group of engineers and technicians headed by our founder, John K. Northrop, who were dedicated to the development of aircraft of advanced design. Jack knew everyone and everyone knew him. He was immediately available to solve problems as they arose, whether they involved an aircraft design, a policy dispute, or a personnel matter.

As the company's production activities grew during World War II, a personnel department was added to handle employment, draft deferments, recreation, Bond drives, wartime wage controls and, incidentally, the day-to-day personnel problems that arose. Throughout this explosive growth, Jack Northrop made every effort to maintain the close relationship with the personnel that he had enjoyed in those early days, and he was extraordinarily successful. He knew more Norcraftors by their first name than anyone else in the plant. His door was always open and, more important, people walked through it. It became common knowledge that if you couldn't get a problem resolved elsewhere, you could go to Jack and it would get fixed. So naturally the load got heavier. Many times the problems Jack handled dealt with employee discipline, and most often he would see to it that nothing really bad happened to anyone. He was that kind of guy. However, some people who got favorable decisions from Mr. Northrop really didn't deserve his help, and others who did, wouldn't go or couldn't get to him in time. Inconsistencies grew along with demands on his time, and it became apparent that a better way of handling personnel complaints and problems was needed.

Recognizing this need, Roger McGuire, a manager in what by then had become the Industrial Relations Department, proposed in 1946 that the company adopt a formal grievance procedure with arbitration as its final step. To suggest that a nonunion company adopt a formal grievance procedure was unprece-

---

*Corporate Director, Industrial Relations, Northrop Corporation, Century City, Los Angeles, Calif.

dented at that time, and to propose that management expose its theretofore unilateral personnel decisions to the scrutiny of an outsider for validation or rejection was nothing short of revolutionary. To compound this madness, the procedure was to be made available not to just the production and maintenance personnel, but to all nonsupervisory employees, hourly and salaried alike.

For a nonunion company to take such a step required both sensitivity and courage: a sensitivity to the needs and desires of the people of Northrop and to the company's management climate at that time, and the courage to open up important internal judgments to outside decision-makers.

In the usual case the adoption of a grievance procedure with arbitration requires neither sensitivity nor courage, but merely a desire to obtain a no-strike clause in a union contract. In Northrop's case, the only negotiations were within the management structure of the company, and I am sure they were intense. The final result, however, was that Northrop was, I believe, the first nonunion manufacturing company to adopt formal grievance machinery for both hourly and salaried personnel which terminates in final and binding arbitration.

Now, lest I appear to be "the complete Northrop chauvinist" and/or extremely naive, let it be noted that our sensitive and courageous predecessors in management had had their sensitivity heightened and their courage bolstered by two union elections in 1945. While the employees chose not to be represented (the first time by an uncomfortably slim margin), it became clear that even though the company provided wages, hours, and working conditions as good or better than others in our industry, a significant gap existed in our procedure for conflict resolution which required a new approach.

Three elements were viewed as essential if this new approach was to be successful: First, the formalized procedure through which facts are discovered and unresolved grievances may seek resolution by appeal to higher levels of management, and finally to arbitration. Second, clearly written and universally distributed personnel policies and standards of conduct, providing for progressive discipline. Third: An organization of people with the responsibility of assisting employees in the resolution of their grievances. I don't think anyone in our industry had ever heard of an ombudsman in 1946 so they were called Employee Relations Representatives.

The grievance procedure adopted in 1946 is essentially the same as that which we have today and closely parallels the four-step procedures found in many union contracts. It addresses not only the concerns of the employee who feels he has been unfairly terminated, but those many other areas of work-related problems that arise. Our employee handbook, "Working with Northrop," provides that any nonsupervisory employee may file a grievance ". . . when they feel they have not been treated in accordance with company policy." In actual practice, this language is interpreted quite broadly and anyone with a real work-related complaint will get access to the grievance procedure.

The matters dealt with in the grievance procedures are just about those you would expect in any industrial organization. Discipline and discharge are the most frequently grieved subjects. Other subjects would include the application of seniority in layoff situations, distribution of overtime, report time pay, shift selection, job classification, promotion, and on and on.

The first step of the procedure, which must be taken within five working days of the event that precipitated the grievance, is an informal discussion between the employee and his immediate supervisor. Quite often this step is initiated upon the counsel of an employee relations representative to whom the employee has come with a problem or complaint. Most grievances are settled at this point and that, of course, is the goal of the procedure—to resolve problems at the earliest possible stage and within the organization in which the employee works.

If, after presenting his problem to his supervisor, quite often with the assistance of the employee relations representative, the employee is not satisfied with the result, he or she (and with increasing frequency, she) may take the second step in the procedure by filing a grievance notice. The employee relations representative will assist the employee in writing his grievance and will then conduct a more formal investigation to ensure that all of the facts are known and that the underlying problems which may have led to the stated grievance are discovered, if possible.

The employee relations representative then acquaints the appropriate higher level of management, called the administrative officer, with the grievance and the discovered facts relating to it. The administrative officer may then make a decision or may call for a conference of the grievant, the supervisor involved, and the employee relations representative in an effort to resolve the grievance. In any event, he must, within ten working days after receiving the grievance, render a written decision.

If the administrative officer's decision is unacceptable to the grievant, the decision may be appealed within five days to the third step in the procedure—the Management Appeals Committee. This committee consists of the division vice president responsible for the organization in which the employee works, the division vice president of human resources, and the corporate vice president of industrial relations or his designee, selected by him from a panel of corporate directors and vice presidents of human resources from other divisions.

To assist the committee at the hearing and in its deliberations, the employee relations representative prepares a folder for each member of the committee. The folder contains the grievance notice, the administrative officer's decision, and the grievance appeal. It also contains a statement of the facts as determined by the employee relations representative, the stated positions of the grievant and the management, an analysis of the case, and copies of any record or other documentation that bears upon the case.

On an appointed date, the committee meets with the grievant and the employee relations representative. The facts are reviewed and the employee tells his side of the story and may support his position by calling witnesses, if he chooses to do so. The immediate supervisor and any other management or staff employees who can add to a full understanding of the problem provide the committee with their views of what "really" happened.

This hearing with the Management Appeals Committee is conducted quite informally. The process is again one of fact-finding, and the members of the committee participate directly by careful and thorough questioning of each witness. If need be, a hearing will be continued in order to develop additional facts or meet with necessary but unavailable witnesses. At the conclusion of the hearing, the committee members discuss and evaluate the evidence presented and reach a decision—often unanimous, occasionally two to one. This decision is then prepared by the employee relations representative, reviewed by the committee members and, when acceptable to them, signed. Within two weeks of the hearing, the written decision is delivered to the aggrieved employee.

If, despite this application of collective wisdom by members of the Management Appeals Committee, the employee's grievance is still not resolved to his or her satisfaction, it may be appealed to the fourth and final step of the procedure—final and binding arbitration.

The question of who shall arbitrate the grievance is decided by mutual agreement between the grievant and the company, represented by an employee relations manager. If mutual agreement cannot be reached—which is seldom—a list of five qualified arbitrators is obtained from an appropriate source, such as the state conciliation service. (FMCS has declined to provide lists to us for the past few years on the grounds that their charter limits their services to disputes between companies and their certified bargaining representatives.) The final selection is made by each party alternately striking names until only that of the selected arbitrator remains.

After agreement is reached, the selected arbitrator is contacted and a date is set for the hearing. This alone has become something of a problem. The popularity of certain experienced arbitrators either make them practically unavailable, in which case the selection process must be repeated, or the date must be set weeks or sometimes months after the decision to arbitrate has been reached. I know the answer, and frequently we do select less well-known arbitrators.

At this point it is well to note that it is extremely rare for the company to allow a case to go to arbitration unless it is convinced that its position is supportable, both on the facts and in its equitable aspects. All other cases are resolved at one of the earlier steps of the procedure. Apparently, we are not always correct in this evaluation, however, because arbitrators do from time to time make decisions that favor Northrop grievants. But despite this, I have maintained that the company has never "lost" an arbitration case. The lessons learned are almost always worth the costs incurred. Arbitration keeps a dear school, but antediluvian supervisors will learn no other—with apologies to Poor Richard and Dr. Franklin.

In the arbitration hearing, the company is represented by an employee relations manager experienced in arbitration and familiar with the case. The employee may represent himself or may elect to be represented by counsel of his own choosing. If so, that is an expense that the grievant must bear. All other costs of arbitration and the grievance procedure which preceded it are borne by Northrop, including the pay of all witnesses and that of the grievant during the processing of the grievance.

It is this point in the procedure which has been of great concern to us. Throughout the processing of the grievance, up to the point of arbitration, the grieving employee has been counseled by an employee relations representative who, by the time the grievance reaches arbitration, probably knows more about the case than the grievant himself. However, the grievant cannot avail himself of this expertise in the arbitration but must, at this point, seek his own paid counsel or represent himself against an expert.

The company's employee relations managers feel that this is a weakness in the system that may be manifested in a number of ways. Where the employee represents himself, his lack of knowledge of the procedure often unduly delays the proceedings; the imbalance of the experience and skill of the grievant vis-à-vis an employee relations professional forces the arbitrator to take a more active role than he might otherwise do; the arbitrator, if he feels that the contest is uneven, may unconsciously give the grievant the benefit of more doubts than he is really entitled to; and, finally, as in one case, an arbitrator may even refuse to render a decision due to the lack of adversary counsel.

At our regular Interdivisional Industrial Relations Committee meeting later this month, the Employee Relations Subcommittee will recommend the adoption of a new option for the grievants who plan to take their cases to arbitration. In addition to the current choice of obtaining paid outside counsel or representing himself, the employee will be permitted to choose as counsel the employee relations representative who has helped him through the steps of the grievance procedure, or a member of the employee relations staff of a division other than his own. If this option is exercised, the division at which the case arose will transfer funds to cover the preparation and hearing time of the selected counsel to the division at which he or she works. In this way the employee will be provided counsel without cost, and I believe that the arbitration process will be expedited and due process better served.

I hope and believe that this recommendation will be adopted and, knowing our employee relations people as I do, I can assure you that any employee who chooses to employ this option will find that he has a real advocate working in his behalf.

Even without this latest wrinkle, the system of grievance handling now employed by Northrop has been in effect for 35 years —and it works. Basically, it works because we want it to work and take pains to see that it works. And it works because we have good people working hard to make it work.

Our employee relations people are all degreed specialists with experience as industrial relations generalists. They are selected on the basis of their ability to communicate at all levels and to understand and apply Northrop's industrial relations philosophy in those many cases where the facts don't quite square with an established rule or policy. They serve the long-range goals of the company in maintaining fair and equitable treatment of employees by daily application of knowledge and mature judgment, and I am very proud of them.

They are counselor, shop steward, and business agent for the aggrieved employee. They are also the counselor and sometimes the conscience of management. They walk a thin line on a hard road, and they do it very well. However, the thing that makes managers listen and employees believe is the existence of the grievance procedure and, most important, the potential that in any given case management's decision may be judged by an impartial arbitrator outside the influence of management.

I have come to believe that without final and binding arbitration, a system of internal grievance handling, whether it be a simple "open door" policy or a more formal system, runs great risk of losing credibility in the eyes of the employees.

A further and very practical benefit flows from a system that uses arbitration; it forces the establishment of written personnel policies, rules, and regulations which add certainty and consistency to the treatment of personnel.

Perhaps the most beneficial effect of such a grievance system is that it makes people think before they take actions which may result in a grievance. No system will ever substitute for good supervisory judgment, but it may help some supervisors to exercise it, knowing that sometime in the future an independent arbitrator may be asked to judge the propriety of the action taken.

This, then, is Northrop's way of providing due process in a nonunion industrial environment, and I recommend it for your consideration. I do not believe that it is the only way, but I do believe it has significant advantages over the creation of a new bureaucracy to further reduce the nation's productivity by ensuring—without understanding—that every "T" is dotted and every "I" is crossed. Nor do I feel that further legislative, judicial, or bureaucratic barratry is called for in this area. We are all plentifully supplied with potential causes of action. It would seem that the sole remaining unprotected class consists of non-veteran white males under the age of 40 who are not engaged in union activity, an OSHA complaint, or a worker's compensation case, and who do not work at Northrop. Everyone else has at least one forum to which to appeal.

As an industrial relations pragmatist, I would also caution those who keep a supply of wood stakes handy to drive into the heart of the doctrine of "termination-at-will" (an unfortunate term which has little real relevance today), that in doing so they may loose a far greater evil on society than the one they seek to destroy.

I would also ask those who believe that the Northrop system of grievance handling is just the thing they need in their company to be very careful. We should be cautious, in viewing a system that works well elsewhere, not to jump to the conclusion that it will work as well for us. This is true whether we are looking at another company's policy or procedure or the laws of other nations. A different history, a different cultural environment, or a different legal heritage can vastly alter the practical application and results obtained from a system that works to perfection elsewhere. That which the Japanese have found to be a serene solution could be a nightmare of frustration in litigious California. And a 35-year-old grievance system that works well at Northrop could be a disaster installed overnight for widgit workers in Waukegan.

III. PROTECTION AGAINST UNJUST DISCIPLINE:
AN IDEA WHOSE TIME HAS LONG SINCE COME

THEODORE J. ST. ANTOINE*

Introduction

The law seems able to absorb only so many new ideas in a given area at any one time. In 1967 Professor Lawrence Blades of Kansas produced a pioneering article in which he decried the iron grip of the contract doctrine of employment at will, and argued that all employees should be legally protected against abusive discharge.[1] The next dozen years witnessed a remarkable reaction. With a unanimity rare, if not unprecedented, among the contentious tribe of labor academics and labor arbitrators, a veritable Who's Who of those professions stepped forth to embrace Blades' notion, and to refine and elaborate it —Aaron,[2] Blumrosen,[3] Howlett,[4] Peck,[5] Stieber,[6] and Summers,[7] to name only some. But the persons who ultimately counted the most, the judges and the legislators, hung back. In the 1960s the country had taken vast strides, at both the federal[8] and state[9] levels, to stamp out discrimination in employment based on such invidious and particularized grounds as race, sex,

---

*Member, National Academy of Arbitrators; Professor of Law, University of Michigan, Ann Arbor, Mich.

[1]Blades, *Employment at Will vs. Individual Freedom: Of Limiting the Abusive Exercise of Employer Power,* 67 Colum. L. Rev. 1404 (1967).

[2]*Cf.* Aaron, *Constitutional Protections Against Unjust Dismissals from Employment: Some Reflections,* in New Techniques in Labor Dispute Resolution, ed. Howard J. Anderson (Washington: BNA Books, 1976), 13.

[3]Blumrosen, *Strangers No More: All Workers Are Entitled to "Just Cause" Protection under Title VII,* 2 Ind. Rels. L.J. 519 (1978).

[4]Howlett, *Due Process for Nonunionized Employees: A Practical Proposal,* in Proceedings of the 32nd Annual Meeting, Industrial Relations Research Association, ed. Barbara D. Dennis (Madison, Wis.: IRRA, 1980), 164.

[5]Peck, *Unjust Discharges from Employment: A Necessary Change in the Law,* 40 Ohio St. L.J. 1 (1979).

[6]Stieber, *The Case for Protection of Unorganized Employees Against Unjust Discharge,* in Proceedings of the 32nd Annual Meeting, Industrial Relations Research Association, ed. Barbara D. Dennis (Madison, Wis.: IRRA, 1980), 155.

[7]Summers, *Individual Protection Against Unjust Dismissal: Time for a Statute,* 62 Va. L.Rev. 481 (1976).

[8]*E.g.,* Equal Pay Act, 77 Stat. 56 (1963), 29 U.S.C. §206(d) (1976); Civil Rights Act of 1964, Title VII, 78 Stat. 253 (1964), as amended, 42 U.S.C. §2000e (1976 & Supp. II 1978); Age Discrimination in Employment Act, 81 Stat. 602 (1967), as amended, 29 U.S.C. §621 (1976 & Supp. III 1979).

[9]All the states have comprehensive laws against discrimination in employment except Alabama, Arkansas, Georgia, Louisiana, Mississippi, Texas, and Virginia. Fair Employment Practices Manual 8A (Washington: BNA, 1980), 451:102–107.

religion, national origin, and age. It was as if we needed a pause to catch our breath before venturing on into more open and exposed territory. Now, as we enter the 1980s, there are signs of quickening interest by both courts and legislatures in broader protections for employees' job interests, and the time seems ripe for an appraisal of where we have arrived and where we may be headed.

I see no reason to retrace at length the trail that has been blazed by my many predecessors. My principal purpose will be to consider the numerous practical problems that must be resolved if we are to effectuate the concept of protecting employees generally against unjust discipline. First, however, I shall briefly survey the existing body of law, both here and abroad, with special emphasis on the significant changes occurring in the United States over the past two decades. Following that will come a summary of the various major proposals for dealing with the unfair treatment of employees. Finally, I shall focus on some concrete suggestions concerning appropriate procedures and remedies.

Existing Law of Employee Discipline

United States

It is an oft-told tale that the rule making employment arrangements of indefinite duration contracts at will, terminable by either party at any time, is not a rule which has roots deep in the English common law,[10] but one which sprang full-blown in 1877 from the busy and perhaps careless pen of an American treatise writer.[11] However dubious may have been the precedent he cited,[12] his pronouncement was admirably suited to the *zeitgeist* of an emerging industrial nation. Before the nineteenth century was out, our courts could confidently assert: "All [employers] may dismiss their employees at will, be they many or few, for good cause, for no cause or even for cause morally wrong, without being thereby guilty of legal wrong."[13]

---

[10]Summers, *supra* note 7, at 485; Blackstone, Commentaries on the Laws of England 1 (Philadelphia: Robert Bell, 1771), 425–426 (general hiring of menial labor for an unfixed term presumed to be for a year).

[11]Wood, Law of Master and Servant (Albany, N.Y.: John D. Parsons, Jr., 1877), 272–273.

[12]For detailed criticism, see Note, *Implied Contract Rights to Job Security*, 26 Stan. L.Rev. 335, 340–345 (1974).

[13]*Payne* v. *Western & A.R.R.*, 81 Tenn. 507, 519–520 (1884).

Three quite different groups of employees have managed to escape these harsh strictures. The first consists of the minuscule handful of persons whose knowledge or talents are so unusual and valuable that they have the leverage to negotiate a contract for a fixed term with their employer. Second, over half of the approximately 15 million employees of federal, state, and local governments are protected by tenure arrangements or other civil service procedural devices.[14] The third category, of course, is composed of the workers covered by collective bargaining agreements, 80 percent of which expressly prohibit discharge or discipline except for "cause" or "just cause."[15] Union membership in the United States, however, has now declined to less than 20 percent of the total labor force.[16] We may thus assume that something like three-quarters of our 100-million workforce operates under contracts at will. Extrapolating from such figures and from the arbitration records of the American Arbitration Association and the Federal Mediation and Conciliation Service, Cornelius Peck has estimated that at least 12,000 to 15,000 nonunion workers are discharged or disciplined annually whose cases would have been arbitrated if they had been subject to a collective agreement.[17] About half these disciplinary actions would presumably have been found unjustified. Perhaps even more important, Peck suggests that as many as 300,000 disciplinary cases a year arising in the nonunionized sector might have been subjected to negotiation and possible settlement if mandatory grievance procedures had been available. Jack Stieber calculates that about one million private industry employees with more than six months service are fired in a typical year without recourse to grievance and arbitration procedures.[18] He thinks that about 50,000 would be reinstated if they could appeal to impartial tribunals.[19] The gravity of the problem needs no further elaboration.

The first significant inroads on the doctrine of contract at will were made in situations where employers had retaliated against

---

[14]Peck, *supra* note 5, at 8–9.

[15]*Id.*, at 8.

[16]Bureau of Labor Statistics, Handbook of Labor Statistics—1978, Bull. No. 2000 (Washington: U.S. Government Printing Office, 1979), 507; New York Times, July 13, 1980, §3, p. 1, col. 1.

[17]Peck, *supra* note 5, at 10.

[18]Stieber, *supra* note 6, at 160.

[19]Letter from Jack Stieber to author, dated April 29, 1981. The estimate will appear in a forthcoming article, and is based on extrapolations from figures in the unionized sector.

employees for exercising their civil rights or declining to act unlawfully. These included cases where workers were fired for serving on a jury,[20] for filing a workers' compensation claim,[21] or even for refusing to give perjured testimony.[22] Plainly, such egregious instances of retaliatory discipline enabled the courts to invoke overarching concepts of "public policy" without reaching the question of whether an employer needed a positive justification for his action. They were akin to decisions that, while a landlord may ordinarily evict a tenant at the end of a lease for any reason or for no reason, he may not evict because the tenant has filed charges under the housing code.[23] Even so, right through the 1960s and 1970s other courts continued to apply the contract-at-will principle with full rigor. A secretary's discharge was sustained, for example, when she went against her immediate supervisor's order and indicated her availability for jury service, even though a senior partner in the firm had said she should do her civic duty.[24] And a court left untouched the dismissal of a long-time salesman for a steel manufacturer because he complained to his superiors and ultimately to a company vice president, justifiably as it later proved, that a new tubular casing could seriously endanger anyone using it.[25]

Another breakthrough occurred in *Monge* v. *Beebe Rubber Co.*,[26] when the New Hampshire Supreme Court extended the concept of retaliatory discharge to an action on an oral employment contract for an indefinite term. A female worker had been fired after rejecting her foreman's sexual advances. The court concluded:

> "We hold that a termination by the employer of a contract of employment at will which is motivated by bad faith or malice or based on retaliation is not in the best interest of the economic system or the public good and constitutes a breach of the employment contract."[27]

Monge may be said to go beyond the earlier retaliation cases because it did not involve the assertion of a statutory right

---

[20]*Nees* v. *Hocks*, 272 Ore. 210, 536 P.2d 512 (1975).

[21]*Sventko* v. *Kroger Co.*, 69 Mich. App. 644, 245 N.W.2d 151 (1976).

[22]*Petermann* v. *Teamsters Local 396*, 174 Cal. App. 2d 184, 344 P.2d 25, 44 LRRM 2968 (1959).

[23]*See, e.g., Edwards* v. *Habib*, 397 F.2d 687 (D.C.Cir. 1968), *cert. den.* 393 U.S. 1016 (1969).

[24]*Mallard* v. *Boring*, 182 Cal. App. 2d 390, 6 Cal. Rptr. 171 (1960).

[25]*Geary* v. *United States Steel Corp.*, 456 Pa. 171, 319 A.2d 174 (1974).

[26]114 N.H. 130, 316 A.2d 549 (1974).

[27]*Id.*, at 133.

or other clearly enunciated public policy. It stops short, however, of imposing any affirmative obligation on an employer to demonstrate a reasonable basis for adverse personnel action.

Michigan edged closer to a broader requirement of just cause for discharge in certain circumstances with its two 1980 decisions in *Toussaint* v. *Blue Cross & Blue Shield of Michigan* and *Ebling* v. *Masco Corporation.* [28] Toussaint and Ebling had been employed in middle management positions for five and two years, respectively. Each had been told upon hiring that he would be employed as long as he "did the job." Toussaint had also been handed a personnel manual that stated it was company "policy" to release employees "for just cause only." The court held that a jury could find that a provision forbidding discharge except for cause had become part of the indefinite term contracts either by "express agreement, oral or written," or, in Toussaint's case, as a result of "legitimate expectations grounded in his employer's written policy statements set forth in the manual of personnel policies."[29] Although the Michigan approach opens the door for a court to infer a just cause provision from an employer's overly hearty welcome to sought-after employees, there are a couple of important qualifications. First, the factual basis for the inference, by its very nature, is likely to be found only in dealings with higher level personnel, not rank-and-file workers. Second, the employer can eliminate the protection simply by refraining from any assurance about the reasons for termination.

A further wrinkle was added by the Supreme Court of California in *Tameny* v. *Atlantic Richfield Co.* [30] An employee alleged he had been discharged for refusing to participate in an illegal scheme to fix retail gasoline prices. The court held that the plaintiff could sue not only in contract but also in tort for a wrongful act committed in the course of the contractual relationship. The practical significance of this is that the employee is entitled to pursue compensatory tort and punitive damages, which are not generally available in contract actions. The Supreme Court of New Jersey has also sustained a cause of action

---

[28]408 Mich. 579,.292 N.W.2d 880 (1980).
[29]*Id.*, at 598–599. *Accord: Cleary* v. *American Airlines, Inc.*, 168 Cal. Rptr. 722 (Cal. App. 1980); *Pugh* v. *See's Candies, Inc.*, 171 Cal. Rptr. 917 (Cal. App. 1981). *See also Fortune* v. *National Cash Register Co.*, 373 Mass. 96, 364 N.E.2d 1251 (1977) (duty of fair dealing).
[30]164 Cal. Rptr. 839 (Cal. Sup. Ct. 1980).

in both tort and contract when an employee is discharged for "refusing to perform an act that violates a clear mandate of public policy."[31]

Despite these salutary developments, however, the blunt reality is that even in the most enlightened American jurisdictions, unorganized private employers need make no positive showing of cause before ridding themselves of an unwanted employee.

Western Europe

The story is quite different concerning job terminations in most of the rest of the industrial world. The International Labor Organization recommended in 1963 that there should be a "valid reason for such termination connected with the capacity or conduct of the worker or based on the operational requirements [of the employer]."[32] Protection against unfair discharge is afforded by statute in all Common Market countries and in Sweden and Norway.[33]

"Unfair" is variously defined, but the differences in phraseology seem to indicate little if any difference in meaning.[34] An American arbitrator would not feel uncomfortable applying the standards. Ordinarily, there must be advance notice for a discharge, but summary dismissal may be allowed for "flagrant" misconduct or "urgent cause." The burden of proving a "fair" discharge generally rests on the employer. Compensation for periods that vary from country to country is the usual remedy for an unfair dismissal. Reinstatement is rarely authorized and even more rarely employed.

The common pattern in Western Europe is to try discharge cases before specialized labor courts or industrial tribunals.[35] Typically these are tripartite, with a professional judge or legally trained individual serving as chairman, and with laypersons drawn from the ranks of employers and employees serving as associates.

---

[31]*Pierce v. Ortho Pharmaceutical Corp.*, 84 N.J. 58, 417 A.2d 505 (1980).

[32]*Recommendation No. 119, Employer Discipline: I.L.O. Report*, 18 Rutgers L.Rev. 446, 449 (1964).

[33]Stieber, *supra* note 6, at 157–159; *see also* Summers, *supra* note 7, at 509–519. Canadian employees covered by the federal Labour Code are also protected. Howlett, *supra* note 4, at 166. Japan and many other non-European countries provide protection as well. Committee Report, *At-Will Employment and the Problem of Unjust Dismissal*, 36 The Record 170, 175 (1981).

[34]Stieber, *supra* note 6, at 157–159; Summers, *supra* note 7, at 509–519.

[35]Summers, *supra* note 7, at 510–519.

Proposals for Ensuring "Just Cause"

At this late date I take it as a given that employees, generally, should be protected, generally, against unjust discipline. Anyone not convinced about this premise is commended to the writings of the illustrious band I have previously cited.[36] But the consensus on objective is not matched by any consensus on means.

To begin with, there is a dispute over the appropriate theory to employ. Blades in his seminal article thought that contract doctrine was so weighted down with the baggage of mutuality of obligation and consideration that it should be shelved in favor of the "more elastic principles" of tort law.[37] Most of the early decisions upholding an employee's cause of action for "abusive discharge" did indeed proceed on the basis of a prima facie tort.[38] Moreover, tort law has the advantage of permitting a wider range of remedies, including punitive damages where appropriate. Yet tort law, grounded as it is in rather nebulous notions of "public policy," has inherent limitations. Often a judge will not be persuaded that an individual injury has risen to the height of an offense against public policy—witness the case of the hapless steel salesman.[39] More fundamentally, public policy may be too coarse a net to catch the more personalized wrong; how should we classify the unwanted overtures of the macho foreman?[40]

Responding to these concerns, a number of commentators have argued that the action should sound in contract rather than tort. Thus, Professor John Blackburn of Ohio State contends that implying a right not to be discharged without good cause would actually conform to the probable intent of the parties to the employment relation.[41] It would also enlarge the scope of employee protection, extending redress to any dismissal not supported by cause instead of restricting relief to malicious or abusive discharges. Blackburn even views the loss of punitive damages as a gain for healthy personnel relations, since he believes the goal should be a make-whole remedy and not a com-

---

[36]*See* notes 1–7, *supra.*
[37]Blades, *supra* note 1, at 1422.
[38]*See* cases cited in notes 20–22, *supra.*
[39]*See* note 25, *supra.*
[40]*See* note 26, *supra.*
[41]Blackburn, *Restricted Employer Discharge Rights: A Changing Concept of Employment at Will,* 17 Amer. Bus. L.J. 467, 482 (1980).

bined penalty and windfall. *Monge,* the case of the rebuffed foreman, relied on an implied contract theory, and *Toussaint,* involving oral assurances and written personnel policies, seemed to intermingle express and implied contract.

I see no reason for having to choose between tort and contract law. Either or both would seem appropriate, as the occasion warrants. For me the more important questions are whether we seek common law or statutory solutions and what kinds of tribunals, procedures, and remedies we ought to provide. Here, too, there is disagreement. Summers, for example, is satisfied that the courts are unwilling "to break through their self-created crust of legal doctrine,"[42] and that we must look to the legislatures for the vindication of employees' rights. Peck, on the other hand, believes legislation is so much the product of organized interest groups that almost by definition unorganized workers are an ineffective lobby and must turn to the courts for redress.[43]

Both these assessments contain a good deal of truth. With the benefit of several years' extra hindsight and the further perspective provided by the 1980–1981 decisions from California, Michigan, and New Jersey, I am prepared to say that it is not at all impossible a solution will be fashioned by the judiciary. But the courts are likely to be long on generalization and short on detail when it comes to spelling out procedures, remedies, and the like. At the same time, even though the legislatures may not wish to take the initiative for a whole fistful of understandable political reasons, they may be goaded into action by the boldness of some courts. Furthermore, it is entirely conceivable that at some point employers themselves might support legislation on the ground the compromises and greater exactness of a statutory solution are preferable to the broad strokes and blurred outlines often produced by an innovative judiciary. The upshot may be that in a number of states the process will go through two stages. The first few steps, halting, tentative, or even blundering, will be taken by the courts, and then the legislatures will be almost compelled to move in and provide a more definitive blueprint.

A critical factor in securing legislative relief may be the attitude of organized labor. It is about the only interest group one can identify that might be willing to take the lead in promoting

[42]Summers, *supra* note 7, at 521.
[43]Peck, *supra* note 5, at 3.

such a cause. A common assumption, however, is that unions will not favor legislation protecting employees against arbitrary treatment by employers because it will eliminate or detract from one of the unions' prime selling-points in their efforts to organize the unorganized. I cannot deny this possibility, but I think it would be as short-sighted as was organized labor's initial hostility toward the Fair Labor Standards Act.[44] First, and not insignificantly, organized labor could profit considerably from refurbishing its image as the champion of the disadvantaged. Second, and perhaps more practically, a universal rule against dismissal without cause should actually prove beneficial to unions in their organizing drives. Now, when a union sympathizer is fired in the middle of a campaign, it must be established by a preponderance of the evidence that he or she would not have been discharged but for the exercise of rights protected by the Labor Act.[45] That is frequently a burden too heavy to bear. With a just cause requirement generally applicable, it would be up to the employer to show that some positive, acceptable basis existed for the discharge. Finally, I believe there is a strong likelihood that just cause standards will act more as a spur than a hindrance to union organizing. The promise of fair treatment will be held out to employees; the promise may remain a tantalizing and unrealized dream, however, unless there is present the means to actualize it. Constant, effective representation and advocacy is the surest way to ensure any right. That is the lesson for unions and the unorganized to heed.

In addition to the possible reservations of organized labor, some neutrals in industrial relations might oppose a statutory just cause requirement for fear that it would erode such worthy values as voluntarism, private initiative, and creativity, and more particularly the collective bargaining process itself. I, too, treasure the unique American institution of union-employer bargaining, but when even so hardheaded an observer as John Dunlop can be found rhapsodizing on its "beauty,"[46] I think we should all be wary about being carried away by the mystique of the process. Collective bargaining, after all, is a means and not an end. The objective is the betterment of the individual work-

---

[44]Dulles, Labor in America (New York: Thomas Y. Crowell, 1960), 283–285.

[45]*Miller Elec. Mfg. Co.* v. *NLRB,* 265 F.2d 225, 43 LRRM 225 (7th Cir. 1959); *NLRB* v. *West Point Mfg. Co.,* 245 F.2d 783, 40 LRRM 2234 (5th Cir. 1957); *cf. Wright Line,* 251 NLRB No. 150, 105 LRRM 1169 (1980).

[46]Dunlop, *The Social Utility of Collective Bargaining,* in Challenges to Collective Bargaining, ed. Lloyd Ulman (Englewood Cliffs, N.J.: Prentice-Hall, 1967), 168, 173.

ing person. When less than a quarter of the labor force is currently afforded protection against unjust discipline, I feel the needs of the other three-quarters outweigh some theoretical risk to traditional bargaining processes. Even then, assuming history is any guide, we underrate the flexibility and resilience of collective bargaining if we believe it cannot adapt to, and indeed exploit, a new legal environment.

Statutory Arbitration

If employees are to be fully and effectively protected against unjust discipline, new specialized legislation will eventually be necessary. The judiciary, as we have seen, may be able to respond to extreme cases and to the atypical situations of middle-management personnel. But the courts have no capacity to construct an administrative apparatus for enforcement purposes, and their more formalized processes are not readily accessible to rank-and-file workers. Nor do I see much hope, as do Peck[47] and Blumrosen,[48] in either the Constitution or existing civil rights legislation. To me the former route seems barred by the courts' increasing reluctance to expand the "state action" concept,[49] and the latter by the need to accord some modicum of respect to the legislative intent to forbid job discrimination only on the specified bases of "race, sex, religion, national origin, age," and the like.[50] It comes down, then, to a matter of further legislation. A federal statute would seem foredoomed in this period of national retrenchment. State legislation appears more promising, and it offers the additional advantage of the opportunity for some healthy experimentation with alternative procedures. During the past few years bills have been drafted in such states as Connecticut,[51] Michigan,[52] and New Jersey[53] to provide "just cause" protection to unorganized workers. In the remainder of this paper I shall consider some of the principal issues almost any statutory proposal will have to confront. Obviously, there will often be substantial values in competition, and more

---

[47]Peck, *supra* note 5, at 26–42.
[48]Blumrosen, *supra* note 3.
[49]*See, e.g., Moose Lodge No. 107* v. *Irvis,* 407 U.S. 163 (1972).
[50]See text at note 8, *supra.*
[51]Conn. Comm. Bill No. 5151 (1975).
[52]At the time of writing, Michigan Representative Perry Bullard had completed the fourth draft of a proposed bill and was planning to introduce it shortly.
[53]N.J. Assembly Bill No. 1832 (1980).

than one choice could be supported. My own suggestions will try to take account of both the ideal and the politically feasible.

"Just Cause" Standard

The first question can be disposed of the easiest. The statute should articulate a standard for lawful discharge or discipline in terms of "just cause" or equivalent language, without further definition. Even in Western European countries having nothing like the body of American arbitral precedent interpreting "just cause" requirements, there has apparently been little difficulty in applying broadly phrased statutory criteria. Any effort at specification is bound to risk underinclusiveness. The decision-makers can be counted on to flesh out "just cause" in the same way as have the arbitrators.

The statute should probably remain discreetly silent on such items as the burden and the quantum of proof. The differing standards that have been applied by public tribunals in job discrimination cases and by private arbitrators under collective bargaining agreements will tug in opposite directions. Concrete cases would appear to provide the best vehicle for dealing with such issues.

Protected Classes of Employees

It is hard to argue in principle that any employee should be subject to an unjust termination. Still, when one reaches the presidency of the Ford Motor Company, it does not seem wholly unfitting that one accepts the risk of being confronted one day by an announcement from the chairman of the board, "I'm getting rid of you because I don't like you." Beyond that, there are practical reasons for excluding certain classes of employees from the protection of a statute.

Managers and Supervisors. In the higher ranges of management, one official's evaluation of another's business judgment may become so intertwined with questions of fair personal treatment that the two cannot be separated. That does not reach down to the level of shop foremen and other supervisors, who are excluded from the organizational protections of the National Labor Relations Act because they are management's immediate representatives to rank-and-file employees and any union that may be bargaining for them. This concern about potential conflicts of interest plainly does not apply to "just cause" legislation, and supervisors as such should be covered. More troubling is the position of middle-management personnel, who are among the most exposed and vulnerable. Unfortunately, our lexicon of industrial relations usage does not contain a convenient term distinguishing middle management, whom we should protect, from higher management, whom we may wish to exclude. I would suggest pointing the direction with as serviceable a definition as we can muster, and leaving the rest to interpretation.

Probationary Employees. There is almost a presumption that an employer will not dismiss an employee unfairly in the early days of employment—otherwise, why hire? Moreover, the first few weeks or months of employment enable the employer to size up the new recruit and assess his or her performance on the job. On the other hand, it is not until an employee has been part of an establishment for some measurable time that he can reasonably feel he possesses anything like an equity in his position. For all these reasons it is generally recognized in collective bargaining agreements and elsewhere that so-called "probationary" employees are not entitled to just cause protections. Howlett would make the probation period one year;[54] Summers and the Michigan and New Jersey bills opt for six months.[55] The latter seems adequate to me.

Small Employers. Theoretically, job protections should not depend on the size of the employer. Indeed, arbitrariness and individual spite may well be more common on the part of an idiosyncratic sole entrepreneur than on the part of a large, structured corporation. Nonetheless, we feel uneasy about intruding too quickly into the sometimes intensely personal relationships of small, intimate establishments. There is also concern about not dissipating our resources in an endless pursuit of minor culprits instead of concentrating on the major malefactors. A suitable dividing line, at least at the outset, would seem to be employers having between ten[56] and fifteen[57] or more employees.

Public Employees. Public employees generally have constitutional guarantees against the deprivation of their "vested" job

---

[54]Howlett, *supra* note 4, at 167.
[55]Summers, *supra* note 7, at 525; Mich. draft bill, §3(1); N.J. Assembly Bill No. 1832 (1980), §1.
[56]Summers, *supra* note 7, at 526; Mich. draft bill, §3(2).
[57]Civil Rights Act of 1964, as amended, 42 U.S.C. §2000e(b).

interests without due process. Approximately half also have
more specific civil service or tenure protections against unjust
dismissal. At least the latter group, as the Michigan bill pro-
poses, could properly be excluded from any new statutory
procedures. In addition, since American employment legislation
has traditionally differentiated between the public and private
sectors, it may be politically advantageous to maintain that distinction by limiting any new protections to private industry.

Organized Employees. Most of the arguments in favor of just
cause requirements have been phrased in terms of protecting
"unorganized" workers. The Michigan bill expressly excludes
employees "protected" by a union contract.[58] Furthermore,
there is at least some potential for a federal preemption problem
in covering unionized workers, as any state statute would necessarily affect collective bargaining under the NLRA. The risk is
slight, however, since the Supreme Court has taken a liberal
attitude toward state regulation in the areas of employment
discrimination,[59] unemployment compensation,[60] and similar
welfare concerns.[61] The issue must be faced as a matter of policy, then, whether to include workers subject to a collective
bargaining agreement.

Except for the possible conservation of limited administrative
resources, I see no justifiable grounds for treating organized
employees differently from the unorganized with respect to
basic statutory protections. If we conclude that workers in general are entitled to invoke a just cause standard, the same public
policy should extend to all, regardless of the existence of parallel protections in a collective bargaining agreement. There is
precedent for such an approach in both the NLRA and civil
rights legislation, which clearly extend to workers who are also
covered by antidiscrimination guarantees in their union contracts.[62]

For me the difficult question is the proper relationship of
statutory and contractual rights and remedies, when both are

[58]Mich. draft bill, §3(1). New Jersey more specifically limits protection to an employee
"without the benefit of . . . a collective bargaining agreement that contains a grievance
procedure covering these matters which terminates in binding arbitration." Assembly
Bill No. 1832 (1980), §1.
[59]*E.g., Colorado Anti-Discrimination Comm'n v. Continental Air Lines,* 372 U.S. 714, 52
LRRM 2889 (1963).
[60]*New York Tel. Co. v. New York State Dept. of Labor,* 440 U.S. 519, 100 LRRM 2896 (1979).
[61]*See, e.g., Teamsters Local 24 v. Oliver,* 358 U.S. 283, 297, 43 LRRM 2374 (1959).
[62]*General American Transp. Corp.,* 228 NLRB No. 102, 94 LRRM 1483 (1977); *Alexander
v. Gardner-Denver Co.,* 415 U.S. 36, 7 FEP Cases 81 (1974).

available. Summers would give the contract priority to the extent of requiring a disciplined employee to exhaust the contractual grievance procedure, and would make any arbitral award that is obtained final and binding.[63] But he would not let the union enter a binding settlement with the employer, as it now may do under *Vaca* v. *Sipes*,[64] subject only to its duty of fair representation toward the employee. Instead, if the union declines to arbitrate under the contract, Summers would permit the employee to proceed on his or her own to the neutral tribunal provided by the state. He believes only "the most stubborn individual" would persist in the face of the union's settlement. From my experience with the United Automobile Workers' Public Review Board, I suspect there are more such "stubborn individuals" about than Summers imagines. Otherwise, I find his conclusions reasonable, but not entirely logical. For example, if the statutory right is so powerful that the union cannot waive it, why should not the employee be able, like an employee charging employer discrimination under section 8(a)(3) of the NLRA,[65] to circumvent the grievance procedure completely, instead of being compelled to exhaust contractual procedures first? My own inclination would be to put more trust in the flexibility of collective bargaining, and to leave some of these questions for future resolution amidst the counterpoint of particular facts, negotiated tradeoffs, dollar costs, and the union's overriding duty of fair representation. I see no reason here to engage in the same close scrutiny of union, employer, or arbitrator conduct that may be appropriate in dealing with such sensitive and divisive issues as race and sex discrimination.[66]

Discipline Covered

Advocates of employee protection have usually talked about protection against discharge, the so-called economic "capital punishment" of industrial relations. That is dramatic. But an extended suspension, a demotion, a denied promotion, or an onerous job assignment, while not as blatant, can be almost as devastating. Such job actions should be regarded as the functional equivalent of discharge. The Michigan bill may be politi-

---

[63]Summers, *supra* note 7, at 528.
[64]386 U.S. 171, 64 LRRM 2369 (1967).
[65]*General American Transp. Corp.*, *supra* note 62.
[66]*See, e.g., Alexander* v. *Gardner Denver Co.*, *supra* note 62; *Glover* v. *St. Louis-San Francisco Ry.*, 393 U.S. 324, 70 LRRM 2097 (1969).

cally astute in the way it puts the matter, in effect creating a "constructive discharge," though it requires the employee to engage in a variation on Russian roulette: "Discharge includes a resignation or quit that results from an improper or unreasonable action or inaction of the employer."[67]

European experience indicates that protections against unjust discipline will inevitably force inquiries into an employer's handling of "redundancies," that is, layoffs or other employee reassignments to meet economic downturns or reduced production demands. Otherwise, there is simply too much opportunity to disguise unfair treatment of an individual employee as part of an employer's overall reaction to business oscillations. This hardly imposes an oppressive burden on employers. All they need do is establish almost any sort of rational, verifiable criterion—seniority, skills, past productivity, etc.—as the basis for their job determinations, and they are practically impervious to challenge.

Adjudicators and Procedure

A new statute could pick and choose across a broad spectrum of possible enforcement devices. Most persons would probably rule out the courts as too formal, too costly, and already overloaded. Existing administrative agencies, either the labor relations boards or the civil rights commissions, are more likely candidates. Robert Howlett, the former chairman of the Michigan Employment Relations Commission, favors placing administration in the hands of state labor departments.[68] He feels the hearing officers of the conventional labor relations agencies are more attuned to organizational than to individual concerns. He also believes the whole proposal would face less political opposition if it were divorced from the usual union-employer regulatory context. My view is that a question like this is best answered by reference to the governmental structure and industrial relations climate of each state.

More significant, I think, than the locus of administration is whether we follow the hearing officer-agency model or the arbitration model. I hope I am not merely exhibiting crass professional bias when I join the overwhelming majority of my fellow arbitrators who have addressed the issue in concluding that

---

[67]Mich. draft bill, §2(3).
[68]Howlett, *supra* note 4, at 167.

arbitration is the superior procedure for "just cause" determinations. Adopting the arbitration format would immediately make available the vast body of arbitral precedent concerning substance and procedure that has been developed in countless decisions over the years. It would permit the use of an established nucleus of experienced arbitrators, and of the growing number of young, able aspirants who are caught in the vicious circle of being denied experience because they have no experience. It would facilitate maximum flexibility, at least until more is learned about future caseloads, because there would be no need to engage a large permanent staff at the outset. It would leave open the option, however, of utilizing a mix, as does New York, of "staff" arbitrators and of free-lancers drawn from a panel for ad hoc assignments. The relative informality and speed of arbitration—though both those qualities are now often much eroded—should also appeal to rank-and-file employees. Finally, just cause rulings do not call for the minute technical expertise that may be essential in a permanent hearing officer specializing in unemployment compensation or Social Security claims.

Although arbitration is the customary capstone of collectively bargained grievance procedures, only a small percentage of the grievances that are filed reach arbitration. Arguably the whole system would collapse if all claims went to the final step. Most are settled or dropped along the way. It would seem highly desirable to have some comparable sieve in the statutory procedure. The most obvious would be a preliminary mediation stage of minimum duration, and the Michigan bill so provides.[69] Howlett would have an official in the administering agency make a "reasonable cause" determination before a case could go to arbitration.[70] I agree such a requirement makes sense, at least if the state is to bear the major share of the cost of the proceedings.

Another advantage of the arbitral model is that the award is final and binding, without the need for agency adoption or review as in the case of a hearing officer's report or decision. Ordinarily, of course, a private arbitration award will not be set aside by the courts unless the arbitrator exceeded his jurisdiction or the award was obtained by fraud, collusion, or similar

---

[69]Mich. draft bill, §6(2) (30 days).
[70]Howlett, *supra* note 4, at 169.

means. That ought to be the standard here. Since a statutory arbitrator is imposed on the parties, however, there may be considerable pressure to adopt the stiffer "substantial evidence" standard. Moreover, some state constitutions require that rulings by public agencies and officials be supported by "competent, material, and substantial evidence on the record considered as a whole."[71] If a "substantial evidence" requirement obtains, one way or the other, it raises the grim prospect of verbatim transcripts, with all their attendant delays and added costs. Although some persons seem to eye a tape recorder in a hearing room the way certain Indians are said to view cameras —as if cameras were out to capture their souls—the sponsor of the Michigan bill was persuaded to accept this cheap, handy device as a sufficient means of documentation,[72] and I should hope others would follow suit.

Remedies

Arbitrators under labor contracts have demonstrated both ingenuity and common sense in devising a range of remedies to counter unjust discharge and other discipline. They have, for instance, evolved the cardinal principle that the punishment must fit not only the offense but also the offender. What is suitable for the short-term employee of spotty record is not right for the long-time veteran of irreproachable deportment. Presumably statutory arbitrators will temper their judgments accordingly.

More specifically, remedies for unjust discharge in the United States have traditionally included reinstatement with or without back pay. In Europe reinstatement is the exception. Apparently it is felt that the lone, unwanted employee can seldom regain a comfortable position in his old workplace, and it is better to award him severance pay and let him go. A number of American experts also seem to believe that reinstatement is unfeasible without the presence of a labor union to support the restored employee. I think awarding severance pay in lieu of reinstatement is an option the arbitrator should have. But I see no reason for precluding reinstatement out of an exaggerated regard for the employee's psychic well-being. American workers are probably more transient than their European

---

[71]E.g., Mich. Const. 1963, Art.VI, §28.
[72]Mich. draft bill, §10(5).

counterparts, and they are used to handling unfamiliar job situations. A reinstatement order also gives them extra bargaining leverage in working out any future adjustment with the employer. I would grant reinstatement when it seemed appropriate, and let the employee decide what use to make of the award.

Costs

The arbitrator's fee and expenses under collectively bargained arrangements are normally shared, 50-50, by the parties, although occasionally the loser pays all. Each side bears its own representation costs, if any. A few years ago my former colleague, Harry Edwards, calculated that the typical one-day hearing costs a union $2200;[73] that would be a prohibitive figure for many individual employees, especially those out of work. Clyde Summers declares that "in principle" under a statutory scheme the state should cover administrative costs and the arbitrator's fee, just as it bears the expense of courts and judges.[74] He would allow a nominal filing fee, perhaps $100, to discourage frivolous claims. Howlett would require such a fee at the point a case is referred to arbitration by a screening officer.[75]

In theory one cannot fault that approach. But there may be practical problems in implementing it. There is now a strong tradition in the collective bargaining sector that the parties shall pay the arbitrator. Although a few states, like Connecticut and Wisconsin,[76] provide arbitrators at public expense, the trend has been, in a kind of reversal of Gresham's Law, for privately paid arbitrators to replace publicly paid arbitrators. Thus, prior to the Taft-Hartley Act, the old United States Conciliation Service furnished free arbitration through staff personnel. Now, of course, the FMCS simply offers parties the names of private arbitrators. New York continues to provide a choice of staff arbitrators paid by the state and "panel" arbitrators whom the parties must pay.[77] But Robben Fleming reports that "the

[73]Edwards, *Problems Facing Arbitration Process,* in Labor Relations Yearbook—1977 (Washington: BNA Books, 1978), 206.
[74]Summers, *supra* note 7, at 524.
[75]Howlett, *supra* note 4, at 169.
[76]Summers, *supra* note 7, at 524; Mueller, *The Role of the Wisconsin Employment Board Arbitrator,* 1963 Wis. L.Rev. 47, 49.
[77]Summers, *supra* note 7, at 522.

amount of free service is declining by deliberate choice of the state agency."[78] The list of private arbitrators is publicized and the availability of staff personnel is not. Moreover, in a period of severe financial stringency for many state governments, the prospect of one more new and perhaps substantial expense is sure to generate even further opposition to a proposal that is not going to elicit universal acclaim in any event. The Michigan bill has heeded the counsel of prudence and provided that the employer and the employee "shall bear equally" the cost of the arbitrator.[79]

Elite private arbitrators, I regret to have to observe, undoubtedly have a personal interest in this debate over costs. If the state pays the bill, the state will almost certainly, like Connecticut, set the rate.[80] That may be fine for fledgling arbitrators, but it may not be adequate for financing many trips to Maui. I shall leave to others any necessary development of this somber theme, expressing only a modest hope that we may comport ourselves more gracefully and responsibly than some other professions in the perceived face of rampant socialism.

Conclusion

Protection against unjust discipline is an idea whose time has long since come. The common law of contract, tort, or even property needs only a small adjustment to accommodate this new concept. More to the point, statutory relief for this long-neglected abuse of the unorganized worker can now be likened to a moral imperative for conscientious legislators and for all those who labor in the field of industrial relations.

This is not "uncharted territory," as some timid courts have exclaimed.[81] This is terrain that has been carefully mapped in thousands of arbitration decisions since the Second World War. That body of arbitral precedent and a large and potentially much larger body of arbitrators stand ready to be drawn upon in the forging of a new set of statutory guarantees. The debates that remain over this detail or that detail should not obscure one central fact. In the 15 years or so since Blades enunciated his

---

[78]Fleming, The Labor Arbitration Process (Urbana: University of Illinois Press, 1965), 51.
[79]Mich. draft bill, §8(1).
[80]Summers, *supra* note 7, at 522.
[81]*Geary* v. *United States Steel Corp.*, 456 Pa. 171, 174, 319 A.2d 174 (1974).

thesis, many other experts have joined the chorus. Not a single respected and disinterested voice has been heard to suggest there is any valid, substantial reason for opposing the requirement of just cause.[82] No such reason has been suggested, in my judgment, because there is none.

Comment—

HENRY B. EPSTEIN*

We have heard three excellent and interesting descriptions of novel experiments designed to give a measure of job security to unorganized workers.

In my opinion, careful analysis will show that these are the exceptions which prove the rule. In the American labor-management situation, there is no effective substitute for the protections given a discharged employee by a well-written and administered discharge and arbitration section and an active union. In order to compare the present situation in an organized company with the novel cases described today, I have to review the benefits of unionized grievance procedures, as I see them.

The first and most important factor is the general labor-management climate. Employees who might be discharged in an arbitrary fashion in an unorganized employment situation will usually be treated differently in a unionized environment—depending on the labor-management climate at that time.

Job security for unionized employees encompasses much more than the submission of unsettled discharges to final and binding arbitration. The process includes negotiating the exact language under which discharges are permitted, careful training of stewards and union staff on the contract language, use of a multistep grievance procedure with emphasis on settling cases at the lowest possible level, screening cases for arbitration, screening arbitrators, actually presenting the arbitration case,

---

[82]At the time I first uttered these words in Maui, I believed them to be literally true. I underestimated the Academy membership's almost infinite capacity for differences of opinion. Immediately several "respected and disinterested" voices were heard to challenge the whole concept of a law requiring "just cause" for the discipline of unorganized employees—primarily, as I understand it, for the reasons mentioned in the text accompanying notes 44–46, *supra.* But I have decided to let my original phrasing stand; at least to date no one has seen fit to commit his contrary views to the permanency of print.

*Special Representative, American Federation of State, County, and Municipal Employees, Honolulu, Hawaii.

and finally, paying for the arbitrator, transcripts, lost wages, and other expenses.

As one who has spent almost all of my working life in the labor movement, I obviously think this is a good system that works well for the average discharged union member. It is not a perfect system. As those of you in the audience know, unions vary in effectiveness in their handling of discharge cases. It also has to be pointed out that the decision to take a case to arbitration is a political one.

However, the political situation in a union works to the discharged employee's advantage. The political pressure is on the union to back up the discharged member and get favorable results. It is very difficult for a union to refuse to take a discharge case to arbitration.

How does this compare to the novel cases described today?

The British Experience

As Professor Hepple points out very well, the British approach to notice of dismissals and grounds for dismissal is much different from the American one. Unions in Britain have not negotiated discharge and arbitration procedures similar to our typical American union agreement. Instead, anger about unfair dismissals has been expressed in wildcat walkouts by union members. I must say that this sounds as if it's good for the union members' emotions, though it must be tough on the overall labor-management situation.

After reading Professor Hepple's excellent paper, I get the impression that the British legislation is really an attempt to have a government body serve as an extension of union agreements to take care of unfair dismissal cases. The British tribunals perform the same functions as arbitrators perform in the American system.

The British legislation excludes coverage for employees in their first year of employment and completely excludes all employers with 20 or less employees. It is very possible that the most unfair discharges occur at small business establishments, and they are completely uncovered under this scheme.

The system obviously has the advantage of forcing employers to adopt clear rules on employee conduct and to be careful and build up a solid case before discharging an employee. In my experience, this is the same effect a union agreement has on a newly organized employer. Clear and fair policies on discharge are a two-edged sword, but inevitable when procedures exist to give greater protection to employees.

Professor Hepple points out that most cases are resolved informally, before coming to a formal hearing. The bottom line is that very few employees win their cases before the tribunals and that enforcement of decisions is difficult, except in industries where unions are strong. Even under the British experiment, the well-organized unions give their members a benefit which is greater than that available to unorganized workers.

Northrop Corporation

As Mr. Littrell points out, the Northrop experiment is unique. I find it hard to believe that many other companies would agree in advance to pay the entire cost of an arbitrator who may overturn an important management decision.

I have no reason to doubt the sincerity and good intentions of Northrop and the working of the grievance and arbitration system. The company admits candidly that the procedure has helped to keep the unions out.

The policy permits employees to appeal the application of company policy in their cases, but the employees have no say in the adoption of company policy.

The aggrieved employee is advised by employee relations representatives who "walk a thin line on a hard road," according to Mr. Littrell. There is now recognition that the employee is at a disadvantage in the presentation of a formal arbitration case and there are attempts being made now to improve that situation.

There appear to be several pluses in the system, as described by Mr. Littrell. It does emphasize getting settlements at the lowest possible level, and the existence of a grievance procedure with teeth does keep management on its toes. The test, it seems to me, comes when there is a major challenge to company decisions. How do those well-educated and diplomatic personnel men who walk a thin line react when top management says, "You've got to decide which side you're on"? Another test must come when dealing with the troublesome employee—the one with a lot of complaints and grievances. Does he get full and enthusiastic representation, or is he counseled to leave the company because he doesn't really fit in?

Northrop is giving its employees many of the benefits and procedures of a union agreement without the need to have a union. An interesting subject for a research project would be to determine whether it would have been cheaper for Northrop to have become unionized and to have worked out these procedures through normal collective bargaining. I suspect it would have been better for the ulcers of those employee relations reps walking a thin line in the personnel department.

Professor St. Antoine's Overview

Professor St. Antoine's presentation is a comprehensive overview of all possible considerations in connection with unjust discipline. Because of its comprehensive nature, it's possible to easily find something to agree with and something to question in the paper.

The review points to the three categories of American workers who presently have protection against unfair discipline. An interesting sidelight is that unionized public employees are in two of the three categories. The first public employee collective bargaining agreement I negotiated in Hawaii gave an employee the option of choosing whether to use the contractual grievance procedure or the established civil service appeal procedure.

Professor St. Antoine then estimates the number of employees who are terminated every year without any protection or rights. Several court cases are cited to point to a growing trend of courts to protect employees who have been unfairly disciplined. To me, these cases sound like isolated cases in which a sympathetic judge grasped at straws to help an employee who was obviously unfairly treated.

A lot of the thought in the presentation follows the theme of giving unorganized workers the protections and benefits unions have built up for their members over the years.

Consciously or unconsciously, every union negotiator goes through many of the same processes employed by Professor St. Antoine. Even if the negotiator is using a model contract from union headquarters, there are certain key points to watch. For example, a good contract section should cover not only discharge, because there are other forms of serious discipline. Be sure to write in "all" discipline or itemize: "discharge, suspension, demotion, etc." Also, a discipline section is meaningless unless there is strong language about layoffs, so that a layoff can't be used as a hidden way to get rid of an unwanted employee. Then there's the problem of coverage. Over the union's objections, probationary employees are usually excluded, so try to make the probationary period as short as possible.

A well-rounded approach is going to require going over all these grounds that have been travelled earlier by the unions. If the goal is to bring a measure of justice to employees previously unprotected, I find it hard to justify excluding employees of small businesses and middle management. They are probably the ones who need the protection more than other groups.

I agree with Professor St. Antoine that this is not a matter for the courts to handle. Placing these new functions in existing government agencies will also create problems. Look at the tremendous backlog of EEOC cases. Agencies like the Legal Aid Society and the Public Defender often find themselves plagued with huge caseloads, tiny budgets, and inexperienced staffs.

I really question the assumption that this is an idea whose time has come. Legislation to prohibit discrimination because of race, sex, religion, and age came slowly and only after major pushes by interested constituencies. It is still not adequately enforced and will probably face a weakening in the present political climate. If some of the laws are not repealed, they will be weakened by budget cuts and indifferent enforcement.

If you took a public opinion poll today and asked people whether they felt "unjust dismissals" should be controlled, you would probably get a very high percentage of yeses. If you asked the same people: "Do you think that an American businessman should have the right to manage his business efficiently and remove people he feels are interfering with the efficiency of his business?" you would probably also get a large "Yes."

Because of this contradictory thinking, I question whether this is really an idea whose time has come.

Probable Union Position

Would American unions support legislation similar to the British law, if it were introduced in Congress?

It would be hard not to support such a measure. Unions would support such a proposal for the same reasons that they support minimum wage legislation, national health insurance, OSHA, and antidiscrimination legislation. Most antidiscrimination crusades have originated elsewhere and then received the support of the labor movement. Sometimes this is with mixed feelings, as when the affirmative action movement conflicts with traditional union positions on seniority.

The American labor movement does have a social conscience. It still sees itself as the spokesman for all working people, organized and unorganized.

While American unions would probably support such a proposal, I do not see such a plan succeeding in the immediate future. I don't see any great enthusiasm among unions for such a change since the membership is pretty well protected by the present contract language and procedures. And, in all honesty, I cannot see the Reagan Administration and a conservative Congress supporting a proposal for another government agency and greater restrictions on American business.

CHAPTER 3

OUTER LIMITS OF INTEREST ARBITRATION: AUSTRALIAN, CANADIAN, AND UNITED STATES EXPERIENCES

I. Notes on the Australian Scene

Sir John Moore*

In order to understand the industrial relations scene in Australia, it is necessary to understand the institutional framework of tribunals. There are a number of tribunals, both federal and state, which handle industrial disputes, but the Australian Conciliation and Arbitration Commission is the predominant one. It is composed of a president, ten deputy presidents, and 25 commissioners. The president must be a lawyer; eight of the deputy presidents are lawyers and all have the title and status of judges. Of the other deputy presidents, one is a well-known labor economist and the other is an expert in the industrial relations field. They, too, have the status of judges. The 25 commissioners come from a variety of backgrounds including unions, employer organizations, employers, and the public sector. However, upon appointment they lose their representative status and are not to be seen as union or employer representatives. One of the deputy presidents and two of the commissioners are women.

All members of the Commission are appointed by the central government. They are appointed until the age of 65 years and have a virtually unchallengeable tenure of office.

The Commission is divided into panels, each of which consists of a deputy president and two or three commissioners. The president arranges the panels and assigns to each a group of industries which then become the responsibility of the panel.

There is a statutory requirement that when an employer or a union becomes aware of an industrial dispute, the dispute must

---

*President, Australian Conciliation and Arbitration Commission, Sydney, Australia.

be reported to the Commission. Members of the Commission are also required to keep themselves informed of matters relating to their industries and can act on their own motion. When a dispute has been reported, it is referred automatically to the deputy president in charge of the appropriate panel who decides which member of the panel will deal with it. That member then arranges appropriate action to handle the matter.

There is a further statutory requirement that the first step should be conciliation. Therefore, the parties are required to confer either with or without the Commission member to attempt to settle their differences. Failing this, the matter will go to arbitration by the member concerned. However, if he has been in the conciliation conferences, objection can be taken to his arbitrating, in which case another member of the Commission takes over.

The arbitration is normally an open hearing, though the Commission has power to sit in private. The hearing rooms are like court rooms and are often called "courts." They physically resemble other courts inasmuch as the Commission sits on a bench, there is a bar table, and so on. This is because the arbitration is essentially conducted as an adversary proceeding, and broad Commission proceedings follow the pattern of ordinary litigation—for example, oral evidence under oath, addresses, and the like. However, to the lawyers, proceedings before the Commission are quite dissimilar to those in the courts. The rules of evidence are not enforced, there is often hearsay evidence, there is tender of documents without proof, and there is a great deal of latitude allowed to those appearing. Lawyers are permitted to appear by leave of the Commission and consent of all parties or, if there is no consent, there are special circumstances which make legal representation desirable. In fact, in almost all cases of moment there is legal representation of one or all parties, and a small bar has grown up which specializes in industrial matters.

It is also quite common for inspections of work to take place to assist the Commission to determine the matter. These, again, are quite informal and are not subject to the stricture that they must be supported by oral evidence in a formal way. Indeed, statements, generally unsworn, made by both employers and employees about the work are often taken down during an inspection and subsequently treated as part of the evidentiary material.

When the arbitration has been completed, the Commission, after taking time to consider the matter, will give its decision and the reasons for it. The decision may take a number of forms, the most important one being an award. A complete award as a matter of law contains the minimum contract of employment which may be entered into for the particular job or jobs covered by the award. Common clauses include rates of pay, hours of work, annual leave, and special payments for particular kinds of unpleasantness or arduousness. Many awards of the Commission are quite long and complex, this being the result of many years of having to deal with special situations that require special remedies. The employees bound by the award are usually bound by reference to the union to which they belong, and the employers bound are either named or bound as members of the employer organization to which they belong.

It should be emphasized that the award is the minimum contract of employment. It is legally permissible for an employer to offer and for an employee to accept better terms of employment than the award specifies, and this happens quite often. Another important fact is that the provisions of an award can be enforced by special and simplified means; for example, an employee claiming underpayment can recover by a much simpler method than he could at common law, but the claim would have to be confined to underpayment according to the award.

In addition to proceedings before a single member, which is the norm, there is an internal appeal system within the Commission to a Full Bench, which comprises at least three members, of whom two must be presidential members—that is, the president and a deputy president or two deputy presidents. The composition of appeal benches is a matter for the president, as is also the time and place of hearings. There is a strict time limit on the making of appeals, 21 days, and the appeal will not be considered unless the Full Bench, in hearing, is of the opinion that the matter is of such importance that it is in the public interest to do so.

There is another procedure whereby a matter before a single member can, on the application of a party or the Minister of Industrial Relations, be referred to a Full Bench of the Commission. Whether or not the matter is referred is a decision for the president to make, who, before referring it, must be of the opinion that the matter is of such importance that, in the public interest, it should be referred. There is also a provision that empowers the president himself to refer a matter to a Full Bench, and the Minister of Industrial Relations may seek a review of a particular matter by a Full Bench.

Finally, there are certain fundamental matters of industrial significance which can be dealt with only by a Full Bench. They are standard hours of work, increases in rates of pay based on grounds related to the national economy, minimum wages, and annual leave or long-service leave. Individual members of the Commission can deal with these matters only if they are giving effect to principles laid down by a Full Bench.

Conferences

The procedures outlined above are rather simpler than those often found in actual practice. The movement from conciliation to arbitration does not mean that conciliation has ceased. At all times during arbitration proceedings, even before a Full Bench on reference or appeal, if the parties or the Commission sees an opportunity to resolve a situation by conciliation, a conference will take place. This happens quite often, especially before individual members, and results in either a complete agreement on all issues or an agreement on some, leaving the remainder to be arbitrated.

Conferences usually deal with individual disputes, although even in those cases there may be many issues to be talked about. However, the conference approach has been used by the Commission for the purpose of exploring the possibility of consensus on much broader issues. Hence, in 1977 a conference called by a Full Bench was convened under the chairmanship of the president to consider broad-ranging issues; it became known as the "Inquiry into Principles of Wage Fixation." Present at the conference were representatives of four leading trade union councils, namely, the Australian Council of Trade Unions, the Council of Australian Government Employee Organisations, the Australian Council of Salaried and Professional Associations, and the Council of Professional Associations, as well as representatives of the Australian Public Service Federation (state public servants), the National Employers Policy Committee, the Master Builders Association of Australia, the Commonwealth government, and the governments of the states of New South Wales, Victoria, Queensland, South Australia, and Western Australia.

The conference started on 25 May 1977 and continued until 13 April 1978. Its purpose was to see what degree of consensus could be reached among all the parties in the industrial relations area about the proper principles to be applied in the fixation of wages. Each party was invited to submit written papers expounding its particular views, which were circulated and discussed and, in some cases, were replied to in writing. The papers were produced in a volume separate from the report itself, and they disclose the care with which submissions were made.

Although a considerable amount of disagreement remained, the amount of agreement was most useful. In two areas about which it was considered there might be significant disagreement, agreement was readily reached. One was that award wages should continue to be expressed as total wages as distinct from an earlier and long-continued practice of expressing them as a basic wage and a secondary wage. That is of real practical importance because, under the old system, the basic wage was altered more frequently than the secondary wage and often on different criteria. The other was that national wage cases should continue to be at the core of a methodical system of wage fixation.

The matters which were not agreed to were the subject of a hearing before a Full Bench of the Commission (comprising seven members) which resulted in an arbitrated decision on all relevant outstanding matters. On the question of an orderly and central wage-fixing system, the Full Bench decided that it should continue.

Since then the principles of wage fixation have been the subject of further conferences and inquiries, and these have led to the formulation of a revised set of principles, announced on 7 April 1981. The main points are set out in Appendix 1 to this paper.

Types of Proceedings

There are, speaking very broadly, three types of proceedings that come before the Commission:

1. Factory disputes where the issues are likely to be reasonably confined.

2. Industry disputes when a claim is made to cover wages and working conditions for a whole industry. In these cases issues are normally much wider than in the factory disputes and the proceedings are more complex. In both of these cases, however,

there will be the mix of conciliation and arbitration that I have
mentioned earlier.

3. National wage cases are cases in which the level of wages
generally is considered in relation to the broadest issues regarding the national economy and independently of any particular
industry. There had been national wage cases of varying kinds
occurring yearly from the early 1960s until 1975. In April of that
year the Commission decided that it would adopt a new approach which continued, with various modifications, until September 1978 when a new form evolved. The package was further
modified in April 1981.

Relationships with Governments

The Commission and its predecessor were established by the
central government, under its power in the Constitution to make
laws with respect to "conciliation and arbitration for the preven-
tion and settlement of industrial disputes extending beyond the
limits of any one state." The power, which has been the subject
of innumerable decisions of the High Court of Australia, does
not permit the Commonwealth government to legislate directly
on industrial matters except with respect to its own employees
or in its own territories. It can only set up machinery to deal with
industrial disputes.

This has resulted in the creation of a body—namely, the Commission—whose decisions may have significant economic reper-
cussions. The Commission has attempted on a number of
occasions to spell out its relationship with the government.
In its National Wage decision of May 1976, the Commission
said:

> "First, the Commission is a body independent of governments,
> unions and employers. It should not be seen as an arm of govern-
> ment which formulates wage decisions simply to 'fit in' with eco-
> nomic policy. The Commission treats all submissions on their merit.
> "Second, in relation to the Commonwealth's submission that in
> the present circumstances we should give greater weight to eco-
> nomic considerations, while the distinction between economic and
> industrial arguments is useful for analytic purposes, the economic
> consequences of any decisions which the Commission makes on
> wages cannot be evaluated in isolation from the industrial conse-
> quences, because of their interaction. In practice, the task of the
> Commission is to weigh all the relevant considerations in order to
> come to a decision which may reasonably be expected to produce

the best overall result. What may appear from a certain viewpoint to be the best wage decision for economic recovery, may turn out to be wrong when industrial considerations are brought to bear on the decision.

"Third, in formulating a set of principles for wage fixation we have tried to approach the question of wage fixing not as the resolution of each dispute as an isolated and independent case but as the determination of inter-related matters within a 'system' in which short term advantages or disadvantages may have to be balanced against long term costs or gains. We have taken this approach in the light of the experience of self-defeating sectional wage settlements of the last few years culminating in the wage explosions of 1974. We believe that this approach will enable the Commission to perform its task of preventing and settling industrial disputes in a more rational, more orderly and more equitable manner with advantages to the economy and to industrial relations.

"Fourth, we should emphasise that it is not for the Commission to offer advice on the proper economic policy for the Government to pursue. But the Commission believes it should draw attention whenever necessary to the industrial implications of economic policies in so far as they bear on wage demands and on the decisions of the Commission. We pointed out in our April 1975 decision that we were impressed with the contention that 'the size of wage demands, especially in a period of rapid price change, is related to the level and structure of personal income taxation; and that the viability of our wage fixing principles will depend in part on the Government's constant sensitivity on this point. . . . It goes without saying that fiscal action which adds to costs and prices will have a direct and rapid effect on wage movements through indexation.' "

Its relationship with state governments is a little more complex. As will have been seen, they participate in national wage cases and in other significant cases and make submissions, but, in addition, because awards of the Commission have the force of federal law, these awards can and in some cases do render inoperative state laws to the extent of any inconsistency.

Compulsory Arbitration

The Australian system is often described as compulsory arbitration. This description not only overlooks the fact that conciliation is most significant, but it also overstates the compulsory nature of the jurisdiction. There are, however, some degrees of compulsion.

First, there is a requirement on unions and employers to notify the Commission of disputes, and it is these notifications.

which start the whole procedure of the Commission outlined above. There is no special form or method of giving notice, though, in the case of applications for complete new awards or national wage cases, there are accepted forms.

There is a proceeding, called a compulsory conference, whereby a member of the Commission can require people to attend and for which there is a penalty for nonattendance. Compulsory conferences are not infrequent, but the question of penalty does not arise because the summons are normally obeyed.

The Commission also has the power common to most tribunals of being able to summon before it witnesses and to compel the production of documents.

Awards made by the Commission are binding upon the parties to the dispute, including members of organizations bound by the award. Awards may be cancelled for various kinds of noncompliance, but this is quite rare.

The Conciliation and Arbitration Act contains a number of provisions imposing penalties for breaches of the act and nonobservance of awards, but in practice these have not been used against unions for the past decade.

Unions and the System

Central to the workings of the system is the registering of organizations of both employees and employers. Without such bodies, the system could not work because the dispute making and settling requires some representation; in other words, it cannot be done between individuals.

There is a central register on which can be put organizations of employers who have on average not less than 100 employees throughout the preceding six months and organizations of employees comprising not less than 100 members. There is a formal registration proceeding at which objections to the registration are heard and decided by the industrial registrar, subject to appeal. The registration of an organization gives it corporate status.

The act requires that the rules of an organization shall provide for proper election of officers, including the secret ballot, and if the election is direct as distinct from collegiate, by secret postal ballot. There are quite a number of other statutory requirements with which union rules must comply. There is also a prohibition on the incitement to boycott awards or to encourage members not to comply with them.

The statute prohibits rules of certain kinds and, in particular, rules that are "oppressive, unreasonable or unjust." Members of organizations can and do challenge rules under this provision. A member can also apply for an order requiring compliance with rules.

Individuals are entitled by law to become members of an appropriate union and, if that is refused, they can seek a court declaration of entitlement. Conscientious objectors can obtain a certificate from the registrar that conscientious beliefs do not allow them to be members of organizations. There are other provisions in the act prescribing that organizations shall keep certain records, including accounting records and audits. There is also provision for judicial inquiries into disputed union elections, in which cases a new election may be ordered.

Finally, there is a power to cancel the registration of a union on a number of grounds, one being that it has failed to comply with the act, and another that it has willfully neglected to obey a court order.

Public Interest

The theme of the public interest runs through the statute creating the Commission. In the definition clause, for instance, the expression "industrial matters" is defined to include "having regard to the interests of the persons immediately concerned and of society as a whole."

There are references to the public interest in both the reference and appeal provisions. There cannot be a reference to a Full Bench unless the president has formed the opinion that, in the public interest, it should be referred, and an appeal is not considered unless the appeal bench decides that the matter is of such importance that, in the public interest, it should be considered.

The Commission has the power to decline to deal with an industrial dispute on the ground, amongst others, that further proceedings are not desirable in the public interest.

In a proceeding before a Full Bench, the Minister for Industrial Relations has the statutory right to intervene in the public interest on behalf of the Commonwealth government.

The expression "public interest" has never been defined by the Commission because it has taken the view that each case should be decided on its own facts.

Interest Arbitration

When considering any limitations on interest arbitration in Australia, it is necessary to bear in mind that there are legally established tribunals that are constantly dealing with disputes about interests. It follows that the limits on interest bargaining are to be found in the jurisdictional limitations of the tribunals rather than in any philosophical concept. Jurisdiction limitations arise from a combination of the Australian Constitution and the statutes which create the various tribunals. Central to these limitations is the word "industrial." I do not propose to go into the constitutional limitations. It is sufficient to say that the Australian Constitution gives limited power to the central government and the residue to the states. In the field of industrial relations, the power of the federal government is somewhat circumscribed and, as a result, some matters cannot be dealt with by the Australian Commission. Conversely, there are some jurisdictional limitations on the state systems, but it would not be fruitful to attempt to explore this constitutional maze.

The important and only general restraint is found in the word "industrial." All acts of Parliament creating the various Australian tribunals are essentially based on the concept of what is commonly called the master and servant relationship. If something arises out of that relationship, then the tribunal can deal with it. In some limited situations, the matter is taken further by deeming certain relationships to be that of master and servant. For instance, taxi drivers who own their own vehicles can be deemed to be employees, although the legal relationship is not one of master and servant. Therefore, if there is a dispute over matters arising out of the relationship of master and servant, it is industrial and capable of being dealt with by an industrial tribunal. Such a dispute may be about an individual or a whole union membership; that is, it may be a factory or an industry dispute, but nevertheless it can be dealt with. It is necessary to interpolate that there is no clear distinction drawn between interests and rights disputes and, on occasion, one may merge with the other. The legal capacity of an individual to enforce his rights in the civil courts is not really taken away, but except for claims as definite as an underpayment of wages, claims tend to be brought to the industrial tribunal. What may originate as a "rights" dispute may become an "interest" dispute. For example, the basic contract (commonly known as an award) may give rise to a "rights" dispute in an industry, but the result may be that the basic contract is varied so that what started as a dispute over a right may result in an alteration of the contract itself.

The word "contract" is not commonly used in Australia. The great bulk of the workforce is covered by "awards" that have been made by the various tribunals, some by consent, some by arbitration, and others by a mixture of both. Parenthetically, the word "arbitration" in the Australian scene tends to mean the creation of rights, not the ascertainment of them. There still is the common law concept of "arbitration" as a noncurial method of dealing with disputed issues, but in common parlance it means the act of creating rights arising from disputes about interests.

The law prescribes that an award must be made for an expressed period of time, but power is given to vary awards during their currency—and this frequently happens. As a result, the actual termination of an award may not be very important because it will have been kept up to date by variations during its currency. Although in some industries the unions insist on reconsidering many major conditions, particularly wages, on the expiry of an award, some unions do not.

There are, however, two limitations. The first, which is not very significant, is that the industrial tribunals will not normally act on the motion of an individual. Central to the whole arbitration system is the creation of unions. The system has both fostered them and, in the eyes of some, weakened them. It has fostered their creation because a system such as the Australian one must rely on representative parties and not on individuals. The allegation that the system has weakened them comes from the view that the mere existence of a permanent umpire to rule on disputes tends to make those involved in the system too reliant on that umpire.

The trade union movement has been, broadly speaking, based on the U.K. system. Thus, Australia has a mix of craft unions and industry unions. The craft unions, as their name implies, are related to the occupation of their members, and they tend to represent similar tradesmen—for example, fitters irrespective of the industry in which they are employed. Fitters in the metal fabricating industry as well as in many other industries in which they perform maintenance functions are all members of the same union. There are, however, some industry unions. It is part of the centralized system that unions become registered with industrial tribunals at both the state and federal levels. Their right to represent their members is determined by their registered constitution, and there are no problems of recognition except in the vexed areas where registered unions' rules are not mutually exclusive or where new processes or industries have occurred. Optimally, there should be only one union for each type of job, but this degree of perfection has not been achieved and, indeed, some of Australia's most intransigent problems come from demarcation disputes between two unions.

The Australian system would not work without unions, and the Australian system is heavily unionized. In 1901, 6.1 percent of the workforce belonged to unions; in 1978 the figure had increased to 57 percent. At the same time the number of unions had grown to 372. Thirty percent of the unions have a membership of less than 500, and only 3.2 percent have a membership of more than 80,000. Trade unions are significant in both the white-collar and blue-collar fields, and in both the public and private sectors. Many of them have identifiable political affiliations, the great bulk of them supporting the labor party.

Another limitation on jurisdiction can be more serious, although it is fairly vague. It has been held that industrial tribunals cannot interfere with managerial rights and that employers must be able to conduct their businesses without interference by tribunals. There is no clear-cut line between managerial and nonmanagerial. Every decision by an arbitration tribunal to some extent interferes with managerial rights. Nevertheless, there is an insistence that there is this limit to the powers of an arbitration tribunal, indefinite though it may be. An example of this limitation is the decision that an award requiring butchers' shops to close on Saturday mornings is not an industrial matter because it does not involve the master-servant relationship (R. v. Kelly (1950) 81 CLR 64).

In practice, awards cover many facets of the master-servant relationship. It is not possible to give details of all the subject matters dealt with, but it may be of interest to know the subject matters covered by one of our principal awards, namely, the Metal Industries Award 1971. It is to be noted that this award is alive and well, although nominally it ceased to exist on 30 June

1972. As a matter of law, all awards continue to remain in effect after their expiry date until superseded, and as a matter of practice unions and employers are content to allow the award to continue by keeping it up to date with variations. The award itself is over 100 pages of print, but as a matter of interest and to show the detail that is covered in awards, appended are both the index to the award and the clause describing its incidence (see Appendix 2).

There are, however, some clear limitations on the power. The tribunal cannot make awards for superannuation because, ex hypothesi, superannuation occurs after the relationship of master and servant has ended (*Hamilton Knights* case (1952) 86 CLR 283). On the other hand, the right to wear a union badge while on duty can be the subject of an arbitration decision (*The Tramways* case (1913) 17 CLR 680). Some state government employment cannot, by its nature, be in an industry, but some government employment can (Engineers case (1920) 28 CLR 129). The list could go on, but the principle is clear. If the matter is industrial, that is, if it involves the relationship of master and servant and it is in industry, then the tribunals have jurisdiction.

It should be added that the tribunals do not form part of the ordinary court system and that, except in limited ways, their decisions are not subject to appeal. However, the High Court of Australia has jurisdiction to prevent the Australian Commission from wrongly exercising jurisdiction and to compel it to exercise jurisdiction. This is done through prerogative writs, and there is a fairly steady flow of them. Subject to such jurisdictional restraints, decisions of the tribunals cannot be challenged in the ordinary courts.

PRINCIPLES OF WAGE DETERMINATION

In considering whether wages, salaries or conditions should be awarded or changed for any reason either by consent or arbitration, the Commission will guard against any contrived arrangement which would circumvent these Principles. It would be inconsistent with these Principles for wages, salaries or conditions to be awarded or changed extravagantly, the effect of which would be to frustrate the Commission's general intentions.

Regardless of the reasons for increases in labour costs outside national productivity and indexation, regardless of the source of the increases (award or overaward, wage or other labour cost) and regardless of how the increases are achieved (arbitration, consent or duress), unless their impact in economic terms is negligible, the Australian economy cannot afford indexation.

In the event of industrial action taking place on a scale such as to signify general rejection of the Principles, the Commission will declare these Principles to be formally abandoned. Where industrial action of a serious and protracted nature is confined to specific industries or groups of employees, a party may apply for the benefits of any national wage adjustment to be withheld from these industries or groups.

National Adjustments

1. First Review

(a) Upon publication of the March quarter CPI, other than in exceptional and compelling circumstances, the Commission will adjust its award wages and salaries for 80 percent of the December and March quarterly movements in the six-capitals CPI. . . .

2. Final Review

(a) Upon publication of the September quarter CPI, the Commission will give consideration to adjusting its award wages and salaries for: the 20 percent remaining from December and March quarterly movements in the six-capitals CPI, the total June and September quarterly movements in the six-capitals CPI, [and] productivity movements.

(b) The Commission will treat price movements as of prime importance. Relevant to the Commission's consideration will be the state of the economy and any question of discounting. . . .

Other Adjustments

In addition to the above increases, the only other grounds which would justify increases in wages or salaries are:

3. Changes in Work Value

Changes in work value arising from changes in the nature of work, skill and responsibility required, or the conditions under which work is performed.

4. Anomalies

The resolution of anomalies and special and extraordinary problems by means of the Conference already established to deal with anomalies and in accordance with the procedures laid down for them.

5. Inequities

(a) The resolution of inequities existing where employees performing similar work are paid dissimilar rates of pay without good reason. Such inequities shall be processed through the Anomalies Conference and not otherwise. . . .

(b) In dealing with inequities, the following over-riding considerations shall apply: the pay increase sought must be justified on the merits, there must be no likelihood of flow-on, the economic cost must be negligible, [and] the increase must be a once-only matter.

(c) The requirements of (a) and (b) above shall be observed in the Anomalies Conference and by a Full Bench to which an inequities application might be referred. The peak union councils must initiate these claims and, in particular, assist in the resolution of issues as to possible flow-on.

6. Allowances

Allowances may be adjusted from time to time where appropriate, but this does not mean that existing allowances can be

increased extravagantly or that new allowances can be introduced, the effect of which would be to frustrate the general
intention of the Principles. . . .

7. First Awards and Extensions of Existing Awards

(a) In the making of a first award, the long-established principles shall apply, i.e., the main consideration is the existing rates
and conditions (General Clerks Northern Territory Award).
(111 CAR 916)

(b) In the extension of an existing award to new work or to
award-free work the rates applicable to such work will be assessed by reference to the value of work already covered by the
award.

(c) In awards regulating the employment of workers previously covered by a State award or determination, existing rates
and conditions prima facie will be the proper award rates and
conditions.

METAL INDUSTRY AWARD 1971

PART 1 – WAGES EMPLOYEES

1. – TITLE

This award shall be referred to as the "Metal Industry Award, 1971". **(A1)**

2. – ARRANGEMENT (C1)

Metal Industry Award, 1971—Contd.

Metal Industry Award, 1971—Contd.

AMENDED – 7.2.80

Metal Industry Award, 1971—Contd.

AMENDED – 7.2.80

Metal Industry Award, 1971—Contd.

3. – INCIDENCE OF AWARD (E4)

(a)   This award shall apply in the States of New South Wales, Victoria, Queensland, South Australia and Tasmania.

(b)   Subject to the exceptions and exemptions prescribed by this award, the industries and callings covered by this award are the engineering, metal working and fabricating industries in all their branches, and all industries allied thereto and include –

1.   Mechanical and electrical engineering.
2.   Shipbuilding and repairing.
3.   Smithing.
4.   Boilermaking and erection and repairing.
5.   Bridge and girder construction and erection, and repairing.
6.   Steel fabrication, construction and erection, and repairing.
7.   Welding.
8.   Tool, die, gauge and mould making.
9.   Sheet metal working.
10.   Metal moulding.
11.   Diecasting.
12.   Stovemaking and repairing.
13.   Agricultural implement making and repairing.
14.   Metal pressing and stamping.
15.   Porcelain enamelling.
16.   Manufacture of porcelain enamels, oxides, glazes and similar materials.
17.   Metal machining.
18.   Ironworking.
19.   Iron and steel pipe making and fabrication.
20.   Window frame making and repairing.
21.   Safe and strong-room making and repairing.
22.   The manufacture, erection and installation, maintenance and repair of all forms of electrical machinery, apparatus and appliances, including valve and globe manufacturing.
23.   Radio, telephone and x-ray manufacturing, maintaining and repairing.
24.   Manufacture of insulation materials and articles.
25.   Wet and dry battery manufacturing and repairing.
26.   Manufacture, erection, installation, maintenance and repair of electrical advertising equipment including neon signs.
27.   Manufacture, erection, installation, maintenance and repair of fluorescent lighting.
28.   The drawing and insulation of wire for the conducting of electricity.
29.   The manufacture and repair of recording, measuring and controlling devices for electricity, fluids, gases, heat, temperature, pressure, time, etc.
30.   The production by mechanical means of industrial gases (other than coal gas).
31.   The making of canisters, drums and other metallic containers.
32.   Galvanising, tinning and pickling.
33.   Electroplateware manufacturing.
34.   Electroplating of all types.
35.   Processing of metals such as sherardizing and bonderizing.
36.   Lift and elevator making, repairing and maintenance.
37.   Plastic moulding, casting or fabricating in synthetic resins, or similar materials and including the production of synthetic resins, powders, tablets, etc., as used in such processes.
38.   Melting and smelting of metals.
39.   Refrigerator manufacturing, maintaining and repairing.

Metal Industry Award, 1971—Contd.

40. Perambulator manufacturing and repairing.
41. Making, manufacture, installation, maintenance and repair of ventilating and air-conditioning plant and equipment.
42. Metal furniture manufacturing and repairing.
43. Kitchenware manufacturing.
44. Metallic toy and sporting goods manufacturing.
45. The making, assembling, repairing and maintenance of vehicles (except where such work is at present covered by another Federal award.)
46. The manufacture of bolts, nuts, screws, rivets, washers and similar articles.
47. The manufacture of bright steel bars, rods, shafting, etc.
48. Making, manufacture, installation, maintenance and repair of scales and machines for measuring mass and equipment.
49. Making, manufacture, installation, maintenance and repair of watches and clocks, including cases.
50. Making, repairing, reconditioning and maintenance of motor engines, and/or parts thereof, and of the mechanical and electrical parts including the transmission and chassis of motor cars, motor cycles and other motor driven vehicles.
51. The making of metal motor-body parts.
52. Japanning, enamelling, painting and etc. of metallic articles.
53. Hand and machine engraving.
54. Badge and name-plate manufacturing, including chemical engraving.
55. Manufacture, testing and repair of water fittings.
56. Manufacture of any article or articles from metal wire.
57. Installation of all classes and types of electrical wiring equipment and plant, and the repair and maintenance thereof.
58. Generation and distribution of electric energy.
59. Manufacture of ceramic articles for use in the metal trades industries.
60. Making, manufacture, treatment, installation, maintenance, repair and reconditioning of any article, part or component, whether of metal and/or other material in any of the foregoing industries.
61. Sorting, packing, despatching, distribution and transport in connection with any of the foregoing.
62. Making, manufacture, installation, construction, maintenance, repair and reconditioning of plant, equipment, buildings and services (including power supply) in establishments connected with the industries and callings described herein and maintenance work generally.
63. Every operation, process, duty and function carried on or performed in or in connection with or incidental to any of the foregoing industries.

All descriptions of industry or callings set out in this clause wherever expressed may be read either alternatively or collectively in any combination whatsoever.

4. – PARTIES BOUND (E3)

This award shall be binding upon –

(a) Elsewhere than in Queensland –

    (i) The organisations of employees mentioned in Schedule "A" and the members thereof respectively;

    (ii) all employees whether members of an organisation of employees mentioned in Schedule "A" to this award or not, engaged in any of the occupations, industries or callings specified herein;

    (iii) Metal Trades Industry Association of Australia, Metal Industries Association, South Australia, Metal Industries Association, Tasmania and the Victorian Chamber of Manufactures and members of such organisations of employers; and

Metal Industry Award, 1971—Contd.

(iv)   the employers specified in Schedule "B".

(b)   In Queensland –

(i)   Metal Trades Industry Association of Australia and the members thereof as to all employees whether members of an organisation of employees or not engaged in any of the occupations, industries or callings specified herein; and

(ii)   the organisations of employees mentioned in Schedule "A" hereto and the members of such organisations of employees.

5. – DATE AND PERIOD OF OPERATION

This award shall come into operation on and from the beginning of the first pay period to commence on or after 24th November, 1971 and shall remain in force until 30th June, 1972.

6. – CONTRACT OF EMPLOYMENT

WEEKLY EMPLOYMENT

(a)   Except as provided in sub-clause (c) hereof employment shall be by the week. Any employee not specifically engaged as a casual employee shall be deemed to be employed by the week.

PART TIME EMPLOYMENT OF FEMALES

(b)   (i)   A female employee may be engaged by the week to work on a part-time basis for a constant number of hours less than forty each week. A female so engaged shall be paid per hour one fortieth of the weekly award wage prescribed herein for ' the work she performs.

(ii)   A female engaged on a part-time basis shall be entitled to payments in respect of annual leave, public holidays and sick leave arising under this award on a pro-portionate basis calculated as follows: –

(1)   Annual Leave (E8)

Subject to the provisions of Clause 25 –

- Where the female has completed twelve months' service on or after 1st December 1974 – four weeks' leave at the number of fixed hours normally worked each week.

- Where the female has complete twelve months' service on or after 8th April 1974 and prior to 1st December 1974 – three weeks' leave plus 1/12th of a week's leave for each month of service completed on or after 1st January 1974 at the number of fixed hours normally worked each week.

- Where the female is entitled to pro-rata leave on termination or at a close down in accordance with this award for each completed week of service she shall receive an entitlement in accordance with the following formula –

$$\frac{\text{Number of fixed hours worked each week} \times 4}{52}$$

(2)   Public Holidays

Where the normal paid hours fall on a public holiday and work is not performed by the female she shall not lose pay for the day.

Where the female works on the holiday she shall be paid in accordance with Clause 22 of this award.

(3)   Sick Leave

During the first year of any period of service with an employer she shall not be entitled to leave in excess of the fixed number of hours worked

Metal Industry Award, 1971—Contd.

each week. Provided that during the first six months of any period of service with an employer, sick leave shall accrue at the rate of one-sixth of the fixed number of hours worked each week for every completed month of service. Provided further that on application by the employee during the seventh month of employment and subject to the availability of an unclaimed balance of sick leave the employee shall be paid for any sick leave taken during the first six months and in respect of which payment was not made.

During the second and subsequent years of any period of service with an employer she shall not be entitled to leave in excess of an amount calculated as follows —

$$\frac{\text{Number of fixed hours worked each week} \times 8}{5}$$

(4) Bereavement Leave (C1)

Where a part-time female employee would normally work on either or both of the two working days following the death of a close relative which would entitle an employee on weekly hiring to Bereavement Leave in accordance with clause 26 of this award, the female shall be entitled to be absent on Bereavement Leave on either or both of those two working days without loss of pay for the day or days concerned.

(iii)   A part-time female who works in excess of the hours fixed under her weekly contract of employment shall be paid overtime in accordance with Clause 21 of this award.

(iv)   The unions respondent to this award are at liberty to apply to vary the provisions of this clause at any time should the circumstances relating to the employment of females on a part-time basis so require.

CASUAL EMPLOYMENT (E8)

(c)   A casual employee is one engaged and paid as such. A casual employee for working ordinary time shall be paid per hour one-fortieth of the weekly award wage prescribed herein for the work which he or she performs, plus 20 per cent.

TERMINATION OF EMPLOYMENT

(d)   (i)   Employment except in the case of casual employees, shall be terminated by a week's notice on either side given at any time during the week or by the payment or forfeiture of a week's wage as the case may be.

(ii)   Notwithstanding the provisions of paragraph (i) hereof the employer shall have the right to dismiss any employee without notice for malingering, inefficiency, neglect of duty or misconduct and in such cases the wages shall be paid up to the time of dismissal only.

(iii)   Where the employee has given or been given notice as aforesaid he shall continue in his employment until the date of the expiration of such notice. Any employee who having given or been given notice as aforesaid without reasonable cause (proof of which shall lie on him) absents himself from work during such period shall be deemed to have abandoned his employment and shall not be entitled to payment for work done by him within that period. Provided that where an employer has given notice as aforesaid. an employee other than a casual employee, on request, shall be granted leave of absence without pay for one day in order to look for alternative employment.

II. THE CANADIAN EXPERIENCE

Frances Bairstow*

Canada is generally considered to have interest arbitration practices that are a hybrid of U.S. and Canadian laws and policies. This myth has been encouraged because of the strong resemblance between the U.S. and Canadian approaches in grievance arbitration in the private sector.

But Canada "does its own thing" in interest arbitration. Each province has a distinctly different conception of "the public interest," based on its economic, political, and social climate. The federal approach is notably innovative in that it provides optional procedures, giving the bargaining agent the right to choose either arbitration or a strike when an impasse is reached —of course, after conciliation has failed. Suffice it to say here that interest arbitration with or without "essential services" features is the prevailing mode and is sufficiently similar to U.S. approaches so as not to warrant lengthy description.

What I would prefer to do here is to describe briefly and comment on mediation combined with arbitration as practiced in some major labor-management relationships in Canada. I cannot characterize this development with the significant label of "trend" because mediation-arbitration certainly has not become widespread. It has, however, made an enormous contribution in such industries as the port of Montreal and the major Canadian railways. Under the guidance of Chief Judge Alan Gold of Montreal, an Academy member, and with the active encouragement of our federal mediation service, major improvements have been effected—certainly so far as the longshoring industry in Quebec is concerned, where there has been labor peace for nearly ten years, a situation no one would have predicted in the turbulent 1960s.

Its extension to other industries has been limited by the reluctance of other parties to try something new and by a conspicuous shortage of arbitrators brave enough to engage in this form of Russian roulette. I like to live dangerously and have accepted such an intriguing assignment with Air Canada and the Flight Attendants. Having had experience as a mediator and arbitrator,

*Member, National Academy of Arbitrators; Director, Industrial Relations Centre, McGill University, Montreal, P.Q.

I find this heady stuff. When you sit there with the parties, separately or together—listening, persuading, cajoling, looking dour or relieved—your responsibility is a heavy one. Every lift of your eyebrow can be interpreted as a signal to the parties as to how you might eventually decide an issue if agreement is not reached. There may not necessarily be hard and fast rules about signing-off clauses if agreement is reached. In fact, both sides may insist on returning to square one if fondly held notions of what they have to have are rejected.

Several conclusions are apparent from my own experience and from those of my colleagues who have been involved in these med-arb situations:

1. If med-arb is to succeed, it cannot be imposed. The resentment in such an event would be counterproductive.

2. The mediator-arbitrator has to have a higher degree of credibility with the parties than an arbitrator who is used in one case and need not be seen again.

3. The mediator-arbitrator must *be* more, or become more, knowledgeable about the industry, the union, or the individuals than the normal practicing arbitrator. The process continues over a long period of time and can be very exhausting. There is the danger of venturing into perilous waters—of being asked to deal with issues that are not strictly collective bargaining matters, but may be in the area of human relations.

4. Add one more significant consideration—if fired as mediator-arbitrator, a thick skin is required to bolster the ego.

But arbitrators are expendable, and mediator-arbitrators are the most expendable.

III. THE U.S. EXPERIENCE

ARVID ANDERSON*

The selection of a New Yorker to speak on the topic of "The Outer Limits of Interest Arbitration" is quite logical because I recognize that many persons consider New York as far out as one can get in public-sector labor relations. It will be my task to describe some of the pioneering features of the New York City Collective Bargaining Law to illustrate some of the limits of interest arbitration. Before doing so, I want to express my appreciation to the Program Committee for affording me the privilege of sharing this platform with our distinguished Canadian and Australian colleagues because those countries have been in the forefront of the development of interest arbitration and had binding arbitration long before its use became widespread in the United States.

I also want to take a few moments to set forth a national basis for these remarks. I recognize that there are important and innovative private-sector examples of interest arbitration, such as the Experimental Negotiating Agreement in the steel industry and certain transportation contracts. This paper will be concerned with the public sector, however. The rapid growth of public-sector unions in the 1960s was followed in the 1970s by the passage of binding interest arbitration laws in order to resolve disputes over new contract terms. With the strike almost universally forbidden as a means of impasse resolution, an alternate method was needed to resolve public-sector disputes and to stimulate the bargaining process.

As Samuel Johnson once declared, there is nothing as likely to focus a man's attention as the certainty that he is to be hanged in the morning. Similarly, the decision to strike or to take a strike is a powerful stimulus to the bargaining process. Experience is demonstrating that the decision to submit an issue to arbitration also stimulates decision-making and collective bargaining by government employers and their employees' representatives.

The enactment of laws banning strikes and providing for interest arbitration as an alternative means of dispute settlement cannot provide an absolute guarantee against strikes in a free

---

*Member, National Academy of Arbitrators; Chairman, Office of Collective Bargaining, New York, N.Y.

society. However, the record to date of the near absence of strikes where interest arbitration laws have been enacted requires a closer look, particularly by those who believe it is not possible to have collective bargaining without the right to strike. I say the near absence of strikes because the record has not been perfect. Last month a two-day strike of firefighters and police superior officers occurred in the city of Yonkers, New York.[1] To my knowledge, this was the first serious strike since the passage of New York State's interest arbitration law some seven years ago.[2] Happily, the matter was resolved with an agreement to go to interest arbitration.

Twenty-two jurisdictions have passed statutes providing for some form of binding interest arbitration to resolve disputes over new contract terms.[3] For the most part, such statutes apply to police and firefighters or to other public safety employees, such as prison guards, or to employees of mental hospitals. However, in some states, for example, Connecticut, Iowa, and Wisconsin, and in the City of New York, the statutes apply to most employees of local government and, in Iowa, also to employees of the state.[4]

Arbitration statutes provide a variety of procedures. Some of these are:

- Conventional arbitration of all unsettled claims.
- Selection of the last offer of the employer or of the union on an issue-by-issue basis.
- Selection of the last offer of the employer or of the union, or the fact-finder's report as a single package.
- Selection of the last offer of the employer or of the union, or the fact-finder's report on an issue-by-issue basis.
- Separating the dispute into economic and noneconomic issues and employing one of the selection procedures outlined above.[5]

Some interest arbitration statutes provide for arm's length

[1]909 *Government Employee Relations Report* 34 (April 20, 1981).

[2]Ch. 724, §3, [1974] N.Y. Laws 1883 and Ch. 725, §3, [1974] N.Y. Laws 1887 (codified at N.Y. Civ. Serv. Law §209(4) (McKinney Supp. 1977)).

[3]The 22 jurisdictions which currently have interest arbitration statutes are Alaska, Connecticut, Delaware, Hawaii, Iowa, Maine, Massachusetts, Michigan, Minnesota, Montana, Nebraska, Nevada, New Jersey, New York, Oregon, Pennsylvania, Rhode Island, Washington, Wisconsin, Wyoming, New York City, and the City of Eugene, Ore.

[4]Conn. Gen. Stat. Ann. §7-472-473 (1979); Iowa Code Ann. §20.22 (1978); Wisc. Stat. Ann. §111.77 (Supp. 1979); N.Y. Admin. Code, Ch. 54, §1173-7.0(c) (2) (1980).

[5]For an analysis of interest arbitration procedures used in the various jurisdictions, *see* Public Employment Relations Services Information Bulletin, Vol. 1, No. 1 (February-March 1978).

judicial proceedings, while others are designed to encourage direct negotiations and settlement by the parties, aided by mediation-arbitration (med-arb) procedures. Final-offer procedures are growing in popularity because they give the parties a much greater role in the arbitration process. Experience is showing that final offer in particular encourages bargained settlements.

Most interest arbitration statutes provide detailed procedures governing the scope and conduct of the arbitration, as well as comprehensive criteria to guide the arbitrators. Most arbitration statutes also provide for limited judicial review and, where that has not been done, the courts have implied that such review is authorized.

Legal Challenges

Interest arbitration statutes have been challenged on the ground that arbitration involves an illegal delegation of legislative authority to a nonelected, nonaccountable arbitrator. Other challenges charge that some arbitration statutes lack adequate guiding criteria for the arbitrator or conflict with other statutes. Civil Service and Cap Laws—the latter are laws which limit the taxing or budgetary authority of local governments—are examples of state laws with which arbitration statutes may conflict.

In other litigation, the issues of separation of powers, due process, equal protection of the laws, home rule, and the power to tax have been considered.[6] Most state courts have held that interest arbitration does not constitute an illegal delegation of legislative authority provided there are in the statute carefully defined limits and criteria to guide the arbitration process and provisions for due process and judicial review.[7]

While legal challenges will continue, it seems safe to conclude at this point that the biggest hurdle for interest arbitration is not in the constitutional challenges still pending before some of the

---

[6]For a comprehensive and thoroughly documented discussion of legal challenges to interest arbitration statutes, see Charles J. Morris, *Interest Arbitration: Panacea's Art or Pandora's Box?*, paper presented at a conference sponsored by the Continuing Legal Education Society of British Columbia, at Vancouver, B.C. (April 18, 1980), available from the author: Professor of Law, Southern Methodist University School of Law, Dallas, Tex. 75275.

[7]*See, e.g., City of Richfield* v. *Local 1215, Int'l Ass'n of Fire Fighters,* 276 N.W.2d 42 (Minn. 1979); *Town of Arlington* v. *Board of Concil. and Arbit.,* 370 Mass. 769, 352 N.E.2d 914 (1976); *City of Amsterdam* v. *Helsby,* 37 N.Y.2d 19, 332 N.E.2d 290, 371 N.Y.S.2d 404 (1975).

state courts. The real test will be whether interest arbitration procedures work to the satisfaction of public employers and employees and reflect appropriate concern for the public interest. If they do, then the process will survive. If arbitration, in practice, fails to provide a reasonable alternative to the strike, then the process will not survive. But that will be a political rather than a legal decision.

The New York City Experience

The extensive experience of Iowa, Michigan, New Jersey, New York State, Pennsylvania, and Wisconsin with interest arbitration could serve to illustrate the limits of binding arbitration. However, this paper will focus on the New York City experience.

New York City has had binding interest arbitration for nearly a decade.[8] The law applies to about 200,000 city employees who are represented by some 50 different unions, but it does not apply to the city's teachers and transit workers. The latter are covered instead by the New York State Taylor Law, and under that law the interest disputes of only police and firefighters must be submitted to final and binding arbitration. The Taylor Law permits local governments to enact local public employment relations "provisions and procedures" provided they are "substantially equivalent" to the Taylor Law.[9] In the exercise of this local option, New York City enacted the Collective Bargaining Law (NYCCBL), which provides procedures for the resolution of bargaining impasses, including mediation and the issuance of a final and binding report by an impasse panel.[10] The law is administered by the tripartite Board of Collective Bargaining, a body composed of three neutral members, two labor members and two city members.[11] The two city members serve at the pleasure of the mayor and the two labor members are chosen by the Municipal Labor Committee (MLC), a voluntary association of city unions. The three neutral members are chosen by the unanimous vote of the city and labor members for staggered three-year terms.[12] The city and the MLC equally share the cost of the fees paid to two of the neutral members as well as the

---

[8]N.Y.C. Local Law No. 2, [1972] N.Y. Local Laws 158–160.
[9]N.Y. Civ. Serv. Law §212 (McKinney 1973).
[10]New York, N.Y. Admin. Code, Ch. 54, §1173-1.0 to §1173-13.0 (1976 & Supp. 1980–81).
[11]New York, N.Y. Charter, Ch. 54, §1171 (1977).
[12]*Id.*

salary of the third, who is the chairman of the Board and full-time director of the Office of Collective Bargaining.[13]

As originally enacted in 1967, the NYCCBL contained provisions for fact-finding which were advisory only.[14] Nonetheless, the City of New York maintained a policy of voluntary compliance with impasse panel recommendations. In 1969, the Taylor Law was amended to require the mayor of the City of New York to submit a plan dealing with the need for a specified final step in the impasse procedures.[15]

In order to develop proposed finality procedures for submission to the state legislature, a series of meetings was conducted among representatives of the City of New York, the Municipal Labor Committee, and the Office of Collective Bargaining. The reluctance of the MLC and of the mayor's office to conform New York City procedures to the Taylor Law as it then stood, by requiring legislative action in bargaining impasses, was strongly concurred in by the city council leadership. The city legislators did not wish to play the part of referee in labor disputes between the mayor and the public employee unions. The council was also reluctant to become involved in disputes between unions where, for example, it would have to determine which union should get the most: police, fire, or sanitation. So long as the unions were denied the right to strike, they preferred a finality method where the ultimate decision would be made by third-party neutrals. Therefore, a system of finality with a form of compulsory interest arbitration was agreed upon and enacted by the New York City Council in 1972.[16]

An impasse in negotiations is deemed to exist when the Board of Collective Bargaining, upon the director's recommendation, "determines that collective bargaining negotiations . . . have been exhausted, and that the conditions are appropriate for the creation of an impasse panel. . . ."[17] Once the impasse determination is made, a panel is chosen by submitting to the parties a list of seven persons drawn from the roster of neutrals maintained by the Office of Collective Bargaining.[18] The parties indi-

---

[13]*Id.*, §§1170–1171.
[14]*See* N.Y.C., Local Law No. 53, 1 [1967] N.Y. Local Laws 449–450.
[15]Ch. 24, §11, [1969] N.Y. Local Laws 79–80.
[16]N.Y.C. Local Law No. 2, 1 [1972] N.Y. Local Laws 158–160 (codified at New York, N.Y. Admin. Code, Ch. 54, §1173-5.0(a)(8), §1173-7.0(c)(3)(e), §1173-7.0(c)(4), and §1173-7.0(f) (1976)).
[17]New York, N.Y. Admin. Code, Ch. 54, §1173-7.0(c)(2) (1976).
[18]*Id.*, §1173-7.0(c)(1)–(2).

cate their preferences in numerical order and the director appoints those persons who are the most mutually acceptable choices.[19] Impasse panels usually consist of one person, but three persons may serve by agreement of the parties or at the determination of the director absent such agreement.[20] Inclusion on the roster of neutrals maintained by the Board of Collective Bargaining is by unanimous vote of the labor and city members of the Board.[21] The fees and expenses of mediation and impasse panels are shared by the public employer and public employee organization which are parties to the dispute,[22] as is the cost of the mandatory stenographic record made in impasse panel hearings.[23]

The NYCCBL grants impasse panels the power to mediate, hold hearings, compel the attendance of witnesses and the production of documents, review data, and take whatever action it considers necessary to resolve the impasse. If an impasse panel is unable to achieve voluntary agreement of the parties, settling an impasse within a reasonable period of time as determined by the director, it is required, within such period of time as the director prescribes, to render a written report containing findings of fact, conclusions, and recommendations for terms of settlement.[24]

Experience has shown that even if the parties do not reach formal agreement through the panel's mediatory efforts, and a report with recommendations is issued, very often the report reflects the parties' advice to the panel as to certain informal agreements existing between them.[25]

The NYCCBL specifies the following criteria which an impasse panel is to consider in making its recommendations for the terms of settlement:

"(1) comparison of the wages, hours, fringe benefits, conditions and characteristics of employment of the public employees involved in

---

[19]*Id.*, §1173-7.0(c)(2).

[20]*Id.*, §1173-7.0(e).

[21]The NYCCBL requires only a majority vote, including one city and one labor member (§1173-7.0(c)(1)). However, in practice, inclusion on the roster has been based on unanimous approval.

[22]New York City Office of Collective Bargaining, Revised Consolidated Rules §9.3 (1972).

[23]*Id.*, §5.10.

[24]New York, N.Y. Admin. Code, Ch. 54, §1173-7.0(c)(3)(a) (1976).

[25]*See* Anderson, *The Impact of Public Sector Bargaining: An Essay Dedicated to Nathan P. Feinsinger*, 1973 Wis. L.Rev. 986, 1101. *See also* Doherty, *On Factfinding: A One-Eyed Man Lost Among the Eagles*, 5 Pub. Personnel Mgt. 363, 366 (1976); Grodin, *Political Aspects of Public Sector Interest Arbitration*, 1 Indus. Rel. L.J. 1, 14 (1976).

the impasse proceedings with the wages, hours, fringe benefits, conditions and characteristics of employment of other employees performing similar work and other employees generally in public or private employment in New York City or comparable communities; (2) the overall compensation paid to the employees involved in the impasse proceeding, including direct wage compensation, overtime, and premium pay, vacations, holidays and other excused time, insurance, pensions, medical and hospitalization benefits, food and apparel furnished, and all other benefits received; (3) changes in the average consumer prices for goods and services, commonly known as the cost of living; (4) the interest and welfare of the public; (5) such other factors as are normally and customarily considered in the determination of wages, hours, fringe benefits and other working conditions in collective bargaining or in impasse proceedings."[26]

Additionally, since 1978, when the state legislature amended the Financial Emergency Act of 1975 (FEA), impasse panels in New York City have been required to accord substantial weight to the City's financial ability to pay when considering demands for increases in wages or fringe benefits.[27] Financial ability to pay is defined by the Act as "the financial ability of the city . . . to pay the cost of any increase in wages or fringe benefits without requiring an increase in the level of city taxes existing at the time of the commencement of [the impasse proceeding]."[28] Even before the enactment of the above-described legislation, the Office of Collective Bargaining had consistently interpreted the statutory criterion "interest and welfare of the public" to include consideration of the employer's financial ability to pay.[29]

The NYCCBL does not specify a time within which the impasse panel must submit its report and recommendations; this decision is left to the director. The statute does provide that the report shall be made public within seven days of its submission to the parties, but this time may be extended up to 30 days upon consent of the parties and with the approval of the director.[30] The latter provision has the purpose of allowing the parties to

[26]New York, N.Y. Admin. Code, Ch. 54, §1173-7.0(c)(3)(b) (1976).
[27]Ch. 201 [1978] N.Y. Laws, §23.3(a).
[28]Id., §23.3(h).
[29]For example, in Community Action for Legal Servs. Inc. v. Legal Servs. Staff Ass'n, Case No. I-110-74, slip op. at 4–5 (Nov. 13, 1974), the single-member impasse panel noted that: ". . . I am bound by the requirements of the City Labor Law [section 1173-7.0(c)(3)(b)] which requires that I take into account the interest and welfare of the public. This has come to mean the ability of the City to pay and the extent to which the services rendered may have to be curtailed if funds are unavailable."
[30]New York, N.Y. Admin. Code, Ch. 54, §1173-7.0(c)(3)(d) (1976).

conclude a negotiated agreement prior to publication. If a contract is negotiated during this time, the report will not be released except upon consent of the parties. If a contract is not being negotiated during this period, the parties must, within ten days of receipt of the panel's recommendation, notify each other and the director of their acceptance or rejection.[31] If no notification is received, the recommendations are deemed accepted. Accepted recommendations become binding on both parties unless implementation of any provision thereof requires the enactment of a law.[32] In such a case, the provision does not become binding until the appropriate legislative body enacts such a law. This limitation was enacted to deal with both the political and constitutional questions of delegation of legislative authority. For example, if sufficient funds are not in the budget, the panel report cannot be implemented until the funds are made available.

A party who rejects, in whole or in part, the panel's recommendations can appeal to the Board of Collective Bargaining for review.[33] A notice of appeal must be filed with the Board and served on the other party within ten days of the rejection.[34] The Board may also review a panel's recommendations on its own initiative.[35] While appeals are normally decided upon the pleadings, the parties may present oral argument and/or submit briefs to the Board.[36] Review is based on the record and evidence before the impasse panel[37] and is guided by the statutory criteria set forth above, including a requirement, pursuant to the 1978 FEA amendments, that before proceeding to other issues the Board must make a threshold determination as to whether a recommendation for an increase in wages or fringe benefits is within the City's financial ability to pay.[38] If the determination is negative, the matter is immediately remanded to the panel for further consideration. If the threshold determination is in the affirmative, the Board may proceed to review the panel's recommendation with respect to other issues.

The Board has adopted a standard of review for impasse

---

[31]*Id.*, §1173-7.0(c)(3)(e).
[32]*Id.*
[33]*Id.*, §1173-7.0(c)(4)(a).
[34]*Id.*
[35]*Id.*
[36]*Id.*, §1173-7.0(c)(4)(b).
[37]*Id.*
[38]Ch. 201 [1978] N.Y. Laws, §23.3(b).

panel determinations comparable to the test applied by the courts in reviewing administrative agency decisions under Article 78 of the New York Civil Practice Law and Rules.[39] This entails examining the record to determine whether the parties were given a fair hearing and whether there is substantial support for the result reached by the panel. The Board will not ordinarily substitute its judgment for that of the impasse panel.

The Board may, by majority vote, affirm or modify the recommendations of the impasse panel, in whole or in part, or, if it finds that the rights of a party have been prejudiced, it may set aside the recommendations.[40] If the Board fails to issue a final determination within the time periods prescribed in the statute, the recommendations of the impasse panel are considered to have been adopted by the Board.[41] A final determination of the Board is binding upon the parties and constitutes an award within the meaning of Article 75 of the Civil Practice Law and Rules governing arbitration in New York State.[42] The binding effect of a Board determination, like the decision of an impasse panel, is qualified by the proviso that it is subject to legislative action when its implementation requires the enactment or amendment of a law.[43]

Board decisions may be appealed to the state courts although there have been only two such appeals to date, both unsuccessful.[44] A threshold determination by the Board that an impasse panel's recommendations concerning increases in wages or fringe benefits are or are not within the City's financial ability to pay is subject to appeal in a special proceeding in the appellate division, New York State's intermediate appellate court.[45] Such a proceeding is given preference over all other cases except those relating to the election law. The standard of review differs from the standard applied to other aspects of Board decisions. It is a de novo review of the entire record solely for the purpose of determining whether an award of an increase in wages or fringe benefits was within the City's financial ability to pay.[46] All

---

[39]N.Y. Civ. Prac. Laws §7803 (McKinney 1981).
[40]New York, N.Y. Admin. Code, Ch. 54, §1173-7.0(c)(4)(c) (1976).
[41]*Id.*, §1173-7.0(c)(4)(d).
[42]*Id.*, §1173-7.0(c)(4)(f).
[43]*Id.*, §1173-7.0(c)(4)(e).
[44]*Higgins* v. *Anderson, et al.*, 97 LRRM 2481 (N.Y. Sup. Ct., N.Y. Cty., Spec. Term, Pt. 1, 1977); *City of New York* v. *Patrolmen's Benevolent Ass'n*, unpublished opinion (N.Y. Sup. Ct., N.Y. Cty., Sept. 30, 1977—J. Kirschenbaum).
[45]Ch. 201 [1978] N.Y. Laws, §23.3(e).
[46]*Id.*, §23.3(f).

questions other than the questions relating to the threshold determination may be reviewed in the same proceeding, however, under Article 75 standards, even though the issues would otherwise have been subject to review in the New York Supreme Court.[47] This procedure has not been utilized to date and is scheduled to sunset out on December 31, 1982,[48] which will be after the next round of City negotiations.

When New York City's final and binding impasse procedures were first introduced, critics claimed that the procedures would encourage the use of third parties in fashioning contract settlements to the detriment of concerted efforts at the bargaining table. The experience to date does not support this contention, however. In the nine years since the adoption of finality in impasse procedures, only 8.6 percent or 51 of 592 reported contract settlements used the process. Of these 51 impasse cases, the panel's recommendations were accepted by the parties in 39; twelve cases were appealed to the Board for final determination. In ten cases, the report and recommendations of the impasse panel were affirmed, while the Board acted in two cases to reduce the award in order to conform the recommendations to the City's fiscal plan.[49]

Unique Features

There are several features in the New York City law which I believe are unique, or at least distinctive. First of all there is a nonjudicial appellate procedure for the review of impasse panel recommendations by the Board of Collective Bargaining. While numerous statutes, including that of New York State, provide for judicial review, only New York City provides for appellate review of interest arbitration awards, prior to judicial review. Arbitrators are familiar with certain nonjudicial appellate procedures for grievance arbitration awards, for example, in the steel and coal industries and under the Federal Labor Relations Authority.[50] The two-step appellate procedure was included in New York City's statute to guard against irrational awards and against disparate awards for employees of the same employer.

---

[47]Id.

[48]Id., §23.3(i).

[49]1980 Annual Report prepared by the Office of Collective Bargaining, at 15.

[50]Some surveys have shown that as many as one in six federal sector awards are appealed to the Federal Authority. 908 GERR 9 (April 13, 1981).

Another distinctive feature of the NYCCBL is the use of the word "impasse" rather than the word "arbitration." The word was adopted in part for semantic reasons because of the antipathy of public employee unions toward the concept of binding arbitration. The term impasse is also used because the impasse panels are empowered to mediate as well as arbitrate and because their recommendations are not final and binding if they are rejected and appealed to the tripartite Board of Collective Bargaining within ten days. This procedure imports a degree of flexibility in the arbitration process which is directed at accommodation rather than adjudication in interest disputes.

The New York City law is also unique in its inclusion of a specific statutory provision to resolve disputes over the scope of bargaining[51] and, thus, the scope of the impasse proceeding. Only mandatory subjects or jointly agreed upon permissive subjects may be considered by the panel. In most other jurisdictions such disputes are resolved through the improper or unfair labor practice route which, I believe, casts in an unnecessarily pejorative light good-faith disputes as to whether certain subjects are proper for interest arbitration.

The NYCCBL also contains a status quo provision which precludes public employees from engaging in a strike and prevents the employer from making any unilateral change in working conditions until a collective bargaining agreement is concluded or until a specified period of time after an impasse panel is appointed or after its report is submitted, whichever is sooner, and including any period during which an appeal to the Board of Collective Bargaining of an impasse panel's recommendations is pending.[52] The terms and conditions contained in the expired contract remain in effect during this time. The status quo provision has the salutary effect of protecting the bargaining process and preserving the relationship between the parties during impasse proceedings.

The Board of Collective Bargaining also has the power to consolidate impasse proceedings[53] and, while this procedure has not yet been exercised to force an unwilling party to arbitration, the threat of such action has eliminated certain lock-step

---

[51]New York, N.Y. Admin. Code, Ch. 54, §1173-5.0(a)(2) (1976); New York City Office of Collective Bargaining, Revised Consolidated Rules §7.3 (1972).

[52]New York, N.Y. Admin. Code, Ch. 54, §1173-7.0(d) (1976) as amended by Int. No. 856-A, Council of the City of New York, §10 (1980).

[53]N.Y.C. Office of Collective Bargaining, Revised Consolidated Rules §13.12 (1972).

parity demands by city unions. I refer to those disputes where one union, usually a member of the uniformed forces, will seek to insure that its wage or salary level will always be higher than that of another group; the perennial problem of police-firefighter parity is an example. It is generally recognized that such a demand in New York City bargaining would lead to Board exercise of its power of consolidation, thus making all parties affected by the demand parties to the impasse proceeding.

The New York City Collective Bargaining Law proviso that any portion of an arbitration award which requires the enactment of a law cannot go into effect until the law is enacted appears to have been sufficient to prevent any impermissible invasion of legislative authority. Most states' interest arbitration laws require legislative approval of all awards. However, New York's Taylor Law specifically states that such approval is not required.[54] I believe that New York City's limitation is sound, both politically and constitutionally.

Another limit on arbitration in the New York City law is the provision for judicial review. As mentioned above, there have been only two challenges to the Board's review of impasse panel awards in the nearly ten-year history of the finality procedures, both of which were unsuccessful.[55]

Lessons to Be Learned

What are the lessons to be learned from New York City's near-decade of experience with interest arbitration? The first lesson is that the process works. One of the major tests of a public-sector bargaining law providing for arbitration in a jurisdiction which outlaws the strike is whether strikes have occurred. Since the enactment of the New York City law, there have been only three strikes over new contract terms and nearly 600 individual contracts were negotiated during this period. There was a five-and-a-half hour firefighter strike in 1973 which was settled by arbitration, a ten-day strike of off-track betting clerks in 1979, and a one-week strike of interns and residents in 1981 which is now being submitted to binding arbitration.

Another measure of whether the law works has been the degree of utilization of arbitration and the related question of

---

[54]N.Y. Civ. Serv. Law §209(4)(c)(vi) (McKinney Supp. 1980–81).
[55]*See* note 44 *supra.*

whether arbitration has had a chilling effect on collective bargaining. Contrary to predictions, there has been a very low utilization rate; only 8.6 percent of all contract disputes have required the use of impasse procedures. And more than half of that number represent awards which were the confirmation, in whole or in part, of the bargaining process of the parties. There has clearly been no chilling of the bargaining process.

It is also important to add that interest arbitration awards have not been used primarily to determine the basic wage pattern of the city and its major unions. For the most part, wage patterns have been established by collective bargaining. Of course, wage disputes can go to interest arbitration and some awards concern attempts to increase the basic wage pattern of the city. Others involve special conditions of employment, such as whether or not one-man supervisory patrols should be implemented in the Police Department,[56] or what the proper rate of compensation should be for two-man sanitation crews assigned to do the work previously performed by three-man crews.[57] A "salary review panel" has been established to resolve disputes over salaries required to attract and retain employees in skilled occupations and professions such as nurses, engineers, and computer operators.[58]

The effectiveness of the process may also be gauged by comparison of arbitration awards with negotiated settlements. As mentioned, there were only two cases during the nearly ten-year period where the awards were found to be inconsistent with negotiated settlements. In the appellate process, these awards were reduced by the unanimous decisions of the tripartite Board of Collective Bargaining to conform the awards to the city's basic wage patterns. It is also significant that less than one-fourth of all impasse panel awards have been appealed to the Board of Collective Bargaining and that no awards have been successfully appealed to the courts.

Is the experience in New York City transferable? I believe it is, and I respectfully suggest that the appellate procedures should be considered by other jurisdictions. A variant of this concept exists in Massachusetts where the law provides for the

---

[56] *Sergeants' Benevolent Ass'n and Lieutenants' Benevolent Ass'n* v. *City of New York,* Case No. I-145-79 (October 3, 1980).

[57] *City of New York* v. *Uniformed Sanitationmen's Ass'n Local 831,* Case No. I-157-80 (January 15, 1980).

[58] *See, e.g., New York State Nurses Ass'n* v. *City of New York (Health and Hosps. Corp.),* Case No. I-154-80 (October 24, 1980).

submission of interest disputes to a Joint Labor-Management Committee (JLMC).[59] While the enactment of Proposition 2½ has curtailed the power of the JLMC to issue awards which are binding on municipal legislative bodies, the record of the JLMC shows that a statewide tripartite labor-management committee to determine local conditions of employment for police and firefighters by arbitration works well.[60]

I also suggest that the New York City procedures for resolving scope of bargaining issues and the requirement that impasse panel awards cannot become final and binding if they require the enactment of a law until such a law is enacted are worthy of consideration by other jurisdictions which are constantly worried about the scope of an arbitrator's authority and the enforceability of the award.

Most of this paper has focused on procedures, but equally if not more important is the role of the arbitrator. In New York City only persons unanimously approved by the tripartite Board of Collective Bargaining serve as members of impasse panels. This prescreening process has contributed to the mediation efforts of the impasse panels and to the acceptance of the awards. We have been fortunate in obtaining the services of highly qualified persons to serve as arbitrators to deal with the complex questions in municipal labor disputes. But if New York City and the other 21 jurisdictions with interest arbitration are to maintain good records, then it will be necessary for the best arbitrators to continue to be willing to do the "heavy lifting" that is required in interest arbitration cases. I am quite aware that interest arbitration can be hard and financially hazardous work, but I have confidence that the members of this Academy will accept their share of the responsibility in order that interest arbitration may continue to be a viable alternative to the strike for resolution of public-sector collective bargaining disputes.

Lastly and more importantly, the New York City impasse procedures have worked because the parties have wanted them to work. The New York City law was jointly drafted by the parties and they have a stake in its success. Procedures, no matter how well designed, are not of much use without a commitment to use them properly when they are needed. There has been a commitment by city administrations and the major labor

---

[59]Ch. 1078 §4 [1973] Mass. Acts, as amended by Ch. 154 [1979] Mass. Acts.
[60]*Commonwealth of Massachusetts Joint Labor-Management Committee for Police and Fire,* a report by Professor John T. Dunlop, reported in 884 GERR 46 (October 20, 1980).

unions since the beginning to make the collective bargaining process work. Consistent with such a commitment, labor and management in New York have used the impasse procedures in a limited number of instances and for the purpose of supplementing the collective bargaining process, rather than as a substitute for collective bargaining. In sum, the parties in New York are persuaded that interest arbitration is the better way to resolve disputes over new contract terms.

CHAPTER 4

REMEDIES: NEW AND OLD PROBLEMS

I. Remedies in Arbitration: Old Problems Revisited

David E. Feller*

The topic for today's discussion is "Remedies: New and Old Problems." That naturally suggests a bifurcation of the discussion, and I have chosen that portion which reasonably can be said to fit under the rubric of "old problems."

The subject is, indeed, an old one in the annals of the Academy. I have no intention of reviewing what has been said in the prior proceedings on this subject, but I wish to note that the first formal paper dedicated to the problem was that of Emmanuel Stein more than 20 years ago.[1] Since then the subject has been addressed by, among others, Robben Fleming in the *Virginia Law Review*,[2] and by papers delivered by Robert Stutz,[3] Peter Seitz,[4] Sidney Wolff,[5] and Lou Crane,[6] not to speak of innumerable commentators on their papers, among whom I am numbered, as well as discussion of remedies in papers not specifically addressed to that subject.[7]

---

*Member, National Academy of Arbitrators; John H. Boalt Professor of Law, University of California, Berkeley, Calif.

[1]*Remedies in Labor Arbitration,* in Challenges to Arbitration, Proceedings of the 13th Annual Meeting, National Academy of Arbitrators (Washington: BNA Books, 1960), 39.

[2]*Arbitrators and the Remedy Power,* 48 Va. L.Rev. 1199 (1962).

[3]*Arbitrators and the Remedy Power,* in Labor Arbitration and Industrial Change, Proceedings of the 16th Annual Meeting, National Academy of Arbitrators (Washington: BNA Books, 1963), 54.

[4]*Remedies in Arbitration,* in Labor Arbitration—Perspectives and Problems, Proceedings of the 17th Annual Meeting, National Academy of Arbitrators (Washington: BNA Books, 1963), 165.

[5]*Id.,* at 176.

[6]*The Use and Abuse of Arbitral Power,* in Labor Arbitration at the Quarter Century Mark, Proceedings of the 25th Annual Meeting, National Academy of Arbitrators (Washington: BNA Books, 1973), 66.

[7]*See, e.g.,* Cox, *Arbitration in the Light of the* Lincoln Mills *Case,* in Arbitration and the Law, Proceedings of the 12th Annual Meeting, National Academy of Arbitrators (Washington: BNA Books, 1959), 24, 38; Aaron, *Arbitration in the Federal Courts: Aftermath of the Trilogy,* in Collective Bargaining and the Arbitrator's Role, Proceedings of the 15th Annual Meeting, National Academy of Arbitrators (Washington: BNA Books, 1962), 60, 69; Fischer, *Implementation of Arbitration Awards,* in Arbitration and the Public Interest, Proceedings of the 24th Annual Meeting, National Academy of Arbitrators (Washington: BNA Books, 1971), 126.

Although not specifically and directly involved with the remedy question, then Dean St. Antoine's address to the Academy in Toronto in 1977[8] furnishes me with what I think is the best takeoff point for a re-examination of some of the remedy problems which have been discussed over the years before the Academy. Ted's paper purported to be a refutation of a controversial speech I made to the Academy the year before.[9] That speech has been widely misinterpreted. It was deliberately put in provocative language for the purpose of arousing controversy and succeeded, at least, in doing so. But that is neither here nor there. What I want to do today is to emphasize my essential agreement with Ted and to take his thought a bit further. What he said, in supposed disagreement with me, was that an arbitrator is essentially the parties' "contract reader." When the arbitrator interprets the agreement, as applied to the particular situation in front of him, his result should be treated as if it were written *in haec verba* into the agreement. When a court is called upon to enforce the award, it is essentially being called upon to enforce what the arbitrator has inserted into the agreement with the consent of the parties.[10]

I emphasize Ted St. Antoine's statement as to the function of the arbitrator because it contrasts with the view of Robben Fleming in his 1962 article on "Arbitrators and the Remedy Power." In that article Fleming described the arbitrator as "in effect, the enforcer of the agreement."[11] He is not. His function, no more and no less, is to say what the agreement means. And —this is my first thesis—this is not only his function in determining whether a violation has occurred, it is also his function, and his only function, when it comes to the question of remedy. To put the matter affirmatively, it is my view that an arbitrator's sole function in deciding what remedy should be given, where he finds that the employer has not complied with the rules set forth

---

[8]*Judicial Review of Labor Arbitration Awards: A Second Look at* Enterprise Wheel *And Its Progeny*, in Arbitration—1977, Proceedings of the 30th Annual Meeting, National Academy of Arbitrators (Washington: BNA Books, 1977), 29.

[9]*The Coming End of Arbitration's Golden Age*, in Arbitration—1976, Proceedings of the 29th Annual Meeting, National Academy of Arbitrators (Washington: BNA Books, 1977), 97.

[10]Although purportedly in opposition to my view of the arbitrator's function, this is essentially my position. What I add, and what Ted does not appear to agree with, is that the arbitrator's role as "contract reader" derives from the function of grievance arbitration in the collective bargaining relationship as a substitute for the strike rather than as a substitute for litigation in the courts, but that disagreement is immaterial for present purposes.

[11]*Supra* note 2, at 1222.

in the collective agreement, is to determine what the agreement says about remedy. In so doing, he is performing a quite different function than a court is performing when it determines what remedies for breach of contract should be awarded.

I have previously written about this at some length.[12] Let me repeat here, in brief compass, what I said about eight years ago and what I still believe to be the essence of the matter. The arbitrator's function is not to award damages. What he sometimes does may look like damages. Indeed, when back pay is involved, his order looks like damages because it involves the payment of money. But it is not. It is what the arbitrator finds is the remedy provided for in the agreement. As the parties' "contract reader," the arbitrator determines what remedy is provided for in the agreement and awards it.

Sometimes, although rarely, the agreement says just that. The Jones and Laughlin agreement with the Steelworkers says (or said), "The decision of the Board will be restricted as to whether a violation of the Agreement as alleged in the written grievance . . . exists and if a violation is found, to *specify the remedy provided in this agreement*"[13] (emphasis added). Neither the United States Steel nor the Bethlehem Steel agreements contain the emphasized language, but I think I can say without much hesitation that the arbitrators involved do not consider their functions to be different because of the presence or absence of those words.

Perhaps I should pause here to say what should have been said in the beginning. I am speaking specifically and exclusively to grievance arbitration under what has been called the standard form in this country, a form in which the arbitrator's jurisdiction consists only of resolving disputes as to the proper interpretation or application of the agreement. The agreement may add a specific limitation that the arbitrator may not alter, add to, or detract from the terms of the agreement, but the result is the same: the arbitrator is limited to reading the contract for the parties and telling them what it means as applied to the particular factual situation presented.

This is equally true, of course, in a suit for breach of contract. When a buyer or seller brings suit for breach of contract of sale,

---

[12]Feller, *A General Theory of the Collective Bargaining Agreement,* 61 Calif. L.Rev. 663, at 749, 778–791 (1975).

[13]*See* Alexander, *Discretion in Arbitration,* in Arbitration and the Public Interest, Proceedings of the 24th Annual Meeting, National Academy of Arbitrators (Washington: BNA Books, 1971), 84, 96.

or even when an employee brings suit for breach of an individual contract of employment, a court's function is to determine whether in fact the contract, properly read, has been violated. There, however, the similarity ends. In a suit for breach of contract, the rules governing remedies are determined by what the society, as it expresses its will through legislation or judicial determination, deems appropriate.[14] Those rules governing remedies are external to the agreement, may not in fact correspond to the intention of the parties, and may in some instances not fully compensate the wronged party for the injury suffered. Thus, for example, although the parties may specify a penalty for failure to perform an agreement, modern law will, by and large, not enforce that penalty. As Corbin put it: "[I]t has seemed to [the courts], that, in case of breach of contract, justice requires nothing more than compensation measured by the amount of the harm suffered. Penalties and forfeitures are not so measured."[15]

It was not always thus. Recall Portia's defense in The Merchant of Venice. Shylock had specified in his loan to Antonio that upon failure to repay at the stipulated time, Antonio should forfeit a pound of flesh. Portia's successful defense was not that the penalty specified bore no relationship to the harm suffered by the failure to perform on time. Nor was it that the sum owed had in fact been tendered, although late. It was assumed by all that upon nonperformance of the contractual obligation, the penalty, neither more nor less than one pound of flesh, and without any blood, became due. Today the defense, even if the penalty were a specified sum of money, would be that it is unenforceable except to the extent of the harm proved to be suffered by reason of the nonperformance of the contract.

This is emphatically not true of the remedies specified in a collective bargaining agreement for a violation of the terms of the agreement. Penalties are routinely awarded without regard to the question of whether they can be said to constitute "liquidated damages," or whether there is any damage at all. If the

---

[14]*See* Farnsworth, *Legal Remedies for Breach of Contract,* 70 Col. L.Rev. 1145 (1970). Professor Farnsworth sets out seven critical choices involved in the system of judicial remedies, among which are the choice between relief to redress breach rather than compulsion to perform, and the choice between substitutional relief (*i.e.,* damages) rather than specific performance. These choices, he argues, are influenced by the free enterprise economy. He concludes that "all in all, our system of legal remedies for breach of contract, heavily influenced by the economic philosophy of free enterprise, has shown a marked solicitude for men who do not keep their promises." *Id.,* at 1215–1216.
[15]5 Corbin, Contracts 334 (1964). *See also* Restatement of Contracts, §339(2).

agreement provides for the award of one day's pay for each individual claim filed against a railroad for a change in scheduling practices, the Adjustment Boards routinely enforce that penalty, although it is not specified as liquidated damages and, in fact, there is no showing that the aggrieved employees suffered any monetary loss or hardship from the violation of the agreement.[16] Many of the rules governing compensation include penalties and are negotiated as such: premium pay for hours worked on Saturday and Sunday, or before or after the normally scheduled hours, is often intended to penalize improper scheduling. The punitive character of these compensation rules is evidenced by the magnitude of such premiums as compared to the much smaller premiums for shift work, or by comparing the premiums paid for Sunday work in most industries with those provided in continuous process industries or others where Sunday work is normally expected.

The distinction is sometimes explicitly made in the agreement, as in the early case of *Public Service Electric & Gas Co.*[17] Walter Gelhorn there offered the following definitions of "premium pay" and "penalty pay," as those terms were used in the contract:

> " 'Premium pay' may be defined as an extra wage granted for special effort; it is earned by that effort, as for example, by working overtime or on seven consecutive days or on a holiday. It is compensatory in purpose and effect. 'Penalty' pay, on the contrary . . . is, rather, punitive in character, being an impost upon an employer in the nature of a fine for failure to carry out some understanding."

A more modern example is provided by the agreement in *Ralph's Grocery Co.*[18] The agreement there provided that if bargaining unit work was performed by nonbargaining unit employees (in that case book or advance salesmen), the union would notify the employer in writing. If thereafter there was a further similar violation within six months, "damages" for such willful violation would be calculated by computing the amount of pay, and the value of the fringe benefit costs, which would have been incurred by the employer if the work had been done by a bargaining unit employee. If a second violation occurred

---

[16]The courts, at least under the Railway Labor Act, not recognizing the difference between remedies provided for in a collective agreement and damages, have, wrongly I submit, refused on occasion to enforce such awards. *See, e.g., Railroad Trainmen* v. *Denver & R.G.R.R.*, 338 F.2d 407, 409–410 (10th Cir. 1974).

[17]2 LA 2 (1946).

[18]70 LA 1001 (T. Roberts, 1978).

within the six-month period, the multiplier would be increased by one digit for each violation. This ascending "damage" calculation obviously bore no relationship to the damage actually suffered because of the violation and was inserted as a penalty. Yet I think few, if any, arbitrators would refuse to enforce those provisions if, in fact, a series of willful violations within the six-month period were proven. Conversely, as Tom Roberts held in that case, no award could be given for the first violation other than a declaration that the agreement had been violated. The arbitrator was to award only the remedies provided in the agreement. No remedy could, therefore, be given because the agreement itself specified no remedy except for the second and successive violations within a six-month period.

I immediately hear the objection. It can perhaps be best put in the words of Archibald Cox in the paper he delivered to the 12th Annual Meeting of the Academy: "Arbitrators frequently fashion remedies for breach of a collective agreement without a shred of contract language to guide them. Although a few agreements prescribe the remedy for an unjust discharge, the majority simply forbid discharge without just cause."[19] How then can it be said with any degree of reality that in awarding back pay, an arbitrator is merely acting as the parties' "contract reader" and applying the remedy that he finds in the agreement? The answer is, I submit, that arbitrators frequently find, and should find, implicit in an agreement, although nowhere expressed, obligations and rules. To take the discharge case one step further, assume that an agreement contains no provision at all limiting discharges to situations in which there is "just cause." It is now too well established to warrant dispute, I submit, that, at least if the agreement contains a seniority provision, the limitation on the employer's power to discharge is implicit in the agreement and can be enforced, although there is not a shred of language indicating that there is any such limitation.[20] The arbitrator, in reading a collective bargaining agreement, reads not only the words of that agreement, but also the commonly accepted standards which the parties may be assumed to have agreed upon even if they fail to express them in words. The authority to act as the parties' "contract reader" includes the authority to read into the contract those provisions which the

---

[19]Cox, *supra* note 7, at 38.
[20]*See* Cox, *Reflections Upon Labor Arbitration,* 72 Harv. L.Rev. 1482, 1502 (1959). *Cf.* Feller, *supra* note 12, at 749.

arbitrator finds can reasonably be expected to have been assumed to exist by the parties even if they fail to signify it by words.

Indeed, one of the characteristics of the collective bargaining agreement is that much must be necessarily implied. What parties address themselves to in the agreement are the problems or the uncertainties which they recognize as requiring resolution, one way or the other. What is assumed to exist is often simply assumed, and not expressed.

I can think of one familiar example. The first of the *Steelworkers Trilogy* was the *American Manufacturing Company* case.[21] I will recall for you what the issue was in that case. An employee was injured on the job and filed a workers' compensation claim. It was settled on the basis of a partial permanent disability. He then sought to return to work. The employer refused to re-employ him. A grievance was filed and the employer refused to arbitrate.

What is interesting about *American Manufacturing* for present purposes is not the arbitrability question that the Supreme Court decided, but the ground on which the court of appeals held that no arbitrator could possibly find that the grievance should be sustained. The reason was that the contract contained a seniority provision which gave preference in the filling of vacancies to employees based on seniority only if their abilities were relatively equal. The court assumed that the seniority provision was applicable to a worker seeking to return to his job after absence due to an injury. The grievant, having received a settlement for his workers' compensation claim based on a claim of partial and permanent disability, could not possibly, the court said, be found to have the ability to perform his job relatively equal to that of an uninjured employee. Now, obviously, if the agreement had said that an employee off because of injury was entitled to return to his job if he could perform it—the test that the arbitrator ultimately found to be the test—it would have been clear that the seniority provision for the filling of vacancies had nothing to do with the case. What is interesting for present purposes is that the agreement contained no such provision. Indeed, after having looked at what must be hundreds of collective bargaining agreements, I have rarely seen one which establishes the proposition that an employee who leaves his position

---

[21]*United Steelworkers* v. *American Mfg. Co.*, 363 U.S. 564, 46 LRRM 2414 (1960).

because of sickness or injury is entitled to return to it if he can perform the work of the position. But I imagine most arbitrators would assume that to be the case, as ultimately the arbitrator did in *American Manufacturing,* even though there are no words in the agreement so stating.

So it is with respect to remedy. Agreements rarely, if ever, specify that if a seniority grievance is granted, the grievant who was denied a position, or a promotion, is entitled to back pay. Arbitrators routinely award it nevertheless, as they do overtime pay when an employee is improperly denied the opportunity to work overtime, or straight-time pay when an employee is denied recall rights under the agreement.

My argument so far has been only that the arbitrator, in awarding remedies, should award only those which he finds implicit in the agreement. That does not advance us very far if we assume that the parties normally intend to provide implicitly in their agreement that the arbitrator shall have authority to award damages or, to put it in the words used by those arbitrators who have awarded damages, "by necessary implication the parties contracted for arbitration on the implied condition that if a violation were found an arbitrator could frame an appropriate remedy to undo the wrong that has been done."[22] Or, as an arbitrator in a second case put it, "It has always been the law that where there is a wrong there must be a remedy; and absent a specific limitation on possible remedies, a Court or arbitrator should order a remedy which is based on principles of equity and justice."[23] If a collective agreement can be read as authorizing an arbitrator to "frame an appropriate remedy to undo the wrong that has been done," or, as in the second case quoted, to "order a remedy which is based on the principles of equity and justice," then my first proposition does not advance the inquiry very far, but simply changes the locus of the source of the arbitrator's authority.

My second proposition, therefore, is that unless the contrary is stated in the agreement, as it sometimes may be, the primary authority implicitly granted to the arbitrator is the authority to award specific performance of the provisions of the agreement. There has been much discussion—foolish, I believe—as to the authority of an arbitrator to issue an injunction. The argument

---

[22]*Schott's Bakery,* 69-1 ARB ¶ 8118 (Joseph H. Jenkins, 1968), at 3397–3398.
[23]*Vallejo Times-Herald,* 76-2 ARB ¶ 8746 (Francis R. Walsh, 1976), at 6720.

is foolish, I submit, because that is all that an arbitrator ever does, or should do. When an arbitrator orders the company to reinstate a grievant, he is issuing an injunction. When an arbitrator directs the company to remedy a condition that is unsafe, he is issuing an injunction. He is ordering the company to take specific action.

Common law courts, of course, had no such power. They were limited to a finding that the defendant, because he had breached a contract, was indebted to the plaintiff for a specific sum of money which we today refer to as damages. As Oliver Wendell Holmes put it in *The Common Law:* "The only universal consequence of a legally binding promise is, that the law makes the promissor pay damages if the promised event does not come to pass. In every case it leaves him free from interference until the time for fulfillment has gone by, and therefore free to break his contract if he chooses."[24] In my view, the usual meaning of a collective bargaining agreement is precisely to the contrary. The parties intend that the employer have an obligation to perform in accordance with the contract, not the option of performing or paying the damages. And the remedy power which the parties give to the arbitrator is the authority to order the performance that the contract requires.

At common law, the judicial focus was on the damage suffered by the promisee in return for the promisor's exercise of his option not to perform but to pay. Complex rules, such as, for example, those governing when interest was payable, were developed. In collective agreements there are also rules governing the payment of money, but they perform a different function: filling a time gap. If it were possible to have an instantaneous grievance and arbitration procedure, in which all violations of the rules set forth in the agreement could be instantly grieved and decided, the only remedy power of the arbitrator would be to order the employer to do that which the contract specifies he should do.

The concept of an instantaneous procedure, like the concepts of infinity and a perfect vacuum, is impossible of achievement but serves as a conceptual end point defining the rules governing the process. There must always be a time gap between the uncorrected event upon which the grievance is based and the arbitrator's determination that the event constituted a failure of

---

[24] *The Common Law* (1881) 301.

the employer to comply with the rules. The usual function of a money award is precisely to fill that time gap. Many collective agreements contain rules limiting money awards, but those rules are almost never phrased in terms of limiting "damages." To the contrary—and I believe the terminology precisely reflects the kind of remedial power they envisage—the rules speak in terms of "retroactivity." What the parties normally intend is that the arbitrator's order to perform can be made retroactive to fill the time gap between the event and the specific performance ordered by the arbitrator. If the grievant should not have been discharged, the arbitrator orders him reinstated and orders the employer to pay the sum he would have paid if it were known at the time of the discharge that it was improper. Back pay, which is ordered to fill the time gap between the event and the decision (or, more properly, the action of the employer in complying with the decision) may look like damages because it involves the payment of money, but it is not.

If the parties wish to limit the amount payable, they do not limit damages but the period of retroactivity. The United States Steel agreement, in referring to monetary awards, calls them awards "involving the payment of monies for a retroactive period."[25] And it limits the back pay in a seniority case in the following way:

> "Awards of the Board may or may not be retroactive as the equities of a particular case may demand but . . . the effective date for adjustment of grievances relating to . . . seniority cases shall be the date of the occurrence or nonoccurrence of the event upon which the grievance is based, but in no event earlier than 30 days prior to the date on which the Complaint For was initiated. . . ."[26]

Where even stricter limitations are intended, the agreement then provides, as an exception, that:

> "If the Company recalls the wrong employee from a layoff to a job in a pool, it will not be liable for any retroactive pay to the employee who should have been recalled, with respect to any period prior to 4 days, or the beginning of the payroll week, whichever is later, after receipt by the Company of a specific written notice. . . ."[27]

Again we have a parallel in the development of judicial remedies. When courts of equity filled the gap created by the inability

---

[25]Agreement between United States Steel Corporation and United Steelworkers of America (1977), Sec. 7(E).
[26]*Ibid.*, Sec. 7.
[27]*Ibid.*, Sec. 13(L)(6)(b).

of the common law courts to direct action, they sometimes awarded money. This was not damages, but, rather, a direction that the defendant perform the obligation to pay money.[28] The usual form of an arbitrator's back pay award follows the equity form rather than that of the law courts. The judgment at law reads that the plaintiff recovers so much money; the decree in equity, that the defendant is ordered to pay the sum.[29]

There is, however, a difference. The arbitrator does not issue an order specifying in dollars and cents the amount to be paid, as a court must if its order is to be enforced. An arbitrator orders reinstatement with back pay, leaving to the parties the determination of the amounts which the agreement requires to be paid for the period in which the grievant was not permitted to work, or was not given the position which the seniority provisions require.

This leads to my third proposition: The power to order specific performance, retroactively if necessary, which the parties may be assumed to have vested in the arbitrator is ordinarily limited to the payment of sums calculated in terms of the collective bargaining agreement, not by measures external to it.

In many cases, of course, measurements derived from the rules of the agreement are available. They may, however, bear little or no relationship to the "damage" caused by the breach of the agreement. Reporting pay is a classic example of a remedy, usually provided in the agreement, for failure of management to provide the notice of the nonavailability of work which the agreement requires. Whether the reporting pay be two, four, or eight hours, it bears no relationship to the hardship or inconvenience the employee may suffer as a result of the failure of management to give notice.

Where there is no measure internal to the agreement which

---

[28]". . . [E]quity acts specifically, and not by way of compensation; which embodies a general principle running through the whole system of chancery jurisprudence. The principle is that equity aims at putting parties exactly in the position which they ought to occupy; giving them in *specie* what they are entitled to enjoy. . . . Thus equity decrees the specific performance of a contract, and does not give damages for its breach." Bispham, *The Principles of Equity* (10th ed., McCoy, ed., 1925), 81.

"The efficiency of the English courts of equity in granting specific relief has been increased by the power conferred upon them of giving damages . . . by virtue of the Statute 21 and 22 Vict., c. 27, commonly known as Sir Hugh Cairns's Act, which provides that the courts may . . . grant that relief, which would otherwise be proper to be granted by another court—i.e., award damages. Before this act the law had been the other way." *Id.,* at 630.

Today, of course, law and equity have been merged.

[29]Cooke, *Powers of Courts of Equity,* 15 Col. L.Rev. 106, 108 (1915).

can be applied, it follows that, unless the contrary is stated, there can be no monetary award at all. Assume, for example, a rule in a collective agreement, or in a rule authorized by the collective agreement, that an employee shall not smoke in designated areas. An employee smokes. The plant burns down. Now in that case, if the employer discharged the employee, an arbitrator would find that the employee had violated the agreement and the discharge would be sustained. But suppose the employer filed a grievance asking for damages in the amount of the value of the burned establishment. Should an arbitrator order the employee to pay damages? I submit he should not. There is nothing in the agreement by which the damage can be measured.

It may be objected to in this example that most agreements do not provide for employer grievances and, hence, the claim for damages for breach of the no-smoking provision could not be heard at all. Suppose we try an example not subject to that objection: a violation of the safety and health provision of an agreement. Whatever the nature of the particular provision, assume that the employer has acted or failed to act in such a way that an arbitrator would sustain a grievance claiming it was being violated. Ordinarily the arbitrator in such a situation would order the employer to remedy the unsafe condition. Or, if the case arose as the result of an employee's refusal to work under the unsafe conditions, the question might be whether he was justified in so doing. But suppose there is no grievance and the employee works and suffers serious injury as a result of the violation of the agreement. If a grievance is filed by an employee (or by an employee's spouse if the violation was serious enough to cause death) requesting damages for the harm reasonably foreseeable as a consequence of the violation, should the arbitrator, in the absence of language specifically giving him that power, issue such an award? I submit he should not.

To take another example: Suppose that an agreement specifies that employees shall be given a choice of vacation periods and that vacations, once scheduled, shall not be changed except under specified circumstances. Further, suppose that an employer, having scheduled an employee for a particular vacation period, then reschedules that vacation to a later time under circumstances not permitted by the agreement. Suppose that the employee, obedient to the direction of the employer, appears for work during his originally scheduled vacation and, as a consequence, suffers damage of an entirely predictable kind:

the deposit he paid on a vacation cabin was lost, the schedules of his wife and children had to be rearranged, and he was generally subjected to considerable inconvenience. Should an arbitrator, given these facts, assess the entirely foreseeable damages suffered and award them to the employee? I think not. Some agreements do, indeed, provide for reimbursement for such losses. But, in the absence of a specific remedial provision, should an arbitrator reasonably read the contract as providing for such relief? The answer should be no.

Sometimes a specific performance remedy can be found in cases such as that last given. Suppose the unpermitted vacation schedule change was to assign a shut-down period as the employee's vacation and give him vacation pay for the weeks of shut-down. An arbitrator, if he later found after the originally scheduled vacation period had passed that the violation was willful, might conclude that the employee had not received the vacation required by the agreement and order the employer to provide an additional period off from work, with pay, in order to comply with the terms of the agreement.[30] That might, in fact, be of greater value than the damage suffered by the employee, but it would be a remedy implicit in the agreement and measured by its terms.

The working foreman is, of course, another familiar example. The appropriate approach to that problem was eloquently set forth by Ben Fischer, a learned and experienced advocate, now retired, at the 1971 meeting of the Academy:

> "Management says: 'Foremen won't work.' And when they do work, management says: 'That's wrong. We're going to look into this and do something about it.' They do, and the foreman is told not to work—and this keeps going on and on until you go to arbitration, and then you've got a new kind of remedy. Now the arbitrator says that the foreman shouldn't work.
> "And the way you implement this is by giving the foreman a copy of the award, and if he can read he knows he violated the contract. Perhaps management takes him aside, if he can't read, and explains it to him. But nothing happens. If you think it's a great deal of satisfaction to a union member to say, 'We won!' when it costs us $1,200 to get this little lecture to the foreman, you are quite wrong. People are not concerned with this sort of elusive victory.
> "I don't know that this is the arbitrator's problem; I think it is the parties' problem. It seems to me that in responsible collective bargaining at this late date, if you're going to say that there is a rule,

---

[30]*Cf. Bethlehem Steel Co.*, 37 LA 821 (R. Valtin, 1961).

then you ought to say that there should be some penalty for its violation. When a member of the union violates a rule, there's a penalty; there's not much of a problem involved in that. When management violates a rule, there ought to be a penalty, and it is not primarily—in my judgment—the responsibility of the arbitrator to fashion such a remedy. If he can do so, God bless him—and I'll help him if I can—but I'm not going to lose sight of the fact that it is the contract itself that really fashions the remedy."[31]

Shortly after Ben made that statement, the basic steel agreements were indeed amended to provide a remedy, and one which bears no necessary relationship to the kind of remedy that a court would provide for breach of contract. The basic steel agreements were amended in 1971 to provide that if a supervisor performs work in violation of the agreement and the employee who otherwise would have performed the work can reasonably be identified, the company would be required to pay such employee two hours' pay or, if greater, the rate for the time which that employee would have worked on the job if the supervisor had not violated the agreement.[32] This penalty apparently having been proven to be inadequate, the provision was modified in 1974 to provide a minimum of four hours' pay.[33] The fact that the identified employee may have been fully paid for the time, and thus would receive double pay for a minimum of four hours, is immaterial. The provision is plainly a penalty measured in terms of the agreement and would be enforced as such by an arbitrator under the agreement irrespective of the lack of damage.

There is an exception to the rule that, unless otherwise specifically provided, the only monetary arbitral remedies should be those measured by computations internal to the agreement. That exception is the deduction of outside earnings from back pay. My thesis that the arbitrator, in ordering a remedy, simply directs the employer to do, retroactively, what the arbitrator finds he should have done, including the payment of money to a grievant who has been discharged wrongly or has been improperly laid off, would lead to the result that there should be no deduction for outside earnings during the period of absence from the workplace.[34] Yet agreements often provide for a de-

---

[31]Fischer, *supra* note 7, at 132.
[32]Section 2-A-3 (1971).
[33]Section 2-A-3 (1974).
[34]Deductions for periods when the employee was sick or would have been laid off, even if not improperly earlier discharged or laid off, are proper under this formulation

duction for outside earnings, and arbitrators almost uniformly provide for such a deduction even where there is no language directing them to do so. The only exception is the case where the remedy is set forth in words in the agreement and does not provide for such a deduction.[35]

Ben Fischer, whom I have already quoted at length, has criticized this practice,[36] but it can be regarded as a fixture of the industrial scene. It arises, I suspect, because arbitrators feel that it would be somehow unjust to permit the grievant to enrich himself because of the employer's violation of the agreement. But even here I can maintain my thesis that the arbitrator is acting as the parties' contract reader rather than acting as a court would in assessing damages. Given the existence of provisions for the deduction of outside earnings in many agreements, it is perhaps proper for arbitrators to assume that the parties contemplated such a deduction even though they do not say so in so many words. Although the parties generally do not include remedial provisions that require computations or assessments of amounts not based upon the wage or other formulas contained in the agreement, they clearly have the power to do so.

In any event, the deduction of outside earnings does not correspond to what a court would do in assessing damages. In court, damages for breach of a contract of employment normally include interest. Arbitrators rarely award it. In court there is a deduction for the amount the dischargee earned or could have earned in other employment but there is also a counterbalancing addition of any costs that he incurred in seeking other employment, whether or not successful. I have yet to see an arbitrator's decision that enhances the back pay due an employee by an assessment of the costs that he incurred in unsuccessfully attempting to "mitigate damages."

There is, I submit, no duty to "mitigate damages" because the arbitrator does not award damages. There is, or should be, therefore, no requirement that the employee seek other employment and no deduction from back pay because of his failure to do so. I concede that arbitrators often speak in terms of the duty

---

since the employer would not have paid the employee for those periods even if there had been no violation of the agreement.

[35]See *United States Steel Corp.*, 40 LA 1036 (C. McDermott, 1963). The agreement has since been modified to permit the offset, but to also give the arbitrator discretion to modify or eliminate it "where circumstances warrant."

[36]Fischer, *supra* note 7, at 133.

to mitigate damages and sometimes do, indeed, refuse to award back pay for periods in which it can be shown that the employee did not seek alternative employment.[37] But the cases in which an employer raises this defense are, at least in my opinion, rare, as are the agreements providing for such a duty. That fact indicates to me that the parties do not really regard this as an element to be considered in determining the appropriate arbitral remedy in a discharge case.

The provision for the deduction of outside earnings in an order of reinstatement with back pay can serve as an illustration of the limitations of my thesis. It is not my thesis that there is something inherent in the nature of the arbitration process that restricts the arbitrator to remedies calculable by use of the wage and other formulas of the agreement. It is my thesis that arbitrators, in awarding remedies rather than damages, are awarding only the remedies that they find inherent in the agreement and that, by and large, the remedies which the parties prescribe in the agreement, and those which can be found to be implicit in it even if not described in words, are so measured.

The parties can always provide otherwise, and they sometimes do. It is perfectly possible for an employer and the union to specify in their agreement that if an employee's grievance is sustained, the arbitrator shall have authority to award damages to him such as a court would in the case of a breach of an individual contract of employment. I have not been able to find an example of that kind of provision, but it is certainly conceivable that the parties could write one. And there are cases in which the parties provide for damage remedies for the employer in arbitration—not against the employees, but against the union. In the *Drake Bakeries* case,[38] the Supreme Court ordered arbitration of an employer claim for damages for an alleged violation of a no-strike clause. My own view is that *Drake Bakeries* was wrongly decided on its facts. But we can take the agreement as read by the Court as an exemplary one under which a damage remedy not calculable by provisions internal to the agreement can be awarded. Insofar as an agreement so provides, however, it is really not grievance arbitration in the usual sense. It does not involve adjudication of the rules governing the relationship

---

[37]*See, e.g., E. F. Hauserman Co.*, 64 LA 1065 (Rankin M. Gibson, 1975), citing judicial precedents in suits for damages. *Contra: Dubuque, Lorenz, Inc.*, 66 LA 1245 (A.V. Sinicropi, 1976).

[38]*Drake Bakeries, Inc.* v. *Local 50, Bakery Workers*, 370 U.S. 238, 50 LRRM 2440 (1962).

of employer and employee, but the quite different matter of the contractual rights between union and employer. It is not provided as a substitute for the strike, but as an alternative form of litigation. Arbitration of employer claims for damages are more properly analogized to commercial arbitration than to grievance arbitration, and my view is that the presumption of arbitrability which the Supreme Court has specified in the case of grievance arbitration is wholly inapplicable.[39]

There are examples of provisions in which the parties have consciously given the arbitrator the authority to do more than simply provide a retroactive remedy for grievances, strictly defined. A remedial problem very much akin to the problem presented by the situation where a foreman works in violation of the agreement but without any loss of pay to any employee is presented by provisions, now fairly common as a consequence of the Supreme Court's *Fibreboard* decision,[40] requiring the employer to enter into discussions with the union before contracting out work. The remedy to be applied where an arbitrator finds a violation of a provision not prohibiting the contracting out but simply requiring prior discussions presents obvious difficulties. They were addressed in the 1977 basic steel agreements by simply giving the arbitrator broad remedial power. Where the employer fails to give notice of contracting out and the failure to give notice deprives the union of a reasonable opportunity to suggest and discuss practicable alternatives, the United States Steel agreement provides that "the Board shall have the authority to fashion a remedy, at its discretion, that it deems appropriate to the circumstances of the particular case." That language is significant not only because of the discretion it vests in the arbitrator, but also because of its negative inference. The parties seem to have assumed, correctly in my view, that in the absence of that language, the arbitrator might find no remedy implicit in the agreement which would be meaningful.

The next question remains, however, as to why arbitrators should have the limited role I have described. Is it a function of the nature of the arbitration process, or is it a function of the collective bargaining process? The answer is, I believe, a bit of both. There is nothing in arbitration as such that would prevent arbitrators from acting the way courts do: taking testimony as to

---

[39]The argument is more fully spelled out in Feller, *supra* note 12, at 800–803.
[40]*Fibreboard Paper Products Corp.* v. *NLRB,* 379 U.S. 203, 57 LRRM 2609 (1964).

the damage suffered by the grievants and issuing an award in dollars and cents. Commercial arbitrators do that all the time. Indeed, that is their principal function. But, at least with respect to grievance arbitration, there are serious limitations on the competence of arbitrators to make such determinations. Our judicial system has evolved an enormous set of procedures designed to facilitate the adjudication of such questions as damages. There are, first of all, discovery procedures which in many cases involve more time and effort than the trial of a case itself. There are provisions governing the allocation of court costs. There are somewhat elaborate provisions governing offers of settlement and the consequences to a party that refuses an offer of settlement and receives less than the offered amount at trial. All of these procedures are meant to facilitate the disposition of claims that will end up in a monetary award in dollars and cents. None of them is available in grievance arbitration. The reason they are not is that the parties have not provided the arbitrator with these tools. And the reason they have not goes back to the collective bargaining process out of which grievance arbitration arises.

If one looks at the history of grievance arbitration in this country, one will find, in every instance in which it was opposed, the theme that the parties opposing the use of arbitration did not want third parties telling them how to run the business (or, today with school boards, in telling them how to run the schools). Grievance arbitration attained the stature that it has today as a substitute, not for litigation, but for the strike. It became acceptable as such a substitute because the arbitrator was limited to the function of reading the agreement for the parties. The strike, for which arbitration is the substitute, was not normally directed toward the payment of damages by the employer, but directed toward compelling action by it. Just so, the remedies that an arbitrator has available are remedies directed at action, retroactive in some cases, but limited to actions of the kind called for by the agreement, including the payment of monies measured by the terms of the agreement. Although it is stretching the analogy quite far, what the parties have in effect done might be said to reinstitute what used to be the rule with respect to the bond under seal. Upon failure of the employer to meet the condition set forth in the bond, the penalty provided for therein, and only that penalty, must be paid, whether or not that penalty adequately redresses the injury or, indeed, much more than adequately redresses the injury.

What I have said here in a sense parallels what I have said on the subject of the application of "external law." I have argued that arbitrators, unless specifically authorized to do so by the agreement, should limit their determination as to what action is or is not required by the agreement to the terms of that agreement, including the terms which the arbitrator may find implicit in it, although not spelled out, and should ignore the requirements of the external law.[41] Just so, my view here is that in determining remedies, the arbitrator should not analogize himself to a court and award remedies of the kind that a court would award, but should limit himself to awarding the remedies that he finds either explicitly or implicitly within the agreement.

It is perhaps appropriate to insert here a comment on a particular class of cases: the cases in which the National Labor Relations Board defers to arbitration under its *Collyer* doctrine.[42] It is uncertain at this moment where the Labor Board stands with respect to *Collyer*. The last definitive announcement was that the Board would not defer to arbitration cases involving complaints of violation of individual rights, that is, complaints involving claimed violations of Section 8(a)(3) of the Act, but would defer to arbitration in cases involving complaints of violation of the duty to bargain expressed in Section 8(a)(5).[43] The deferral of such cases poses obvious remedial problems. Suppose parties, subservient to the Board's direction, do submit to the arbitrator the question of whether the employer has refused to bargain in violation of Section 8(a)(5) of the Act, but do not specify what remedy the arbitrator is permitted to award. The Labor Board, if it found a violation, is authorized by statute to order the offending party to cease and desist from the violation "and to take such affirmative action . . . as will effectuate the policies of this Act."[44] Further, the statute specifically provides that "such order may require such person to make reports from time to time showing the extent to which it has complied with the order."[45] The Board has utilized a variety of remedies in order

[41]Feller, *supra* note 9.
[42]*Collyer Insulated Wire,* 192 NLRB 837, 77 LRRM 1931 (1971).
[43]*General American Trans. Corp.,* 228 NLRB 808, 94 LRRM 1483 (1977); *Roy Robinson Chevrolet,* 228 NLRB 828, 94 LRRM 1474 (1977).
[44]Section 10(c).
[45]*Ibid.*

"to effectuate the policies of the Act." It normally requires that the parties bargain. Where the act constituting a refusal to bargain is unilateral action, it may order the employer to rescind that action. In *Fibreboard* the Board ordered the employer to recreate its maintenance department and to pay back pay to the employees it terminated when it contracted out its maintenance work without first bargaining with the union. The Board routinely orders the posting of notices. Where it finds an egregious violation, it may go further and order the employer to assemble the employees and read to them, or permit a Board agent to read to them, the findings of the Board and its order. It may order the employer to give the union access to bulletin boards, or to provide the union with the names and addresses of employees.[46]

Should an arbitrator in a case deferred to him by the Board assume the power to grant such remedies if he finds them appropriate? Again, if the parties stipulate that he may issue such orders as the Board might issue, the parties may be deemed to have authorized him to engage in a continuing policing role. But unless they do so, I submit, he should not. He has neither the jurisdiction nor the physical capability to police compliance with his order. The Labor Board carefully separates the process of deciding whether a violation has occurred and determining the general nature of the remedial order to be issued, on the one hand, and the determination of whatever sums may be due and whether the order has been complied with on the other. The latter function is performed by the regional offices, each of which has an individual designated as the "compliance officer" whose function it is to assure compliance with the Board's order after it has been issued. No such facilities are available to the arbitrator, nor should he assume authority to police compliance with his order unless the parties specifically indicate that he should do so.

All that I've said thus far should have been phrased in descriptive terms: a statement of what arbitrators in fact do. It has largely been phrased, however, in normative terms: what arbitrators should do. The reason is that, in preparation for this paper, I attempted to read at least a sampling of the recent

---

[46]*J.P. Stevens & Co.*, 239 NLRB No. 95, 100 LRRM 1052 (1979), enforced in part, *J.P. Stevens & Co.* v. *NLRB*, 623 F.2d 322, 104 LRRM 2573 (4th Cir. 1980). The Board had also ordered the payment of the union's negotiating and litigation expenses. The court remanded that portion of the order to the Board for further explication.

reported arbitrators' decisions dealing specifically with remedies. Any such survey is subject to a serious qualification. As we all know, only a small proportion of arbitrators' decisions are submitted for publication, and only a small proportion of those submitted are, in fact, published. The editors of the publishing agencies naturally and understandably choose to publish those decisions that add something new to those already published. Decisions that simply follow well-established norms are not new, but simply repetitive, and, hence, are usually not published. A survey of the published decisions, therefore, will tend to give greater weight than should be given to what the statisticians call "outliers."

Statisticians, as a matter of routine, disregard "outliers" in doing regression analysis. Reliance on published decisions as indicating what arbitrators in fact do, to the contrary, gives undue weight to the "outliers." Despite this qualification, however, a sampling of the reported decisions produces such a significant number that do not correspond to what I have described as the proper scope of the arbitrator's remedial power that it is fair to conclude that what I have described as what arbitrators should be doing is not, in fact, a fair description of what at least a number of them are doing.

Let me give you a few examples. I have already said what I believe the arbitrator's function should be when presented with a claim for damages as a result of a violation of a safety and health provision. When I last wrote on this subject, in 1973, I was able to say that I could find only a single published decision in which an arbitrator had awarded damages to a grievant injured as a result of a violation of a safety and health provision, and in that case the arbitrator's powers were not limited to interpretation and application of the agreement. This is no longer the case. I have found at least one in which an arbitrator awarded not only back pay for the period in which the grievant lost time because of an injury caused by a violation of the safety and health provision of the agreement, but also the cost of the drugs prescribed by his physician and mileage for the cost of his transportation to his physician.[47] (Presumably he did not order payment of the physician's fees only because that was already covered by workers' compensation.)

That decision may be fairly classified as an "outlier." But

---

[47] *Vallejo Times-Herald*, 76-2 ARB ¶ 8522 (Francis R. Walsh, 1976).

surely it would be presumptuous to describe the soon-to-be-president of the National Academy of Arbitrators as an "outlier," so let me describe to you a series of three decisions in the same case issued by that arbitrator.[48]

The case involved the discharge of two employees who refused, on October 3, 1974—the dates are important—to agree to work a changed schedule that was to begin on October 8. They were instantly discharged. On October 4, still before the change in schedule was to take place, they recanted and asked for reinstatement. The company refused. A charge of violation of Section 8(a)(3) was filed with the Labor Board because it appeared that the discharge of at least one of the grievants was in part motivated by a desire to get rid of a troublemaker, that is, a shop steward who had been filing a large number of grievances. The Board, under its then application of *Collyer* to 8(a)(3) cases, deferred to arbitration. The arbitrator, quite properly, refused to address the statutory issue since the case could be resolved under the contract. In his award, dated May 7, 1975, he found that the grievants had unequivocally offered to retract their refusals and to accept the disputed work assignments without any condition other than the pursuit of their claim that the assignments were improper. Accordingly, he ordered that they "be reinstated effective October 4 without loss of pay, computed on the basis of the straight-time hours they would otherwise have worked but for their wrongful separation from the payroll." So far, so good: specific performance retroactive to October 4. He then went on to specify that "any monies received by them in lieu of their wages, including unemployment compensation, shall be deducted from the sum due them and they shall submit sworn statements of such earnings to the Employer as a condition precedent to receipt of back pay." This point is perhaps questionable, but certainly not contrary to accepted practice. Finally, he ordered that the hearing should remain open and jurisdiction be retained until June 15, 1975.

Before that date both parties asked the arbitrator for resumption of the hearing with respect to the sum due the grievants, as well, apparently, as to whether the employer was obliged to reinstate them. The employer introduced testimony that the grievants would have been laid off by November 1974. The arbitrator, after citing and discussing the California Code of

[48]*Farmer Brothers Co.,* 64 LA 901 (E.A. Jones, 1975), 65 LA 884 (1975), 66 LA 354 (1976).

Civil Procedure and the United States Arbitration Act, concluded that this evidence should have been tendered at the first
hearing and could not, therefore, be considered. The union
sought an award of its costs, including attorneys' fees, on the
ground that the company had unwarrantably and unreasonably
abused the post-award procedure provided for in the first
award. The arbitrator rejected this claim in view of the specific
provisions in the agreement specifying that each party should
bear its own costs. The award was that the employer and the
union should comply forthwith with the terms of the May 7,
1975, award. Again, however, the arbitrator retained jurisdiction, this time until October 31, 1975.

Sure enough, the case came back again. From his third opinion in the same case, it appears that subsequent to the second
award the employer offered to pay one of the two grievants, the
trouble-making shop steward, back pay from the date of his
discharge to May 7, 1975, the date of the first award, provided
he would accept layoff status and agree that he would not accept
any recall. Reinstatement and back pay had been given neither
grievant. The arbitrator was duly enraged. "The employer," he
said, "has purposely retained and converted to its own use monies long overdue, that are rightfully the Grievants." Accordingly, he issued a new award. There was to be added to the
accrued back pay health and welfare payments and prorated
vacation time, and this liability should continue to accrue until
an unconditional offer of reinstatement was made. But, under
this third award, there would be no subtraction of unemployment compensation payments. Furthermore, to the sums thus
calculated there was then added interest at 10 percent, compounded daily. The employer and the union were to seek concurrence on the sum due, and upon failure to concur each was
to submit his proposal and the arbitrator would choose one or
the other. The hearing was again left open and jurisdiction
retained. There is no report as to whether any further proceedings became necessary.

This very distinguished arbitrator's outrage at the employer's
refusal to comply with his award is understandable. As he said,
the employer did not have one scintilla of justification for its continuing failure to comply with the award of May 7, 1975.[49] But,

[49]It is not quite true, as he said it was, that the award was entirely unambiguous. It
did not specifically include the health and welfare payments or the vacation accruals, nor
did it specify as the final award did that there should be deducted federal and state
paycheck withholdings. But that was not a fault in the first award. Arbitrators, in my view,

despite his understandable indignation, the arbitrator, I submit, had no authority whatsoever to order the payment of interest or to eliminate the deduction of unemployment compensation payments if it were proper in the first place to provide for their deduction. Either the agreement should be read as providing for a deduction of unemployment compensation payments, or it should not. Either the agreement provided for interest payments on back pay—as most do not—or it did not. Most arbitrators do not award interest because it is not normally included as a contractual remedy. A court, when called upon to enforce an arbitrator's award, could indeed provide for interest. Indeed, it could direct the employer to comply upon penalty of contempt and jail (a remedy which the arbitrator apparently did not enter-tain). The additional burden he did place upon the employer might well have been imposed by a court determined to do justice and equity, and undoubtedly was so imposed by the arbitrator for that purpose. In so doing, however, I submit that he exceeded his function as an arbitrator.

There is a story that Judge Learned Hand, when departing from one of his meetings with Justice Holmes, said, "Do justice." Holmes is reported to have replied, "My job is not to do justice but to see that the game is played according to the rules." Holmes was not speaking of remedies and of arbitration. But his thought is apt. The arbitrator's function is not to do justice, even with respect to remedies. His function is to read the contract, including its provision as to remedies, and to tell the parties what those provisions mean as applied to the particular case. Where the agreement is silent, he may find implied in it, as the common law of industrial relations, the kind of remedies customarily provided in collective agreements or by arbitrators. Those remedies are almost universally injunctive in nature and, where the payment of money is involved, based on calculations interior to the agreement. The remedy in a particular case may be more or less than justice. But, as the parties' "contract reader," the arbitrator's function ends when he tells the parties what the remedy provided in their agreement is and directs performance of that remedy.

This is, concededly, a narrow view of the arbitrator's function. But the institution of grievance arbitration as we know it today

---

do not direct the specific form of calculation; they simply tell the employer to pay what he should have paid if the wrongful discharge had not taken place.

has been built upon the assumption that arbitrators are not courts and do not have the power, unless they are expressly given it, to see that justice and equity are done. They are, and should be, restricted to performing the narrow function that the parties have given them. Concededly, in determining the meaning of an ambiguous contractual provision, or in determining what remedy should fairly be read into an agreement, the arbitrator should choose the alternative among those offered to him which best corresponds to what he believes the parties intended and that, in turn, may involve an assumption that the parties intended to do that which is right as the arbitrator sees it. But surely an arbitrator should not read an agreement as providing for the deduction of unemployment compensation and not providing for interest on back pay when it is first presented to him and then, when the employer refuses to comply, read that same agreement as not providing for a deduction of unemployment compensation and providing for interest at 10 percent.

It takes discipline to issue an award that the arbitrator firmly believes does not do justice to the parties. It takes, to push the analogy further, the same kind of discipline that, under the *Steelworkers Trilogy*, requires a court to enforce an award interpreting a collective bargaining agreement in a way which the court believes is plainly erroneous and unjust. I am sure you are all familiar with the cases in which a court, through one device or another, has failed to exercise that kind of discipline because, in the court's view, the result reached by the arbitrator was plainly wrong and did an injustice to one of the parties. I regret such instances. I'm sure that everyone in this audience does. There are at least an equal number of cases, however, in which arbitrators, bemused perhaps by the freedom from review which the disciplined courts have granted them, or perhaps only confused by the similarity of orders for back pay to the damage remedy available in the courts, have not imposed upon themselves the discipline which I urge they should. I hope, although I doubt, that everyone in this audience also agrees.

II. REMEDIES: ANOTHER VIEW
OF NEW AND OLD PROBLEMS*

ANTHONY V. SINICROPI**

Two Views of Arbitral Remedial Authority

David Feller has expressed a point of view emphasizing what he feels *should* be the basis or foundation of arbitral remedy power. In addition, he has thoroughly explained why that power should be narrowly circumscribed. I have elected to concentrate on what arbitrators do with respect to formulating remedies and on what basis they predicate their actions. In doing so, it is important to note that these conclusions are based on published arbitration awards. The danger of relying on published arbitration awards has already been voiced by Professor Feller. Despite his admonition, I am of the view that these published awards are indeed reflective of the trends that have developed with regard to remedies in "arbitration." On that basis, I feel a review of the findings is useful.

There are two perspectives from which to examine arbitral remedy power.[1] One is based on the "legal" authority of the arbitrator to formulate a specific remedy under the labor agreement. The other is based on a policy foundation, that is, what the likely effect, or impact, of a specific remedy will be on the collective bargaining institution.

A review of the "legal-authority" concept must include an examination of specific contractual provisions as well as of state and federal statutes and the common law. In addition, such a review must examine the judicial response to remedial determinations because, despite the directive of the Supreme Court in the *Steelworkers Trilogy,*[2] state and federal courts are increasingly accepting the invitation to review the merits of arbitrators'

---

*The main body of this paper has been excerpted from Remedies in Arbitration, by Marvin Hill, Jr., and Anthony V. Sinicropi (Washington: BNA Books, 1981).

**Member, National Academy of Arbitrators; J. F. Murray Professor of Industrial Relations and Director, Industrial Relations Institute, University of Iowa, Iowa City, Iowa.

[1] *See, e.g.,* Fleming, *Arbitrators and the Remedy Power,* 43 Va. L.Rev. 1199, 1201 (1962); Stein, *Remedies in Labor Arbitration,* in Challenges to Arbitration, Proceedings of the 13th Annual Meeting, National Academy of Arbitrators (Washington: BNA Books, 1960), 39.

[2] *Steelworkers* v. *American Mfg. Co.,* 363 U.S. 564, 46 LRRM 2414 (1960); *Steelworkers* v. *Warrior & Gulf Navigation Co.,* 363 U.S. 574, 46 LRRM 2416 (1960); *Steelworkers* v. *Enterprise Wheel & Car Corp.,* 363 U.S. 593, 46 LRRM 2423 (1960).

awards under the premise of determining contractual restrictions on arbitral authority.[3] As a result, a truly innovative, yet fair, arbitrator may face the hazard of having his awards overturned.

In analyzing remedial power under the policy concept, it is essential to understand that the focus is not on whether the remedial measure is permissible under the collective bargaining agreement or the law but, instead, on how the measure, if awarded or implemented, might affect the collective bargaining institution.

It should not be assumed that policy and legal-authority concepts are independent. Clearly, they are often interdependent and, when taken in combination, affect the formulation and application of arbitral decisions.[4]

Any examination of arbitral remedial authority, whether from a legal-authority or policy point of view, must address the question of what the arbitrator's function should be within the "private rule of law" established by the collective agreement. Arbitral opinion is divided on this question.

Some arbitrators and practitioners would equate the arbitrator's remedy power with that of a court on contractual disputes. This approach has been advanced by Arbitrator Sidney Wolff[5] and has been characterized by Arbitrator David Feller[6] as: "What is the proper measure of damages in a suit for breach of a labor agreement which happens to be decided by an arbitra-

---

[3]See, e.g., St. Antoine, Judicial Review of Labor Arbitration Awards: A Second Look at Enterprise Wheel and Its Progeny, in Arbitration—1976, Proceedings of the 30th Annual Meeting, National Academy of Arbitrators (Washington: BNA Books, 1978), 29; Christensen, Judicial Review: As Arbitrators See It, in Labor Arbitration at the Quarter-Century Mark, Proceedings of the 25th Annual Meeting National Academy of Arbitrators, National Academy of Arbitrators (Washington: BNA Books, 1973), 99–114.

[4]The late Dean Harry Shulman, Sterling Professor of Law at the Yale Law School, noted in a Holmes Lecture that appeared in the Harvard Law Review, 68 Harv. L.Rev. 999 (1955), that collective bargaining is not concerned merely with the return for employees' services. Rather, collective agreements are pacts adopted to set up systems of industrial democracy in complex industrial societies. Shulman writes: "No matter how much time is allowed for the negotiation, there is never time enough to think every issue through in all of its possible applications, and never ingenuity enough to anticipate all that does later show up." Dean Shulman went on to state that the parties recognize that all contingencies have not been anticipated and that, in any event, there will be many differences of opinion as to the proper application of the standards used by arbitrators. Clearly, Shulman recognized that both legal-authority and policy factors are present in the collective bargaining arrangement and that the grievance-arbitration mechanism is designed to address and incorporate both of those concepts.

[5]Wolff, The Power of the Arbitrator to Make Monetary Awards, in Labor Arbitration—Perspectives and Problems, Proceedings of the 17th Annual Meeting, National Academy of Arbitrators (Washington: BNA Books, 1964), 176–193.

[6]See Feller, Discussion of Remedies in Labor Arbitration, in Labor Arbitration—Perspectives and Problems, id., at 194.

tor?"[7] Under this approach, arbitration is viewed as a speedy and informal way of dealing with what is essentially a suit for breach of contract. Hence, the basic remedies available in breach-of-contract cases—damages, restitution, and equitable remedies—may, unless proscribed by the agreement, be awarded by the arbitrator, who essentially acts as a surrogate for a judge. Questions concerning the propriety of a specific remedy may readily be understood by reference to Corbin or Williston. As one observer has stated: "[T]he never-say-die Willistonian view . . . [is] that a contract is a contract is a contract, and that although some contract rules are too narrow to qualify as full-fledged principles, the general principles . . . of contract law are always applicable."[8]

At the other extreme is the view that the arbitrator's only function is to explicate what is implicit in a collective bargaining agreement. David Feller, in his classic piece, "The Coming End of Arbitration's Golden Age,"[9] and in his paper at this meeting, argues that arbitration is not a substitute for judicial adjudication, but a method of resolving disputes over matters which, except for the collective bargaining agreement and its grievance-arbitration machinery, would be subject to no governing adjudicative principle at all. Arbitration is an adjudication against standards, but the standards are not those which would be applied by a court charged with adjudicating a contractual dispute. Labor arbitration requires treatment different from that accorded commercial arbitration cases, Feller contends, since in the commercial setting arbitration is a substitute for litigation rather than a system to avoid industrial strife.

For this reason arbitration of labor disputes has functions quite different from arbitrations under an ordinary commercial agreement. Feller argues that it is important to draw a sharp distinction between the role of the arbitrator in construing and applying the collective bargaining agreement and that of an

---

[7]Id., at 194–195.

[8]Mueller, *The Law of Contracts—A Changing Legal Environment,* in Truth, Lie Detectors, and Other Problems in Labor Arbitration, Proceedings of the 31st Annual Meeting, National Academy of Arbitrators (Washington: BNA Books, 1979), 204–217. In *Local 636* v. *J.C. Penney Co.,* 484 F.Supp 130, 103 LRRM 2618 (W.D.Pa. 1980), a federal district court, in determining whether an employer was contractually bound to arbitrate, stated: "Although the technical rules of contract do not necessarily control all decisions in labor management cases, normal rules of offer and acceptance are determinative of the existence of a bargaining agreement. . . ." *Id.,* at 2620.

[9]Feller, *The Coming End of Arbitration's Golden Age,* in Arbitration—1976, Proceedings of the 29th Annual Meeting, National Academy of Arbitrators (Washington: BNA Books, 1976), 97–139.

arbitrator functioning as an adjudicator of contractual controversies subject to resolution under the general law of contracts.
In another article he states:

> "[Y]ou must recognize the impropriety of questions such as: 'What
> is the proper measure of damages in a suit or arbitration for breach
> of contract?' 'Can an arbitrator issue an injunction?' 'Can he give
> punitive damages?' All those questions are exactly the same . . .
> questions that you *do* address—to a court of law in which you are
> suing for breach of contract.
>
> "When you arbitrate, however, you are not suing through an
> informal domestic tribunal. . . . You are not using an informal
> tribunal as a substitute for a lawsuit when you establish a system of
> grievance arbitration. You are establishing a completely different
> kind of machinery, and it is therefore improper to measure an award
> as if it were the kind of damage judgment which the courts would
> render. You should not put the question in that focus or framework
> at all. The real question is: 'What is the proper function of an
> arbitrator in settling a grievance under a contract?' "[10]

The majority view, as argued by Addison Mueller,[11] is probably somewhere between the views of Wolff and Feller, namely,
that collective bargaining agreements are special types of contracts[12] with respect to which the principles of ordinary contract
law, though not strictly applicable, are nonetheless helpful to
arbitrators because they tap the wisdom of the past. Although
the parties are free to make the arbitrator the equivalent of a
judge formulating remedies in a contractual dispute, in general
the parties do not anticipate that he will act in such a fashion.
If, as claimed by the Supreme Court, the arbitrator is usually
chosen because of the parties' confidence in his knowledge of
the "common law of the shop," it is expected that he will draft
remedies that may not explicitly be authorized within the four
corners of the agreement. After all, the Court, in *Warrior &
Gulf,*[13] has stated that "the industrial common law—the practices of the industry and the shop—is equally a part of the
collective bargaining agreement although not expressed in it."[14]
Justice Black has likewise declared that "a collective bargaining
agreement is not an ordinary contract for the purchase of goods

---

[10]Feller, *supra* note 6, at 194–195.

[11]Mueller, *supra* note 8; *See, e.g., Metal Specialty Co.,* 39 LA 1265 (Volz 1962); *Coca Cola Bottling Co.,* 9 LA 197 (Jacobs 1947).

[12]In this regard, *see* Feller, *A General Theory of the Collective Bargaining Agreement,* 61 Calif. L.Rev. 663 (1973).

[13]*Steelworkers* v. *Warrior & Gulf Navigation Co., supra* note 2.

[14]*Id.,* at 2419.

and services, nor is it governed by the same old common-law concepts which control such private contracts."[15]

Whichever view one endorses—the extreme positions may not necessarily be mutually exclusive since an agreement may be explicit in specifying the remedy that is to apply if a violation is found—it is the author's premise that the parties in the arbitration procedure spend much time on the merits of the dispute, as they should, and sometimes almost as much time on the question of arbitrability, which perhaps they should not. The matter of an appropriate remedy, if addressed at all, is usually noted merely by asking the traditional question: "If so, what shall be the remedy?" While in some cases this will be sufficient, in others the remedy is far from apparent and is not easily determinable.

In view of the potentially great impact of an arbitration decision and the limited judicial review available to the parties, it is puzzling to note the extent to which remedy issues have been ignored by the parties and practitioners alike.

Discipline and Discharge—Problem Areas

Perhaps the most frequently encountered remedy problems arise in the disciplinary area. Reinstatement with full benefits is usually not a problematic factor, but conditional reinstatement with back pay, reinstatement without back pay, and obligation for mitigation of damages all present difficulties that will be touched on briefly.

Last Chance or Conditional Reinstatement

Under this structure, arbitrators have provided that an employee be reinstated, but not until the occurrence of some future event (condition precedent); or, an arbitrator may provide for reinstatement, but if some event or condition materializes in the future, the remedy shall no longer be binding on the employer (condition subsequent). Some common examples of both types of conditional remedies are noted as follows:

---

[15]*Transportation Communications Employees Union* v. *Union Pacific R.R.*, 385 U.S. 157, 160, 63 LRRM 2481, 2482 (1966). *See also, Emery Freight Corp.* v. *Teamsters Local 295*, 356 F.Supp. 974, 81 LRRM 2393 (E.D.N.Y. 1972), citing *Columbia Broadcasting System* v. *American Recording & Broadcasting Assn.*, 293 F.Supp. 1400, 69 LRRM 2914 (S.D.N.Y. 1968) ("collective bargaining contract not necessarily governed by common law principles").

In an example of a remedy conditioned upon an event subsequent to reinstatement, an arbitrator[16] considered the discharge of an employee who allegedly concealed on his employment application his problem with hand eczema. Finding that the condition was not work-related, the arbitrator reinstated the grievant, but placed him on probation for five years, with the provision that if at any time during that period the grievant was unable to perform a full schedule, including overtime, he should immediately be terminated.[17]

Where it is demonstrated that the basis of a discharge was due not to an intentional individual fault of the grievant, but rather to a defect in mental or physical capacity, arbitrators have not hesitated to order reinstatement conditioned upon a proper showing of mental or physical fitness. Remedies in this area range from merely requiring the employee to submit to a physical examination,[18] to undertaking serious long-term mental therapy. As an example, one arbitrator[19] found that a discharge for excessive absenteeism was improper because the employee demonstrated that his poor attendance was due to an alcohol problem. As a remedy, the arbitrator converted the discharge to a disciplinary layoff and, effective as of the date of the award, ordered the grievant immediately to place himself in the care of a hospital rehabilitation center and carry out whatever recommendations it should make, including submission to long-term hospital treatment and/or Alcoholics Anonymous. The arbitrator also directed the employer to reinstate the grievant unconditionally within six months provided that the rehabilitation center certified that the grievant was able to work. If the conditions were not met, the arbitrator declared that the grievant could be treated as a voluntary quit.

Another arbitrator[20] was called upon to consider the discharge of an employee who was diagnosed as a manic-depressive with no clear prognosis. In reversing the discharge, the arbitrator stated:

"Although cause for discharge is not *always* based on fault on the employee's part, it normally requires such a finding. For example,

---

[16]64 LA 1129 (1975).
[17]*Id.*, at 1132.
[18]*See* Elkouri and Elkouri, How Arbitration Works (Washington: BNA Books, 1975), at 649–650. *See also Atlas Metal Parts Co.*, 67 LA 1230 (Kassoff 1977); *Lever Bros.*, 66 LA 211 (Bernstein 1976); *MGM Grand Hotel*, 65 LA 261 (Koven 1975).
[19]67 LA 847 (1976).
[20]*Consolidated Foods Corp.*, 58 LA 1285 (1972).

cases of chronic illness, lack of requisite skill in job performance and the like are not normally analyzed in terms of fault; yet in such cases inability to do the work, or continuous unreliable attendance, are regarded as disqualifying conditions over a period of time.

". . . Fault has no place in this situation. Since Grievant was helpless to prevent what he did while mentally ill and since Management could not reasonably be expected to tolerate his conduct, it would seem more reasonable to remove him from the work place until one of two things occur.

"1. He fully recovers and can establish his recovery to the reasonable satisfaction of Management's physicians, or to a board of those psychiatrists chosen jointly by a physician selected by Management and a physician designated by the Union on Grievant's behalf.

"2. He reaches retirement age. If he reaches retirement age first, he should be retired under the pension plan then current. . . ."[21]

In *Johns-Manville Perlite Corp.*, [22] the arbitrator converted a discharge into a two-year suspension where the record indicated that the employee was schizophrenic. The arbitrator found that discharge was inappropriate, in part because it would result in the grievant seeking employment elsewhere and merely passing the problem on to another employer. Ordering an indefinite suspension not to exceed two years from the date of the award, the arbitrator attached the following conditions:

"1. The Grievant places himself under the care and treatment of a qualified psychiatrist for treatment of his mental illness.

"2. That when at any time within the two-year period the Grievant's psychiatrist declares the Grievant recovered, or that his illness is and can be controlled so that he can function in a factory environment without engaging in disruptive conduct attributed to his illness, the Union and Management are to agree on an independent psychiatrist, or in the absence thereof, a Board of three psychiatrists, consisting of one selected by the Company, one by the Union, and a third selected by the two psychiatrists selected by the parties, for the purpose of evaluating the Grievant. Such independent psychiatrist or Board's evaluation shall be determinative of the issue herein and if favorable to the Grievant's employment, he is to be reinstated without back pay but with full seniority and other contractual benefits as if he had been on a leave of absence. If unfavorable to the Grievant, the suspension is to be converted into a discharge."

Where it was shown that an employee's weight problem placed undue restrictions on his capacity to perform assigned

[21]*Id.*, at 1288.
[22]67 LA 1255 (Traynor 1977).

work, the arbitrator overturned a discharge,[23] with the following conditions:

"If the grievant undertakes a program to reduce his weight under the care of his physician, and is successful within a period of one year in reducing his weight within the normal and optimum limits for an adult of his age and height, as determined by the Company Medical Director, and can produce a medical certificate that he can work without restrictions, he shall be reinstated to the labor classification with his seniority as of the date of his termination. If he is so reinstated he will be on probation for attendance for one year. . . . If his absences exceed the average for all employees at the plant he may be terminated. . . . The arbitrator retains jurisdiction to decide any questions as to this award."

In *Newkirk Sales Co.,*[24] the arbitrator found that an employer did not have just cause to discharge an employee who had a proven disability. Although the employee had been restricted by his doctor from lifting in excess of 200 pounds—and the employer's workers' compensation insurance carrier had determined that he had suffered a permanent partial disability of 16 percent—the arbitrator nevertheless held that the standard of "just and sufficient cause" presupposes some wrongful act on the part of the grievant. The arbitrator refused to reinstate the grievant to his old position even though the employee had performed his old duties for eight weeks after his return to work. The arbitrator reasoned that there was no evidence that his reinstatement would not create a risk to himself, to his fellow workers, and to customers. Absent evidence that the grievant would not recover sufficiently to perform the required tasks, the arbitrator ordered the employer to carry the grievant on a "suspended" status for a period of three years, or until such time as medical proof was established that he could perform all the requirements of his job.

Arbitrators have frequently ordered reinstatement conditioned upon the nonrecurrence of the conduct giving rise to the initial disciplinary penalty. Often referred to as "last chance" remedies, they are applied in a variety of situations. For example, in cases where an employee is discharged for excessive absenteeism, an arbitrator may find mitigating circumstances and order reinstatement, but condition it upon some satisfactory level of attendance in the future.

---

[23]*Reynolds Metals Co.,* 71 LA 1102 (Bothwell 1978).
[24]61 LA 1144 (Hutcheson 1973).

Similarly, an arbitrator conditioned a reinstatement order on the fact that if within the 12-month period from the date of reinstatement the grievant was again charged with habitual absenteeism, it would be considered a third offense and he would be subject to the usual contractual provisions.[25] The arbitrator considered the initial discharge for absenteeism as a suspension and, accordingly, designated it as equivalent to a second offense under the agreement.

In yet another absenteeism case, the arbitrator stated that a common remedy where discipline is upheld, but discharge is found to be too severe, is to reduce the penalty to a suspension and to place the grievant on permanent probation in case of future offenses, thus placing the burden and responsibility on the employee if he or she wants to retain employment.[26]

In *Intalco Aluminum Corp.*,[27] the arbitrator ordered conditional reinstatement of an employee who was discharged after pleading guilty, in a criminal proceeding, to an unlawful delivery of marijuana. Finding that there was no evidence that the employee's conduct had adversely affected the employer, the arbitrator nevertheless stated that he would fashion a remedy to insure the legal rights of the grievant and to protect the employer's right to pursue its objectives with minimal interruption and disturbances. The grievant was ordered to be reinstated without back pay and with loss of seniority from his discharge to the date of reinstatement. In addition, the reinstatement was conditioned upon the following: "(a) [I]f the Grievant is found to possess marijuana on Company property, the Company is free to discharge him at will. (b) [I]f the Grievant is again found guilty of selling or buying marijuana outside the Company premises by a court, the Company is free to discharge him at will."[28] The arbitrator further provided that the grievant would lose all further protection under the just cause provision of the contract in criminal matters, absenteeism, and tardiness.[29]

An arbitrator declared authority for arbitrators to condition remedies upon some special act or promise by an employee and ordered the reinstatement of an employee who was discharged

[25]*Menasha Corp.*, 71 LA 653 (Roumell 1978).
[26]*Stevens Shipping & Terminal Co.*, 70 LA 1066, 1972 (1978). *See also Microdot, Inc.*, 66 LA 177 (Kelliher 1976).
[27]68 LA 66 (LaCugna 1977).
[28]*Ibid.*
[29]*Ibid. See also Inmount Corp.*, 58 LA 15 (Sembower 1972) (any recurrence of disruptive activity); *United Tel. Co.*, 58 LA 1246 (Seinsheimer 1972) (company rules).

for calling in sick during a period when he was attending to his private garage business.[30] In reinstating the grievant, the arbitrator nevertheless designated that the following conditions must be maintained for a period of one year after reinstatement:

> "The Grievant shall waive in writing any sick and accident benefits during the period prior to his reinstatement.
> "The Grievant prior to reinstatement is to cease and desist from any outside business or employment and continue to do so during said (1) one year period. The Grievant shall furnish the Company with an affidavit that he has discontinued his business."[31]

Policy Considerations Under Conditional Reinstatement

Although conditional reinstatement is commonly used in arbitration, arbitrators ought to proceed with caution before formulating such remedies. One recurring problem in conditioning the terms of reinstatement is illustrated in the following decision:[32] In an arbitration involving an employee with alcohol problems, the arbitrator ordered the employee to be reinstated to his former job as soon as he was medically cleared to return to work. In this regard, a doctor's review was ordered, with the arbitrator retaining jurisdiction over possible disputes over implementation of this aspect of the decision. Moreover, the grievant was mandated "to refrain from, resort to or indulgence in alcoholic beverages at any time." The arbitrator similarly retained jurisdiction over the grievant "with respect to discipline meted out on a charge of imbibing alcoholic beverages for the purpose, only, of insuring that the fact of violation of the mandate . . . transpired."

The grievant was subsequently returned to work, but thereafter was suspended after being arrested for reckless driving and having drugs and alcohol in his possession. The employer requested an arbitration to authorize a termination "in light of [the grievant's] . . . incident involving alcoholism." The record, however, indicated that the supervisor who effected the employee's suspension asserted that the suspension was attributable to the grievant's excessive absenteeism.

The arbitrator in the second arbitration involving the same grievant declared that the actual narrow ground on which jurisdiction was reserved was plainly limited to discipline meted out

---

[30]*Microdot, Inc.,* 66 LA 177 (Kelliher 1976).
[31]*Id.,* at 180.
[32]*City of Sandusky,* 73 LA 1237 (Keefe 1979).

144 ARBITRATION ISSUES FOR THE 1980s

on a charge of imbibing alcoholic beverages, and not at all with respect to absenteeism. Consequently, the arbitrator reasoned that if the complaint related only to attendance infractions, the charge would not automatically position the arbitrator to hear the case. He further noted that management was requesting him to terminate the grievant under the conditions of the prior award, to which he correctly responded that arbitrators do not impose discipline. They simply pass judgment on actions which have been taken. Finally, in holding that the suspension should continue, the arbitrator issued an additional set of conditions, including an order for the grievant to present himself to the arbitrator for readmittance to work at the end of a six-month recovery period.

It is important to stress that a conditional reinstatement may, in the abstract, be a suitable way of dealing with an industrial problem. In the final analysis, however, the parties must implement the award and, in the process, it is not uncommon that the conditions imposed by the arbitrator will cause another round of litigation in the arbitral forum,[33] which, in turn, may create continued antagonism between the parties. The arbitrator, rather than acting as the parties' contract reader, instead becomes a "legislator" and an important and sometimes unwanted fixture in the grievance process.

Another problem involves the terms of the conditions themselves. If the conditions are deemed to be repugnant to a statute or some public policy, the award is subject to reversal if appealed. To illustrate: in *Douglas Aircraft Co.* v. *NLRB*,[34] the Ninth Circuit considered an award where back pay was denied for two reasons: (1) a pattern of abusive and uncivil conduct by the grievant, and (2) the grievant's refusal to agree to a settlement worked out by the union and the employer, which called for reinstatement, arbitration of the back pay issue, and withdrawal of the unfair labor practice charge. The General Counsel of the NLRB issued a complaint alleging that the discharge was an unfair labor practice and that the arbitrator's award was repugnant to the National Labor Relations Act. The company and the union then requested the arbitrator to clarify his decision. The

---

[33]As in *Taystee Bread Co.*, 52 LA 677 (Purdom 1969); *Bethlehem Steel Corp.*, 54 LA 1090 (Porter 1970); *Kurz Kasch, Inc.*, 68 LA 677 (Imundo 1977); *Story Chemical Corp.*, 65 LA 1257 (Daniel 1976).
[34]See Hill and Sinicropi, *Collateral Proceedings,* in Evidence in Arbitration (Washington: BNA Books, 1980), 60–68.

arbitrator responded that there was no evidence that the grievant's union activities were a reason for his firing, and that the
two reasons for denying back pay were each independent and
sufficient. Although an administrative law judge recommended
deference to these arbitral findings and dismissal of the unfair
labor practice charge, the NLRB found that the arbitrator's
award was clearly repugnant to the purposes and policies of the
statute and refused to defer to it. The Ninth Circuit, while agree-
ing with the Board that the conditioning of an award of back pay
on surrender of an unfair labor practice charge is repugnant to
the Act, nevertheless held that the NLRB abused its discretion
in not deferring since the two reasons given for denying back
pay were independent and not cumulative.

Finally, the various arbitration reporting services publish numerous awards where reinstatement is conditioned upon a
designated period of "probation" or "good behavior." Such
conditions are ambiguous and potentially troublesome. For example, if an employee is reinstated and placed on probation,
does this indicate that the employee is to be treated as a "probationary employee" (however these employees are treated), or
does it mean that if the reinstated employee is found to have
engaged in any violation of the agreement (as opposed to disciplinary offenses), he is subject to discharge with full access to the
grievance-arbitration procedure? Again, it is important to note
that the parties are faced not only with administering their negotiated agreement, but also with the possibility that the conditions imposed by the arbitrator may themselves be subject to
interpretation.

In addition to reinstatement, back-pay questions are of grave
concern and the decisions in this area demonstrate a wide diversity of reasoning. There is no genuine issue concerning the
power of an arbitrator to make a monetary award of back pay.
Even where this power is not expressly provided for in the
collective bargaining agreement,[35] or expressly requested in the
parties' written submission to the arbitrator, arbitrators have

---

[35]BNA reports that reinstatement with back pay for employees improperly discharged
is required in 43 percent of the contracts it surveyed—44 percent of the manufacturing
agreements and 40 percent of the collective bargaining agreements in nonmanufactur-
ing. BNA states that 63 percent of these provisions grant full back pay, 34 percent leave
the amount awarded to the arbitrator, and 4 percent place a limitation on the amount
awarded. In some instances unemployment compensation or money earned from other
jobs is deducted from back pay. Basic Patterns in Union Contracts (Washington: BNA
Books, 1979), at 9.

held that the power to decide the disciplinary issue includes the power to formulate a remedy including, but not limited to, back pay. It must be remembered, however, that the parties may, through appropriate contractual language, limit the amount of back pay that may be awarded by an arbitrator. For example, in *Columbus Show Case Co.,*[36] the arbitrator ruled that a back-pay award must be limited where the contract provided that "awards or settlements shall in no event be made retroactive beyond the date on which the grievance was first presented by the employee to his foreman." Similarly, the arbitrator, in *Yellow Taxi of Minneapolis,*[37] ordered reinstatement with only 10 days' back pay pursuant to an agreement which limited any make-whole compensation to 10 days' pay.

It is noteworthy that even where the contract specifically designates or limits the amount of back pay that is to be awarded in a disciplinary case, there are reported decisions indicating that arbitrators have not always adhered to such constraints.

Back Pay Without Reinstatement

When an arbitrator finds that discharge was improper, he has a range of remedies; he may grant reinstatement with full, partial, or no back pay. Infrequently, an arbitrator may award back pay but not order the grievant reinstated. Thus, in *Safeway Stores, Inc.,*[38] the arbitrator held that reinstatement was inappropriate where the grievant's behavior was not correctable. Although the contract provided that an employee may not be discharged except for just cause, the arbitrator pointed out that such a remedy would be justified since nothing in the parties' bargaining history, contract language, or other precedent precluded him from ordering back pay without reinstatement. Attention is called to his reasoning:

> "It is important to note that the Agreement is silent with regard to any mandated remedy. Neither party quarrels with the view that the Arbitrator has the authority under the Agreement to provide for reinstatement with back pay with interest. But what is significant is that the Arbitrator under this Agreement is not mandated to fashion any particular remedy. The parties could have bargained for such a contractual provision. Limitations upon arbitral remedial discretion

---

[36]64 LA 1148 (Leach 1975).
[37]68 LA 26 (O'Connell 1977).
[38]64 LA 563 (Gould 1974).

are not unknown to American labor-management contractual relations. But under this collective bargaining agreement, the arbitrator was provided remedial flexibility."[39]

The arbitrator also found that the discharge was not for cause, since "procedural due process" guarantees were violated. Specifically, he found that the agreement provided that "before a regular employee is discharged for incompetency or failure to perform work as required, he shall receive a written warning (with a copy to the union), and be given opportunity to improve his work." Since the union did not receive copies of the written warnings until five days before the discharge, it was denied the opportunity to counsel with the employee, as was clearly provided in the agreement. Accordingly, back pay without reinstatement was ordered.

In another situation where an employee, found to have been improperly discharged, had secured employment elsewhere and did not desire to be reinstated, the arbitrator, in *American Building Maintenance Co.,*[40] found a back-pay remedy appropriate. Noting that the agreement spoke only in terms of reinstatement, and was silent about relief where the discharged employee had secured alternate work, the arbitrator nevertheless held that the failure of the parties to include this contingency in the agreement should not work to the detriment of an otherwise improperly discharged employee.[41]

While arbitrators and parties are not of the same view regarding the specificity of the back-pay remedy and the retention of jurisdiction by the arbitrator, it appears that when the remedy can be specifically formulated, it should be; and when this is inappropriate, the arbitrator, with the concurrence of the parties, should retain jurisdiction for a specified period of time, and such jurisdiction should be exercised only in the event the parties cannot reach accord on the extent of the remedy.

Computing Back Pay

In computing back pay, the principle of "make whole" relief for an employee who was wrongfully discharged has been uniformly applied by the NLRB and the courts where an unfair

---

[39]*Id.*, at 570.
[40]58 LA 385 (McDonald 1972).
[41]*Id.*, at 397.

labor practice has been found. Thus, the Supreme Court has declared: "[A]n order requiring reinstatement and back pay is aimed at 'restoring the economic status quo that would have originated but for the company's wrongful refusal to reinstate.' . . ."[42]

Similarly, the Eighth Circuit has stated: "The amount which serves as the basis for the back pay award is the amount which the employee discriminated against would have earned but for the discriminatory act. It is grounded upon the rate of compensation normally to be expected during that period."[43]

The Fifth Circuit has voiced this principle as follows:

> "[T]he 'make whole' concept does not turn on whether the pay was wholly obligatory or gratuitous, but on the restoration of the *status quo ante*. . . . The Board's discretion to take such affirmative *remedial* action as will effectuate the policies of the Act included more than placing the employee in position to assert contractual or legally enforcible obligations. 'Back pay' . . . includes the monies, whether gratuitous or not, which it is reasonably found that the employee would actually have received in the absence of discrimination."[44]

The Court of Appeals for the District of Columbia has stated the policy reasons for allowing back pay as "make whole" relief:

> "The purpose of requiring that the employer make the discriminatee whole in such a case has a two-fold objective. First, the back pay remedy reimburses the innocent employee for the actual losses which he has suffered as a direct result of the employer's improper conduct; second, the order furthers the public interest advanced by the deterrence of such illegal acts."[45]

Arbitrators have borrowed from court and Board decisions and applied similar "make whole" concepts when ordering back-pay relief. The arbitrator in *Alliance Mfg. Co.*[46] advanced the following principle for awarding back pay:

> "The theory upon which back pay is awarded a discharged employee upon reinstatement is the same theory upon which courts of law award damages for breach of contract of employment, viz., to make the employee whole for the loss sustained by reason of his discharge. The purpose is to put him in the same position finan-

---

[42]*Golden State Bottling Co.* v. *NLRB*, 414 U.S. 168, 84 LRRM 2839, 2847 (1973), citing *NLRB* v. *J.H. Rutter-Rex Mfg. Co.*, 396 U.S. 258, 263, 72 LRRM 2881 (1969).
[43]*NLRB* v. *Columbia Tribune Pub. Co.*, 495 F.2d 1385, 86 LRRM 2078 (8th Cir. 1974).
[44]*Nabors* v. *NLRB*, 323 F.2d 686, 54 LRRM 2259 (5th Cir. 1963). *See also Segarra* v. *Sea-Land Service Inc.*, 581 F.2d 291, 99 LRRM 2198 (1st Cir. 1978).
[45]*NLRB* v. *Madison Courier, Inc.*, 472 F.2d 1307, 80 LRRM 3377, 3382 (D.C. Cir. 1972).
[46]61 LA 101 (1973).

cially that he would have been in had the discharge not occurred."[47]

In the same regard, Ralph Seward has stated:

"The ordinary rule at common law and in the developing law of labor relations is that an award of damages should be limited to the amount necessary to make the injured party 'whole.' Unless an agreement provides that some other rule should be followed, this rule should be followed, this rule must apply."[48]

It is of interest to note that Archibald Cox has observed that back pay awards are punitive as well as compensatory:

"[T]he company pays twice when it improperly discharges a man or violates his seniority. It pays back wages and also pays the person who took the grievant's place. And the 'only justification for an award of back pay is that there is no method of doing perfect justice.' Thus the dilemma lies in being forced to choose between denying the employee an adequate remedy or forcing the employer to pay twice for the same work. When the employer causes the loss, however innocently, it is more just that he should be forced to suffer a denial of contract rights without a remedy."[49]

Some practitioners, however, have questioned whether "make whole" relief can ever be fully effectuated in the arbitral forum. Ben Fischer, in an appearance before the National Academy, has argued as follows:

"You never make a discharged employee whole by putting him back to work. In this day and age, when workers are developing dignity and status in the community and in their family, and you operate almost in an industrial gold-fish bowl, you can't make him whole. He was offended; he was embarrassed; his family was embarrassed. 'I saw your husband the other day. Isn't he working? What's the matter?' Do you reply, 'He was fired'? Or, 'He's ill'? Or, what do you do to avoid the stigma? How do you make that whole? What do you do about the guy who loses his car, whose TV is picked up, who has to borrow money and pay interest, who loses his home? We've had those cases. How do you make him whole?"[50]

Although arbitrators are by no means legally or otherwise bound to apply damage principles developed by the Board and the courts under Taft-Hartley, many of the concepts and policy

---

[47]*Id.*, at 103.

[48]*International Harvester Co.*, 15 LA 1, 1 (Seward 1950).

[49]*Electrical Storage Battery Co.*, AAA Case No. 19–22 (Cox 1960), as cited in Fairweather, Practice in Labor Arbitration (Washington: BNA Books, 1973), at 294.

[50]*See* Fischer, *The Implementation of Arbitration Awards—The Steelworkers' View,* in Arbitration and the Public Interest, Proceedings of the 24th Annual Meeting, National Academy of Arbitrators (Washington: BNA Books, 1964), 133–134.

reasons applicable under the Act have been incorporated by arbitrators in formulating "make whole" relief for a breach of a collective bargaining agreement.

Employee's Obligation to Mitigate Damages

In determining remedies, the question of the employee's obligation to mitigate damages often arises. Professor Feller has stated that he finds no reasonable basis for a grievant to mitigate damages. However well-grounded that view happens to be, the majority position seems to be to the contrary. The view preferred by most arbitrators is simply that the grievant's failure to mitigate damages reduces the employer's liability. In this respect, except in unusual circumstances, arbitrators require that an aggrieved employee has a duty to attempt to mitigate any loss he might suffer as a result of the employer's improper assessment of discipline. One arbitrator has stated this principle as follows: "I believe that in a discharge or similar situation, that the employee is obligated to minimize his damages; he is required to make reasonable efforts to obtain gainful employment; he may not sit at home 'licking his chops' in anticipation of the large money award that may be in the offing."[51]

Under a contract providing that an unjustly discharged employee "shall be . . . paid for all time lost," another arbitrator held:

"It is commonly and generally recognized that the purpose of a contract provision calling for payment of 'all time lost,' where disciplinary action or discharge has been found to be without justifiable cause, is to compensate and indemnify the injured employee and make him whole for loss of earnings suffered by him as a result of the inappropriate exercise of judgment by the Company. The loss of earnings is usually to be measured by the wages he would have earned for the period they were improperly denied him, subject however, to a recognized duty and responsibility reposed in the employee to mitigate, so far as reasonable, the amount of that loss. If, as a result of employee's action or inaction, he has failed to mitigate the loss, then to the degree of such failure he is himself partially responsible."[52]

Another arbitrator has declared:

"A grievant has the responsibility of lessening his damages, if possible. He cannot fairly expect to sit back and reject the economic

---

[51]Wolff, *supra* note 5, at 178.
[52]*Love Brothers,* 45 LA 751, 756 (Solomon 1965).

resources at hand to tide him over the period of his dispute with his employer. Here [G] chose to undertake a four months project of building his home. It would hardly be equitable to allow him to compel his employer to underwrite that project."[53]

A difficult issue within the employment context is determining what constitutes a "willful loss of employment." Court decisions, Board rulings, and arbitration awards reveal that an employee is not entitled to back pay to the extent that he fails to remain in the labor market, refuses to accept "substantially equivalent" employment, fails to search for alternative work, or voluntarily quits alternative employment without good reason.[54] Particularly troublesome is determining what constitutes similar employment which, if not accepted, will constitute failure to avoid loss and, thus, a reduction in back pay. The Court of Appeals for the District of Columbia has declared:

"A discriminatee need not seek or accept employment which is 'dangerous, distasteful or essentially different' from his regular job. . . . Similarly, he is not necessarily obligated to accept employment which is located an unreasonable distance from his home. . . .

". . . [T]here is no requirement that such a person seek employment which is not consonant with his particular skills, background, and experience."[55]

The Fifth Circuit has likewise stated: "In order to be entitled to backpay, an employee must at least make 'reasonable efforts' to find new employment which is substantially equivalent to the position [which he was discriminatorily deprived of] and is suitable to a person of his background and experience."[56]

The First Circuit has ruled that the principle of mitigation of damages does not require success but only an honest good-faith effort, and an employee is held "only to reasonable exertions in this regard, not the highest standard of diligence."[57]

Applying this principle, the arbitrator in *Albertson's Inc.*[58] stated that even those arbitrators who recognize a duty to mitigate damages may not require the employee to use more than

---

[53]*Olson Brothers, Inc.*, 61-3 ARB ¶8855 at 6678 (Jones 1961).
[54]*NLRB* v. *Mastro Plastics Corp.*, 354 F.2d 170, 174, No. 3, 60 LRRM 2578 (2d Cir. 1965), *cert. denied*, 384 U.S. 972 (1966).
[55]*NLRB* v. *Madison Courier, Inc.*, 472 F.2d 1307, 80 LRRM 3377, 3384–3385 (D.C.Cir. 1972).
[56]*NLRB* v. *Miami Coca Cola Bottling Co.*, 360 F.2d 569, 575, 62 LRRM 2155 (5th Cir. 1966).
[57]*NLRB* v. *Arduini Mfg. Co.*, 394 F.2d 420, 422–423, 68 LRRM 2129 (1st Cir. 1968).
[58]65 LA 1042 (Christopher 1975).

"ordinary diligence" to obtain other work. In that decision an assistant manager in a retail food store was discharged after he refused to give up his interest in an outside business venture. Before dismissing the grievant, however, the employer had given him the option of accepting a clerk's position if he insisted on retaining his interest in his business. Granting the grievant full back pay, the arbitrator held that the mitigation rule does not require an employee to accept unsuitable or "lower rated work" and that, since the grievant received a large income as assistant manager, it would have been difficult for him to secure the same or a substantially equivalent position in the immediate labor market.

This principle was again voiced by the arbitrator in *Crowell-Collier Broadcasting Co.,* [59] where he held that a radio disc jockey, improperly discharged because of poor station ratings, could not be faulted for not searching for alternative employment.[60]

At some point in the mitigation process an employee may be reasonably required to lower her/his expectations concerning alternative employment. As the Sixth Circuit noted in *NLRB* v. *Southern Silk Mills:*[61]

> "We are of the opinion, however, that the usual wage earner, reasonably conscious of the obligation to support himself and family by suitable employment after inability over a reasonable period of time to obtain the kind of employment to which he is accustomed, would consider other available, suitable employment at a somewhat lower rate of pay 'desirable new employment.' The fact that a married woman employee is being supported by her husband during the discharge period should not relieve her of the obligation to accept suitable employment. The failure . . . under the conditions existing in the present case, to seek or take other suitable employment, although at a lower rate of pay, over a period of approximately three years, constitutes to some extent at least loss of earnings 'willfully incurred.' "[62]

One caveat, however, has been noted by the D.C. Circuit:

> "If the discriminatee accepts significantly lower-paying work too soon after the discrimination in question, he may be subject to a reduction in back pay on the ground that he willfully incurred a loss

---

[59]45 LA 635 (Jones 1965).
[60]*See also McLouth Steel Corp.,* 23 LA 640 (Parkers 1954); *Airquipment Co.,* 10 LA 162 (Aaron 1948); *Honeywell, Inc.,* 51 LA 1061 (Elson 1961).
[61]242 F.2d 697, 700, 39 LRRM 2647 (6th Cir.), *cert. denied,* 355 U.S. 821, 40 LRRM 2680 (1957).
[62]*Id.,* at 700

by accepting an 'unsuitably' low-paying position. On the other hand ... if he fails to 'lower his sights' after the passage of a 'reasonable period' of unsuccessful employment searching, he may be held to have forfeited his right to reimbursement on the ground that he failed to make requisite effort to mitigate his losses."[63]

Cases have arisen where an employee rejects an offer of reinstatement without back pay and thereafter pursues the matter in the arbitral forum. Should refusal to accept reinstatement preclude the employee from receiving an award of back pay past the period where the employee refused employment?

In *Cagles, Inc.,* [64] the arbitrator considered this problem where the employer offered to reinstate the grievant, without back pay, two weeks after her discharge. The grievant refused and, in a subsequent arbitration, was reinstated without back pay from the date she refused reinstatement until the date of the award. Because the employer made an offer of reinstatement albeit without back pay, the arbitrator reasoned that this was effectively a "two-week layoff for which it had just cause." The grievant's refusal was accordingly used to mitigate the employer's back-pay liability.

The difficult case is where the employer offers the employee *unconditional* reinstatement without back pay, the offer is rejected, and the employee is subsequently reinstated by an arbitrator. In a case similar to this condition, an arbitrator, declaring what appears to be the better rule, held that the employer could not mitigate a back-pay obligation where an employee refused an improper transfer to a lower paying job *at a time when the employee could not subsequently challenge the action:*

"Having held that the transfer . . . was unjustified, it necessarily follows that she should be made whole for her full loss unless she was obligated to accept the transfer and thereby to mitigate her damages. Under the peculiar facts here, however, I cannot find that she was so obligated. My conclusion on this might be different if, at the time of the incident, the parties had been bound by a collective bargaining contract which included a grievance procedure affording her protection in securing a retroactive adjustment of her monetary loss while continuing at work in her new job. But there was no such contract in existence at the time and had she accepted the transfer to an inferior job, it would clearly have constituted a full settlement of her grievance, as she had no right, nor was she given the opportunity by the Company to accept the transfer conditionally. As testified

---

[63]*NLRB* v. *Madison Courier, Inc., supra* note 55, at 3855.
[64]48 LA 972 (King 1967).

by the Company, the only alternatives she had were to accept the transfer or terminate her employment."[65]

The arbitrator, citing a decision from the Tenth Circuit, went on to state that in similar circumstances, where an employee had refused an undesirable job offer by the employer, there had been no mitigation of the employer's liability:

> "They [the employees] were in effect discharged from the jobs they were entitled to hold. Under the circumstances their refusal to accept the discriminatory jobs was not willful. While they should be charged with earnings actually received and with earnings not received because of the unjustifiable refusal to take desirable new employment, they should not, in our opinion, be charged with the earnings they would have received at the discriminatory jobs proferred them."[66]

Selected Problems in the Nondisciplinary Areas

Although a number of problems in the nondisciplinary area could be considered, in the interest of time and space I have decided to address only a few of them on a random basis.

Vacation Scheduling

Arbitrators are split in their views concerning the remedy that should apply when an employee has been improperly denied a preference in vacation time. One view is that monetary damages should be assessed against the employer since forcing an employee to take a vacation at a rescheduled time causes an inconvenience for him. On the other hand, a significant number of arbitrators have held that no effective remedy is possible in such a case because the employee is not damaged merely by being forced to take a vacation at a different time (as opposed to being denied a vacation). Still other arbitrators have reasoned that if there are any damages, they are not of the type that can be compensated in the arbitral forum. What follows are a few examples of those positions.

In *Combustion Engineering, Inc.,*[67] the collective bargaining agreement provided that "a scheduled extended vacation shall not be changed without at least 60 days' notice to the employee, unless the employee consents to the change in the schedule."

---

[65]*Gardner-Richardson Co.,* 11 LA 957, 962 (Platt 1948).
[66]*Id.,* citing *NLRB* v. *Armour & Co.,* 154 F.2d 570, 18 LRRM 2469 (10th Cir. 1946).
[67]61 LA 1061 (Altrock 1973).

The arbitrator held that the employer was not justified in rescheduling extended vacations of six employees for a poststrike period and, as a remedy, ordered payment for the vacation weeks the grievants were forced to take on an unscheduled basis.

In *Bethlehem Steel Corp.,*[68] the arbitrator found that back pay was a proper remedy when the employer, contrary to the explicit terms of the contract, failed to give timely notice of a change in the employees' vacation preference. In making the award, the arbitrator explained that there was a problem of timing with regard to the remedy:

> "For those grievants whose preferred dates have already passed, by the time this decision is issued, it is of course impossible to grant their requests, and back pay is the obvious alternative. . . .
> "Some of the grievants' preferences are still chronologically possible to grant, however, calling for specified weeks in late November or early December. In those cases, I think management should be given the alternative of granting those weeks or pay in lieu thereof. It would not be proper, in my view, simply to direct that the weeks be granted, since that might create severe operational problems."[69]

It is interesting that the arbitrator did not credit the employer's argument that an award of back pay would be improper since that remedy had not been discussed in the earlier steps of the grievance procedure. Finding that all but one of the grievants asked to be "made whole," the arbitrator reasoned that this was an effective request for back pay and that, at any rate, it was well within an umpire's discretion to award back pay as an alternative to the requested weeks when granting those weeks was inappropriate or impossible.[70]

In *Lucky Stores, Inc.,*[71] the arbitrator considered what remedy should apply for an employer's failure to secure the union's permission before allowing employees to take vacations outside of a stipulated vacation period. In this case, the arbitrator noted, no employee was injured, monetarily or otherwise. The injury was to the labor organization and the collectivity that it represented. The appropriate remedy, the arbitrator reasoned, was one that would correct the situation that caused the violation— the employer's lack of awareness of the requirement that the

---

[68]48 LA 223 (Gill 1966).
[69]*Id.,* at 226–227.
[70]*Id.,* at 227.
[71]70-1 ARB ¶8271 (Feller 1969).

union's consent should be secured before making changes in the schedule. The employer was accordingly ordered to issue a notification to the appropriate supervisor at each store covered by the agreement to prevent similar violations in the future.

A number of arbitrators have directed employers to compensate employees for unemployment compensation payments lost as a result of improperly scheduled vacations during a shutdown.[72] One arbitrator, after finding that an employer violated the agreement by requiring employees to take vacations during a two-week plant shutdown, ordered lost unemployment compensation payments to the affected employees. In making that award, the arbitrator reasoned that the claim for unemployment compensation was for a "distinctly monetary and measurable loss":

> "Looking at the situation from a realistic rather than a technical point of view, however, there is simply no doubt that the men lost out on unemployment compensation benefits *because of the Company's violation of the contract in the first place.* This was a definite monetary loss, and I think it falls squarely within the language of the Award which is here to be applied—'The appropriate employees shall be made whole by the Company for whatever losses, if any, they suffered because of the action by the Company.'"[73]

It is noteworthy that 21 employees were affected during the first week of the shutdown and 38 during the second week, yet only two employees actually filed claims with the unemployment compensation bureau. The arbitrator, nevertheless, did not find it improper to award all employees relief, since the claims of the employees who had filed were rejected by the bureau and it was reasonable to assume that the other employees had concluded that their claims would similarly be denied.[74]

A contrary result was ordered by an arbitrator in *Scovill Mfg. Co.*[75] Because the employees were required to take the second week of a plant shutdown as a vacation period, the arbitrator provided an extra week of vacation with pay. His reasoning in that decision is instructive:

> "[I]t may be argued that giving them another week's vacation [with pay], as requested, would have the effect of giving them an *extra*

---

[72]37 LA 134 (Gill 1961).
[73]*Id.,* at 137. *Accord: Cone Mills Corp.,* 29 LA 346 (McCoy 1957); *Caterpillar Tractor Co.,* 23 LA 313 (Fleming 1954).
[74]*Id.,* at 139.
[75]31 LA 646 (Jaffee 1958).

week off with pay. But this argument loses sight of the fact that these girls suffered damage, and the question before us is how we ascertain the amount. And there *was* damage, even if it is difficult to assess its precise amount. What the Company did in violation of the Agreement did cause them inconvenience which may be inferred to be substantial, and presumably some monetary loss as well. One of the difficulties in fixing the precise amount of loss is, of course, the fact that it would undoubtedly vary to some extent from girl to girl. But although the Company acted in good faith in what it did . . . the fact remains that it was its breach which has created the uncertainty.
. . .

"On the whole, I believe that it is not unreasonable to infer that the resulting inconvenience plus some monetary loss was in general equivalent to one week's pay for each of the twelve employees with whom we are presently concerned. Even if there can be an element of uncertainty as to the scope of the damages, as distinguished from its existence, it would be more speculative to try to assess an offset credit to the Company. Moreover, the monetary assessment of an imponderable like inconvenience is hardly more difficult than trying to assess the value of pain and suffering to an injured plaintiff in an accident case."[76]

Some of the arbitrators have refused to award monetary damages of any kind where employees are forced to take a vacation during a shutdown but, nonetheless, have ordered that the employees be rescheduled for a vacation of their choosing.[77]

Absence of a Remedy. Where employees were not allowed to exercise their contractual preference for vacation, some arbitrators have found that there could not be an effective remedy. The following reasoning explains this point:

"An arbitrator is authorized to assess damages, but these damages must be related to the losses suffered by the aggrieved party. In the instant case the difficulty in determining a proper remedy lies in making a determination of just what damages an individual employee has suffered, when he was forced to take his extended vacation at a time other than his original first preference. With some employees it will make no real difference, as the time selected was one of personal preference, rather than one based upon personal

---

[76]*Id.*, at 651. *Accord: U.S. Steel Corp.*, 33 LA 82 (Garrett 1959). Of interest is *Parchment Co.* v. *Paterson Parchment Paper Co.*, 282 U.S. 555, 51 S.Ct. 248 (1931), a decision cited by Arbitrator Jaffee, where the Court stated that the wrong having been proven, the risk of uncertainty as to the scope of damage is on the party who committed the breach, and recovery may be had even if the extent of damage is only an appropriate inference. *See also Westinghouse Electric Corp.* v. *IBEW.* 56 F.2d 521, 96 LRRM 2084 (4th Cir. 1977).

[77]*Harlo Products*, 59 LA 613, 620–621 (Howlett 1972); *Interstate Industries, Inc.*, 46 LA 879 (Howlett 1966) (fixing of vacation period); *Huebsch Originators*, 47 LA 635 (Merrill 1966) (no specific relief awarded absent request for remedy by union).

needs. For some others there may be circumstances, such as personal needs, family requirements or long range plans, which might
actually cause a real injury to the employee. . . .
    "Therefore, for those grievants who have already received their
extended vacation, I cannot find any effective remedy."[78]

It is noteworthy that the arbitrator rejected the union's request
that each grievant be given another extended vacation at a time
of his own choosing, financed by the employer.

In a 1958 case, an umpire denied a union request for monetary damages where vacations had been accelerated to avoid
layoffs. The umpire reasoned as follows:

"The complaint in these grievances was not against a *denial* of
vacations; it was concerned entirely with the *dates* on which the
grievants were required to *take* their vacations. And though the
grievants may justly feel that—because of the changes in dates—
their vacations in 1957 were less happy and enjoyable than they
otherwise would have been, the Umpire does not see how he can
hold that they had no vacations at all or how—for that matter—he
can assign a monetary value to the grievants' mental discomfort."[79]

Although the arbitrator declined to award damages, he did point
out, however, that the employer's action in accelerating the
vacations was taken in the good-faith belief that the contract
permitted such action—a belief to which the union had contributed by its failure to protest such accelerations in the past.
The arbitrator made it clear that in cases of "repeat" violations,
deliberately forcing an employee to take an accelerated vacation, an award of back pay would be appropriate.[80]

Another arbitrator similarly found no effective remedy where
employees were forced to take one week of vacation during a
period of work shortages. Rejecting the union's claim for another week of vacation with full vacation pay, at a time of their
choice, he declared:

"As to 'another week of vacation,' the reality of the situation is that,
at the time of the writing of this decision, the 1959 vacation year is
over. It is clearly not for the arbitrator to order that the vacation year
be elongated. The most that he could hold is that the grievants be
reimbursed a week's vacation pay in lieu of taking a vacation. Even
this, however, would be 'too much.' As the result of the Agreement
violation here found, the grievants did *not* lose a week's vacation pay
—for there is no disputing the fact that they could not have worked

---

[78]*Pittsburgh Steel Co.*, 42 LA 1002 (McDermott 1964).
[79]Umpire Decision No. 498, cited in *Bethlehem Steel Corp.*, 48 LA 223, 225 (Gill 1966).
[80]*Bethlehem Steel Co.*, 31 LA 857 (Seward 1958).

on their scheduled Iron Power Plant operations during the week in question."[81]

Still, the arbitrator found that what the employees lost was "whatever they would have been entitled to had they been laid off from their jobs." He noted that the record did not reveal whether the grievants would have been laid off "to the streets" or merely demoted to other jobs. The parties were accordingly directed to "reconstruct the situation as best they can," paying each grievant the sum to which he would have been entitled had there been a layoff.[82]

One arbitrator has characterized a monetary award for improper changing of vacations as "punitive" in nature:

> "The union asserts that the remedy in this case should be additional vacation pay for all those employees who took their vacations at the time scheduled by the company under the pressure of the company.
>
> "The legal principles concerning damages and remedies, however, cannot justify such a remedy. The company correctly says adopting the proposed remedy would be punitive rather than a compensatory matter. . . .
>
> "The short answer concerning damages in this case is that no damage has been shown. The board of arbitration has no power to award damages where damage has not been shown."[83]

Summary. Apart from unemployment compensation losses, most claims arising out of rescheduling of vacation periods are for nonmonetary losses, such as inconvenience. Absent special circumstances, such as the case where a rescheduling is made with full knowledge that the agreement is being violated, the better view is not to award monetary damages for the mere inconvenience of employees. This view is perhaps best expressed by an analogy offered by one arbitrator:

> "I think that it can hardly be doubted that an employee who is fired from his job is subjected to much greater 'inconvenience,' to put it mildly, than an employee who is forced to take his vacation at a time not of his own choosing. The uncertainty about his future

---

[81]*Alan Wood Steel Co.*, 33 LA 772, 775 (1960).

[82]*Id.*, at 775. *But see Bethlehem Steel Co.*, 37 LA 821, 823–824 (Valtin 1961) (remedy of vacation pay was appropriate in accordance with past awards under similar contract where employer failed to give employee first choice of vacation and failed to offer employee second opportunity to state preference).

[83]*ACF Industries*, 39 LA 1051, 1057 (Williams 1962). *Accord: Pittsburgh Steel Co.*, 42 LA 1002, 1008 (McDermott 1964) (no punitive remedy); *Philip Carey Mfg. Co.*, 37 LA 134 (Gill 1961) (employees were not entitled to one week's pay as "punitive" damages for "inconvenience" resulting from employer's designation of plant shutdown as vacation period in violation of contract). *Lucky Stores Inc.*, 70-1 ARB ¶8271 (Feller 1969) (no authority to issue a punitive sanction).

status, the worry over whether a serious blot on his record will be removed, the problem of keeping financially afloat while his case is being adjudicated (presumably with no unemployment compensation payments to cushion him in the meantime)—these matters and others all add up to a vastly more impressive catalogue of inconvenience and hardship than anything we are talking about here. And yet it has never to my knowledge been the practice to go beyond back pay for actual loss of wages in fashioning a remedy for unjust discharge. . . .

". . . [T]here is no established concept of which I am aware to the effect that contract violations involving no monetary loss to employees are to be remedied by payments based on inconvenience or designed as punitive damages."[84]

Employers' Claims for Damages

One other area which is not often encountered, but nevertheless presents difficult questions, is that of employers' claims for damages. There is no uniform rule for determining when a claim for damages arising out of a breach of the no-strike clause will be arbitrable since what is subject to arbitration depends upon the particular contract at issue. For example, where the parties' agreement provided for arbitration of all disputes and all grievances involving an act of either party or any conduct of either party, the Supreme Court, in *Drake Bakeries* v. *Bakery & Confectionery Workers*, [85] held that an employer's Section 301 damage action against the union for breach of the no-strike clause should be stayed pending arbitration of the damage claims. It is especially worth noting that the Supreme Court found that the determination of damages may be particularly suited to arbitration:

"If the union did strike in violation of the contract, the company is entitled to its damages; by staying this action, pending arbitration, we have no intention of depriving it of those damages. We simply remit the company to the forum it agreed to use for processing its strike damage claims. That forum, it may be true, may be very different from a courtroom, but we are not persuaded that the remedy there will be inadequate. Whether the damages to be awarded by the arbitrator would not normally be expected to serve as an 'effective' deterrent to future strikes, which the company urges, it is not a question to be answered in the abstract or in general terms. . . . The dispute which this record presents appears to us to be one particularly suited for arbitration, if the parties have agreed to arbitrate."[86]

---

[84]*Philip Carey Mfg. Co.*, 37 LA 134, 136 (Gill 1961).
[85]370 U.S. 254, 50 LRRM 2440 (1962).
[86]*Id.*, at 2455. See also *Capital City Telephone Co.* v. *Communications Workers*, 575 F.2d 655, 98 LRRM 2438 (8th Cir. 1978); *Pietro Scalzitti Co.* v. *Operating Engineers Local 150*,

In this same regard, one arbitrator has argued that an arbitrator needs no special grant of authority to award an employer monetary damages for a breach of the no-strike agreement:

> "If we justify an award of damages to an employee for a contract breach on the theory of implied power to formulate a remedy, why must we insist upon a special grant of authority to award damages for a violation of the no-strike covenant?
>
> "When arbitration is properly invoked, no purpose can be gained by determining a breach has occurred and then remitting the parties to the courts to determine damages."[87]

While the parties are free to make such claims arbitrable, there is some authority to support the theory that an employer's claim for damages arising out of a breach of the no-strike clause is not accorded the traditional strong presumption in favor of arbitrability.[88] As pointed out by David Feller and others, adjudication of damage claims is not a substitute for industrial strife, but rather a substitute for litigation. The presumptions that apply to grievance arbitration under the *Trilogy* standards may simply be inapplicable.[89] Absent a submission as to the issue of damages, an arbitrator ought to proceed with caution before concluding that the parties have in fact vested him with authority to make a monetary award for such a breach.

Elements of Damages

A review of arbitral authority indicates that arbitrators have invariably applied damage principles adopted by the courts when awarding monetary relief for breach of no-strike clauses. Under both Sections 301 and 303 of Taft-Hartley,[90] the amount of damages recoverable are "actual" or "compensatory" damages, representing those damages directly caused by the breach of the collective bargaining agreement or other illicit activity. Both arbitrators and courts have required that these damages be foreseeable and within the reasonable contemplation of the parties. At the same time, however, it is not necessary that the damages be calculated with precise specificity so long as the existence of some damage is certain. Thus, in *Sterling Gravure*

---

351 F.2d 576, 60 LRRM 2222 (7th Cir. 1965); *Minnesota Joint Board Clothing Workers* v. *United Garment Mfg. Co.,* 338 F.2d 195, 57 LRRM 2521 (8th Cir. 1964).

[87]Wolff, *supra* note 5, at 185–186.

[88]*See, e.g., Welded Tube Co.* v. *Electrical Workers,* 91 LRRM 2027 (E.D.Pa. 1975); *Affiliated Food Distributors* v. *Local Union No. 229, International Brotherhood of Teamsters,* 483 F.2d 418, 84 LRRM 2043 (3d Cir. 1973).

[89]Feller, *supra* note 6, at 198.

[90]29 U.S.C. §§187(a) and (b).

Co., [91] the arbitrator, in computing damages for a breach of a no-strike clause and an illegal secondary boycott, stated this principle as follows:

> "Once the threshold question of direct and proximate cause is answered in the affirmative, the amount claimed in damages demands a less rigid test. 'Reasonable estimates' or 'a fair and just approximation' are acceptable, and economic losses caused by a union's unlawful conduct or breach of contract need not be proven with mathematical certainty. . . . However, while the wronged party need not establish damages with exactitude, a court will not allow damages to be recovered by mere indulgence, speculation or guesswork. . . .
>
> "Upon a determination that the injured party is entitled to recover for the breach of contract, the theory is that the resulting damages were presumed foreseeable by the offending party's unlawful conduct. . . ."[92]

When direct and proximate cause has been established, arbitrators have allowed recovery for a variety of economic losses sustained by employers as a result of an "illegal" strike or boycott. The most comprehensive review of damage awards is contained in the opinion of Arbitrator Joseph Gentile in *Dan J. Peterson Co.,* [93] and cited at length are selected components and corresponding cases analyzed by Gentile as a summary of the possibilities in this area.[94]

Abandonment of Independent Project Caused by a Strike. In *Lewis* v. *Benedict Coal Corp.,* [95] the Court of Appeals for the Sixth Circuit considered, in a Section 301 action, an employer's claim for damages for losses sustained on an independent project abandoned during a strike. Although the court found that the strike contributed to the decision to abandon the project, it held nevertheless that such abandonment was not a foreseeable consequence of the strike for which damages could be awarded.

Attorney's Fees. While recovery of attorney's fees incurred in prosecuting an action under Section 301 is unlikely, it may nevertheless be possible to obtain such fees in the arbitral forum.[96]

---

[91]79–2 ARB ¶8325 (Kaplan 1979).

[92]*Id.,* at 4354.

[93]The leading case is *Hadley* v. *Baxendale,* 9 Exch. 341, 156 Eng. Rep. 145 (1854), cited by Arbitrator Kaplan in *Sterling Gravure Co., supra* note 91, at 4355.

[94]66 LA 389 (1976).

[95]For corresponding citation, the reader is urged to review Arbitrator Gentile's decision at 66 LA at 392–398.

[96]*See* Marvin Hill, Jr. and Anthony V. Sinicropi, Remedies in Arbitration (Washington: BNA Books, forthcoming), Ch. 11, notes 39–42 and topic titled "Awarding Attorneys' Fees."

Consultant's Fees Expended as a Result of a Strike. Where evidence exists that consultants were hired as a result of an improper strike, such fees may properly be awarded as compensatory damages.

Costs of Obtaining Goods Elsewhere to Sell to Customers During a Strike. Arbitral authority supports awarding lost profits as well as the difference between the cost in obtaining goods from other suppliers and the lower price at which the employer then resells to customers. As an example cited by Arbitrator Gentile, in *Mercer, Fraser Co.,*[97] the arbitrator allowed an employer to recover from the union profits lost as a result of an illegal strike. In addition, the company was awarded the difference between the company's cost in obtaining concrete from other suppliers and the lower price at which it was then resold to customers.

Depreciation. Where it can be demonstrated that actual depreciation results from nonuse of tools or equipment, such depreciation may properly be awarded. While there is authority to the contrary, the better rule in this regard would appear to be that depreciation estimates for mere accounting purposes are not controlling as a measure of damages as a result of actual depreciation from nonuse of equipment. Thus, in *Master Builders Assn. of Western Pa.,*[98] the arbitrator disallowed a claim of depreciation on equipment idled during a strike. This denial was based on the fact that the tools and equipment were not in actual use during the strike, and the evidence did not establish any actual depreciation from nonuse.

Destruction of Business. In the extreme case where a business has been completely destroyed, there is precedent for allowing recovery of the value of the business.

Equipment (Owned by Company) Idled by a Strike. Both arbitrators and courts have appropriately awarded the fair rental value of idled equipment. For example, in *Foster Grading Co.,*[99] the arbitrator ruled that an employer was entitled to recover damages for a two-day work stoppage in violation of a no-strike agreement called by a union steward at a construction site. As items of damages, the employer was awarded (a) labor costs for supervisors and office men; (b) the fair rental value of the employer's own equipment which sat idle for two workable days (the rental value to be computed from monthly rental figures based on the

---

[97] 70-2 ARB ¶8615 (Gentile 1970).
[98] 67-1 ARB ¶8243 (Kates 1967).
[99] 52 LA 198 (1968).

18th edition of Monthly Rental Rates by Associated Equipment Distributors); (c) the actual rental value of six pickup trucks and other equipment rented from rental companies prorated on a daily basis; and (d) the prorated costs of maintenance and protection of traffic. And in *Denver Building Trades Council* v. *Shore*, [100] the Colorado Supreme Court stated:

> "[T]he rule has generally been adopted that where through unlawful or wrongful acts of defendants heavy equipment has been kept idle and the work expected to be accomplished thereby delayed, the fair rental value of such equipment during the period of prevention of its use is generally adopted as a proper measure for determining the extent of damage."

Equipment Rented Idled by Strike. Where it is demonstrated that, because of an improper strike, rented equipment was not used or, alternatively, it was necessary to keep the equipment longer than was originally planned, the arbitrator may properly award damages for equipment idled by the strike.

Freight Loss and Damage. Damages for loss and damages to any freight caused by strikers may properly be awarded in either the court or arbitral forum.

Inability to Receive Shipments of Goods During Strike. An inability to receive deliveries of raw materials during a strike may result in a damage award to the employer.

Insurance. In *Vulcan Mold & Iron Co.,* [101] an arbitrator awarded the pro-rata portion of fire and other insurance for the period of the illegal strike. Similarly, in *Master Builders Assn.,* [102] an arbitrator awarded as damages the amount paid to extend a builder's risk insurance to cover completion of a job delayed by an improper strike.

Interest. [103] In general, it has not been the practice of arbitrators to award interest as part of the traditional "make whole" package, primarily because (1) the parties rarely request it in the submission or argument, and (2) it is not considered customary in the forum. It is clear, however, that unless a contract specifically prohibits the awarding of interest, such assessments may be made and have been made by arbitrators. Nevertheless, it is the exception rather than the rule to award interest, and when

---

[100]36 LRRM 2578 (1955).
[101]70-1 ARB ¶8080 (Kates 1970).
[102]50 LA 1018 (McDermott 1968).
[103]*See* Hill and Sinicropi, *supra* note 96, Ch. 11, notes 1–15 and topic titled "Awarding Interest."

it is done it usually is the result of some dilatory tactic by an employer.

Labor Costs. Arbitrators and courts have awarded various categories of labor costs as damages for a breach of a no-strike agreement. Such an award of damages may include compensation for any of the following:

(a) Direct pay to idle workers. In *Mason-Rust* v. *Laborers Local No. 42,* [104] the federal district court awarded call-in pay for workers unable to work because of an illegal work stoppage, as well as fringe-benefit costs incurred as a result of the employees' showing up for work.

(b) Overtime pay required to catch up on work delayed due to a strike. In *Sheet Metal Workers* v. *Sheet Metal Co.,* [105] the Court of Appeals for the Fifth Circuit, in a damage action under Section 303 of Taft-Hartley, allowed recovery of overtime pay required to catch up on delayed work, provided that the employer could demonstrate that such damages were purely compensatory. In so ruling, the court declared: "Section 303 is purely compensatory, all elements of damages must be directly related to or caused by the unlawful secondary activity."

(c) Recovery of portion of wages paid to workers working at a reduced rate of efficiency. The District Court for the Eastern District of Missouri, in *Mason-Rust* v. *Laborers Local No. 42,* [106] stated that damages due to reduced efficiency could not be awarded where the job at issue was still in its planning stage, and hence any award would be speculative. However, in *A.I. Gage Plumbing & Supply Co.* v. *Local 300,* [107] the California District Court of Appeals ruled that, by virtue of an illegal strike, some plumbers had a more difficult time installing pipes and thus were made less productive. Damages were accordingly awarded to persons who worked at a reduced efficiency rate. In making such an award, the court stated the general principle which is applied in awarding damages:

> "In an action against the union under Section 301 for damages caused by a breach of a no-strike provision in a contract, the measure of damages recoverable is the actual loss sustained by the plaintiff as a direct result of the breach. . . . Such loss would be that which may reasonably and fairly be considered as arising naturally

---

[104]306 F.Supp. 934, 72 LRRM 2743 (E.D.Mo. 1969).
[105]384 F.2d 101, 65 LRRM 3115 (5th Cir. 1967).
[106]*Supra* note 104
[107]50 LRRM 2114 (1962).

from the particular breach of contract involved and which may reasonably be supposed to have been in the contemplation of the parties at the time the agreement was entered into in the event of such violation. . . . Damages stemming directly from a strike with which the collective bargaining contract was concerned and which contained a 'no strike' clause are clearly within the contemplation of the parties."[108]

Loss of Goodwill. An employer may appropriately claim loss of reputation resulting from the inability to deliver orders on time, or loss of company goodwill due to the inability to accept new orders or fill old ones.

Overhead Expenses. In *United Electrical Workers* v. *Oliver Corp.*, [109] the Court of Appeals for the Eighth Circuit stated:

"Overhead expense is the necessary cost incurred by a company in its operation which cannot be easily identified with any individual product and which by accepted cost accounting procedures is spread over or allocated to the productive labor, which is labor performed in the processing of the company's products. Such expenses do not fluctuate directly with plant operations. They are expenses necessary to keep the company on a going concern basis and are based upon the company's production which is planned for a year in advance. They are constant regardless of fluctuations in plant operations. When productive labor in a plant is reduced for any period to less than the normal, the company sustains a loss in expenditure of necessary overhead for which it receives no production."[110]

Finding that the plant had operated at 52.5 percent of normal production, the court concluded that a jury could indeed determine that its loss amounted to 47.5 percent of overhead for which no return was received in the form of productive labor.

Similarly, in *Canadian General Electric Co.*, [111] an employer was allowed to estimate its overhead by taking a percentage of overhead costs for a year, determined by the ratio of the number of working hours lost during the strike to the total number of hours worked for the year. The arbitrator included in the calculation of overhead the following items: depreciation on fixed assets; insurance premiums, mainly for fire insurance; rent of outside property used for storage; salaries of office and managerial staff; local taxes; telephone and telegraph service; traveling expenses; and heat. In making such an award, the arbitrator declared: "[I]t

---

[108]*Id.,* at 2117, 2119.
[109]205 F.2d 376, 32 LRRM 2270 (1953).
[110]*Id.,* at 387, 2278.
[111]18 LA 925 (1952).

is axiomatic that the company is not entitled to double recovery," but, as summarized by the arbitrator, an award of these overhead expenses in conjunction with lost profits was allowable, because they were not overlapping.

Another example cited by Arbitrator Gentile was *Belmont Smelting & Refining Works, Inc.,* [112] where the employer requested damages for daily overhead expenses, including wages and salaries paid to nonbargaining-unit employees. The arbitrator suspended assessment of the requested damages, but indicated that breach of the conditions of suspension (that is, another work stoppage) would result in the imposition of the requested damage on the union.

In *Vulcan Mold & Iron Co.,* [113] a wrongful work stoppage resulted in a 75 percent loss in production. The arbitrator awarded damages for utilities used during the strike, but reduced the employer's request by one-third on the theory that utilities were used less during the strike. The arbitrator refused to make an award for supervisors' salaries where it was determined that the supervisors performed bargaining-unit work during the strike rather than regular supervisory functions.

Penalties for Late Completion. Any penalty suffered as a result of an illegal strike may appropriately be awarded as compensatory damages. Thus, the U.S. District Court for the Western District of Kentucky, in *Wells* v. *International Union of Operating Engineers,* [114] allowed an employer to recover $35 per day for 35 days for a late completion. Where the employer has the option to extend the time for delivery, however, it may not be appropriate to award recovery of damages even where the delay was caused by a strike.

Pension Liability. Any pro-rata portion of fringe benefits, including pension payments, that accrued during a strike may be awarded as damages. The arbitrator, however, should be satisfied that the lost benefits in fact relate to the strike period.

Lost Profits. It is well settled that an arbitrator or a court may award profits lost as a result of illegal strike activity. In addition, an award may be made for profits likely to be lost in the future. For example, in *Abbott* v. *Local 142 Plumbers,* [115] the Court of Appeals for the Fifth Circuit, in a Section 303 action, sustained

---

[112]68-1 ARB ¶8342 (Gentile 1968).
[113]*Supra* note 101.
[114]206 F.Supp. 414 (W.D.Ky. 1962).
[115]429 F.2d 786, 74 LRRM 2879 (5th Cir. 1970).

a lower court award of $11,218 for profits lost as a result of illegal picketing. In that case the court stated:

> "Having established disruption of the project and a lower than average rate of return on the project the plaintiffs introduced evidence showing that the low rate of profitability was not attributable to causes other than the picketing. Proof was introduced demonstrating that: (1) the project was bid in the customary manner; (2) the bid was neither excessively high nor inordinately low; (3) factors which had resulted in lower than average profits on other Abbott jobs (e.g., torrential rains, incompetent labor, unusually small size of project, discounts to religious institutions) were absent from this project; and (4) nothing about this job was especially complicated or challenging."[116]

The court sustained the lower court's determination that the loss of profits should be measured by calculating the difference between the actual profit on the picketed project and the average profit made by the employer.

Likewise, in *Canadian General Electric Co.*,[117] the employer was permitted to approximate lost profits by taking a percentage of the total profits of all operations of the company, as measured by the proportion of "shipping costs" attributable to the particular plant at issue. After a measure of the yearly profit attributable to that plant was obtained, the amount of profits lost due to the strike was calculated by taking a percentage of the estimated total, determined by the ratio of working hours lost to the total available during the year.

Protection of Freight During a Strike. In *Overnite Transportation Co. v. International Brotherhood of Teamsters*,[118] the Supreme Court of North Carolina, in a Section 303 case, allowed recovery of $16,662 expended for guards necessary to protect freight service from strikers.

Punitive Damages.[119] Generally, arbitrators have not awarded "damages," and when such awards have been issued, they have been limited to the amount which is necessary to make the injured employer whole. The major problem this area holds for arbitration is that arbitrators are not in agreement as to whether such a remedy is "punitive" or "compensatory." The bottom

---

[116]*Id.*, at 790, 2881.
[117]*Supra* note 111.
[118]257 N.C. 18, 50 LRRM 2377 (1962), *cert. den.*, 371 U.S. 862, 51 LRRM 2267, *rehearing den.*, 371 U.S. 899.
[119]*See* Hill and Sinicropi, *supra* note 96, Ch. 9, notes 20–33 and topic titled "Punitive Remedies."

line in this area seems to be whether the contract prevents a "punitive" or "compensatory" remedy and/or whether such a remedy is reasonable in light of the arbitrator's findings.

Recovery Where Business Is Operating at a Loss Before the Strike. There is arbitrator-cited authority for the proposition that where the company is operating at a loss prior to an illegal strike, it is entitled to recover fixed charges until operations return to normal, but no more than the amount by which the overall loss is aggravated by the strike.

Salaries of Nonbargaining-Unit Employees. Amounts paid to supervisory and nonbargaining-unit personnel necessarily retained by the company while the illegal strike is in progress may be awarded as compensatory damages. Before such an award is made, it should be clearly established that supervisors did not perform bargaining-unit work. Thus, in *Vulcan Mold & Iron Co.,*[120] the arbitrator refused to make an award for supervisory expenses during a strike where it was demonstrated that no supervisory functions were performed. And in *Master Builders Assn.,*[121] an arbitrator denied a claim for damages as a result of reduced efficiency of supervisors who had 26 rather than 36 workers to supervise during a strike. The arbitrator stated that the supervisors had to be paid the same no matter how many men had to be supervised. In addition, there was evidence that they performed unit work during the strike.

Telephone and Telegraph Charges. Additional telephone and telegraph expenses incurred as a result of a strike have been allowed by both arbitrators and courts.

Travel Expenses. Travel expenses incurred because of an improper strike may appropriately be awarded as compensatory damages.

Factors Used in Considering Damages

As a final note on this topic, arbitrators have generally relied on the testimony of experts, including certified public accountants, in determining the amount of damages arising from a temporary shutdown.[122]

---

[120]*Supra* note 101.
[121]*Supra* note 102.
[122]*See, e.g.,* the discussion of Arbitrator David Kaplan in *Sterling Gravure Co., supra* note 91.

Individual Liability for Breach of a No-Strike Clause

Section 301(b) of Taft-Hartley[123] provides, in relevant part: "Any money judgment against a labor organization in a district court of the United States shall be enforceable only against the organization as an entity and against its assets, and shall not be enforceable against any individual member or his assets."

When a union is found liable for damages in violation of the no-strike clause of a collective bargaining agreement, its officers and members are not liable for those damages. The Supreme Court, in *Atkinson* v. *Sinclair Refining Co.,* [124] made it clear that "where the union has inflicted the injury, it alone must pay." The Court, however, specifically did not reach the issue of whether the officers or members of the union could be liable for activity, not on behalf of the union, but in their personal and nonunion capacity.[125]

To date, the lower courts are split with respect to the issue of members' liability for unauthorized individual acts. The better weight of authority, however, is that individual members may not be held financially liable for the consequences of a "wildcat" strike conducted without union authorization or approval. As stated by the Court of Appeals for the Seventh Circuit, "the primary remedy of *Sinclair* is discharge or discipline of individual defendants."[126]

Adopting this same line of reasoning, this writer believes that the better rule is for an arbitrator not to award damages against any individual for a breach of the no-strike agreement, but rather to limit such a monetary award to assessments against the union.

It is important to stress that arbitrators exercise considerable discretion in awarding damages for a breach of the collective bargaining agreement. This is especially true when violations of the no-strike clause are found. One arbitrator has stated that merely the finding of a violation does not necessarily imply that damages will be awarded:

"Finding a violation of the no-strike clause by the union does not automatically bind the arbitrator to an award of full compensatory damages, any more than finding that an employee has been dis-

---

[123]29 U.S.C. §185(b).
[124]370 U.S. 238, 50 LRRM 2433 (1962).
[125]*Id.,* at 249, note 7.
[126]*Sinclair Oil Corp.* v. *Oil, Chemical & Atomic Workers Int'l Union,* 200 F.2d 312, 48 LRRM 2045 (7th Cir. 1961).

charged without just cause automatically binds an arbitrator to award full back pay upon reinstatement. There are principles of equity as well as principles of contract to be considered. These principles must be applied in a manner designed to serve the best interests of the continuing bargaining relationship."[127]

Summary

This brief and random treatment indicates that there are indeed diverse positions taken by arbitrators with respect to remedies. What is apparent is that an arbitrator's powers with respect to remedies are plenary, provided they are not unfaithful to the agreement. In this respect it appears that the arbitrator's remedy powers have a wider range of authority in the disciplinary area than with respect to contract issues. Moreover, there often are unique or unusual remedies provided by arbitrators. However, when such unusual remedies are applied, they are often subject to more pitfalls and further complications. Nevertheless there are occasions when reliance on such unusual remedies is necessary and even expected. It is in this connection that it is instructive to take note that arbitration is a private system which continues to be flexible and adaptable to the peculiar needs of the parties in each dispute. While the average case lends itself to the usual remedy, it is not unexpected, nor has it been the experience as reflected in the published awards, that unusual awards and remedies have been issued.

Comment—

Robert S. Katz*

The title and focus of our program is "Remedies: New and Old Problems," and my limited role is to comment upon the papers presented by our principal speakers, Professors David Feller and Anthony Sinicropi. Although both papers treat the same topic, their perspective is quite different. Professor Feller offers us a provocative and philosophical view of how arbitrators should approach the issue of remedies. In contrast, Professor Sinicropi has provided us with a highly informative catalogue of how arbitrators have decided the issue of remedies in a variety

---

[127]*Mercer, Fraser Co.,* 70-2 ARB ¶8615, at 5037 (Eaton 1970).
*Torkildson, Katz, Jossem & Loden, Honolulu, Hawaii.

of situations. In light of the purely informative nature of the Sinicropi paper, my comments will deal primarily with Professor Feller's theory of how arbitrators should act. In doing so, however, I do not mean in any way to denigrate the value of Professor Sinicropi's work, which will soon be out in book form and I, for one, will be in line to purchase my own copy.

I would like to begin my own commentary on Professor Feller's paper with a brief confession. After reading his introductory reflections on his prior intellectual disagreement with another distinguished member of this Academy, Professor Theodore St. Antoine, my first reaction was that, as a former student of Professor St. Antoine, I should decline to proceed further on the basis of an irreconcilable conflict of interest. But upon further reflection, my intellectual curiosity, which had been so strongly piqued by Professor St. Antoine during those idyllic days at Ann Arbor, and my own sense of gratitude to Professor Feller for all that he has contributed to the growth of industrial arbitration (and, coincidentally, my own livelihood) compelled me to read on and thereby learn, to my great relief, that the prior disagreement, like my conflict of interest, was more apparent than real.[1] So, having been freed of all ethical considerations, I plunged ahead into the provocative challenge of Professor Feller's philosophical discourse on how arbitrators should approach the issue of remedies and, to my pleasant surprise, found myself mostly in agreement with both Professor Feller and Professor St. Antoine.

The first and perhaps central viewpoint expressed by Professor Feller and, incidentally, Professor St. Antoine as well is that arbitrators are "contract readers" and not "contract enforcers." Accordingly, in deciding what remedy to impose, the arbitrator ". . . must decide what the agreement says about [the appropriate] remedy" rather than undertaking the role of a judge and unilaterally determining what the remedy should be. In Professor Feller's view, "as the parties' 'contract reader,' the arbitrator determines what remedy is provided for in the agreement and awards it." As a lawyer representing employers and having been raised on Professor St. Antoine's frequent reminder that even Justice Douglas, in *Steelworkers* v. *Enterprise Wheel & Car Corp.,*[2]

---

[1]*See* St. Antoine, *Judicial Review of Arbitration Awards: A Second Look at* Enterprise Wheel *and Its Progeny,* in Arbitration—1977, Proceedings of the 30th Annual Meeting, National Academy of Arbitrators (Washington: BNA Books, 1977), 31–34, 51.
[2]363 U.S. 593, 597, 46 LRRM 2423 (1960).

expressly recognized that an arbitrator, in awarding a remedy, "does not sit to dispense his own brand of industrial justice," but rather is restricted to interpreting and applying the collective bargaining agreement, I find nothing in Professor Feller's characterization of the arbitrator's role as a "contract reader" with which to quarrel seriously.

To the contrary, it is my own opinion that the apparent recent increase in successful judicial challenges to arbitration decisions and the reluctance of our Supreme Court to grant a greater role to arbitration in our federal labor statutory scheme stems primarily from the tendency of arbitrators to characterize themselves as "industrial judges" and then to assume that, like their judicial counterparts in our society at large, they have been ordained by their employer and union nominators to promulgate some Solomon-like judgment which incorporates all of the most progressive teachings of modern-day sociology, psychology and philosophy, religion, economics, and so forth. The result of such lofty aspirations is frequently a decision that reflects only the arbitrator's personal vision of what the contract should say to comport with such progressive teachings rather than what the contract does say.

Such a result has little value for the unfortunate first-line supervisors and rank-and-file employees who must strive each day to conform their conduct to the more mundane language of the contract and who look to the arbitrator for a common-sense, straightforward reading of the contract. For unless such a straightforward "reading of the contract" is forthcoming, the contract loses its principal function as a predictable source of how to behave. Since most arbitration today is of the ad hoc variety, which by its very nature means that several different arbitrators with widely different personal prejudices and perspectives will be arbitrating cases under the same contract, Professor Feller's argument that the arbitrator must serve as contract reader, confined to what the parties have stated in their agreement, rather than as a contract enforcer, armed with the authority to frame his own solutions based on his personal vision of what the contract should say, is not only compelling but, in my humble view, necessary if ad hoc arbitration is to retain the confidence of those who must live day to day under collective bargaining agreements.

My principal difference with Professor Feller, and it may be primarily one of method rather than substance, arises from the second part of his theory of how arbitrators should approach the issue of remedies: namely, that "the authority to act as the parties' contract reader includes the authority to read into the contract those provisions which the arbitrator finds can reasonably be expected to have been assumed to exist by the parties even if they fail to signify it by words."

Professor Feller considers the addition of such implied authority as only a minor exception to the objective foundation for arbitration erected by his first and principal contention that the arbitrator serves simply as the parties' "contract reader," which is necessary to legitimize the common practice by arbitrators of awarding reinstatement with back pay in cases of discharge that are found to be without just cause, even though the labor agreement does not expressly provide for such a remedy.

My concern, and therefore disagreement, with Professor Feller's grant of "implied authority" to an arbitrator to read into the agreement those provisions that the arbitrator feels the parties assumed they had already inserted into that agreement is that it invites the all too familiar situation of the exception which swallows the rule. To tell arbitrators, on the one hand, that they must simply "read the contract" and avoid dispensing their own notions of industrial justice, and then to tell them, on the other hand, that they can "read into the contract" whatever they feel the parties assumed they had already inserted in the agreement, may be asking arbitrators to walk too thin a tightrope, especially when we move beyond the basic example cited by Professor Feller for his proposition—the award of reinstatement with back pay, which has received literally universal acceptance by arbitrators—and encounter the far more numerous kinds of remedies about which there is considerable disagreement among arbitrators—interest on back-pay awards, compromised or modified penalties, conditional reinstatements, or retained jurisdiction to permit postaward arbitral oversight hearings.

Moreover, while the exception for "implied authority" to read into the contract provisions deemed necessary and within the reasonable expectations of the parties sounds fine in those cases where the contract permits discharge only for just cause and the arbitrator finds that there was no just cause, it raises serious questions in many other cases, especially those involving contracts that have the commonly included prohibition that the arbitrator's decision may not "amend, change, add to or detract from the language of the contract."[3] I believe that *Torrington* and its progeny require arbitrators to decline Professor Feller's invitation to imply assumed remedies into labor contracts and, instead, to heed more closely the sage words of the late Marion Beatty in *American Sugar Refining Co.:*[4]

> "In grievance arbitrations, arbitrators are employed to interpret contracts, not to write them, add to them or modify them. If they are to be modified, that has to be done at the bargaining table. If this Union is to have 'jurisdiction over work,' it must obtain this at the bargaining table in language which fairly imparts this.
>
> "Arbitrators are not soothsayers and 'wise men' employed to dispense equity and goodwill according to their own notions of what is best for the parties, nor are they kings like Solomon with unlimited wisdom or courts of unlimited jurisdiction. Arbitrators are employed to interpret the working agreement as the parties themselves wrote it.
>
> "I am not unmindful that some arbitrators have read contracting-out restrictions into contracts containing no clear statements on the subject. In contract interpretation, we are trying to ascertain the mutual intention of the parties. We must be guided primarily by the language used. Admittedly, certain inferences may be read into it, but they should be only those inferences which clearly and logically follow from the language used and which reasonable men must have mutually intended. To go far afield in search of veiled inferences or ethereal or celestial factors is a mistake. I believe Labor contracts are much more earthly; they are not written in fancy language purposely containing hidden meanings.
>
> "When an arbitrator finds that the parties have not dealt with the subject of contracting-out in their working agreement, but that the employer is nevertheless prohibited from contracting-out (a) unless he acted in good faith; (b) unless he acts in conformance with past practice; (c) unless he acts reasonably; (d) unless his act does not deprive a substantial number of employees of employment; (e) unless his acts were dictated by the requirements of the business; (f) if his act is barred by the recognition clause; (g) if his act is barred by the seniority provisions of the working agreement; or (h) if his act violates the spirit of the agreement, the arbitrator may be in outer space and reading the stars instead of the contract."

One final comment on Professor Feller's second proposition regarding an arbitrator's "implicit authority to award specific performance of the provisions of the agreement" is appropriate in light of his somewhat intimate connection with the so-called *Steelworkers Trilogy.* While Justice Douglas did state in *Enter-*

---

[3]*Torrington* v. *Metal Products Workers,* 362 F.2d 677, 62 LRRM 2495 (2d Cir. 1966).
[4]37 LA 334, 337–338 (1971).

prise[5] that an arbitrator may look to the "law of the shop" or the so-called industrial common law of the industry involved in the arbitration, I believe the "look" Justice Douglas referred to was limited to looking for guidance reflected in the parties' own undisputed practices to construe an ambiguous contract provision and not looking for new requirements that could be added to the agreement.

Professor Feller's third proposition, that an arbitrator's authority is "ordinarily limited to the payment of sums calculated in terms of the collective bargaining agreement, not by measures external to it," signals a return to his original and principal premise that the arbitrator is a "contract reader" and not a quasi-judicial "contract enforcer." While I have no difficulty with Professor Feller's statement of this proposition, I am again troubled by his suggested implementation of this proposition and especially his compulsion to resurrect his so-called "implicit in the agreement" exception. Thus, in his example of the employer who "willfully" reschedules an employee's vacation, I find his suggestion that, notwithstanding any expressly stated contractual remedy, an arbitrator could "imply" a monetary penalty as an inconsistent bit of backsliding. Such an approach seems to more accurately reflect the very "contract enforcer" role (that is, for every wrong there must be a remedy and all I have to do is devise one for the parties) that Professor Feller claims to have eschewed in favor of the "contract reader" role and to be at odds with the approach of Ben Fischer at the 24th Annual Meeting of the National Academy of Arbitrators,[6] which Professor Feller quotes with approval. You may recall that Ben Fischer's concern was that industrial arbitration was becoming too far removed from the front-line supervisors and rank-and-file employees who have to conform to the requirements of the labor contract. Fischer's approach was to avoid the temptation to fabricate a remedy in the guise of an implicit provision of the agreement and, instead, to send the problem back to the parties to decide through negotiations what remedy they want to impose.

Now I can already hear Professor Feller's retort: namely, that if I am opposed to an arbitrator's "implying" remedies into an

---

[5] *Supra* note 2.
[6] *See Implementation of Arbitration Awards,* in Arbitration and the Public Interest, Proceedings of the 24th Annual Meeting, National Academy of Arbitrators (Washington: BNA Books, 1971), 126-137.

agreement, how else can I justify the traditional arbitral practice of reducing an employee's back pay award by his "outside earnings" or his failure to mitigate his damages when neither is expressly provided for in the agreement. My answer is that both the reductions for outside earnings and failure to mitigate are simply part of the calculations made by the arbitrator in deciding back pay. In other words, if a contract provides for back pay, then inherent therein is the act of calculating the amount of back pay the employee should receive to make him whole, and such calculations, unless expressly limited by contract to a mathematical computation of the missed work hours multiplied by the employee's hourly rate, must include every appropriate element of a back-pay calculation such as actual outside earnings and mitigation of losses.

In closing my comments on Professor Feller's paper, I would be remiss in not thanking him for a thoughtful and provocative paper and reiterating my basic agreement with him and Ted St. Antoine that arbitrators should be "contract readers" and not "contract enforcers." But I would be equally remiss if I did not also reiterate my belief that along with the authority to "read the contract" comes the responsibility to avoid the temptation to add your own epilogue or denouement. Arbitrators, unlike judges, have not been licensed to dispense their own notions of social justice or to expand constitutional *notions* of due process from criminal cases to arbitrations in response to "the felt necessities of our time."

CHAPTER 5

GRIEVANCE ARBITRATION IN THE FEDERAL SERVICE: STILL HARDLY FINAL AND BINDING?

John Kagel*

Traditional Arbitration

Classically, arbitration is a process of dispute resolution where the parties agree to abide by the decision of the arbitrator. Court challenges are essentially limited to protests that the arbitrator has not carried out his agreed-upon function. Provided that he or she does, the award will not be disturbed. Mistakes of law are tolerated on the basis that the parties, having chosen their arbitrator, also chose his or her fallibilities, unless the parties have "limited" the submission by requiring the arbitrator to adhere to the law. Broad discretion as to remedy is allowed unless restricted by agreement. Otherwise only if the underlying contract itself is illegal or the award compels the violation of law will the courts not enforce the arbitrator's remedy.[1]

This broad tradition of the basic traits of arbitration has been in existence since at least the 1600s and has continued unbroken

---

*Member, National Academy of Arbitrators; Kagel and Kagel, San Francisco, Calif.
[1]*See* generally Kagel, *Grievance Arbitration in the Federal Sector: How Final and Binding?*, 51 Ore. L. Rev. 134, 139–140 (1971) (hereinafter Kagel). For cases involving limited submissions, *see e.g., Utah Const. Co.* v. *Western Pac. Ry. Co.*, 174 Cal. 156, 161, 162 Pac. 631 (1916). For cases involving illegal awards, *see e.g., Loving & Evans* v. *Blick*, 33 Cal.2d 603 (1949); *Union Employers Div.* v. *Columbia Typo. Union 101*, 353 F.Supp. 1348, 82 LRRM 2537 (D.D.C. 1973); *Amer., etc. Baseball Clubs* v. *Major League Baseball Players Assn.*, 59 Cal. App.3d 493, 130 Cap. Rptr. 626 (1976). In some instances public policy requirements have not allowed enforcement of decisions or orders to arbitrate over matters which are subject to statutory controls, *e.g., Wilko* v. *Swan*, 346 U.S. 427 (1953) (Securities Act); *Alexander* v. *Gardner-Denver*, 415 U.S. 36, 7 FEP Cases 81 (1974) (Civil Rights Act); *Barrentine* v. *Arkansas-Best Freight System, Inc.*, 450 U.S. 728, 24 WH Cases 1284 (1981) (Fair Labor Standards Act); *World Airways* v. *Teamsters*, 578 F.2d 800, 99 LRRM 2325 (9th Cir. 1978) (Federal Aviation Act); *Teamsters Local 748* v. *Haig Berberian Inc.*, 623 F.2d 77, 105 LRRM 2172 (9th Cir. 1980) (National Labor Relations Act).

178

to the present. It is generally applicable to all manner of disputes including labor disputes, in both the public and private sectors.[2]

Federal-Sector Arbitration

The Civil Service Reform Act of 1978 (CSRA) for the first time codified arbitration as a dispute resolution mechanism for employees in the federal service.[3] In doing so, it broke with tradition in many ways. It adopted a broader definition of a grievance than found in most collective bargaining agreements, and it made arbitration awards reviewable either by courts or administrative bodies, or both. At least three separate channels of review were established, depending on the type of case involved. There are separate channels for (1) "adverse action" cases—suspensions of 14 days or longer up to and including discharge, (2) cases where discrimination by the employer is alleged, and (3) all other cases.

The purpose of this paper is to compare this system with traditional arbitration as described above. For the practitioner —the arbitrator, counsel, or party—to understand this comparison, a detailed analysis of the system is required. Also required is an understanding of the force that agencies extraneous to the dispute in question can bring to bear on the finality of a decision. Particular pitfalls or concerns to the arbitrator and the parties in that system, compared to the traditional model, are outlined.

---

[2]*See* Arbitrium Redivivum or the Law of Arbitration (1694); A Gentlemen of the Middle-Temple, The Compleat Arbitrator (1731); California Law Revision Commission, Recommendation and Study Relating to Arbitration (1960).

[3]Public Law 95-454, 92 Stat. 1111. The pertinent arbitration provisions are found in Title 5, U.S.C., Reorganization Plans 1 and 2, and Executive Order 11491. The latter three survive, even though nonstatutory, where not overruled by statute. *See* Elkouri and Elkouri, Legal Status of Federal Sector Arbitration, supp. to How Arbitration Works, 3d ed., notes 4, 7 (1980) (hereinafter Elkouris supp.). For sources on the predecessor federal service system, *see* Kagel, *supra* note 1; Elkouri supp., *supra* note 3; Gamser, *Back-Seat Driving Behind the Back-Seat Driver: Arbitration in the Federal Sector,* in Truth, Lie Detectors, and Other Problems in Labor Arbitration, Proceedings of the 31st Annual Meeting, National Academy of Arbitrators (Washington: BNA Books, 1979), 268; Porter, *Arbitration in the Federal Government: What Happened to the "Magna Carta"?,* in Arbitration—1977, Proceedings of the 30th Annual Meeting, National Academy of Arbitrators (Washington: BNA Books, 1978), 90; Cooper & Bauer, *Federal Sector Labor Relations Reform,* 56 Chi. Kent L. Rev. 509 (1980); *Legislative History of the Civil Service Reform Act of 1978,* House Comm. on Post Office and Civil Service (1979) (hereinafter *Legis. History*); *Legislative History of the Federal Service Labor Management Relations Statute, Title VII of the Civil Service Reform Act of 1978,* House Subcomm. on Postal Personnel and Modernization of the Comm. on Post Office and Civil Service (1979) (hereinafter *Legis. History Title VII*).

Finally, suggestions for reformation of the codified system are made.[4]

The Grievance and Mandatory Arbitration System

Grievances are defined in the CSRA as complaints covering "*any* matter relating" to employment; the "effect," interpretation, or breach of a collective bargaining agreement; or "any claimed violation, misinterpretation, or misapplication of any law, rule, or regulation affecting conditions of employment. . . ."[5] Excluded from the grievance procedure by statute are matters relating to prohibited political activities, retirement, life and health insurance, "any examination, certification, or appointment," employee classification matters not affecting pay or grade, and removals for national security matters.[6]

Each collective bargaining agreement must contain procedures for settling grievances (including arbitrability) which must be "fair and simple," provide for "expeditious processing," and allow the union or the employer to invoke "binding arbitration."[7]

Adverse Actions

In adverse action cases, the employee must initially and irrevocably opt either to utilize the negotiated grievance procedure including potential arbitration *or* to use the procedures of the Merit System Protection Board (MSPB) as an alternative, statutorily created, decision-making authority.[8]

---

[4]This paper does *not* deal with the scope of bargaining, or lack of it, in the new statute. See Kagel, *supra* note 1, 137, 138, 5 U.S.C. §§7106, 7121(c). *See also* 873 Govt. Emp. Relations Rep. 9 (8/4/80) (hereinafter GERR); Coleman, *The Civil Service Reform Act of 1978: Its Meaning and Roots,* 31 Labor L.J. 200 (1980).

[5]5 U.S.C. §7103(a)(9). By agreement, the parties may reduce the scope of their grievance procedure, 5 U.S.C. §7121(a)(2).

[6]5 U.S.C. §7121(c).

[7]5 U.S.C. §§7121(a), (b). While any employee can raise a grievance, only the union can move it to arbitration. 5 U.S.C. §§7121(b)(3)(A), (C).

[8]5 U.S.C. §7121(e)(1) involving matters arising under 5 U.S.C. §§4303 and 7512 "and similar matters which arise under other personnel systems." There are apparently more than 20 of these. *Legis. History Title VII, supra* note 3, at 1371. The MSPB is a spinoff from the old Civil Service Commission, succeeding to its past adjudicatory functions. See Elkouris supp., *supra* note 3. It is composed of three members appointed by the President, and confirmed by the Senate, to one-time seven-year terms. 5 U.S.C. §§1201, 1202(a), 1202(d). The MSPB has, through statute and extensive regulations, established an "appellate" procedure from agency actions including a "presiding officer" step allowing for prehearing discovery as well as setting forth hearing conduct, including taking of a transcript. An appeal or "review" of the presiding officer's decision can be

An arbitrator hearing an adverse action case is required to find that a removal or a grade reduction for unacceptable performance was supported by substantial evidence. Any other adverse action must be supported by the preponderance of the evidence.[9]

The appeal from an arbitration decision concerning an adverse action is to the U.S. Court of Appeals or Court of Claims.[10] Only the employee can appeal to the courts.[11] And an agency action upheld by the arbitrator can be overturned if, from the record, the court finds the agency action to be arbitrary, capricious, an abuse of discretion, not in accordance with law, obtained without lawful procedures, or unsupported by substantial

---

made to the Board itself which, by its procedures, may hear oral argument and allow for filing briefs. A review may occur when it is "established" that the presiding officer's decision is based on an erroneous misinterpretation of a statute or regulation as shown by a petition for review. See 5 CFR §§1201.4-117. *See also Note, Federal Employment—The Civil Service Reform Act of 1978—Removing Incompetents and Protecting Whistle Blowers,* 26 Wayne L.Rev. 97, 108–110 (1979). The MSPB has ruled it has the authority to reduce penalties in adverse action matters. *Douglas* v. *V.A.,* MSPB Docket No. NY05209013, Apr. 13, 1981, 909 GERR 12, 42 (4/20/81).

[9]5 U.S.C. §§7121(e)(2), 7701(c)(1). The MSPB is bound to these standards under the latter section as well as being required to reverse an agency decision if there was "harmful error" in the application of its procedures or they were not in accordance with law. 5 U.S.C. §7702(c)(2). These latter criteria were not specified to be applied by arbitrators but, presumably, would come before them in any event. The MSPB has defined "substantial evidence" as: "That degree of relevant evidence which a reasonable mind, considering the record as a whole, might accept as adequate to support a conclusion that the matter asserted is true." It has defined "preponderance of the evidence" as: "That degree of relevant evidence which a reasonable mind, considering the record as a whole, might accept as sufficient to support a conclusion that the matter asserted is more like to be true than not true" (5 U.S.C. §§1201.56(c)(1), (2)). The substantial evidence standard is that applied in *Universal Camera* v. *NLRB,* 340 U.S. 474, 27 LRRM 2373 (1951); *Parker* v. *Def. Log. Agency* (MSPB), 850 GERR 7 (2/25/80). *See also* 809 GERR 9–10 (5/7/79), 811 GERR 9–11 (5/21/79). In remarks added to the Congressional Record because the conference report came at the end of the session, which "forced the conference documents to be less helpful than normal," Rep. Ford pointed out that the substantial evidence standard has to be applied by the initial triers of fact. "Therefore, the burden [of the task] is greater than that of an appellate body. They are responsible for developing the record." The triers of fact must decide, before admitting evidence, if it is "reliable, probative, and relevant. The substantiality of evidence must take into account whatever in the record fairly detracts from its weight." *Universal Camera, supra* at 488; II *Legis. History Title VII, supra* note 3, at 2003, 2014–2015. The substantial evidence test was adopted "because of the difficulties of proving that an employee's performance is unacceptable. . . ." *House-Senate Conference Committee Report,* 781 GERR 65 (10/16/78) (hereinafter *Conference Report*). This is probably a lesser standard of proof than applied in many private-sector arbitration cases. *See* Elkouri and Elkouri, How Arbitration Works, 3d ed. (Washington: BNA Books, 1973), 622. For a discussion of this subject generally, *see* Clarke, *Substantial Evidence and Labor Arbitration in the Federal Sector,* 31 Labor L.J. 368 (1980).

[10]5 U.S.C. §§7121(f), 7703. The agency is named as the respondent. 5 U.S.C. §7703(a)(2).

[11]5 U.S.C. §7703(a)(1). *See also* 5 U.S.C. §7703(d).

evidence.[12] Although no trial de novo is held at the circuit court level, the court's statutorily required review amounts to that. The court must look at the agency's action, not the regularity or irregularity of the arbitration process or award.[13]

Once an employee selects his or her avenue of appeal, he or she cannot backtrack.[14] The statute is silent as to what occurs if an employee chooses the route of the negotiated grievance procedure but the union which negotiated it, and which by statute has the exclusive right to bring a case to arbitration, declines to do so or settles the case short of arbitration. Presumably, this is a risk known to an employee when he or she opts for the grievance procedure route. Collateral litigation on the fairness of union representation in such an instance, however, may occur.[15]

Other Nondiscrimination Cases—The FLRA

What is included in this channel are disciplinary cases of up to a 14-day suspension—not harsh enough to be adverse actions—and any other matter covered by a negotiated grievance procedure, keeping in mind the broad types of extra-contractual claims that can be encompassed under the definition of a grievance.[16] In these situations, the negotiated grievance procedure is the sole procedure which may be followed.

After the arbitration hearing, either party to the case may file "exceptions" to the award with the Federal Labor Relations Authority (FLRA) within 30 days of the date of the award. If not, the award is final and the agency must observe it.[17]

---

[12]5 U.S.C. §7703(c). See remarks of FLRA Chairman Haughton, 838 GERR 8 (11/26/79). The mandatory transcript of the MSPB proceedings and the need of the court to have a record should spur the parties, if not the arbitrator, to have a transcript as well. "The provision for judicial review is intended to assure conformity between the decisions of arbitrators with those of the [MSPB]. Under the terms of this subsection, an arbitrator must establish a record that will meet the judicial tests provided for in section 7702...." *Senate Report No. 95-969,* 4 U.S. Code Congressional & Administrative News (Govt. Affairs Comm.), July 10, 1978, p. 2833 (hereinafter *Senate Report*).

[13]*Conference Report, supra* note 9, at 66, states that the statute "adopts the traditional appellate mechanism for reviewing final decisions and orders of Federal administrative agencies."

[14]5 U.S.C. §7121(e)(1).

[15]The union's exclusive right to decide whether or not to take a case to arbitration requires that the decision be made in "good faith." *Senate Report, supra* note 12, at 2832. See *Tidewater Virginia Fed. Emps. Metal Trades Council/IAM Local 441 and Burns and Norfolk Naval Shipyard,* 2/3/81, 901 GERR 8 (2/23/81), regarding unfair labor practices involving union not fairly representing nonmembers.

[16]See text accompanying note 5–7, *supra.*

[17]5 U.S.C. §§7112(b), 7122(b).

The FLRA consists of three members appointed to five-year terms by the President and confirmed by the Senate.[18] It is charged with providing "leadership in establishing policies and guidance relating to matters" under the statutory provisions dealing with federal-sector collective bargaining.[19] Involved with numerous duties roughly equivalent to those of the NLRB, it also is required to "resolve exceptions to arbitrator's awards."[20] It can find an award "deficient" on the basis that "it is contrary to any law, rule, or regulation" or "on other grounds similar to those applied by Federal courts in private sector labor relations."[21]

The FLRA standards of these latter grounds are that the arbitrator's award " 'can[not] in any rational way be derived from the agreement'; or is 'so unfounded in reason and fact, so unconnected with the wording and purpose of the collective bargaining agreement' as to 'manifest an infidelity to the obligation of the arbitrator'; or that it evidences a 'manifest disregard of the agreement'; or that on its face the award does not represent a 'plausible interpretation of the contract. . . .' "[22] Mere disagreement with the arbitrator's decision is insufficient grounds to have a petition for review even considered,[23] and, as in the private sector, disagreements with findings of fact will not set an award aside.[24] But if an arbitrator's award from its face is based on a "nonfact," which misapprehension was not chargeable to the parties, was a matter which is "objectively ascertainable," and was the central matter on which the decision was based, then the award will be overturned.[25]

Additional grounds where the FLRA has indicated it could find an award "deficient" include situations where the arbitrator would determine an issue not included in the subject matter

---

[18]5 U.S.C. §§7104(a)–(c).

[19]5 U.S.C. §7105(a)(1).

[20]5 U.S.C. §7105(a)(2)(H).

[21]5 U.S.C. §§7122(a)(1)(2).

[22]*Army Missile Materiel Readiness Command and AFGE Local 1858,* 2 FLRA No. 6, pp. 5–6. See also *Red River Army Depot and NAGE Local R 14-52,* 3 FLRA No. 32 (1980).

[23]*Ibid. FAA Science and Tech. Assn. and FAA,* 2 FLRA No. 85 (1980); *VA Hospt. and AFGE Local 331,* 3 FLRA No. 34 (1980); *VA and AFGE Local 1985,* 3 FLRA No. 91 (1980).

[24]*VA and AFGE Local 2146,* 5 FLRA No. 31 (1981); *Social Security Admin. and AFGE Local 2193,* 5 FLRA No. 33 (1981), 908 GERR 9 (4/13/81).

[25]*Army Missile Materiel Readiness Command, supra* note 22, citing *Electronics Corp. of America* v. *IUE Local 272,* 492 F.2d 1233, 85 LRRM 2534 (1st Cir. 1974). The burden is on the party seeking to overturn the award. *Social Security Admin., supra* note 24.

submitted to arbitration;[26] if an award was to be so incomplete, ambiguous, or contradictory that implementation of it is impossible;[27] or if the arbitrator failed to conduct a fair hearing by refusing to consider evidence that is relevant or material.[28]

If the FLRA determines that an award is "deficient," it can take such action as it deems necessary, "consistent with applicable laws, rules, or regulations." No direct judicial review is available from either an unappealed arbitrator's award or an FLRA ruling "unless the order involves an unfair labor practice."[29] The FLRA has indicated that if a party does not comply with an award, the winning party must pursue and win an unfair labor practice charge before the FLRA, and then, if the losing party still refuses to comply, the winner will finally get a court-ordered enforcement of the award of the FLRA by the circuitous route of enforcing the unfair labor practice decision.[30]

The FLRA has issued sparse regulations as to how it exercises its authority to review arbitration awards. It does demand strict adherence to the statutory 30-day filing period, requiring that the filing contain the arguments of the petitioner, and then gives 30 days for a response.[31]

Two other areas of FLRA authority directly impact on the arbitration process. First, when a case is being reviewed for

---

[26]*Dept. of Air Force and AFGE Local 1364,* 5 FLRA No. 7 (1981); citing *Dept. of Air Force and AFGE Local 1778,* 3 FLRA No. 38 (1980) and *Fed. Aviation Science and Tech. Assn. Local 291 and FAA,* 3 FLRA No. 38 (1980).

[27]*VA Hospt. and NAGE Local R1-109,* 5 FLRA No. 12 (1981), citing *Steelworkers* v. *Enterprise Wheel & Car Corp.,* 363 U.S. 593, 46 LRRM 2423 (1960); *Bell Aerospace* v. *Local 516 UAW,* 500 F.2d 921, 86 LRRM 3240 (2d Cir. 1974); *UMW Dist. 2* v. *Barnes & Tucker Co.,* 561 F.2d 1093, 96 LRRM 2144 (3d Cir. 1977).

[28]*National Border Patrol Council and INS,* 3 FLRA No. 62 (1980), citing *Harvey Aluminum* v. *Steelworkers,* 263 F.Supp. 488, 64 LRRM 2580 (C.D.Ca. 1967); *Shopping Cart, Inc.* v. *Amal. Food Emps. Local 196,* 350 F.Supp. 1221, 82 LRRM 2107 (E.D.Pa. 1972); *Newark Stereotypers Union 18* v. *Newark Morning Ledger,* 261 F.Supp. 832, 64 LRRM 2024 (D.N.J. 1966), *aff'd,* 397 F.2d 594 (3d Cir.), *cert. den.,* 393 U.S. 954 (1968); Aaron, *Some Procedural Problems in Arbitration,* 10 Vand.L. Rev. 739 (1957).

[29]5 U.S.C. §§7122(a)(1), (2).

[30]*Army Communications Command and AFGE Local 1662,* 2 FLRA No. 101 (1980). *See also* 895 GERR 6 (1/12/81), 5 U.S.C. §§7123(c), (d). Direct judicial review of arbitration awards was not adopted in the CSRA. *Legis. History Title VII, supra* note 3, at 1062. *But see Columbia Power Trades Council* v. *U.S. Dept. of Energy, Bonneville Power Admin.,* 1979–80 Pub. Barg. Cases ¶37,115 (W.D.Wa. 8/22/80). One case to test this question at the time of this writing is *AFGE Local 1286 and FLRA* (D.D.C. No. 80-2015), 905 GERR 8 (3/23/81).

[31]5 C.F.R. §§2425.1, .2. Given governmental hierarchies, including that technical claims of violations of law or regulation may more likely be raised at central headquarters than in more remote areas where the case may have been heard, the timeliness requirement may bar valid exceptions from being considered. In one case the FLRA reconsidered a decision in which a petition had been untimely filed, based on later filed documentation. *Immigration and Naturalization Service and AFGE Local 1656,* Case No. 0-AR-81 (6/26/80).

compliance with law, rule, or regulation, the problem is determining which rules or regulations are to be considered.[32] They must predate the collective bargaining agreement[33] or have been later enacted on less than a government-wide basis because of "compelling need."[34] If so enacted, they may be challenged by the union before the FLRA in an independent proceeding. It appears that the challenge must be made at the time the regulations are sought to be imposed, not for the first time in arbitration.[35] Otherwise, they will be binding on the parties to the arbitration matter. Nonetheless, experience teaches that an arbitrator in the first instance, and the FLRA in the second, need to interpret regulations. Both forums also will be required to determine what legal effect to give those regulations that the parties contend are controlling as to whether they are entitled to be considered as lawful.

The second area where FLRA authority impacts directly on the arbitration process involves a more familiar role for the arbitrator, which has been institutionalized in the legislation. All federal service agreements must contain provisions for arbitrability determinations. Although not specified, the expected route of these determinations—without distinction as to substantive or procedural questions—will be to the arbitrator and, on review, to the FLRA.[36] The FLRA has by decision adopted the private-sector rule that procedural arbitrability determinations are solely for the arbitrator.[37]

This authority has already had specific impact on statutory interpretation. In one instance a probationary employee was fired. He sought to arbitrate his dismissal. The agency contended, and the arbitrator agreed, that the matter was not arbi-

---

[32] See generally Elkouris supp., supra note 3, at 15–19; Smith & Wood, Title VII of the Civil Service Reform Act of 1978: A "Perfect" Order?, 31 Hastings L.J. 855, 879 (1980).

[33] 5 U.S.C. §7116(a)(7), making it an unfair labor practice to seek to enforce a postdated rule or regulation except ones dealing with prohibited personnel practices under 5 U.S.C §2302.

[34] 5 U.S.C. §§7117(a)(2), (3), dealing with duty to bargain.

[35] 5 U.S.C. §§7117(a)(2), (b), 5 C.F.R. §2424.11.

[36] 5 U.S.C. §7121(a)(1). The Conference Report, supra note 9, at 70, stated that all questions concerning orders "to proceed to arbitration will be considered at least in the first instance by the . . . FLRA."

[37] EPA and NFFE Local 1907, 5 FLRA No. 36 (1981), 908 GERR 10 (4/13/81), citing John Wiley & Sons, Inc. v. Livingston, 376 U.S. 543, 55 LRRM 2773 (1964), and Tobacco Workers Local 317 v. Lorillard Corp., 448 F.2d 949, 78 LRRM 2273 (4th Cir. 1971). Strict adherence by the arbitrator to the parties' negotiated grievance procedure will not overturn the award. EPA, supra, citing Chambers v. Beaunit Corp., 404 F.2d 128, 69 LRRM 2732 (6th Cir. 1968); Newspaper Guild Local 10 v. Philadelphia Newspapers, Inc., 87 LRRM 2670 (E.D.Pa. 1974); Amer. Can Co. v. United Papermakers, 356 F.Supp. 495, 82 LRRM 3055 (E.D.Pa. 1973).

trable, based on the statutory exemption from arbitration of "any examination, certification, or appointment." The FLRA reversed, holding that probationary status was not part of any of these.[38]

In another case the FLRA has seemingly adopted a view that even if arbitrability is raised, a case cannot be found nonarbitrable based on the statutory provision reserving specific rights to management. The FLRA held that the impact of that statute was to be resolved either with respect to the merits, or remedy, but if a particular agreement section was alleged to be violated, the management rights statute does not "in and of itself prevent an arbitrator from deciding if there has been a violation of a particular contract provision."[39] These cases portend an apparent willingness by the FLRA to interpret the CSRA broadly, thereby enhancing the substantive and symbolic importance of the bargaining agreement and the arbitration process.[40]

Discrimination Cases

If an employee alleges that an agency action involves discrimination against him or her,[41] an extraordinary system of hearings and appeals comes into play. Fortunately, the arbitration aspects are among the simplest of the tortuous paths that may be followed. The employee has the option to use the negotiated grievance procedure or other routes to pursue his or her claim. Once having opted for arbitration, the employee is foreclosed from pursuing any other procedure, at least until the arbitration award is in.[42]

An appeal from the award not involving an adverse action can be made to the FLRA by either party as in any nondiscrimination case. Thereafter, in that case or in an adverse action case, a variety of things can occur, depending on how the claim is le-

---

[38]*AFGE and U.S. Dept. of Labor,* FLRA Case 0-AR-60, 884 GERR 8, 59 (10/20/80).
[39]*Marine Logistics Support Base and AFGE,* 3 FLRA No. 61 (1980), interpreting 5 U.S.C. §7106.
[40]For reaction to these types of determinations and reaction to FLRA independence generally, *see* address of OPM Asst. Dir. A. F. Ingrassia to Dept. of Defense Labor Management Relations Conference, 1/23/80, 847 GERR 35–37 (2/4/80). *See also* Ingrassia, *Reflections on the New Labor Law,* 30 Labor L.J. 539 (1979), and 848 GERR 9 (2/11/80).
[41]"Discrimination" as used here is synonymous with "prohibited personnel action," including discrimination based on race, color, religion, sex, national origin, age, handicap, marital status, or political affiliation as prohibited by law. 5 U.S.C. §§2302(b)(1)(A–E), 7121(d).
[42]5 U.S.C. §7121(d).

gally characterized. In these instances, the employee can bring his or her claim, now presumably including an unfavorable arbitration decision, to the MSPB, the EEOC, and/or the federal courts.[43] In instances where the MSPB could hear the case initially, it can go to the MSPB, the EEOC, back to the MSPB, and then to a mixed MSPB-EEOC special panel with a neutral member also sitting.[44] From there it can still go to federal court. At these steps and in the courts, the matter may be viewed de novo.

For the curious reader, I have appended two charts with notes prepared by, and with the courtesy of, FLRA Assistant Chief Counsel C. Brian Harris tracing these procedures. I have also included the House-Senate Conference Committee Report, giving its explanation of what Congress has wrought. The reader should note, among other things, the committee's listing of *eight* different times during these processes when an employee has an opportunity to move the matter to the federal court.[45]

Finally, it should be noted that none of this has affected the rights of an employee to go directly to the EEOC, thereby bypassing the entire CSRA scheme, but using it only to raise

---

[43]A case which the MSPB may hear is a "mixed" case. If it had no jurisdiction over the matter, it is a "pure" case. The MSPB's jurisdiction is described as "any personnel action that could be appealed to the MSPB" under 5 U.S.C. §7121(d) and an employee can appeal to the MSPB "from any action which is appealable to the Board under any law, rule, or regulation." 5 U.S.C. §7701(a). OPM has identified 28 categories of instances where this can occur. Eighteen of those identified possibly as being subject to arbitration (and the FLRA may or may not have a broader interpretation) are: adverse actions (5 U.S.C. §7512); removal or demotion for performance deficiencies (5 U.S.C. §4303); overtime pay under the Fair Labor Standards Act (P.L. 93-259); withholding of within-grade salary increases (5 U.S.C. §5335); actions against administrative law judges (5 U.S.C. §7521); OPM administered employment practices, except examinations, certifications, or appointments (5 C.F.R. §300.104); reductions in force (5 C.F.R. §351.901); violations of reemployment priority rights (5 C.F.R. §330.202); restoration to duty after military service (38 U.S.C. §2023) or recovery from compensable injury (5 C.F.R. §353.401); reemployment rights based on movement between executive agencies during emergencies (5 C.F.R. §352.209), following details or transfers to international organizations (5 C.F.R. §353.313), after service under the Foreign Assistance Act of 1961 (5 C.F.R. §352.508), in the Economic Stabilization Program (5 C.F.R. §353.607) and the Indian Self-Determination Act (5 C.F.R. §352.707); grade and salary retention under the CSRA (5 U.S.C. §5337 and 5 C.F.R. §531.517), and termination of such benefits based on refusal to accept a reasonable offer (5 U.S.C. §5366); and removal based on adverse suitability rating (5 C.F.R. §754). Untitled OPM compilation.

[44]The MSPB has, by regulation, determined to view any discrimination appeal from an arbitration award (and in nonadverse action cases, the FLRA) de novo. 5 C.F.R. §§1201.152, 157. See 5 C.F.R. §1201.154 for how the MSPB seeks to deal with late-filed discrimination claims.

[45]See also Elkouris supp., *supra* note 3, at 8–9. Congress bypassed proposals which would have skipped all of this for direct appeal to the district court from either the MSPB or an arbitration decision. Ink, *President's Reorganization Project, Personnel Management Project, Final Staff Report, Dec. 1977, Legis. History Title VII, supra* note 3, at 1483. Instead, Congress became embroiled in determining which could better handle this type of claim, the MSPB or the EEOC. *See* remarks of Sen. Glenn, *Senate Report, supra* note 12, at 2852.

contract or statutory claims and reserving discrimination ones initially for the EEOC and ultimately, if necessary, for the courts de novo.[46]

Noblesse Oblige

By statute, both the FLRA and the MSPB are to be independent agencies.[47] Yet, at least as to the FLRA, there has been one severe instance of failing to so act.

Under the statute, the FLRA ". . . *may* request from the Director of the Office of Personnel Management an advisory opinion concerning the proper interpretation of rules, regulations, or policy directives issued by the Office of Personnel Management in connection with any matter before the Authority."[48]

The Office of Personnel Management (OPM) inherited the managerial authority of the Civil Service Commission. It sets the personnel standards to be followed by federal agencies.[49] On its establishment, the President described OPM's director as "the government's principal representative in Federal labor relations matters."[50] Its management has attacked the FLRA for how it has asserted its authority to date, maintaining that the FLRA has significantly expanded its mandate beyond what Congress intended.[51] Yet, in at least two cases, the FLRA obtained an advisory opinion from OPM as to how to interpret law and relied thereon for its decision. In one case, it was reported that OPM's opinion was contrary to the appealing agency's opinion.[52] In another, OPM's opinion, where it was obtained by the FLRA and then circulated to the parties who didn't comment, was relied on by the FLRA to reverse the award.[53]

This practice, if it becomes one, of getting such opinions is a bad one—not unlike letting the fox into the hen house. In its

[46]5 U.S.C. §2000e-16, Reorganization Plan No. 1, in annot. to 5 U.S.C. §2000e-4 (*see* note 3, *supra*). A de novo court hearing is assured. *E.g., Vetter v. Frosch,* 599 F.2d 630 (5th Cir. 1979). *See* generally Martin, *Equal Employment Opportunity Complaint Procedures and Federal Union-Management Relations: A Field Study,* 34 Arb. J. 34 (1979).
[47]*E.g., Senate Report, supra* note 12, at 2729.
[48]5 U.S.C. §7105(i) (emphasis supplied).
[49]*See* Elkouris supp., *supra* note 3, at 4, 5 U.S.C. §1104(b)(1). The MSPB can review OPM rules and regulations for legality. 5 U.S.C.§§1205(a)(4), (e).
[50]President Carter's message to Congress, May 23, 1978, in annot. to 5 U.S.C. §1101.
[51]*See* note 40, *supra.*
[52]*VA Hospt. and AFGE Local 2201,* 4 FLRA No. 57, 886 GERR 10–11 (11/3/80).
[53]*National Bureau of Standards and AFGE Local 2186,* 3 FLRA No. 98 (1980).

statutorily mandated "leadership" role,[54] the FLRA must, of course, be impartial between labor and management. It has the independent role of determining whether or not to uphold arbitration awards, and it must make those decisions itself. It cannot rely upon the invited opinions of management's principal executive. If OPM wants to participate in the arbitration process, it should do so as a party, and Congress has indicated an intent to allow it to petition to intervene in FLRA exception proceedings.[55] Since it is fair to assume that OPM will attempt to keep track of decisions in which it has an interest, such intervention is far more appropriate a role for management's representative than a participatory role in the decision-making process of the FLRA. Clearly, the FLRA, not OPM, is to make the necessary decisions when exceptions to arbitration awards are lodged.

But the OPM skirmish is only that. A much greater threat to the arbitration process in the federal service continues to come from the Comptroller General. An arm of the Congress, the Comptroller General's legislative role and consummate interference with arbitration prior to the new statute has been well spelled out for the Academy by Alexander Porter and Howard Gamser as well as elsewhere.[56] As the watchdog of the propriety of federal expenditures, it had sharply limited arbitrators' remedy authority, especially the use of back pay to correct contract violations before the CSRA. In fact, the Comptroller General put out its own manual of what remedies were or were not awardable by arbitrators.[57]

Congress, in the CSRA, did two things about this. It first expressly made final an unappealed arbitration award or an FLRA decision, requiring an agency to follow it unimpeded by the Comptroller General. And it amended the Back Pay Act of 1966 to allow monetary recovery for an "unjustified or unwarranted personnel action" which has affected the grievant's pay.[58] It did this notwithstanding at least testimony and half a dozen pleas by the Comptroller General before the appropriate legislative committees. In one such plea it described its role in federal service arbitration as "a positive one. We have upheld

[54]See text accompanying note 19, *supra.*
[55]*Conference Report, supra* note 9, at 70.
[56]Porter and Gamser, *supra* note 3; Kagel, *supra* note 1.
[57]Gamser, *supra* note 3, at 277, note 28.
[58]5 U.S.C. §§5596(b), 7122(b).

most arbitration awards that have been referred to us . . . ,"
stating that it would overrule an arbitration award only as it
would a decision from an agency head.[59] Specific amendments
introduced in the House Committee to this effect were not
adopted.[60]

Undaunted, in September 1980 the Comptroller General
published a new set of regulations. They allow parties to get
advisory opinions, provided the requesting party served the request for that opinion on the other party to the dispute, allowing
that party to file a written response.[61] They allow "arbitrators
and other neutral parties authorized to administer 5 USC Chapter 71" to likewise request such an opinion from the Comptroller General in any case "which is of mutual concern to Federal
agencies and labor organizations." Service of the request is
"discretionary" in this instance.[62]

While admitting that payments pursuant to a final arbitration
award "will be conclusive on GAO in its settlement of accounts"
and "the Comptroller General will not review or comment on
the merits of such an award," the regulations went on: *"However,
such payments made pursuant to such an award do not constitute precedent
for payment in other instances not covered by the award."*[63]

The Comptroller General's regulations are asserted to be
based on statutes giving federal officials the right to opinions as
to whether claims may be paid from government funds, the same
ones on which it pleaded its case to Congress to no avail.

Consider the impact of these regulations: Ideally, parties in
the traditional collective bargaining setting try to do two things.
The first is to settle as many grievances as they can short of
arbitration, and, second, if they go to arbitration, generally they
will use the arbitration award to resolve and give guidance in like
cases that arise between them in the future—at least until their

---

[59]*Legis. History, supra* note 3, at 747; *Legis. History Title VII, supra* note 3, at 1096, 1102, 1103, 1120–1121, 1127.
[60]*Legis. History, supra* note 3, at 693–694; *Legis. History Title VII, supra* note 3, at 1092.
[61]4 C.F.R. §§21.2–4.
[62]4 C.F.R. §§21.5(a), (b). It should be noted that arbitrators are bound to assume full personal responsibility for the decision in each case. Since an arbitrator may not consider submissions of one party that have not been provided to the other, it cannot be
understood how, ethically, an arbitrator could, without such "service," use this process,
even assuming there is no breach of the duty to take full personal responsibility for the
award. *See* NAA, AAA, FMCS, *Code of Professional Responsibility for Arbitrators of Labor-
Management Disputes* (1974), ¶¶59, 125. To the extent that the law may allow the arbitrator to base an award on information not obtained at the hearing, the arbitrator may be
required to disclose it and allow the parties to meet it. *E.g., Calif. Code of Civil Proc.,*
§1282(g).
[63]4 C.F.R. §21.7 (emphasis supplied).

collective bargaining agreement is amended through negotiations. With its historic antipathy to arbitration and its tradition of interference in the federal service collective bargaining process,[64] the Comptroller General has expressed a view that will continue to thwart these goals. As seen, the Comptroller General has only begrudgingly acceded to Congress's will as to actual arbitration awards themselves, contrary to what a grievance and arbitration system is intended to accomplish—to provide means of peaceful and final dispute resolution which thereby reduce employer-employee tensions.

The Statute and the Arbitrator

On the whole, the arbitrator's role in the process retains many of its traditional characteristics. Specific note should be made that, while the CSRA confers subpoena authority on several agencies and officers, arbitrators are excluded from that list.[65] Unlike the private sector where no specific statute may confer such authority, but either state law or reference to the U.S. Arbitration Act has supplied subpoena power,[66] the CSRA is a specific statute which has not included that power for arbitrators. While eventually the general policy of encouraging the use of arbitration may, by extension, include the granting of such authority in federal-sector cases, arbitrators and the parties may have to be content with drawing adverse inferences against those who withhold witnesses or documents that subpoenas ordinarily might produce.[67] One route against a recalcitrant

---

[64]Kagel, *supra* note 1, at 147. *But see* 765 GERR 6–8 (6/26/78) where the Comptroller General recommended the expansion of the scope and fairness of government grievance procedures.
[65]5 U.S.C. §§1205(b)(2), 7105(g), 7132.
[66]9 U.S.C. §7. *See* Kagel, *supra* note 1, at 27. *Great Scott Supermarkets* v. *Teamsters Local 337*, 363 U.S. 1351, 84 LRRM 2514 (E.D.Mich. 1973); Heinsz, Lowry, & Torzewski, *The Subpoena Power of Labor Arbitrators*, 29 Utah L.Rev. 29, 42–45 (1979).
[67]The contention that not listing arbitrators is an expression of congressional intent to exclude them from such authority may distinguish the CSRA from Section 301 of the Labor-Management Relations Act. There, it has been forcefully urged, the policy encompassed in Section 301 itself of favoring arbitration over industrial strife is the source of uniformly applied subpoena power. Heinsz et al., *supra* note 66, 48–51. The same arguments for subpoena authority should apply to the CSRA. *Cf. UPS* v. *Mitchell*, 451 U.S. 56, 49 LW 4378 (1981); *Teamsters Local 135* v. *Jefferson Trucking Co.*, 105 LRRM 2712 (7th Cir. 1980), *cert. den.*, 49 LW 3527 (1981); *Typographical Union* v. *Newspapers, Inc.*, 106 LRRM 2317 (7th Cir. 1981). A Freedom of Information request may be inadequate as a means of providing information. *NTEU* v. *IRS*, 862 GERR 5–6 (4/24/80) (D.D.C. 1980). One device that has been used is to file a discrimination claim (*see* text and note 46 *supra*) while independently pursuing the grievance, and then to use the investigation file as a form of discovery.

party might be an independent unfair labor practice to the FLRA, a time-consuming, collateral process. Moreover, without subpoena authority, nonparty witnesses or information, often crucial, could be beyond the reach of the parties to present to the arbitrator.

The primary impact of the statute on the arbitrator is in the area of interpreting laws, rules, and regulations, unless the parties have negotiated to exclude those considerations from their grievance procedure. This problem existed under the Executive Order predecessors to the statute, and it continues. A higher order of initial sophistication for the arbitrator will be needed to guide the parties to produce the relevant portion of regulations and statutes and administrative agency decisions, such as those of the FLRA, on which the arbitrator is to rely. For, quite clearly, the arbitrator, as the first link in one or more appellate chains, is serving as a magistrate in this regard. He or she should insist on transcripts. The practical burden, however, is on the parties to make the appropriate record on which a proper decision can be made.

That the matter may be reviewed once or multiple times, on a de novo basis, is not a new situation especially as it concerns discrimination, for that can occur in the private sector.[68] Whether reviewing agencies or courts will give deference of any particular kind to arbitrators' decisions, as may occur on at least a limited basis in the private sector, remains to be seen.[69]

The arbitrator will need to know—or at least need to attempt to find out—what particular route his or her decision will take in terms of potential appeal. Adverse actions require the arbitrator to apply statutorily mandated burdens of proof in varying situations. Obviously, knowledge of these requirements is necessary to do the job properly.[70]

In terms of remedy, since the arbitrator acts independently, but nonetheless within the law as he or she interprets it and as it may be reviewed under the statute, a Comptroller General manual of preordained remedies is inappropriate. But, given the Comptroller General's predilection to volunteer its opinion, arbitrators may have to deal with its advisory opinions and adopt

---

[68]*Alexander* v. *Gardner-Denver, supra* note 1.
[69]*E.g., ibid.,* note 21; *Spielberg Mfg. Co.,* 112 NLRB 1080, 36 LRRM 1152 (1955). That the MSPB will not do so in discrimination cases is shown by its regulations. See note 45 *supra.*
[70]*See* note 9 *supra.*

or reject them as the arbitrator independently interprets the relevant law.

One area of remedy deserves mention. The statute specifically authorizes payment of attorney's fees if an employee prevails in a case where he or she wins back pay in a grievance if "warranted in the interests of justice" or, if in a discrimination case, in accordance with the 1964 Civil Rights Act.[71] Arbitrators, accordingly, will be asked, and are authorized, to award such fees. The MSPB, which has the same authority,[72] has issued decisions which allow attorney's fees, maintaining that it has substantial discretion by statute in this regard. It has developed an "illustrative" list of when such fees are warranted: When prohibited personnel practices as defined by statute have been shown to exist; that the agency's action was "clearly without merit" or "wholly unfounded"; where the employee is "substantially innocent" of whatever charges are brought; if bad faith or harassment by the agency has occurred; where gross procedural error prolonging proceedings or resulting in "severe prejudice" has taken place; if a determination has been reached that the agency "knew or should have known it would not prevail on the merits"; or agency officials "unjustifiably fail to undertake prudent fiscal inquiries, which would have led the agency to discover at the outset that the removal action was wholly unfounded." Legal fees which are the responsibility of the appellant-employee's union have been ordered paid by the MSPB.[73] Since the authority of the arbitrator and the MSPB is the same in awarding attorney's fees, at a minimum the former should at least match the latter's standards.[74] Not only would the employee have, in many instances, opted for arbitration instead of MSPB hearings but, further, such payments, being authorized by statute, are thus necessarily within the expectation of the parties as part of the federal sector arbitration process.[75]

---

[71] 5 U.S.C. §§5596(b)(1)(a)(ii), 7701(g)(1), (2).

[72] 5 U.S.C. §7701(g).

[73] 873 GERR 7–8 and cases cited therein (8/4/80); *Conference Report, supra* note 9, 66. See also 899 GERR 8 (2/19/81).

[74] See 824 GERR 5, 33 (8/20/79).

[75] The MSPB has ruled that fee awards must be conservative: "[A] fee award . . . must not provide a windfall to counsel at the expense of the public fisc." The MSPB has required that counsel's customary hourly billing rate, or any special rate if lower, is the starting point for determining the amount of fees, after the amount of billed hours has been scrutinized for duplication or padding. The amount may then be increased for quality of performance, the handling of an unusually unpopular cause, and any contingency factor where considered justified, citing *Lindy Bros. Bldrs.* v. *American Radiator and Standard Sanitary Corp.,* 487 F.2d 624 (6th Cir. 1979) and *Johnson* v. *Georgia Highway*

The Statute and the Parties

Attorney's fees are only one area where the statute has changed or challenged the traditional avenues of a grievance and arbitration system.[76] The burden of these remarks clearly underlines those distinctions without much necessity for further elaboration—review based on law; discovery of law as expressed in regulation; different standards of proof; appeal of all cases, including appeals to the courts on the merits, let alone varied forms of appeal based on varied circumstances; an array of avenues to pursue grievances, some, especially in the discrimination area, with bewildering, if not unknown, consequences. Moreover, there is evidence that the arbitration process has not been fully understood by, nor its nuances of straightforwardly seeking a full, fair, impartial, and final determination fully known to both federal management and union personnel.[77]

The statute can be viewed as requiring unions, without union security clauses to finance their efforts, to bargain about a myriad of subjects except such vital items as wages, but to necessarily include arbitration clauses where grievances may be unlimited in their scope. If a legal duty of fair representation—and potential liability—is imposed on federal-sector unions in their roles as exclusive bargaining agents,[78] there is no reason to expect their experience will not parallel private-sector unions' increased use of arbitration to avoid or minimize liability. But in doing so, they may have to take the case much further since the federal-sector processes are so much more complex. And, at the same time, despite some progress, Congress has apparently not corralled its own watchdog, the Comptroller General.

All should not be viewed negatively by this catalogue. There is vast diversity among federal activities, managers, and unions. Some are very sophisticated and have utilized arbitration under

---

Express, 488 F.2d 714 (5th Cir. 1974), 873 GERR 8–9 (8/14/80). Arbitrators have awarded such fees. *See* 824 GERR 5–6, 33 (8/20/79). It is assumed that if fees are granted, their computation would initially be remanded to the parties, the arbitrator retaining jurisdiction to determine fees if the parties cannot agree.

[76]*Cf. Litton Systems* v. *Local 572,* 90 LRRM 2964, 3177 (S.D.Ohio 1975).

[77]*E.g.,* 803 GERR 29–38 (3/26/79); Sulzner, *The Impact of Grievances and Arbitration Processes on Federal Personnel Policies and Practices: The View from Twenty Bargaining Units,* 9 J. Coll. Neg. in the Pub. Sector 143 (1980). *See also* 908 GERR 9 (4/13/81).

[78]*See* note 15, *supra.* Lack of funding by the prohibition on union security clauses, 5 U.S.C. §7115, or otherwise, early began to take its toll in terms of the ability of unions to finance appropriate administration of a statutory grievance procedure, requiring a narrowing of its scope in bargaining. *See, e.g.,* remarks of A. F. Ingrassia, OPM Asst. Dir., SPIDR 7th Ann. Conf., 839 GERR 6 (12/3/79). *See also* 863 GERR 12–13 (5/26/80).

the new statute to achieve what it can at its optimum—resolution of disputes and reduction of industrial tensions.

Yet, if you recall our model of the traditional arbitration system, you can see that the federal model has strayed from it. While in several important respects it is better than what it supplanted, it still falls short of traditional arbitration in other significant ways. The federal-sector process may work in many instances to provide the kind of resolution of disputes that the traditional model does. But if either party chooses not to have it so work, then, unfortunately, there are numerous pitfalls and traps for the unwary—often for no apparent meritorious reason —written into the statute which can be used for delay or in other dilatory ways.

The result seems to be particularly tragic in the discrimination field. Numerous avenues of appeal have been created for the employee with a token claim, taking a high toll of employer time and money in two or three de novo hearings.[79] But for the employee with a proper and meritorious claim, he or she runs the risk of being thrown out of court for improper or nonexhaustion of administrative remedies, even though he or she may not be able to predict accurately what they are, in trying to get to a federal court which may be the place where that claim can get proper and appropriate recognition. This conclusion is patent from an examination of the statute. Yet the House and Senate conferees seem almost proud of the labyrinth that they created notwithstanding that it almost appears to mock law as a tool of governance.[80]

There had been urgings in the days of the Executive Order that Congress write a statute tailoring grievance arbitration in the federal service to mirror its counterpart in the private sector, maintaining that a statute was required to transfer effectively and fully the private model to the federal-sector job. Those of us who did so[81] did not contemplate what has occurred. It will, I venture, be far more difficult to enact a new statute to untie the complications of the current one that I have reported to you.[82]

---

[79]In this instance the private sector is hardly a model. *See Aponte* v. *Nat'l Steel Serv. Center,* 24 FEP Cases 609, 613 (N.D.Ill. 1980).

[80]*Conference Committee, supra* note 9, reproduced *infra.*

[81]*See e.g.,* Kagel, *supra* note 1, 150.

[82]See remarks of FLRA member Applewhaite, 907 GERR 33 (4/6/81).

Suggestions

But, assuming a new statute were to be adopted, the following are suggestions of what it should contain to correct these problems. This short list does not address broader policy questions such as the scope of bargaining and the permissibility of effective union security clauses.[83]

Nonetheless, it is readily apparent that arbitration as a process in the federal sector is intended to reflect the traditional model of arbitration described earlier. To accomplish this within the context of federal employment, the following should be considered:

1. If a grievance is defined as being broader than the interpretation or application of an agreement to include questions of law, then review of arbitration decisions should be either by the FLRA or, if that body does not review it, by the federal district court. If the FLRA reviews an award and upholds it, a party should be allowed to secure its direct enforcement. Motions to vacate should also be allowed in the district court directly from an FLRA ruling to the contrary.

2. If Suggestion 1 is adopted, then no distinction need be made between types of cases of any kind, except to allow an employee the initial and sole option in adverse action cases as to whether to use the negotiated grievance procedure or an optional one such as the MSPB.

3. Discrimination cases should be handled as they are in the private sector, which assumes a trial de novo after either arbitration or MSPB handling without further ado.

4. The FLRA should require that any nonparty move to intervene if it wishes to participate in FLRA proceedings, and the FLRA should make its own decision.

5. The Comptroller General should be finally and fully eliminated as a factor in grievance and arbitration determinations. If fraud is alleged, already existing criminal process should be used.

6. Subpoena power of the arbitrator should be made specific.

These are relatively simple notions. But within the federal service, if they were to be adopted, the grievance and arbitration

---

[83]Lack of union security fee protection, in the end, may denigrate any effort to move federal service employee representation to the quality and quantity of that provided in the private sector, even as to those matters which may be bargained about or grieved. See note 78 *supra.*

process would then more fully and fairly mirror the traditional arbitration process which has been so successful for resolving commercial disputes for the last four centuries, and labor disputes for at least the last two generations.

APPENDICES

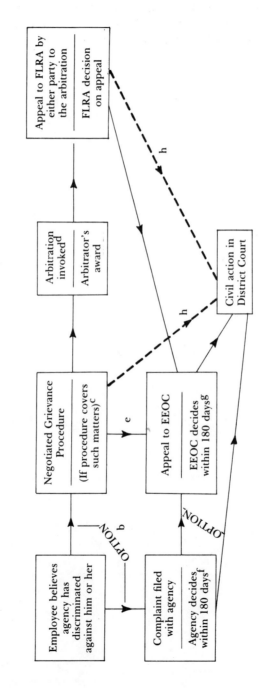

Pure Discrimination Case[a]

Employee believes agency has discriminated against him or her

b OPTION

Negotiated Grievance Procedure
_____
(If procedure covers such matters)[c]

Arbitration invoked[d]
_____
Arbitrator's award

Appeal to FLRA by either party to the arbitration
_____
FLRA decision on appeal

Complaint filed with agency
_____
Agency decides within 180 days[f]

OPTION

Appeal to EEOC
_____
EEOC decides within 180 days[g]

e

Civil action in District Court

h

h

Prepared by Arbitration Division, Federal Labor Relations Authority (B. Harris).

[a] An allegation of discrimination that does not also involve a matter appealable to MSPB.

[b] A complaint of discrimination may, in the discretion of the aggrieved employee, be raised under a statutory procedure or the negotiated grievance procedure, but not both. An employee shall be deemed to have exercised his option at such time as the employee timely initiates an action under the applicable statutory procedure or timely files a grievance in writing under the provisions of the grievance procedure, whichever occurs first. [5 U.S.C. §7121(d).]

[c] Any collective bargaining agreement may exclude any matter from the application of the grievance procedures. [5 U.S.C. §7121(a)(2).]

[d] A grievance not satisfactorily settled under the negotiated grievance procedure shall be subject to binding arbitration which may be invoked by either the exclusive representative or the agency. [5 U.S.C. §7121(b)(3)(C).]

[e] Selection of the negotiated procedure in no manner prejudices the right of an aggrieved employee to request EEOC to review a final decision in a matter involving a complaint of discrimination of the type prohibited by any law administered by EEOC. Such "final decision" could conceivably come at a step of the grievance procedure prior to arbitration. [5 U.S.C. §7121(d).]

[f] An employee may file a civil action in an appropriate district court after 180 calendar days from the date of filing a complaint with his agency if there has been no decision. [42 U.S.C. §200e–16(c).]

[g] An employee may file a civil action in an appropriate district court after 180 calendar days from the date of filing an appeal with EEOC if there has been no EEOC decision. [42 U.S.C. §2000e–16(c); Reorganization Plan No. 1 of 1978.]

[h] An employee has an option, after a final agency action on his or her complaint of discrimination, to appeal to EEOC or to file a civil action in an appropriate district court (see figure). It is unclear as to whether this option exists if the employee chooses to pursue the matter through the negotiated grievance procedure since 5 U.S.C. §7121(d) only refers to the right of an employee to request EEOC to review a final decision. Thus it may be that an employee who chose the grievance procedure would have to go to EEOC before he or she could go to a district court.

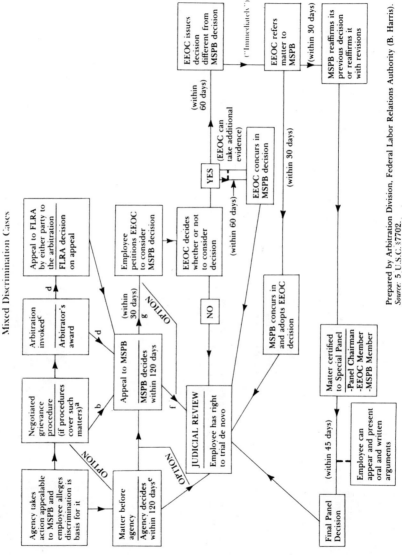

Mixed Discrimination Cases

Prepared by Arbitration Division, Federal Labor Relations Authority (B. Harris).
Source: 5, U.S.C. §7702.

aAny collective bargaining agreement may exclude any matter from the application of the grievance procedures. [5 U.S.C. §7121(a)(2).]

bSelection of the negotiated procedure in no manner prejudices the right of an aggrieved employee to request MSPB to review the final decision. Such "final decision" could conceivably come at a step of the grievance procedure prior to arbitration. [5 U.S.C. §7121(d).]

cA grievance not satisfactorily settled under the negotiated grievance procedure shall be subject to binding arbitration which may be invoked by either the exclusive representative or the agency. [5 U.S.C. §7121(b)(3)(C).]

dEither party to arbitration may file an exception to any arbitration award with FLRA except for an award relating to a reduction in grade or removal for unacceptable performance (5 U.S.C. §4303); or a removal, suspension for more than 14 days, a reduction in grade or pay, or a furlough of 30 days or less (5 U.S.C. §7512). Awards involving these matters may be appealed directly to MSPB. [5 U.S.C. §7122(a); 5 U.S.C. §7121(d).]

eIf the agency doesn't decide within 120 days, an employee may appeal the matter to MSPB or file a civil action in court. [5 U.S.C. §7202(e)(2); 5 U.S.C. §7702(e)(1)(A).]

fAn employee may obtain judicial review of the MSPB decision if the employee doesn't choose to petition EEOC to consider the decision. Also, the employee may file a civil action in court if MSPB doesn't decide within 120 days. [5 U.S.C. §7702(a)(3)(A); 5 U.S.C. §7702(e)(1)(B).]

gFrom this point on, if this path is followed, the total time frame for all the remaining steps may not exceed 180 days or the employee may file a civil action in court. [5 U.S.C. §7702(e)(1)(C).]

House-Senate Conference Committee Report on CSRA

Appealable Actions in Which Allegation of Discrimination Has Been Raised

Both the Senate bill and the House amendment adopt special procedures for resolving appealable actions where an allegation of discrimination is raised. The Senate bill provides that, whenever an issue of discrimination is raised in the course of a hearing before the Board, the Board must notify the EEOC and the EEOC has the right to participate fully in the proceeding. After action by the Board, the EEOC has an opportunity to review the decision and revise it. The Board may then accept the EEOC's decision, or issue a new one. Where the two agencies are unable to agree, the matter is immediately certified to the Court of Appeals for resolution. Before the Court of Appeals, the expertise of both the MSPB and the EEOC is to be given weight in their respective areas of jurisdiction. While the matter is pending in the Court, the EEOC is authorized to grant interim relief to the employee.

The House amendment allows the EEOC to delegate to the MSPB authority to make a preliminary determination in an adverse action in which discrimination has been raised, but it directs the EEOC to make the final determination in such cases. The decision of the EEOC constitutes final administrative determination in the matter, and there is no further review in the courts, unless the employee decides to appeal.

The conference substitute in section 7702 adopts the Senate approach at the administrative level, with some modifications, but it places an administrative tribunal, ad hoc in nature, at the apex of the administrative process, rather than depending upon the Court of Appeals to resolve conflicts between the two agencies. The conference substitute maintains the principle of parity between the MSPB and the EEOC and establishes an appropriate balance in regard to the enforcement of both the merit system principles of Title 5 of the United States Code and Title VII of the Civil Rights Act of 1964 and other laws prohibiting discrimination. At the same time it preserves for EEOC, as proposed in Reorganization Plan No. 1 of 1978, authority for issuing general policy directives implementing Title VII of the Civil Rights Act. This preserves an important policy role for EEOC which it may invoke, consistent with the requirements of law, regardless of the outcome of a particular case. The conference substitute also protects the existing rights of an employee to trial de novo under the Civil Rights Act after a final agency action or if there is no administrative decision after a specified number of days.

Appeals Procedure

This section applies to both employees and applicants. In all mixed cases, that is, cases involving any action that could be appealed to the MSPB and which involve an allegation of discrimination, the MSPB will hold hearings and issue a decision on both the issue of discrimination and the appealable action. The EEOC will not participate in this proceeding. The term "decision" as used throughout this section includes any remedial order the agency or panel may impose under law.

It is expected that the Board will make adequate training and resources available for the training and supervision of these appeals officers provided for in section 7702(a) to avoid the possibility of inadequate preparation for the processing of those appeals matters which involve allegations of discrimination.

The decision of the Board shall be final agency action unless the employee files a petition with the EEOC to reconsider the case. In the case of class actions, the law generally governing the right of one or more members to appeal an initial decision shall be applicable in this case as well. If the EEOC decides to reconsider the MSPB decision, it may remand the case to the Board for further hearing or provide for its own supplemental hearing as it deems necessary to supplement the record. This amends the procedures established in the Senate bill which did not allow the EEOC to take additional evidence. In making a new decision, the EEOC must determine that: (1) the MSPB decision constitutes an incorrect interpretation of any law, rule, or regulation over which the EEOC has jurisdiction; or (2) the application of such law to the evidence in the record is unsupported by such evidence as a matter of law.

If the EEOC concurs in the decision of the Board, including the remedy ordered by the MSPB, then the decision of the Board shall be final agency action in the matter. If the EEOC decision differs from the MSPB decision, then the case must be referred back to the MSPB. The MSPB may accept the EEOC decision, or if the MSPB determines that the EEOC decision

(1) constitutes an incorrect interpretation of any civil service law, rule, or regulation; or (2) the application of such law to the evidence in the record is unsupported by such evidence, as a matter of law, it may reaffirm its initial decision with such revisions as it deems appropriate.

If the Board does not adopt the order of the EEOC, the matter will immediately be certified to the special three-member panel. The panel will review the entire administrative record of the proceeding, and give due deference to the expertise of each agency in reaching a decision. The employee and the agency against whom the complaint was filed may appear before the panel in person, or through an attorney or other representative. The decision of the special panel will be the final agency action in the matter.

Upon application by the employee, the EEOC may, as in the Senate bill, issue certain interim relief as it determines appropriate, to mitigate any exceptional hardship the employee might incur. The bill establishes mandatory time limits to govern the maximum length of time the employing agency, the MSPB, the EEOC, or the Panel may take to resolve the matter at each step in the process. The Act makes compliance with these deadlines mandatory—not discretionary—in order to assure the employee the right to have as expeditious a resolution of the matter as possible. The conferees fully expect the agencies to devote the resources and planning necessary to assure compliance with these statutory deadlines. The bill imposes a statutory requirement that the delays that have been experienced in the past in processing discrimination complaints will be eliminated. Where an agency has not completed action by the time required by this statute it shall immediately take all necessary steps to rapidly complete action on the matter.

It is not intended that the employing agencies, the Board, the Commission, or the special panel would automatically lose jurisdiction for failing to meet these time frames. Congress will exercise its oversight responsibilities should there be a systematic pattern of anybody failing to meet these time frames.

Rights of Employees Under Civil Rights Act

The conference substitute fully protects the existing rights of employees to trial de novo under Title VII of the Civil Rights

Act of 1964 or other similar laws after a final agency action on the matter. Under the Act's provisions, this final agency action must occur within 120 days after the complaint is first filed. After these 120 days, the employee may appeal to the Board or file a complaint in district court in those cases where the agency in violation of the law has not issued a final decision. If the employee files an appeal of the agency action with MSPB, the employee may file a suit in district court any time after 120 days if the Board has not completed action on the matter by that time. Finally, the Act gives the employee the right to sue in district court 180 days after it petitions EEOC to review the decision of MSPB even if the administrative process is not completed by that time, as required by other provisions in the section. Once the employee files a petition with EEOC, however, it may not bring an action in district court until the end of this 180-day period, or until there is final agency action on the matter.

There are in all eight different times when the employee may have the right to bring suit in Federal district court. They are as follows:

1. 120 days after filing a complaint with the employing agency even if the agency has not issued a final decision by that time.

2. 30 days after the employing agency's initial decision.

3. 120 days after filing a petition with the MSPB if the MSPB has not yet made a decision.

4. 30 days after an MSPB decision. If the employee petitions EEOC to review the matter and EEOC denies the petition, the 30-day period in this case runs from the denial of such a petition by EEOC.

5. 30 days after the EEOC decision, if EEOC agrees with the MSPB.

6. 30 days after MSPB reconsideration if MSPB agrees with the EEOC.

7. 30 days after the special panel makes a decision.

8. 180 days after filing a petition with the EEOC for reconsideration of an MSPB decision, if a final agency decision by EEOC, MSPB, or the Panel has not been reached by that time.

If a suit is brought in district court, the rules of equity provide that minor procedural irregularities in the administrative process for which the employee is responsible should not predetermine the outcome of the case.

Special Panel

The special panel will be comprised of one member of the EEOC designated on an ad hoc basis by the Chairman of the EEOC, one member of the MSPB designated on an ad hoc basis by the Chairman of the MSPB, and a permanent chairman who will be an individual from outside the government. The members appointed by EEOC and MSPB to represent the agency in a particular case must be able to represent the views and decisions of the majority of the Board or Commission in that particular case. The chairman will be appointed by the President with the advice and consent of the Senate to a term of six years, and shall be removable only for cause.

The MSPB and the EEOC shall make available to the panel appropriate and adequate administrative resources to carry out its responsibilities under this Act. The cost of such services must, to the extent practicable, be shared equally by EEOC and MSPB.

Because it is anticipated that the special panel will not have to be convened often, the conferees do not expect that it will need substantial resources or administrative support. For instance, the EEOC, because it is larger could provide a convenient place for the panel to meet.

Comment—

JAMES M. HARKLESS*

In his paper John Kagel has cogently outlined for us the new grievance arbitration system in federal-sector employment under the Civil Service Reform Act (CSRA) and compared it to the one that has developed in private-sector employment in this country, primarily since the 1940s. I have no major quarrel with this analysis. However, since receiving Kagel's paper some weeks ago, I have had a problem figuring out why his comment in the title ends with a question mark. I haven't been able to. Therefore, I think it permissible for me to preface my reaction to the main thrust of his paper with a rhetorical question: "So what did you expect already?"

---

*Member, National Academy of Arbitrators, Washington, D. C.

By this response I am suggesting that the employment relationships in the federal service, and the collective bargaining
agreements under the CSRA and the predecessor Executive
Orders which permitted them, are so controlled and affected by
various statutes, rules, and regulations that grievance arbitration within that system necessarily cannot be final and binding
as in the private sector; that to the extent that an arbitrator is
required to interpret external law in order to resolve a grievance
in the federal sector, such a decision should properly be subject
to full review by public bodies charged with the responsibility of
assuring uniform application and interpretation of public policy.
There is no doubt that private arbitrators in the federal sector
not only interpret and apply the terms of the parties' agreement,
but also must consider the provisions of any applicable laws and
regulations. Hence, what has developed in the federal sector
since Executive Order 10988 first granted organizational and
bargaining rights to federal employees in 1962, up to the enactment of CSRA in 1978 which refines and codifies this program,
is another step toward what David Feller described in his classic
thesis at the Academy's 1976 Annual Meeting as "the coming
end of arbitration's golden age."[1]

I realize that Feller was talking about arbitration in the private
sector, and he made it clear that he was referring to the potential
diminution of the special position arbitrators have enjoyed in
this country particularly since the U.S. Supreme Court issued
the *Steelworkers Trilogy* in 1960.[2] As one whose thinking in this
field was lastingly influenced as a third-year law student in attendance at Dean Shulman's great lecture on "Reason, Contract
and Law"[3] in private arbitration systems, I tend to agree with
Feller's observations about the effect of the interposition of
external law on questions arising under private-sector collective
bargaining agreements and his admonition that arbitrators in
this sector should stick to interpreting the terms of the agreement and avoid deciding disputed questions of external law
where the two conflict. However, Feller's arguments and analy-

---

[1]Feller, *The Coming End of Arbitration's Golden Age,* in Arbitration—1976, Proceedings
of the 29th Annual Meeting, National Academy of Arbitrators (Washington: BNA Books,
1976), 97.
[2]*Steelworkers* v. *American Mfg. Co.,* 363 U.S. 564, 46 LRRM 2414 (1960); *Steelworkers* v.
Warrior & Gulf Navigation Co., 363 U.S. 574, 46 LRRM 2416 (1960); *Steelworkers* v.
Enterprise Wheel & Car Corp., 363 U.S. 593, 46 LRRM 2423 (1960).
[3]68 Harv. L. Rev. 999 (1955).

sis also are instructive on why decisions of arbitrators in the federal sector should not be granted the same special status of limited judicial review as in the private sector, except in those instances where the arbitrator is dealing only with interpretation and application of the terms of the collective bargaining agreement.

Feller stated "that arbitration is a substitute for a strike"; that "the parties to the collective bargaining process have substituted for the strike . . . a system of adjudication against the standards set forth in that agreement; but that system of adjudication, since it is not a substitute for litigation, is not the same in principle, historical background, or effect, as the system of adjudication used by the courts to resolve controversies over the meaning and application of contracts."[4] He went on to say:

> "Essential to the Golden Age of Arbitration was the proposition that the rights of employees and employers with respect to the employment relationship are governed by an autonomous, self-contained system of private law. That system consists of a statute, the collective bargaining agreement, and an adjudicatory mechanism, the grievance and arbitration machinery, integral with the statute and providing only the remedial powers granted, expressly or impliedly, in the statute."[5]

Feller then reasoned:

> ". . . that an arbitrator, as the adjudicator of rights under the rules established by a collective bargaining agreement, performs quite a different function from a court in construing a contract of employment. There are a whole set of implicit relationships, not spelled out in the agreement and not confined to any particular employer, which an arbitrator assumes to exist. His so-called expertise is not so much expertise as it is knowledge of the fact that the parties have not called upon him to act as a court in adjudicating a breach-of-contract action, but to act as—perhaps there is no better word—an arbitrator.
> "It is this unique aspect of arbitration, I think, from which the deference of courts to arbitration decisions derives, and this derivation explains why such deference is awarded only when arbitrators remain within their particular area of concern, of jurisdiction if you will—that is, the interpretation and application of the collective agreement. . . ."[6]

---

[4]Feller, *supra* note 1, at 100–101.
[5]Feller, *supra* note 1, at 102–103.
[6]Feller, *supra* note 1, at 106.

He then concluded:

"Thus, the very special status that courts have awarded arbitrators has little to do with speed or informality or, indeed, the special expertise of arbitrators. The status derives from a not always explicitly stated recognition that arbitration is not a substitute for judicial adjudication, but a part of a system of industrial self-governance."[7]

While there are some similarities between this private grievance arbitration system, as Feller describes it, and the federal-sector system which has been patterned after it, the differences are more significant and substantial. Grievance arbitration in the federal system is not a substitute for a strike because federal employees have never had that right. The grievance arbitration system in the federal sector is an adjudicatory one to assure compliance with the collective bargaining agreement, but it is more than that. As the Elkouris point out in their supplement to *How Arbitration Works*, it "is to review or police compliance with controlling laws, rules and regulations by federal agency employers and employees alike."[8] The Elkouris also note that:

"Arbitral disposition of federal-sector grievances will often be governed or materially affected by laws, rules, and regulations apart from the collective bargaining agreement; another highly significant factor is that important areas of unilateral management control in the federal sector exist by statute. For some matters in the federal sector, the collective agreement and custom cannot be made the controlling 'law of the plant.' "[9]

I believe it is because of these differences between federal and public-sector grievance arbitration that federal-sector grievance arbitration decisions should not be accorded the same deference as in the private sector.

This is illustrated by one of the cases to which Kagel referred: *National Council of Field Labor Locals of the AFGE and U.S. Department of Labor.*[10] There, an NAA member ruled that a probationary employee's grievance contesting his termination was not arbitrable. The issue turned completely on the interpretation of applicable statutes. The FLRA reversed the decision essentially on the basis that this interpretation was incorrect. Whether or

---

[7]Feller, *supra* note 1, at 107.
[8]Elkouri and Elkouri, Legal Status of Federal Sector Arbitration, supp. to How Arbitration Works, 3d ed., 1980, 7.
[9]*Id.*
[10]4 FLRA No. 51, issued Sept. 30, 1980.

not one agrees with the reasoning of the arbitrator or the FLRA, it is manifest that a final and binding decision on such a question involving public policy should not be left to a private arbitrator, but should be made by the public body or bodies charged with this function.

Recently the Government Employee Relations Report noted that of the 48 arbitration awards which FLRA has reviewed, five have been found deficient.[11] This is a much lower percentage of reversals or modifications than experienced under the Executive Order. However, the percentage of arbitration decisions appealed to the FLRA is still high. I suspect that this will change and there will be more willingness by the unsuccessful party in an arbitration case to accept it as final and binding, if the current trend in FLRA reversals or modifications continues.

As Kagel has noted, there are some grievances in the federal sector that are subject to court review. Such review in discrimination cases is similar to what would occur in the private sector. However, in adverse actions where an employee is removed or reduced in grade for unacceptable performance, the CSRA mandates that the arbitrator, in considering a grievance on such a matter, can reverse the agency decision only if it is not supported by substantial evidence. I am not certain whether this differs from the "clear and convincing" test that most arbitrators appear to use in discipline and discharge cases. However, it definitely is a change from the "beyond a reasonable doubt" test that some arbitrators apply in certain kinds of discharge cases. In footnote 9 of his paper, Kagel refers to an article in the Labor Law Journal which contains a good discussion of this subject and suggests the substantial-evidence test is similar to the clear-and-convincing rule. To date, no court rulings on arbitration awards in this area have come down. However, it is important, as Kagel has indicated, that arbitrators know of the statutory standard on burden of proof in these cases and properly apply it.

I will leave for John Shearer any comments on Kagel's criticism of the Comptroller General's role in reviewing arbitration decisions. However, I believe this presents much less of a problem with the 1978 amendments to the Back Pay Act and now that the Comptroller General has stopped acting like a bull in a china shop.

---

[11]908 GERR 9 (April 13, 1981).

Comment—

JOHN C. SHEARER*

John Kagel's paper presents me with an awkward situation. Perhaps the most important role of a discussant is to alert the listener or reader to any shortcomings in the paper. If that is all I were to do, I could not justify my trip to Maui. Except for a few relatively minor points on which I have a different view, I have little but praise for this paper. It is scholarly, yet very readable. It deals with matters far more complex than in other areas of arbitration, yet does so clearly and crisply. It fills a vital need in our understanding of an increasingly important area of arbitral activity.

Only in one major area of the paper do I have a significantly different view. Before dealing with it I shall make a few general comments on dispute settlement in the federal sector. Then I shall take issue with a few minor items in the paper and cite a few ways in which I try to deal with some of the major problems Kagel discusses. Finally, I shall present my different views on the matter of remedy and the role of the Comptroller General in reviewing remedies designed by arbitrators.

My reactions to Kagel's paper are those of one who comes from a background of industrial relations and economics rather than law. As such, on the question of external law and private-sector arbitration I am among those who consider external law as generally beyond the scope of private-sector arbitration. In the private sector, my role and my competence are limited to the interpretation and application of the collective bargaining agreement. The courts, not I, are in the business of interpreting law. However, if I consider a legal matter germane to my resolution of a contractual dispute, I do not shrink from applying law, but only if I consider that law to be clear and unambiguous and, therefore, not in need of interpretation. Although I am neither a court of law nor an attorney, I can read and understand clear English. If, on the other hand, the language of the law is not clear and unambiguous as it relates to my contractual issue, I certainly do not presume to interpret it for my arbitral purposes.

Federal-sector arbitration is, of course, a very different mat-

---

*Member, National Academy of Arbitrators; Professor of Economics and Director, Manpower Research and Training Center, Oklahoma State University, Stillwater, Okla.

ter. When I accept a federal case, I am bound by its rules, and the Civil Service Reform Act clearly states that upon review by the Federal Labor Relations Authority my award will be found deficient if it be "contrary to any law, rule or regulation."[1] This adds the word "rule" to the language of Executive Order 11491, which had specified as grounds for a deficiency the violation of "applicable law, appropriate regulation or the order." I know what a law is and what a federal regulation is, but I do not know, nor have I been able to find out, what Congress meant by adding the word "rule" to the list of what arbitrators' awards may not violate. Does "rule" include any work rule that management might promulgate unilaterally, even if it be contrary to the terms of the labor agreement? Fortunately, I have not yet had a case that involves the concept of "rule." If such a case comes along and if the parties do not want an amateur in legal matters thrashing about in this thicket, they should not select me as their arbitrator.

Of course, the parties may spell out in their agreement what rules they agree to bind themselves to. I quote an agreement between an Air Force base and a local of the American Federation of Government Employees:

> "In the administration of all matters covered by the Agreement, officials and employees are governed by existing or future laws and the regulations of appropriate authorities, including policies set forth in the Federal Personnel Manual, by published agency policies and regulations in existence at the time the Agreement was approved, and by subsequently published agency policies and regulations required by law or by the regulations of appropriate authorities, or authorized by the terms of a controlling agreement at a higher agency level."

That is a long list of what, in addition to the content of the agreement, binds both the parties and the arbitrator.

It seems to me that the very broad definition of a grievance which the CSRA specifies is consistent with the obligation of the arbitrator, and especially of the parties, to deal with disputes not only with respect to the terms of the agreement, but also with respect to, in the words of the CSRA, "any law, rule, or regulation affecting conditions of employment."[2] This legal requirement generally works to the advantage of the union, for it

---

[1] 5 U.S.C. §7122(a)(1).
[2] 5 U.S.C. §7103(a)(9).

greatly enlarges beyond the labor agreement their hunting ground for management violations.

As one who believes firmly that arbitration must be final and binding to be of greatest value to the parties and to society, I have been greatly distressed by the fact that federal-sector arbitration lacks this essential characteristic. As Kagel's paper skillfully describes, federal dispute settlement can be a nightmare of appeals within appeals in which the arbitrator's award on some issues may be merely one of many steps in a cumbersome, highly legalistic labyrinth which might delight bureaucrats but which makes a travesty of dispute settlement.

The monster Congress has created here seems in keeping with the cumbersome procedures it previously designed to deal with industrial relations matters, and which contrast sharply with the simple and effective procedures in the private sector. For example, it is not possible for federal agencies to deal with even minor disciplinary matters in an expeditious manner. Before imposing any disciplinary suspension, however brief, the employer must serve formal and detailed notice of the proposed action. The employee may then begin an appeals procedure on this proposed action. I had a case recently where it took management six months to impose discipline on two employees for sleeping on a critical security job, and that discipline was merely three days' suspension. In a similar private-sector situation these sleepers would most likely have been discharged or given lengthy suspensions immediately, with subsequent right to protest management's action.

To me the elaborate protections for employee rights which the federal sector has evolved over the years, and in the absence of effective unionism, now constitute a legacy of unnecessary and wasteful duplication of the protection of employee rights which effective unionism now provides.

I am not thoroughly versed in all relevant laws, rules, and regulations for each agency of the federal government. I am not a student of the Federal Personnel Manual. For me to become expert so that I might, on my own volition, apply all these things in any particular case would cost the parties considerable study time. If they want only arbitrators who are already independently expert, they should cross me off their lists. Practicality and principle argue strongly that it is the responsibility of the parties to acquaint the arbitrator with all the laws, rules, and regulations upon which they rely, including the basis upon which they might subsequently file an exception to the arbitration award.

Because I believe it to be the responsibility of the parties, and in their best interests, to acquaint the arbitrator, in the hearing, with all the relevant laws, rules, and regulations, I make a practice of so notifying them at the beginning of the hearing. I then include in my written opinion the following language:

> "At the hearing the arbitrator notified the parties that it was incumbent on them to present at the hearing 'any law, rule, or regulation' which they consider relevant to the arbitration proceeding or to any subsequent filing of an exception to the arbitration award. The following were all such citations presented at the hearing:"

Whereupon I list all citations and deal with them in my opinion.

Of course, this practice does not bar a party from filing an exception on some other basis, but it specifies my position and may be helpful to the FLRA in any subsequent review.

Now, some lesser points. Kagel discusses the lack of subpoena power by arbitrators. This has different consequences in the federal sector than elsewhere because of the Freedom of Information Act. Under it the employer can be compelled to release documents to the union. In one of my cases involving the Federal Aviation Administration, prior to the arbitration hearing the union had, by expending considerable effort and time, compelled the employer to release to it management's internal memos concerning their strategy on the dispute to be arbitrated. Although the effect of the Freedom of Information Act may be one-sided, I doubt that ordinary subpoena procedures could produce such privileged communications.

Kagel recommends that the arbitrator insist on transcripts, because his is the first link in one or more appellate chains. I do not do so because I regard this as entirely the province of the parties. In my experience, the same parties have different practices at different locations. For me to insist upon transcripts might facilitate challenges to my awards, which I would prefer to be as final and binding as possible.

Kagel's discussion of remedy did not mention one key peculiarity of federal-sector arbitration: the doctrine of "but for." The Back Pay Act of 1966 governs back pay to federal employees. The primary requirement is that once a violation by the employer has been found, in order for back pay to be awarded, there must also be a concomitant and specific finding that but for that violation by the employer, the grievant would have received certain pay that he or she did not receive. This "but for" test is especially significant in promotion cases because an agency has the right to select or not to select from a group of employees on a promotion roster. It is one thing for an arbitrator to find that the employer erred in promoting employee "A"; it is quite another for the arbitrator to award the promotion to the grievant when that person was only one of several other candidates on the promotion roster and the employer is free to reject any of them.

I recently had such a case wherein the evidence persuaded me that "but for" a violation by the Veterans Administration of the regulations dealing with promotion procedures, the grievant would have gotten that promotion. My opinion and award made ample use of the magic term "but for." This case was the only one of my cases which I know to have been reviewed by the FLRA. Its decision, which sustained my award on all counts, also made heavy use of the term "but for."

Kagel's paper expresses considerable concern about the limitations placed on the arbitrator's power to fashion appropriate remedies, ultimately by review of the Comptroller General as to the legality of public expenditure ordered by a third party. Philosophically, I share this concern. However, because legal requirements pervade the use of arbitration in the federal sector, I am not persuaded that there should be an exception for such an important matter as the legality of public expenditures ordered by an arbitrator.

A technique I have used for many years in private-sector arbitration is useful also in the federal sector. At the conclusion of the hearing I routinely ask the union for a precise statement of the remedy they seek. I then offer the employer the opportunity to comment, if it chooses to do so, upon the appropriateness of the remedy sought by the union. I make it clear that any such comment, or lack of comment, on the part of the employer has no implications for the merits of the case. If I sustain the grievance, I often find employer comments to be helpful in fashioning an appropriate remedy while avoiding unintended complications for one or both parties. In the federal sector this same procedure sometimes calls to my attention legal requirements as to remedy which might not otherwise be known to me.

Kagel points to the high cost in employer time and money

when an employee, after losing in arbitration, takes a token claim of discrimination into any of the numerous avenues of appeal for de novo hearings. I would modify his point to the effect that this is taxpayer money which can be lavished on multiple and, I fear, frequently pointless reviews of discrimination and of other grievable matters.

Correspondingly, there seems little reason for employers to prefer finality in arbitration when the costs of appeals are ultimately borne by the taxpayers. I would like to see an objective study of the costs and benefits of dispute settlement procedures in the federal sector. I suspect that the results might be persuasive to an economy-minded administration and Congress to simplify and rationalize dispute settlement procedures, including the restoration of arbitration to a role more closely approximating its key role in the private sector.

I would, therefore, add such a cost-benefit analysis to Kagel's suggestions for improving federal-sector arbitration. I like his suggestions, but I find unrealistic his suggestion No. 5, which would eliminate the Comptroller General as a factor in arbitration. Even if law, rule, and regulation did not dominate the arbitration process, the Comptroller General has the legal obligation to guard the public purse against the ordering by an arbitrator of an illegal expenditure. It would take bold action by Congress, that might raise interesting constitutional questions, to exempt expenditures ordered by arbitrators from the general legal requirements.

I would add another suggestion, designed to discourage the filing of exceptions to arbitration awards. I would like to see a procedure worked out whereby explicit costs are imposed on parties who file exceptions. Perhaps some schedule of heavy fees might be utilized, or a system devised whereby only the loser of such an appeal pays for exercising this right. This might discourage the parties from taking the position they did with me in a recent case. There was a complex threshold issue of arbitrability that involved a matter of two bites at the apple. The employer claimed that the union had lost in an unfair labor practice proceeding and was thereby barred from pursuing the same matter through the grievance procedure and arbitration. The union claimed that the matters at issue were different. Neither party was able to find any precedent, but both announced emphatically that whichever way I ruled on arbitrability, the loser would file an exception. This intent to appeal, before having my decision and reasoning, should be discouraged by making it costly for a party to pursue a weak appeal.

In conclusion, I repeat that I feel that Kagel has done an admirable job of putting into perspective the complex environment in which arbitrators must work in the federal sector. His paper is very helpful to us in discharging our responsibilities in the interests of the parties, the public, and the arbitration process.

CHAPTER 6

HOW OTHERS VIEW US AND VICE VERSA: ADMINISTRATIVE AND JUDICIAL CRITIQUES OF THE ARBITRATION PROCESS

I. ARBITRATION OF TITLE VII CLAIMS: SOME JUDICIAL PERCEPTIONS

BETTY BINNS FLETCHER*

In the last 10 or 12 years, a great deal has been written and said about the role of arbitration and arbitrators in employment discrimination disputes. Several speakers have previously addressed this body on the subject. Many of the problems focused on in these discussions have been settled for us by the Supreme Court in *Alexander* v. *Gardner-Denver Co.,* [1] reinforced by *Barrentine* v. *Arkansas-Best Freight System, Inc.,* [2] a Fair Labor Standards Act case, decided in April of this year. It is now clear, at least, that resort to arbitration never precludes an employee alleging employment discrimination from bringing his or her claim to court. How this doctrine will be applied to employees' claims of unfair labor practices is not at all clear, but that is a subject for another talk.

From the arbitrator's point of view—and indeed from the court's point of view—many questions remain unanswered. Employment discrimination is a rapidly changing and developing field of law, so it is hardly surprising that arbitrators and courts alike, to say nothing of unions, employees, and employers, are continually faced with new and unresolved problems—problems of procedure as well as of substance.

To say that an employee never, or almost never, waives his claim of discrimination by going to arbitration tells us little about what does or should happen in arbitration, or about how the court should treat the arbitration in subsequent litigation. Among the more serious questions which remain are: Should

---

*Circuit Judge, United States Court of Appeals, Ninth Circuit, Seattle, Wash.
[1]415 U.S. 36, 7 FEP Cases 81 (1974).
[2]49 U.S. LW 4347 (April 6, 1981).

arbitration deal with claims of discrimination at all? Are unions competent or motivated to represent employees making discrimination claims? Are arbitrators competent to consider questions of public law? All of these questions could be subsumed in one basic question: What is the role of private bargaining and grievance arbitration in eliminating discrimination in the workplace?

The nature of the problem is graphically illustrated by the Supreme Court's decision in *Emporium Capwell Co.* v. *Western Addition Community Organization.* [3] Several black employees of the Emporium claimed that the Emporium systematically discriminated against blacks in hiring and promotion. The union agreed to file grievances on behalf of the employees and to investigate the charges of racial discrimination. The grievants, however, expressed the view that the grievance and arbitration machinery was inadequate to deal with a systematic problem, and they ultimately refused to participate in the arbitration. Four of the grievants then sought a personal interview with the president of the company. When this was refused, they picketed the store to protest the company's alleged racism. When the minority employees repeatedly refused to stop picketing, they were fired.

Western Addition Community Organization filed an unfair labor practice charge with the NLRB on behalf of the strikers. The Board ultimately held that the discharged employees had been seeking to bargain separately with the company over the concerns of minority employees. This, in the Board's view, threatened to undermine the ability of the union, the exclusive bargaining representative, to bargain with the employer. The picketing was therefore unprotected activity and could properly be the basis of discharge.[4] The District of Columbia Court of Appeals disagreed with the Board and refused to enforce its decision.[5]

The Supreme Court, in turn, reversed the D.C. Circuit and agreed with the Board. In the course of its opinion, the Supreme Court made a number of interesting observations. It pointed out in a footnote that the employees could have, but did not, file a charge with the EEOC.[6] It also noted that no showing had been

[3]420 U.S. 50, 88 LRRM 2660 (1975).
[4]192 NLRB No. 19, 77 LRRM 1669 (1971).
[5]485 F.2d 917, 83 LRRM 2738 (D.C.Cir. 1973).
[6]420 U.S. at 65, note 16.

made that the statutory procedures were too cumbersome to be effective. The Court concluded that the contractual grievance-arbitration machinery, together with the nondiscrimination clause in the contract, was adequate to deal with the problem; and if it was not, under *Gardner-Denver* the claimants would not be precluded from bringing their claim in court. Finally, importantly, and indeed I think most surprisingly to some, the Court held that the employees' substantive rights under Title VII cannot be pursued at the expense of orderly collective bargaining under the NLRA.

The decision obviously implicates a number of policy questions and brings immediately to mind a host of problems. The Court is telling us apparently that minority employees may file charges with the EEOC (or the state agency), or may proceed through their union's contractual grievance-and-arbitration machinery, or may do both, but that they may not work outside the union or statutory procedures to correct what would clearly be unlawful employment practices. Yet the Supreme Court, in *Vaca* v. *Sipes*[7] and elsewhere, has acknowledged that unions themselves have frequently participated in the discrimination proscribed by Title VII. Furthermore, although the union is held to a "duty of fair representation," as a practical matter it must also represent the majority interest or risk losing its support. Are the courts putting unions in an impossible position? Frequently a Title VII claimant's rights must be vindicated at the expense of other employees who have previously benefited from the employer's discrimination. And yet the union is duty-bound to protect those employees as well as those discriminated against.

If the union is unable or unwilling to press the discrimination claim as vigorously as the employee thinks necessary, the employee is relegated to the statutory machinery. However this pursuit, unlike arbitration, must be at the employee's expense; arbitration, of course, is paid for by the union and the employer. A litigated Title VII action frequently consumes three years or more, first in the EEOC's efforts to conciliate, then in the process of discovery and trial. As a result, our court (the Ninth Circuit) is currently considering acts of discrimination which occurred many years ago. The strain a Title VII suit puts on the litigants and their employment relationships is notorious. I understand from practitioners that their clients rarely remain employed by the employer they sue.

---

[7]386 U.S. 171, 64 LRRM 2369 (1967).

I cannot help but think that an employer in the Emporium's position might have been better off dealing directly with the dissatisfied employees, if that were the price of avoiding a Title VII suit. Certainly the minority employees might have fared better, and the union, too, might have escaped a sticky wicket. But the question I want to discuss with you is how arbitration could be made to better serve the parties in cases involving discrimination, and to focus on how the arbitral process has operated in the context of discrimination-based complaints and how it might operate better. The conduct of the *Emporium* employees in end-running both the union and the proposed arbitration is at least evidence of a perception on the part of the employees either that the union was not fully representing them, or that the arbitration process would not serve their best interests. They could have been wrong on either or both scores.

In quest of support for some of my hunches I have been reading in foreign territory for me—arbitration opinions. I must say I find them interesting fare.

In my brief and admittedly very unscientific review of the decisions reported in BNA's Labor Arbitration Reports for the last three years, I have arrived at some interesting conclusions. First, as I'm sure you are aware (which I was not), a large proportion of the reported disputes involve employment discrimination claims. And this is four to six years after the *Gardner-Denver* decision; the fears expressed by the Sixth Circuit in *Dewey* v. *Reynolds Metals Co.*,[8] to the effect that arbitration would not be used if employees got another bite of the apple in a court proceeding, have not been borne out. Neither employers nor unions appear reluctant to use the arbitration machinery to solve Title VII problems, even though the grievant can bring the claim again in court. Almost every decision I read, by the way, involved a nondiscrimination clause in the contract, as well as some reference incorporating into the contract Title VII or similar state statutes. These findings were heartening.

Less heartening by far, I found what seemed to me very little uniformity in the way the arbitrators deal with discrimination claims. From one point of view, this is as it should be. The parties are free to order their contractual relations as they see fit; arbitration is attractive partly because the parties can make it serve their own ends. But that is not a sufficient answer to the

---

[8]429 F.2d 324, 332, 2 FEP Cases 687 (6th Cir. 1970).

problems raised by Title VII claims. The answer depends in part on what we want to accomplish with arbitration. It seems to me that there are several good reasons why arbitrators should be familiar with Title VII and should try to interpret contractual language so as to be consistent with it. If final resolution of the dispute is a goal of arbitration, and surely it should be, then the arbitrator's decision needs to deal with the discrimination claims in a way that minimizes the attractiveness of pursuing the matter in court. If the arbitrator takes too restricted a view of the rights of the grievant, the grievant may resort to litigation more often than might be necessary.

From the grievant's point of view, it is equally important that the arbitrator take as liberal a view of employees' rights as a court would, because the time, expense, and aggravation of a court suit may in fact, if not in law, make arbitration the forum of last resort for many.

Another good reason for the arbitrator to apply Title VII standards more or less as a court would is that that may very well be—should be presumed to be—what the parties intended. Many collective bargaining agreements today contain nondiscrimination clauses; many of these refer specifically to state and federal laws. While the parties probably did not intend for the arbitrator to invalidate contract clauses he or she finds inconsistent with public law (although this also has frequently been done), they probably did intend that the contract be read whenever possible to be consistent with the external law.

A fear which I have heard expressed is that arbitrators who are chosen by the parties, and who depend to some extent on their continued popularity with the parties, may not be willing to enforce fully the strictures of Title VII even if given the power. I am inclined to think such fears are overstated. As I have said, employers and employees have demonstrated their willingness to take Title VII claims to arbitration even after *Gardner-Denver.* If compliance with the demands of a fairly tough-minded arbitrator is the price of avoiding continued unrest and eventual litigation, I think the parties will be willing to accept the arbitrator's decision.

Whether the arbitrator is or should be competent to deal with discrimination claims is a more difficult question. Many arbitrators note in their decisions that they are neither competent nor empowered to interpret and apply external law. Others, by contrast, feel perfectly free to read and apply the statute even when it conflicts with the plain requirements of the contract. Occasionally the parties even request such a ruling. Most often, however, it appears that the arbitrator takes a middle ground: reading the contract in light of the perceived requirements of the statute. This is far preferable in my view to an approach which deliberately ignores external law, especially in those cases where the arbitrator knows the contract, as he or she interprets it, to be possibly or probably illegal. The latter approach is almost certain to lead to litigation sooner or later.

I think it bids fair that so many collective bargaining agreements now contain antidiscrimination clauses. But, as I indicated, I am concerned that the arbitrator's interpretation and enforcement of these clauses is anything but uniform.

Beyond lack of uniformity, the decisions I read suggest that some arbitrators are not familiar with Title VII or the case law surrounding it. One particular type of case I think illustrates the problems. These are the cases in which the employee complains of sexual harassment, something that has only recently been recognized as a violation of Title VII.[9]

While an employee could sue in court for damages due to sexual harassment even if she has not lost her job, in the arbitral context the focus of the dispute will usually be whether the employee was dismissed for nondiscriminatory reasons during the probationary period, for "just cause" thereafter, or denied a promotion for permissible reasons. Of course such a charge will be difficult to prove, either in court or in arbitration, except in the most egregious cases. But arbitrators seem to impose a much higher standard of proof on the grievant than would a court. This may in part have to do with the perceived requirements of the contract; for instance, less is required to discharge a probationary employee than an employee protected by a "just cause" provision. The burden of proof in arbitration is said to be on the probationary employee. Interestingly, however, a court would not make the same distinction. The burdens of proof would be allocated according to the dictates of *McDonnell Douglas Corp.* v. *Green,*[10] regardless of the nature of the action taken against the employee, or the employee's status.[11]

---

[9]See 29 C.F.R. §1604.11 (1980); *Bundy* v. *Jackson,* 24 FEP Cases 1155 (D.C.Cir. 1981); *Barnes* v. *Costle,* 561 F.2d 983 (D.C.Cir. 1977).

[10]411 U.S. 792, 5 FEP Cases 765 (1973). The Supreme Court clarified the requirements of *McDonnell Douglas* in *Texas Department of Community Affairs* v. *Burdine,* 101 S.Ct. 1089, 1093–1095, 25 FEP Cases 113 (1981).

[11]I do not mean to suggest that when a "just cause" provision imposes a higher standard of proof on an employer than a court would under Title VII, that the arbitrator should not apply the contract. The employee is certainly entitled at least to the measure of protection provided by the contract.

In one arbitral decision I read,[12] the arbitrator imposed on the probationary employee the entire burden of proving sexual harassment. He dismissed her testimony as "self-serving," and discounted the testimony of her coworkers. In particular he noted that there was no direct corroboration of the sexual demands allegedly made by her supervisor, although other portions of the grievant's testimony were corroborated. The arbitrator held that her dismissal was not shown to be discriminatory.

I am not suggesting that a court necessarily would ultimately have reached a different conclusion. However, the allegations of sexual demands, the testimony of coworkers, and the fact of the dismissal would at least have made out a prima facie case against the employer under *McDonnell Douglas*. The burden would then have been on the employer to show legitimate business reasons for the firing. The employee would then have had an opportunity to show that the reasons given by the employer were pretextual.

In a much more egregious case, the arbitrator found that the employee's allegations of truly outrageous sexual harassment were true, but that the "Company" did not know about them, even though the employees responsible for her training certainly did.[13] When the company did learn of the incidents, it put a stop to overt harassment, although not to the "cold shoulder" treatment the grievant received. She was nonetheless fired. The company claimed she had failed to learn her job; she countered that she had had no opportunity to learn it because the harassment by her coworkers was so severe.

The arbitrator denied the employee relief on the ground that because the employer didn't know about the harassment, it was not responsible. The arbitrator reached this conclusion by imposing a very high standard of proof on the employee. He first observed that a charge of sexual harassment was akin to a charge of criminal activity, so that the employer should be presumed innocent until proven guilty. The standard of proof he actually employed, however, was preponderance of the evidence rather than beyond a reasonable doubt—not as bad, but still wrong—and he concluded that the employee had failed to show that her employer knew about the harassment.

---

[12]*Paccar, Inc.*, 72 LA 769 (Grether 1979).
[13]*Amoco Texas Refining Co.*, 71 LA 344 (Gowan 1978).

I suggest that the arbitrator asked the wrong questions. Once he concluded that the employee had in fact been harassed, he should have asked: Did the harassment affect her ability to learn the job? Should the employer have taken steps to protect her from harassment? Should it have taken remedial action once it learned of the incidents, rather than allowing other employees to give the victim the cold-shoulder treatment? And it was certainly within the arbitrator's power, without necessarily finding the employer "guilty" of harassment, to require the employer, for instance, to offer the woman employee a second training period (the first period was at best a "hazing" period), during which she would be put in a less hostile environment and allowed to learn her job.

The arbitrator's decision presents a striking contrast to the EEOC's recently issued guidelines for sexual harassment cases.[14] The guidelines state that an employer will be held liable for sexual harassment if any supervisory employee knows of the incidents. Furthermore, the employer is liable if it should have known of the incidents, even if no supervisory employees actually knew of them.[15]

I find it very likely that a court, faced with the same case, would have found a violation of Title VII. Furthermore, if a violation were found, the fact that the employer had put a stop to the conduct after it had continued for several months would not be deemed adequate as a remedy. The employee was still suffering from a severe disadvantage in her training program; that is suggested by the fact that the employer fired her for failing to learn the job. The court could have ordered reinstatement and back pay, as well as other equitable remedies, aimed at preventing similar incidents in the future.

Again, I do not suggest that a court would necessarily have reached a different result—and I certainly do not suggest that the arbitrator was wrong under the contract. What I do suggest is that the case law in this area makes it very attractive for the employee to pursue her claim in court. If the employer lost after the several years usually required for such litigation, it could well be liable for a large amount of back pay. The arbitration in that case does not seem to have fulfilled the function of satisfactorily resolving the dispute between the parties.

---

[14] 29 C.F.R. §1604.11 (1980).
[15] See also, Miller v. Bank of America, 600 F.2d 211 (9th Cir. 1979); Barnes v. Costle, 561 F.2d at 992–993.

Another example of a situation in which courts and arbitrators arrive at widely differing decisions is in the consideration of evidence that tends to show a pattern or practice of discrimination by the employer. Such evidence frequently includes statistical data. I have not read an arbitration of an individual grievance (I am not talking here about systemic or class grievances) in which the arbitrator considered such evidence important. One decision in particular struck me. The grievant claimed that he was fired after his probationary period because of racial discrimination. The union presented evidence that minority employees almost never successfully completed probation under this particular supervisor. The arbitrator held, however, that because no particular "incidents" of racial discrimination involving this particular employee had been shown, his firing was not discriminatory.[16]

In court, on the other hand, statistics may be used to make out a prima facie case of discrimination even in an individual action.[17] Such evidence is frequently, although not always, part of the plaintiff's case. Indeed, it would be difficult in many cases to prove discrimination without the inference raised by statistical disparities.

A systematic study by arbitrators of Title VII, and a conformance to court-blessed standards of proof, would do much to achieve uniformity. Indeed, adherence to the teachings of the two cases I've mentioned, *McDonnell Douglas* v. *Green*[18] and *Texas Dept. of Community Affairs* v. *Burdine,*[19] would suffice, with the caveat that whenever a higher standard is imposed on the employer under the contract, the contract should control.

On a happier note, I have discovered that some arbitrators have pursued some innovative techniques to enforce the requirements of Title VII. The courts are probably not, in general, even aware of these developments (at least this representative of the court confesses ignorance). I refer to several recent cases in which the arbitrator was specifically asked to pass on the legality of a particular course of action.

In one such case the employer was involved in ongoing Title VII litigation.[20] The trial judge had made findings of fact and conclusions of law, but had not yet ruled on the appropriate

---

[16]*Paccar, Inc.,* 72 LA 771 (Grether 1979).
[17]*See, e.g., Heagney* v. *University of Washington,* 642 F.2d 1157 (9th Cir. 1981).
[18]*Supra,* note 10.
[19]*Supra,* note 10.
[20]*Operating Engineers Employers,* 72 LA 1223 (Kramer 1979).

relief. The parties asked the arbitrator to decide whether the employer should discontinue use of the exclusive hiring hall required by the contract but found illegal by the judge. The arbitrator decided that, in light of the judge's decision, the hiring hall could be discontinued despite the express language of the contract.[21]

Another case involved a government contractor which, at the government's informal request, had made unilateral changes in its seniority system.[22] The union protested. The arbitrator found an intractable conflict between the contract and the possible statutory requirements. He therefore ordered the parties to seek an official government opinion on the statutory requirements, and retained jurisdiction pending the result. He also suggested that if such an opinion was not forthcoming, he might seek to join the United States in the arbitration proceeding so that it might be bound by the result. Although the legal effect of such a procedure, as the arbitrator recognized, is extremely doubtful, it does represent a valiant effort by the arbitrator to deal with the problem without remitting the parties to a solution by strike or litigation. I decline to predict how the court would respond to a challenge to the arbitrator's joinder of the United States as a necessary party to the arbitration.

Arbitrators have been called upon to deal with similar situations when statutory requirements change during the life of the collective bargaining agreement. The Pregnancy Amendments of 1978[23] caused quite a problem in this regard. Many contract clauses were plainly illegal under the amendments. Arbitrators have been faced with the question of whether to enforce the contract clauses or to invalidate them under the new law; other disputants have sought an interpretation of new contract clauses written to comply with the amendments. One arbitrator, interpreting a parallel state law, awarded a pregnant employee sick leave, although the contract did not require it and past practice was clearly shown to be otherwise. The arbitrator considered it his duty to read the contract to be consistent with the new legal requirements.[24]

---

[21]I note that the final decree in the case referred to did not require that the exclusive hiring hall be disbanded, but rather that certain referral quotas for minorities be observed. *Commonwealth of Pennsylvania* v. *Local Union 542, International Union of Operating Engineers*, 488 F.Supp. 988 (E.D.Pa. 1980). This does not detract from my point, that the arbitrator made an admirable effort to settle the controversy consistent with the law as he understood it.

[22]*Max Factor & Co.*, 73 LA 742 (Jones 1979).

[23]42 U.S.C. §2000e(k) (Supp. III 1979).

[24]*Muskego-Norway School Dist.*, 71 LA 509 (Rice 1978).

In another case the arbitrator was asked to decide whether the newly written contract clause required disability benefits for an employee who was on pregnancy leave at the time the amendments took effect.[25] The employer had denied the benefits. The arbitrator read the EEOC guidelines and decided that they required benefits to be paid as of the effective date. He concluded that the contract must have been intended to require what the statute required. The employer was instructed to reprocess the grievant's claim for benefits.

Pulling the threads together, I really have a rather simple thesis. I put aside the philosophic and theoretical problems posed by arbitration of discrimination cases: the incompatibility of majoritarian union interests on the one hand and employer goals on the other. I recognize the difficulties of relying on private dispute resolution to vindicate the rights of employees who have been the victims of discrimination and to eliminate that discrimination in the workplace. I look at the tools we have and the realities of the workplace. I conclude that arbitration in the context we know it—grievances under the collective bargaining agreement—is the best tool we have, the best forum for the grievant. And I think arbitrators have it within their power and their grasp to improve the process in order to accomplish the goals of Title VII, in the context of the traditional forum. Some of you are already doing an excellent job.

The advantages of relying on private arbitrators to settle discrimination claims are, of course, first and foremost, that the machinery is already in place; second, arbitration provides speedy dispute resolution by persons knowledgeable about the industry and the players, and persons who are skilled in resolving disputes in a way that does not disrupt ongoing relationships.

The courts and the EEOC are poor instruments for the vindication of individual grievants' claims. There is no commitment or capacity to preserve ongoing relationships. Detailed understanding of the particular business or industry is lacking. The EEOC and the courts face mounting backlogs. In an ideal division of labor, the EEOC and the courts would better serve in the class-action case, the industry-wide problem, leaving the individual grievance to the arbitration process.

Your sense of frustration (not to speak of the employers' and

---

[25]*Northern Indiana Public Service Co.*, 74 LA 604 (Kossoff 1980).

the unions') at the ability of the unrequited grievant to start all over again in the courts can be lessened if you see, as did the Supreme Court in *Gardner-Denver,* that because of the inherent tensions between Title VII goals and the traditional grievance and arbitration procedures there must be an ultimate opportunity to resort to the courts for vindication of such rights. Certainly for now the courts provide a necessary corrective aspect. You, as arbitrators, can offer the parties greater assurance of finality if you can secure for arbitral awards in the discrimination area a deference from the courts not unlike that accorded your awards in other areas.

Arbitrators certainly have the power and the flexibility to achieve this result. My reading has convinced me that you are not reluctant to read and apply external law when you feel the situation requires it. I would urge that the goal of achieving finality makes that effort very worthwhile. To the extent that a fair reading of the collective bargaining agreement can encompass a resolution consistent with Title VII, arbitrators should so decide. To the extent that the arbitrator has in his/her arsenal remedies akin to Title VII remedies, they should be employed.

I conclude with Justice Powell's ultimate sentence in *Gardner-Denver:* "The arbitral decision may be admitted as evidence and accorded such weight as the court deems appropriate,"[26] footnoted with the following words:

> "We adopt no standards as to the weight to be accorded an arbitral decision, since this must be determined in the court's discretion with regard to the facts and circumstances of each case. Relevant factors include the existence of provisions in the collective-bargaining agreement that conform substantially with Title VII, the degree of procedural fairness in the arbitral forum, adequacy of the record with respect to the issue of discrimination, and the special competence of particular arbitrators. Where an arbitral determination gives full consideration to an employee's Title VII rights, a court may properly accord it great weight."[27]

I urge that you accept the challenge.

---

[26]415 U.S. at 60.
[27]415 U.S. at 60, note 21.

II. A Comment on the Role
of Grievance Arbitration
in Public-Sector Bargaining in Hawaii

Edward H. Nakamura*

According to the program, this morning's panel discussion is on "How Others View Us and Vice Versa: Administrative and Judicial Critiques of the Arbitration Process." However, my remarks this morning will be related to the assigned topic only in a peripheral sense. And while the Hawaii experience may be different from that of other states, my remarks will be confined for the most part to a situation in Hawaii because of an ignorance of what is happening elsewhere and because I have reason to believe our experience is by no means unique.

If clear precedent emanating from the Hawaii Supreme Court is still vital, the relationship between the judicial process and the grievance arbitration process in Hawaii is undoubtedly governed by precepts enunciated in the *Steelworkers Trilogy*. While the court earlier had adopted a restrictive view of the authority conferred upon arbitrators, we began marching in cadence with the rest of the country in 1966 when the decision in a case involving an arbitration between Local Union 1260, IBEW, and the Hawaiian Telephone Company was issued.[1] Previously, in a case involving another local of the IBEW, Local 1357, and the telephone company,[2] the court had this to say about an arbitrator's authority:

> "Where an arbitration agreement contained in a collective bargaining agreement does not expressly confer upon the arbitrator jurisdiction to determine legal questions arising under the agreement but does limit his decision expressly to the terms and provisions of the agreement, the arbitrator has no authority to interpret or construe the provisions of collective bargaining but the court must determine the extent of the arbitrator's authority."

However, this narrow approach was unceremoniously abandoned with the following terse comment in the Local 1260 decision of 1966:

---

*Associate Justice, Supreme Court of Hawaii, Honolulu, Hawaii.
[1] *In the Matter of the Arbitration Between Local 1260, IBEW, and the Hawaiian Telephone Co.*, 49 Haw. 53, 411 P.2d 134, 61 LRRM 2390 (1966).
[2] *In the Matter of the Arbitration Between Local Union 1357, International Brotherhood of Electrical Workers, A.F. of L., and Mutual Telephone Co.*, 40 Haw. 183 (1953).

"It is conceded by the company that the law applicable in the case is federal and that the holding in *In the Matter of the Arbitration Between Local Union 1357, International Brotherhood of Electrical Workers, A.F. of L., and Mutual Telephone Company*, 40 Haw. 183, has been 'swept into oblivion.' "

And the court held that:

"The question as to whether there was cause to discharge or suspend the employee under section 6.1 and 6.2 was determined by the arbitrator and so far as the arbitrator's decision concerns the interpretation and application of section 6, this court has no business weighing the merits of the grievance and the award."

The citations of authority made clear that the governing principles thereafter were to be those from the *Trilogy*. The court subsequently echoed similar sentiments in contexts of commercial arbitration.

While the discernible tensions between the judicial process and grievance arbitration in the private sector may be few, the advent of collective bargaining in the public sector has resulted in a regeneration of some old tensions. To put it mildly, our courts are being requested by public employers to reshape the broad powers heretofore entrusted to arbitrators to conform to a much narrower concept of collective bargaining—one which apparently does not allow much room for grievance resolution with the aid of neutral third parties.

The Hawaii Public Employment Relations Act, the ostensible basis for these pleas to redirect the course of grievance arbitration, at least in one sector of collective bargaining in Hawaii, was among the earlier and more comprehensive public-sector collective bargaining laws. Its enactment was mandated by a constitutional amendment approved in 1968. Article XIII, Section 2, of our constitution unequivocally provides that: "Persons in public employment shall have the right to organize for the purpose of collective bargaining as provided by law." The statute implementing this right follows the private-sector model in most of its essential provisions. For example, it permits strikes by public employees, albeit only after the exhaustion of lengthy procedures designed to encourage the settlement of bargaining disputes and after a continuation of services essential to public health and safety has been assured by the designation of essential employees whose participation in strikes is proscribed. I believe the law follows the private paradigm in grievance arbitration, too.

That the private-sector model was selected by the Hawaii legislature is evident from the policy statement in the statute. The legislative declaration of policy reads:

> "The legislature finds that joint-decision making is the modern way of administering government.where public employees have been granted the right to share in the decision-making process affecting wages and working conditions, they have become more responsive and better able to exchange ideas and information on operations with their administrators. Accordingly, government is made more effective. The legislature further finds that the enactment of positive legislation establishing guidelines for public employment relations is the best way to harness and direct the energies of public employees eager to have a voice in determining their conditions of work, to provide a rational method for dealing with disputes and work stoppages, and to maintain a favorable political and social environment.
>
> "The legislature declares that it is the public policy of the State to promote harmonious and cooperative relations between government and its employees and to protect the public by assuring effective and orderly operations of government. These policies are best effectuated by (1) recognizing the right of public employees to organize for the purpose of collective bargaining, (2) requiring the public employers to negotiate with and enter into written agreements with exclusive representatives on matters of wages, hours, and other terms and conditions of employment, while, at the same time, (3) maintaining merit principles and the principle of equal pay for equal work among state and county employees pursuant to sections 76-1, 76-2, 77-31, and 77-33, and (4) creating a public employment relations board to administer the provisions of this chapter."

The obligation to negotiate and enter into written agreements is reiterated elsewhere in the law.

The scope of bargaining decreed by the foregoing thus covers "matters of wages, hours, and other terms and conditions of employment," exactly what employers in the private sector are mandated to bargain on. And while a maintenance of "merit principles and the principle of equal pay for equal work" is also mandated, the objectives of constructive collective bargaining have hardly been inconsistent with these principles.

The negotiated agreements have, to no one's surprise, borne more than a slight resemblance to private-sector agreements, and provisions for the arbitration of grievances, to my knowledge, are included in all agreements covering public employees in Hawaii. But the public employers here, especially in the field of higher education, perceive differences in the laws governing the two sectors that could serve as the means to diminish the scope of bargaining and to circumscribe the authority of third parties to intrude in their relations with employees. They urge that other statutory provisions have rendered arbitrators impotent in large areas where arbitrators traditionally have exercised much authority. The contention is that resort to arbitration on matters such as tenure denials and promotions is foreclosed by the law. The crucial language comes from the section entitled Scope of Negotiations, quoted earlier, and reads in pertinent part:

> "The employer and the exclusive representative shall not agree to any proposal which would be inconsistent with merit principles or the principle of equal pay for equal work . . . , or which would interfere with the rights of a public employer to (1) direct employees; (2) determine qualification, standards for work, the nature and contents of examinations, hire, promote, transfer, assign, and retain employees in positions and suspend, demote, discharge, or take other disciplinary action against employees for proper cause; (3) relieve an employee from duties because of lack of work or other legitimate reason; (4) maintain efficiency of government operations; (5) determine methods, means, and personnel by which the employer's operations are to be conducted; and take such actions as may be necessary to carry out the missions of the employer in cases of emergencies."

Some public employers view the relevant language as an ideal management rights clause that reserves all meaningful personnel actions unto themselves. At first sight, the language appears to lend itself readily to the foregoing view. But a closer look reveals that the public-sector collective bargaining law does not foreclose bargaining as contended. What apparently has been removed from bargaining are civil service protections for employees and the exercise of traditional management functions not subject to mandatory bargaining even in the private sector. There is a definite difference between the challenge of a decision not to fill a position by promotion and a grievance premised on an alleged failure to follow negotiated procedures after a decision is made to fill a position by promotion. But some public employers would even deny an arbitrator authority to determine the latter. And some of our judges have agreed. The Hawaii Supreme Court is scheduled to pass on these crucial matters soon. The law is nonetheless ambiguous, as most pioneering statutes are. It probably would not have been approved if it did not provide different meanings for people with different interests in collective bargaining. The function of the judiciary in such a situation is to reconcile what purportedly is irreconcilable and to furnish interpretations accommodating competing interests within a rational scheme. Its function is never to emasculate a law or create a vacuum.

Arbitrators likewise have a function to supply reasoned decisions consistent with the stated policy of the law in this situation. The judiciary's final determination will undoubtedly be influenced by what arbitrators have said about their role in public-sector bargaining and grievance settlement. The Hawaii Supreme Court has acknowledged the salutary presence of arbitrators in the past; there is no reason why it should not continue to do so and to be influenced by what arbitrators have to say in their area of expertise.

But, in my opinion, arbitrators here in Hawaii and throughout the United States will influence the course of public-sector collective bargaining only to the extent they are willing to participate in this process of attempting to reconcile what may appear irreconcilable by supplying reasoned opinions consistent with concepts of collective bargaining they helped to develop in the private sector. This is definitely not a time for them to be quibbling about the implications of external law and whether arbitrators should or should not heed them. They should be part of the process of determining what the law will be.

III. The Legitimacy of Arbitrating Claims of Discrimination*

Leroy D. Clark**

I disagree with the position taken by Mr. Jenkins, that a federal agency (the National Labor Relations Board) should have sole responsibility for carrying out the national policy in labor relations as evidenced by the National Labor Relations Act (NLRA). I believe that national policy can only be appropriately effected when the citizens who are governed thereby acquiesce in the demands of the law and seek ways of complying without the intervention of federal enforcement agencies. There are many examples of how national policy can be undermined if general compliance without the intervention of law enforcement officials does not occur, such as the experiment with prohibition.

However, I wish to make it clear that there are several features with respect to the laws prohibiting discrimination in employment which sharply distinguish them from the National Labor Relations Act and which make it absolutely mandatory that we keep open access to private efforts at compliance with the law.

In the first place, there is an enormous difference between the number of potential violations of the Civil Rights Act of 1964 and violations under the NLRA. The Civil Rights Act of 1964 covers all employers in the country who employ 15 or more persons. It is probably fair to say that very few companies could claim that, post-1964, they had not engaged in any discrimination in terms of race, sex, national origin, or religion. A similar potential for violations does not exist with respect to the NLRA. While it is possible that any employer engaged in interstate commerce could violate the act by acting improperly with respect to spontaneous collective activity of unorganized workers, the overwhelming bulk of charges are lodged against employers in circumstances where there is a recognized union or where

---

*The speaker preceding Mr. Clark on the panel was Howard Jenkins, Jr., Member, National Labor Relations Board, who did not submit a paper for publication in the Proceedings. Mr. Clark's opening remarks are in response to Mr. Jenkins's position that any matters that are the subject of an unfair labor practice charge ought not to be deferred to arbitration by the National Labor Relations Board.

**Professor of Law, Catholic University, Washington, D.C.; formerly General Counsel, Equal Employment Opportunity Commission. The bulk of the research which informed these remarks was done by Barbara A. Bush while she was special Assistant to Mr. Clark at the E.E.O.C.

there are active attempts by a union to organize employees in order to achieve representative status. Only about one-quarter of the workforce are union members, and there are no current signs that the percentage of union membership will increase dramatically in the foreseeable future. Unfair labor practice charges, therefore, will revolve around the organized workforce, or that small percentage who are involved in organizing drives.

Given the breadth of coverage of the Civil Rights Act and the fact that discrimination is widespread and has been firmly rooted in the mores of the society, if substantial compliance is ever to be achieved, a large part of it must come through employers who recognize their responsibility and actively seek to change their own practices. Arbitration of discrimination claims could be one privately initiated mechanism for doing so.

Additionally, the structure of Title VII of the 1964 Civil Rights Act is quite different from the NLRA. Under the National Labor Relations Act, the authority for sustaining an unfair labor practice charge and, indeed, prosecuting it is lodged exclusively with the NLRB. Title VII, on the other hand, relies quite heavily upon private parties litigating against other private parties and therefore, I believe, implicitly recognizes the possibility that these private parties may develop their own mechanisms for dispute resolution. Moreover, Title VII explicitly builds in a period of conciliation during which, as a factual matter, most charges are resolved. This also suggests that processes other than litigation (that is, arbitration) are compatible with the statutory scheme.

The issue of whether arbitration is a productive way of resolving employment discrimination claims has been debated since the inception of the statute in 1964. The proponents of arbitration suggested that it would be an effective way of reducing the burden of litigation in the federal courts. The prime reason offered in the early comments was that the equal employment opportunity agencies were swamped with massive numbers of charges of discrimination, and the Equal Employment Opportunity Commission (EEOC), in particular, had built up a backlog of cases which often languished in the agency for years without being investigated. This created a serious problem for employers because months could elapse before a matter was brought to them for resolution and, where back pay was at issue, potential damages had mounted in the interim—making it even more difficult to arrive at a settlement. Objectively, the time-lag also made it more difficult for either side to recapture the facts accurately in situations where the parties had to rely on the memories of participants or witnesses.

Despite some strong support for the arbitration of discrimination claims, there were also some severe critics of this approach. The charge was made that arbitration was not geared to the handling of claims of a multiple number of persons who were similarly situated (class-action-type claims), since it had traditionally been limited to adjusting grievances brought by single individuals. It was also noted that conventional arbitration lacks some of the procedural safeguards of litigation, that is, the power to order discovery. Also, under a collective bargaining agreement, the union is one of the parties in an arbitration. However, it may be a party *to* the discrimination, thus compromising it as an adequate representative of the victim of the discrimination. It was also claimed that arbitration is a relatively private, invisible process and, thus, not the best one for the resolution of ambiguities in the statute where a more public forum is needed. Further, in the typical arbitration clause, the arbitrator has no power to reform the contract or to nullify certain provisions in it, which may be necessary in a discrimination case to give full and permanent relief to the grievant or grievants.

The debate around the usefulness of arbitration took a sharply different turn after the decision in the *Gardner-Denver* case.[1] When the Court held that a grievant had a right to a de novo suit in federal court even though he had previously resorted to grievance arbitration, the scholarly comments began to focus on how to invest arbitration with the procedural safeguards mentioned in the *Gardner-Denver* opinion which would give it, if not complete finality, at least some weight in the fact-finding process in a subsequent suit.

After the *Gardner-Denver* decision, there was very little discussion about whether there continued to be a need for arbitration as an alternative to the resolution of discrimination claims by state and federal agencies. This was probably due to the sweeping reforms that were undertaken at the EEOC beginning in 1977. The Commission instituted a rapid-charge and fact-finding process in which the scope of an investigation was sharply limited to the specific claims of discrimination made by

---

[1]*Alexander v. Gardner-Denver Co.*, 415 U.S. 36, 7 FEP Cases 81 (1974).

the charging party, and quick settlements in face-to-face conferences were arranged. (The Commission had previously broadened many investigations of a charge to cover all possible discriminatory practices in the entire company.) With this new approach in place, the 1977 backlog of approximately 130,000 charges had, by December 1979, been reduced by 45 percent, and by December 1980 by 66 percent. The processing time for individual charges was reduced from an average of two years to four months.

One might ask, with this greatly improved efficiency, whether there is any longer a need for utilizing arbitration to settle discrimination charges. I believe that there are a number of reasons which still argue for arbitration being developed as an alternative mechanism. In the first place, the very success and the improved image of the EEOC have perhaps contributed to the fact that many more charges are being lodged with the agency currently than in previous years. In particular, the number of age-discrimination complaints that the agency is now receiving is much higher than was the case when they were handled by the Department of Labor. This increase in the volume of charges is occurring at a time when a new Administration is cutting back general support funds by millions of dollars and has ordered a reduction of the staff by 241 persons by July 1, 1981. There are already projections that the time for processing charges will increase, and thus there is the potential for another backlog developing as in pre-1977 days.

Moreover, there have been severe criticisms of the rapid-charge processing system. The General Accounting Office (GAO) has indicated that, in spot investigations which it undertook, there appeared to be some negotiated settlements under the rapid-charge process system in which there may have been no merit to the charge at all. The dilemma that the GAO criticism presents for the EEOC is that if these "no-fault" mediated settlements cannot go forward without a full-scale investigation, it is inevitable that a backlog will develop again. One cannot completely dismiss the GAO criticism, however, for a random sampling of charging parties showed a high rate of dissatisfaction (48 percent) after they had thought about the settlements they had received through the rapid-charge process. This was true even though a look at the dollar figures would show that there was a higher return per charging party under the rapid-charge processing system than before its adoption. Ultimately, however, it must be admitted that a less than full investigation with quick negotiated settlements may create a certain kind of cynicism about the total process among both the charging parties and the respondents. Neither is forced to take responsibility for the true merits of a claim, for respondents may simply feel that they are buying their way out of a nuisance situation and the charging party whose case has no merit is never made to take responsibility for that fact. Arbitration may be a viable solution to many of these problems, and it certainly is a less resource-consuming compromise.

There is the question of whether arbitration can fit within the current statutory scheme or whether amendments to the statute might be necessary if arbitration were to be undertaken on a large scale. Under Title VII, fact-finding may occur in a state agency's administrative process or in a suit in federal court as well as in the EEOC procedures. Since the *Gardner-Denver* case suggested that, where arbitration was conducted with certain safeguards, the federal court could give some weight to the arbitrator's findings of fact, it would seem reasonable to argue that the EEOC or, indeed, a state agency could give similar weight to an arbitrator's findings in their own proceedings. The only problem with that reading of the statute is that the only instance in which the statute explicitly authorizes the EEOC to take into account the findings of another agent is with respect to state and local antidiscrimination commissions. Thus, one might read the statute as not authorizing the EEOC to grant any weight to other fact-finding forums. A more important problem, however, is that arbitration loses a great deal of attractiveness as a remedy if it cannot be made final and binding on all of the participants. However, even if the federal commission took into account the findings of an arbitrator in its "reasonable cause" findings, it is clear that this would not completely preclude a grievant from subsequently resorting to litigation, under the *Gardner-Denver* decision.

The view that there is an absolute right to a trial de novo in the federal court under Title VII, despite prior arbitration, was recently reinforced in the case of *Barrentine* v. *Arkansas-Best Freight System*. [2] The Court was dealing with arbitration under the Fair Labor Standards Act (FLSA), but its dictum references to *Gardner-Denver* showed that even the dissenting judges who

---

[2] 49 LW 4347 (April 6, 1981).

thought that the FLSA could be interpreted to accommodate final and binding arbitration of minimum wage claims did not believe that this was an appropriate interpretation of Title VII. The Court is thus unanimous in that view of *Gardner-Denver*. Therefore, while I think that arbitration ought to be incorporated explicitly within the scheme under Title VII, I believe it is probably best done through amendments to the present statute. An amended statute could respond specifically to some of the legitimate criticisms that have been made of arbitration as a dispute-resolution procedure in certain contexts. For example, I would exclude from arbitration class-action-type claims seeking a reformation of the collective agreement, or situations where there are unresolved areas of the law.

I think that the EEOC, under this amended statutory scheme, ought to train arbitrators in the law of Title VII so that they could apply it in the context of their arbitrations, and that the Commission should be given the funds to pay for the arbitrator and for representation of the employee-grievant. This form of arbitration should be initiated and controlled by the employee and not a union, and it should be available even where the employer has no union. With those limitations and strictures on the arbitration process, I would give the EEOC an oversight review of an arbitrator's decision, similar to that which the NLRB now has, to give minimal assurances that there has been basic compliance with Title VII.

CHAPTER 7

INTEREST ARBITRATION:
CAN THE PUBLIC SECTOR AFFORD IT?
DEVELOPING LIMITATIONS ON THE PROCESS

I. An Overview

WAYNE MINAMI*

Compulsory arbitration has been adopted in many states as an alternative to public employee strikes. As of August 1980, 20 states had such legislation on their books.

Growing just as fast are statutes or constitutional provisions that attempt to limit government spending. At the present time, Hawaii, Nevada, New Jersey, Oregon, and Washington have both a "cap" law and compulsory interest arbitration. How do these "cap" laws affect interest arbitration in the public sector? Today's panel will address the pros and cons of such legislation. My role is to give an overview of the subject.

What are "cap" laws and how prevalent are they? New Jersey was the first state to adopt the process. In 1976 the New Jersey legislature adopted a state spending limit that restricted increases in state spending to increases in personal income. With regard to school districts, counties, and municipalities, the legislature set a 5-percent maximum per year on increases in spending. Colorado's legislature in 1977 approved a measure that limits increases in state spending to a 7-percent increase over the previous year's expenditures.

Probably the most publicized of these spending limitations is Proposition 13 which was approved by California voters in June 1978. By drastically reducing the amount of tax revenues generated from property taxes, Proposition 13 had an immediate impact on the amount of money available to fund negotiated or arbitrated salary increases. The passage of Proposition 13 resulted in a "bail out" law by which the state supplied more than

---

*Attorney, Honolulu, Hawaii.

$4 billion to compensate localities for lost revenues. As a condition for receipt of state bail-out funds, the state required the localities to limit employee wage increases to no more than that accorded state employees, a requirement that placed a cloud over many negotiated salary increases. This confusing situation was not remedied until the California Supreme Court struck down the restriction as an unconstitutional impairment of contract.[1] The bail-out law also attempted to freeze the level of fire and police services by requiring that the level of police and fire protection actually provided in the 1977–1978 fiscal year be continued for the 1978–1979 fiscal year.

The publicity from Proposition 13 fueled taxpayers dissent in other states. In rapid succession, limitations were adopted. Five states—Arizona, Hawaii, Michigan, Tennessee, and Texas—adopted spending or revenue limits in 1978. Four more states—Louisiana, Nevada, Utah, and Washington—adopted limits in 1979. In 1980, Delaware, Idaho, Oregon, and South Carolina continued the trend. As of August of last year, 16 states had such limits applicable to state expenditures or revenues. In addition, nine other states had limits applicable to local government units.

Since these cap laws apply to total spending by a municipality or a state, you may ask: How can they impact an arbitrator? The impact is clearly brought out in a case called *Policemen's Assn.* v. *Town of Irvington.*[2] In that case the Town of Irvington was faced with a maximum 5-percent increase in spending imposed by the New Jersey cap law. Increases in insurance premiums and utilities costs were in excess of 5 percent and eroded the amount available for salary increases for employees. The town, in a final-offer arbitration with the police, offered a 5-percent salary increase. The Policemen's Association asked for substantially more. The town presented evidence that if it had to comply with the union's demand, it would be forced to lay off many essential employees, and it argued that these layoffs would aggravate present "skeleton" crews and hence be detrimental to the citizens of Irvington. The arbitrator, however, found that the union's economic proposals were "more fair and reasonable" than those put forth by the town.

In seeking confirmation of the arbitrator's order, the union

---

[1]*Public Employees* v. *County of Sonoma,* 100 LRRM 3044 (1979).
[2]102 LRRM 2169 (1979).

brought the matter before the courts. The New Jersey Supreme Court made the following finding: The costs incurred in implementing compulsory arbitration awards are subject to the cap law. The court noted that the statute providing for interest arbitration required that the arbitrator "give due weight" to eight enumerated factors and that three of them, (a) "the interests and welfare of the public," (b) "[t]he lawful authority of the employer," and (c) "the financial impact [of the award] on the governing unit, its residents and taxpayers" required the arbitrator to consider a municipality's cap-law restraint prior to the rendition of an award.

Arbitrators can take comfort in the standard adopted for judicial review of the arbitration award. The court inquiry was limited to whether the award was supported by substantial credible evidence in the record and whether the arbitrator gave due weight to each of the eight statutory factors and rendered an award that was "reasonable." The court found that the award was reasonable and enforceable even though the award, when added to other proposed expenses, would result in an increase in total expenditures in excess of 5 percent. The court stated: "The manner in which the Town will comply with the award without running afoul of the Cap Law proscriptions is a matter which neither we nor the arbitrator have the authority to decree." That decision lies with municipal officials.

The court in that case quotes a prophetic assemblyman who was a member of the study commission which proposed the compulsory interest arbitration law:

> "The cap laws have put a new element into this whole picture that makes the work of the arbitrator, I would say, even more difficult than it would have been before because he now has to take into consideration not only the dispute that is before him, but what the requirements of the governing body, whatever it may be—a board of education, a municipality, a county—are in other aspects of governance, what other employees have to get, what the increases in insurance, utilities and all the other things that go into making up a budget represent. So he does have to take that into consideration. It becomes a more complicated process."

It is probable that in every state with a cap law, the government entity will attempt to point out the spending-limit constraints. Under *Irvington,* the arbitrator has to consider the entity's cap situation before rendering his decision. Although he is not automatically bound by its percentage limitations, his decision must be reasonable in light of statutory factors. I think it will be a troublesome area for arbitrators. For example, in many states the spending limitation is determined by the growth in the state's economy or the growth in personal income.[3] If there is no growth as measured by these indicators, can an arbitrator award pay raises and still have his decision considered reasonable? This is more likely to become a problem in California because that state's spending limit is tied in part to increases in population, and some cities have been losing population.

One thing is clear, however. Each arbitrator in a cap-law jurisdiction will have to learn the mechanics of the law. He must know how the cap is calculated, how much has been committed to non-collective-bargaining expenditures, and how much remains for collective bargaining costs. While that may sound simple, in practice it is not. Hawaii underwent its first collective bargaining negotiation under the state's cap law which limits increases in general-fund expenditures to the growth in personal income. Ted Tsukiyama and I served as fact-finders as part of the dispute-resolution process. The state government argued that the spending ceiling limited the amount of their offer. To gauge the true impact of the ceiling, however, it was necessary to focus only on general-fund expenditures. Since many employees were paid by special funds or by federal funds, a separate cost accounting was required. In Hawaii, the governor is required to submit a budget which complies with the spending ceiling. Since that budget would include the negotiated collective bargaining costs, we found ourselves reviewing his budget to find the true constraints. Since the legislature was already in session, it had in the meantime made significant changes in the governor's budget, so it was difficult to get a true reading of what the allocation was.

Our experience is not unique. In another case in New Jersey,[4] an arbitrator had to consider the effect on the cap limit of a shortfall of $1.1 million in anticipated collection of delinquent taxes. All of these technical issues, when raised, have to be considered by the arbitrator in order to meet the standard set forth under *Irvington.* Thus, in addition to issues which all arbitrators are familiar with, such as the inflation rate, comparative pay in other jurisdictions, and the U.S. Department of Labor's

---

[3]Austermann, *The Tax Revolt Transformed,* State Legislatures, July–August 1980.
[4]*New Jersey State Policemen's Benevolent Assn.* v. *City of East Orange,* 164 N.J. Super 436 (1978).

typical-family-of-four statistics, the arbitrator now has a whole new technical and factual topic to consider.

The constraints imposed by these cap laws are alleviated where the legislative body has the power to approve or reject arbitrated or negotiated agreements. For example, in Hawaii the state legislature and the county councils retain that right and, as a result, can review the cost of the agreement in light of other government expenditures and the spending limit. All state legislatures have retained the power to approve or reject state collective bargaining agreements.[5] However, that right is not granted to all county or municipal governments. In those cases the arbitrator has broad authority to determine the fiscal priorities of a city since his award must be funded. I don't know which is the better solution. Where the legislative body retains the right to approve or reject, the arbitrator's decision is clearly not final and may be rejected, as it was in Hawaii in 1979. Where the arbitrator's award is not subject to legislative approval, I expect more court challenges of the awards when municipal officials are faced with a large award that utilizes most, if not all, of the allowable increases.

In addition to the passage of cap laws, the taxpayers' concern over government spending has also resulted in laws that limit or more narrowly define the role of the arbitrator in public collective bargaining. Some of these laws are subtle, such as final-offer arbitration or residency requirements for arbitrators. But there also are more direct ones. For example, the Financial Emergency Act for the City of New York, in recognition of the large salary increases granted employees previously, required arbitration awards rendered pursuant to the city's collective bargaining law to consider and give "substantial weight" to the city's financial ability to pay such increases without requiring increases in the level of city taxes existing at the commencement of arbitration proceedings.[6] In addition, it created the Emergency Financial Control Board which could return awards to the negotiators if the parties had not demonstrated that the agreement was in compliance with wage guidelines.[7]

I also came across a Massachusetts statute which, under certain conditions, limits to 50 percent the amount of contributions

---

[5]See *Minnesota Ed. Assn.* v. *State of Minnesota,* 103 LRRM 2195, 2197 (1979).
[6]See *De Molia* v. *State of New York,* 100 LRRM 2625 (1978).
[7]Anderson, *Local Government-Bargaining and the Fiscal Crisis: Money, Unions, Politics and the Public Interest,* 27 Labor L.J. 512 (1976).

public employers may make to public employees' health insurance premiums.[8]

The New York compulsory arbitration law was amended in 1978 to require arbitrators not just to specify the basis of their findings, but to assign them weight. It also included a provision that the determination of the arbitration panel is subject to review by a court of competent jurisdiction. Citing the above changes, a New York court remanded for further consideration a three-member arbitration panel's decision which the court held did not elaborate sufficiently on its reasons for various contract proposals and thus did not meet the law's requirements.[9]

In summary, I believe the cap laws are here to stay and will probably be passed in more and more states. Public dissatisfaction with government taxes and services will remain high as long as the total tax burden keeps growing, and as long as we have persistent inflation combined with slow growth in personal income. Caps or ceilings provide the mechanism by which the taxpayer can gauge whether his elected officials are controlling growth in government. Whereas the calculation of the limit may be a technical exercise, the taxpayer need only ask, "Did they exceed the ceiling?"

Since salary costs represent a significant portion of any governmental entity's budget, these cap laws will have a pronounced impact on collective bargaining. Indeed, in the *Irvington* case, the town asserted that salaries and fringe benefits account for 75 percent of its overall budgetary appropriations.

If a jurisdiction has a cap law, that law will become a major item of discussion. How the cap law is calculated, how much has been allocated prior to bargaining, and how wage proposals affect the ceiling will be common issues. An arbitrator will have to know the answers to these questions in order to render a reasonable award. In addition to learning an entirely new area, the arbitrator will find his award more likely to be criticized if salary awards exceed the percentage growth for the budget as a whole. Concurrently, as taxpayers, concerned about government spending, see employee salary expenses rise faster than the percentage growth in the municipality as a whole, we will see

---

[8] *See School Comm. of Holyoke* v. *Duprey*, 102 LRRM 3007 (1979), and *Medford School Comm.* v. *LRC*, 103 LRRM 2059 (1979).

[9] *In the Matter of the Application of Buffalo Police Benevolent Assn.* v. *City of Buffalo, State of New York*, Supreme Court of Erie County (Sept. 30, 1980), as reported in 894 GERR 24.

more limitations and restrictions placed upon arbitrators. We have already seen a growing tendency to send arbitration awards to court for review. If the trend continues unabated, there may come a time when interest arbitration no longer provides finality and the process is so cumbersome that its utilization will diminish in the public sector.

I hope that the foregoing has laid out the current trends and the problems that lie on the horizon.

II. A MANAGEMENT PERSPECTIVE*

R. THEODORE CLARK, JR.**

At the outset it is important to note that fiscal limitations on public employers did not start with either the New Jersey "cap" law in 1976 or with Proposition 13 in California in 1978. Fiscal limitations have always been part of the public-sector collective bargaining landscape. Twelve years ago Charles Rehmus wrote an excellent article entitled "Constraints on Local Governments in Public Employee Bargaining" that appeared in the Michigan Law Review.[1] In this article, Rehmus observed that "[t]he financial constraints on local governments constitute the most serious problem they face in coping with public employee collective bargaining."[2] He further noted:

> ". . . Local government administrators are helplessly caught between employee compensation demands, public unwillingness to vote increased operating millage levied on property, and the state legislature's reluctance to allow local governments the freedom to impose income, sales, or excise taxes."[3]

While fiscal limitations are not new, the type of limitations that have been enacted in the past few years are much more restrictive and permit few, if any, escape hatches. Among the most inflexible are the "cap" laws in states like New Jersey,[4] which places a rather absolute limit on the amount a public employer can increase appropriations from one year to the next, and the "lid" laws in states like California,[5] which limit the amount of taxes that a public body can collect. Despite the assertions of some that these limitations give public manage-

---

*The comments in this paper should not be viewed as representing any change in the author's frequently expressed opposition to compulsory arbitration. *See, e.g.,* Clark, *Legislated Interest Arbitration—A Management Response,* in Proceedings of the 27th Annual Meeting, Industrial Relations Research Association (Madison, Wis.: IRRA, 1975), 319. Being a pragmatist, the author must perforce accept compulsory arbitration where a legislature has enacted such a law and its constitutionality has been upheld. Given this reality, the issue then becomes one of attempting to make the process work. It is to this latter topic that the remarks in this paper are directed.
**Partner, Seyfarth, Shaw, Fairweather & Geraldson, Chicago, Ill.
[1]Rehmus, *Constraints on Local Governments in Public Employee Bargaining,* 67 Mich. L.Rev. 919 (1969).
[2]*Id.,* at 924.
[3]*Id.,* at 923.
[4]N.J.S.A. 40A:4-45.1 *et seq.*
[5]Calif. Const., Art. XIIIA, as added by Proposition 13, an initiative measure passed by the electorate on June 6, 1978.

ment a stacked deck in wage negotiations, it should be emphasized that public employers for the most part—especially at the
local government level—did not sponsor or lobby for these
limitations. As a result, when a public employer makes an inability-to-pay argument because of a cap or lid law, arbitrators
should not assume that these limitations were self-imposed. To
the contrary, most of the restrictive limitations that have been
adopted in the past few years have been adopted over the opposition of public employers.

Parenthetically, while public-sector interest arbitrators have
expressed concern over the limitations imposed by cap and lid
laws, they have not voiced similar concerns about state statutes
which prescribe salary and fringe benefit minimums.[6] There are,
for example, numerous statutes establishing minimum salaries,
pensions, sick leave, insurance benefits, premium pay, tenure,
and other terms and conditions of employment of public employees.[7] Since the state legislature is the source of both the
"floor" laws and the cap or lid laws, interest arbitrators must,
as the Supreme Court noted in a somewhat different context in
Arnett v. *Kennedy*,[8] ". . . take the bitter with the sweet."[9]

The cap and lid laws that have been enacted obviously affect
rather directly a public employer's ability to pay and, in a period
of high inflation like the present, public employers will invariably present an inability-to-pay argument based in whole or in
part on the existence of such a law. The major question raised
in those jurisdictions which have both a cap or lid law and
compulsory arbitration is how the interest arbitrator should respond to such an argument.

Substantially all the public-sector interest arbitration statutes
require—either explicitly or implicitly—that financial limitations
on a public employer's ability to pay must be considered by the
interest arbitrator. That was the specific holding of the New
Jersey Supreme Court in *New Jersey State Policemen's Benevolent
Association Local 29* v. *Town of Irvington.*[10] The court ruled that an

---

[6]It would, of course, be beyond the authority of an interest arbitrator to render an
award which would reduce or lower a benefit that is prescribed by statute.

[7]For a broad sampling of such legislative enactments, *see* Lieberman, *Memorandum
Analysis of Preemption Problems with Proposed Federal Bargaining Legislation for State/Local
Employees,* in 593 GERR at E-1 *et seq.* (2-17-75).

[8]416 U.S. 134, 94 S. Ct. 1633 (1974).

[9]*Id.,* at 154, 94 S.Ct. at 1644.

[10]80 N.J. 271, 102 LRRM 2169 (1979).

interest arbitrator must "take account of a municipality's cap law constraints prior to the rendition of an award."[11] Nevertheless, I get the very definite impression that many interest arbitrators wish that ability-to-pay arguments would simply disappear. Russell Smith at the 1971 meeting of the National Academy of Arbitrators, after commenting on the serious problems confronting arbitrators in attempting to assess an inability-to-pay argument, candidly observed that the inability-to-pay criterion, "if deemed to be relevant or required by law to be taken into consideration, is likely to be taken less seriously than others, such as comparison data."[12] My own impression is that the attitude of many arbitrators toward the inability-to-pay criterion ranges from indifference to hostility.[13] I also have the feeling in some cases that while a public employer's ability to pay is considered, it is considered in form only and not in substance.[14]

It is my position that ability to pay is a valid interest-arbitration criterion, especially in the context of cap or lid laws, and that interest arbitrators are duty bound to give it serious consideration when it is raised. My reasons for so contending are several.

In the first place, public-sector interest arbitrators are *not* free agents who can do whatever they please. In this regard, public-sector interest arbitration must be differentiated from private-sector interest arbitration. Interest arbitration in the private sector is not legislatively mandated; rather, it is voluntarily consented to by the parties. Moreover, private-sector interest arbi-

---

[11]*Id.*, 102 LRRM at 2177. *Accord, Town of Arlington* v. *Bd. of Conciliation and Arbitration,* 370 Mass. 769, 352 N.E.2d 914, 93 LRRM 2494 (1976) (an interest arbitrator "is bound to apply the statutory standards in reaching a decision").

[12]Comment by Russell A. Smith, in Arbitration and the Public Interest, Proceedings of the 24th Annual Meeting, National Academy of Arbitrators (Washington: BNA Books, 1971), 180, at 185.

[13]There are some arbitrators, to be sure, that have accorded appropriate weight to the ability-to-pay criterion. *See, e.g., City of Council Bluffs, Iowa and Council Bluffs Assn. of Professional Fire Fighters Local No. 15* (Fact Finder Gundermann 1979) ("What is relevant to this dispute is evidence relating to the City's ability to pay, for if the City does not first have the ability to pay, comparability becomes meaningless"); *Mayor and Council of Baltimore and IAFF Local 734* (Impartial Chr. Galfand 1979), discussed at note 36 *infra; Parma Education Assn.,* 52 LA 800 (Teple 1969). *See generally* Berkowitz, *Arbitration of Public-Sector Interest Disputes: Economics, Politics, and Equity,* in Arbitration—1976, Proceedings of the 29th Annual Meeting, National Academy of Arbitrators (Washington: BNA Books, 1976), 159, at 168 (Ability to pay "is the one criterion that comes closest to getting at the economic realities, and I shall argue that in the public sector it deserves more weight than it has received in the past").

[14]*See, e.g., City of Mount Vernon,* 49 LA 1229, 1233 (Chr. McFadden 1968), in which the panel stated that it would "not ignore" the city's financial condition, but stated that its function was to recommend "a settlement that is fair and equitable." The panel further observed that the city "must raise whatever revenues are necessary in the manner which it deems best."

trators are usually given wide latitude—typically without any explicit standards—in rendering an award.[15] As a result, interest arbitrators in the private sector are literally given the authority to write the parties' contract with virtually no strings attached. This contrasts sharply with the role and function of public-sector interest arbitrators. The prevailing judicial view is that public employers in the absence of legislative authorization do not have the authority to submit unresolved collective bargaining disputes to interest arbitration. For example, the Ohio Court of Appeals in *Xenia City Board of Education* v. *Xenia Education Association*[16] held that a voluntary agreement to submit unresolved collective bargaining issues to binding interest arbitration was null and void. The court ruled that such an agreement ". . . conflicts with and abrogates the board's duties and responsibilities to enter into new collective bargaining agreements for the employment of teachers and other school personnel and to manage the schools in the public interest. . . ."[17] As a result, in substantially all jurisdictions public-sector interest arbitration must be legislatively sanctioned.

While the prevailing majority view is that compulsory public-sector arbitration laws do not constitute an unconstitutional delegation of legislative authority,[18] this does not detract from the fact that there has been a delegation of legislative authority to public-sector interest arbitrators and that such arbitrators are exercising delegated legislative authority. As the Rhode Island Supreme Court noted in *City of Warwick* v. *Warwick Fire Fighters:*[19] ". . . we find that the legislature delegated to each of the arbitra-

---

[15] *See generally* Elkouri and Elkouri, How Arbitration Works, 3d ed. (1974), 745–796. Elkouri and Elkouri note, however, that "[s]ometimes the parties will specify, in their stipulation for arbitrations, the standards to be observed." *Id.,* at 745.

[16] 52 Ohio App. 2d 373, 370 N.E.2d 756, 97 LRRM 2327 (1977).

[17] *Id.,* 370 N.E.2d at 758. *Accord, Trotwood-Madison Teachers Assn.* v. *Trotwood Madison Board of Education,* 52 Ohio App.2d 39, 367 N.E.2d 1233, 96 LRRM 3148 (1977) (". . . we do not believe that the board of education itself may abandon its discretionary authority to enter into agreements with employees"). *See also Maryland Classified Employees Assn., Inc.* v. *Anderson,* 97 LRRM 2179 (Md. Ct. App. 1977) (". . . the prevailing rule . . . [is that] absent such authorization it is invalid for a municipality or charter county to attempt to bind itself in the exercise of legislative discretion over compensation of its employees").

[18] *See, e.g., City of Detroit* v. *Detroit Police Officers Assn.,* 294 N.W.2d 68, 105 LRRM 3083 (Mich. S.Ct. 1980), and the cases cited at note 3 therein. *Contra, Greeley Police Union* v. *City Council of Greeley,* 191 Colo. 419, 553 P.2d 790, 93 LRRM 2382 (1976); *Sioux Falls* v. *Sioux Falls Fire Fighters,* 89 S.D. 455, 234 N.W.2d 35, 90 LRRM 2945 (1975); *Salt Lake City* v. *International Association of Fire Fighters,* 563 P.2d 786, 96 LRRM 2383 (Utah S.Ct. 1977).

[19] *Warwick* v. *Warwick Regular Firemen's Assn.,* 106 R.I. 109, 256 A.2d 206, 71 LRRM 3192, 3195 (1969).

tors a portion of the sovereign and legislative power of the government, particularly the power to fix the salaries of public employees, clearly a legislative function." Rather than being responsible solely to the parties, as would be the case in the private sector, a public-sector interest arbitrator—both in fact and in law—is an extension of the legislature and, as such, is an agent of the legislature in establishing wages and conditions of employment.

It should come as no surprise, then, that the courts have routinely held that public-sector interest arbitrators are public officials. The Rhode Island Supreme Court in the *Warwick Fire Fighters* case held that a public-sector interest arbitrator "is a public officer," and as such "constitute[s] an administrative or governmental agency."[20] The Oregon Appellate Court, in *Medford Firefighters Assn. Local 1431* v. *City of Medford*,[21] ruled that an interest arbitrator appointed by the state PERB "acts in a public capacity."[22] Sometimes the public capacity in which an interest arbitrator acts is explicitly set forth in the applicable statute. For example, the Connecticut teachers statute specifically provides that an interest arbitrator "shall be representative of the interests of the public in general."[23]

Further recognition that public-sector interest arbitrators are public officers whose duties are akin to administrative agencies is evidenced by the standard of judicial review that the courts are increasingly adopting with respect to compulsory arbitration awards. For example, the New Jersey Supreme Court has stated that "the judicial oversight available should be more extensive than the limited judicial review had under [the New Jersey Arbitration Act]."[24] The court held that judicial review of a compulsory arbitration award "should extend to consideration of whether the award is supported by substantial credible evidence present in the record," noting that "[t]his is the test normally applied to the review of administrative agency decisions and is particularly appropriate here."[25]

If it is candidly recognized—as it must be—that public-sector interest arbitrators are public officials carrying out delegated

---

[20]*Id.,* 71 LRRM at 3194.
[21]40 Or.App. 519, 595 P.2d 1268, 102 LRRM 2633 (1979).
[22]*Id.,* 102 LRRM at 2635.
[23]Conn. Gen. Stat. Ann. §10-153f(c)(1).
[24]*Division 540, Amalgamated Transit Union* v. *Mercer County Improvement Authority,* 76 N.J. 245, 386 A.2d 1290, 98 LRRM 2526 (1978).
[25]98 LRRM at 2530. *Accord, City of Detroit* v. *Detroit Police Officers Assn., supra* note 18.

legislative power, it necessarily follows that they have an obligation to give meaning and effect to other legislative enactments such as cap and lid laws. In this regard, the Supreme Court has repeatedly ruled that administrative agencies are required to give effect to competing legislative policies. For example, in *Southern Steamship Co.* v. *NLRB,* [26] the Court stated:

". . . the Board has not been commissioned to effectuate the policies of the Labor Relations Act so single-mindedly that it may wholly ignore other and equally important Congressional objectives. Frequently the entire scope of Congressional purpose calls for careful accommodation of one statutory scheme to another, and it is not too much to demand an administrative body that it undertake this accommodation without excessive emphasis upon its immediate task."[27]

By analogy, public-sector interest arbitrators have not been commissioned to single-mindedly focus on what is a reasonable wage and wholly ignore the effect of a cap or lid law on an employer's ability to pay. Where a public employer makes an inability-to-pay argument, arbitrators must seriously consider it without placing excessive emphasis upon comparability data.

In analyzing the interrelationship between cap and lid laws, on the one hand, and interest arbitration, on the other, it is helpful to consider cap and lid laws as limitations on the authority or discretion that an interest arbitrator would otherwise have. In this regard, limitations on an arbitrator's authority are not a new phenomenon—they have been around for a long time in rights arbitration. Many contracts, for example, provide that in discipline cases the arbitrator is limited to deciding whether there is cause for discipline, with the specific limitation that if the arbitrator finds cause, he/she shall not have the authority to disturb or modify the penalty meted out by the employer. Another example is the following provision in the collective bargaining agreement between the Illinois Board of Governors of State Colleges and Universities and the Illinois Federation of Teachers:

"Where the administration has made an academic judgment such as a judgment concerning application of evaluation criteria in decisions on retention, promotion, or tenure, and a judgment concerning the academic acceptability of a sabbatical proposal, the arbitra-

---

[26]316 U.S. 31, 62 S.Ct. 886 (1942).
[27]*Id.,* at 47, 62 S.Ct. at 894.

tor shall not substitute his/her judgment for that of the administration."[28]

Although many more examples could be cited, arbitrators have not had any real difficulty in complying with such contractual limitations on their authority, even though they might have reached a different result if the limitation in question had not been contained in the parties' agreement.[29] Similarly, public-sector interest arbitrators should treat statutory limitations on their authority in the same way that they would treat contractual limitations on their authority in rights arbitration.

Rights arbitrators get their authority from the parties' agreement, and it is elementary arbitral law that they may not add to, subtract from, or ignore any of the provisions of the contract.[30] As Harry Platt observed many years ago,

> ". . . While both parties have presented strong equitable arguments in support of their respective positions, the Arbitrator's decision here must necessarily rest not on broad moral principles but rather on the rights and obligations imposed by the contract. A contract freely entered into through collective bargaining is not only binding on its makers but on an Arbitrator as well and he cannot, under the guise of construction, ignore its plain terms or rewrite it to suit his own notions of equity. . . ."[31]

By analogy, since interest arbitrators get their authority from the legislature, they likewise may not add to, subtract from, or ignore applicable legislative provisions. The admonition of Justice Douglas in *Enterprise Wheel & Car*—one of the *Steelworkers Trilogy*—that an arbitrator "does not sit to dispense his own brand of industrial justice" is just as applicable to interest arbitration as it is to rights arbitration.[32]

Having established, I hope, that interest arbitrators must give serious consideration to ability-to-pay arguments where they are raised, let me turn now to an examination of the implementation

---

[28]1979–1982 agreement between the Board of Governors of State Colleges and Universities and the AFT Faculty Federation—B.O.G. Local 3500, Art. 16, §10(b)(2), at 41.
[29]*See, e.g., Lucky Stores, Inc.,* 53 LA 1274, 1278 (Eaton 1969).
[30]*See, e.g., Champion Papers, Inc.,* 69-1 ARB ¶8341 (Coffey 1968); *Page Milk Co.,* 76-1 ARB ¶8076 (Quinn 1975). The rule applies even though the contract does not contain a specific limitation on the arbitrator's authority. *See, e.g., Emerson Electric Co.,* 72-2 ARB ¶8674 (Erbs 1973) ("While the agreement does not seem to have the usual clause restricting the power of the arbitrator, . . . the arbitrator recognizes that he is restricted to construing the agreement as written"). *Accord, Viviano Macaroni Co.,* 70-2 ARB ¶8478 (Kindig 1970).
[31]*Bay City Shovels, Inc.,* 10 LA 761, 764 (Platt 1948).
[32]*Steelworkers* v. *Enterprise Wheel & Car Corp.,* 363 U.S. 593, 80 S.Ct. 1358, 46 LRRM 2423 (1960).

of the ability-to-pay criterion in practice. I would agree with the following two observations that Arnold Zack made at the New York University Conference on Labor a number of years ago. First, ". . . the neutrals should be properly concerned with the interrelated subjects of the costs of the compensation package and whether funds are, will be, or can be made available to finance it."[33] Second, ". . . [t]he employer must bear responsibility for the full operation of the governmental unit, and his perspective must be broader than merely concern over the wages of his staff."[34] My concern is that many interest arbitrators would appear to inadequately consider the effect of their awards on other employees and/or the public employer's overall operations. As Howard Block perceptively observed at the 1971 meeting of the National Academy of Arbitrators:

> "In many, if not most, inability-to-pay situations, the impasse is not due to the economic cost of reaching an agreement with the employee group directly involved in the negotiations. . . . The underlying problem for management is to avoid a settlement figure with one group which arouses unrealistic expectancies among large numbers of other employees who are being pressed to go along with a uniform wage policy pegged at a lower rate."[35]

In assessing a public employer's inability-to-pay argument, at least five considerations should be taken into account. First, if the public employer has already settled with one or more bargaining units and the employer is proposing the same basic wage settlement for the unit involved in the interest-arbitration proceeding, the uniform wage policy being proposed by the public employer, as Howard Block has noted, ". . . merits a high degree of support from interest neutrals."[36]

---

[33]Zack, *Ability to Pay in Public Sector Bargaining,* in Proceedings of the NYU 23rd Ann. Conf. on Labor (1970), 403, at 416.
[34]*Id.,* at 411–412.
[35]Block, *Criteria in Public Sector Interest Disputes,* in Arbitration and the Public Interest, Proceedings of the 24th Annual Meeting, National Academy of Arbitrators (Washington: BNA Books, 1971), 161, at 173.
[36]*Id. See also Mayor and Council of Baltimore and IAFF Local 734,* AAA Case No. 14 39 0365 79 J (1979), in which Harry Galfand, the Impartial Chairman, held that the results of the city's negotiations with eight other unions was a "critical factor" in accepting the city's final offer that extended to firefighters what the city had previously negotiated with those eight other unions, noting: ". . . I am not saying that we are absolutely bound to award no greater increase to the Firefighters than the others are scheduled to receive. We are, however, bound to consider the relationship of Firefighters' increases to those of other City employees, and to decide whether some variation is valid and, if so, whether a variation to the extent requested is in order. . . .
"This need to maintain equality, especially when financial conditions have forced the other City employees to accept what is probably less than they are entitled to as well, is one of the most influential factors in the shaping of my decision...." *Id.,* at 5–6, 9.

Second, if the employer has bitten the bullet and taken significant actions to reduce expenditures and to ensure that the misery is being distributed across the board, an interest arbitrator should think twice before rejecting the employer's inability-to-pay argument. If the interest arbitrator awards more than the employer contends it can afford in these circumstances, it necessarily means—assuming the contention is factually premised—that the additional funds will have to come out of somebody else's hide.

Third, consideration should be given to what the employees would have received if they had had the right to strike. As Albert Shanker commented following a New York City teachers' strike in 1975 that lasted less than one week, "A strike is a weapon you use against a boss who has money."[37] At the 1976 meeting of the National Academy of Arbitrators, Monroe Berkowitz observed that public-sector neutrals "must be able to suggest or order settlements of wage issues that would conform in some measure to what the situation would be had the parties been allowed the right to strike and the right to take a strike."[38] Applied in the context of an inability-to-pay argument, interest arbitrators should not award more than the employees would have been able to obtain if they had the right to strike *and* the employer had the right to take a strike.

Fourth, serious consideration should be given to the employer's ability to attract and retain employees. If the evidence shows that the employer has had no difficulty in recruiting new employees and that employee turnover is within or below normal bounds, it would be more than appropriate to give significant weight to the employer's inability-to-pay contention.[39]

Fifth, public-sector interest arbitrators should be hesitant to accept without close scrutiny an argument that employees should be awarded a normal wage increase if the employer is picking up the full cost of increases for energy and other com-

---

[37]Quoted by Dorf, *Mediation and Final Offer Arbitration: A Management Counsel's View,* in Interest Arbitration (1980), 31, 32, proceedings of an IMLR Conference on March 26, 1980.

[38]Berkowitz, *supra* note 13, at 169. *See Sibley County Sheriff's Employees' Assn. and County of Sibley, Minn.,* PERB Case No. 80-PN-1256-A (Arb. Fogelberg, April 29, 1981) in which the arbitrator, in selecting the employer's final offer on salary adjustments, noted that "[w]ere these employees allowed to strike, it is highly unlikely that the ultimate settlement would equal their final demands now submitted to arbitration."

[39]"The existence of long waiting lists of applicants eager for the jobs lends credence to the . . . assumption [that] wages and conditions are sufficient to attract the required number of people. These are reflections of real market conditions that should be given due consideration." Berkowitz, *supra* note 13, at 172.

modities or supplies. While this argument may have some attraction at first blush, a deeper examination of the facts usually demonstrates its fallacies. It is instructive, for example, to determine on a before-and-after basis what percentage of the employer's operating budget is devoted to wages and benefits and what percentage is devoted to supplies and commodities. If there has been no decrease in the percentage of the budget spent on wages and benefits, the argument loses whatever persuasiveness it might have had. Moreover, while the employer probably has no alternative but to pay the going rate for gasoline and oil, the employer might be buying less as a result of energy conservation projects.

Conclusion

Obviously, there is tension between public-sector compulsory arbitration laws, on the one hand, and cap and lid laws, on the other. In grappling with this tension, public-sector interest arbitrators would do well to remember that they are agents of the legislature and that, in carrying out their delegated legislative authority, they must attempt to give effect to *both* legislative policies. If public-sector interest arbitrators fail to fulfill this dual responsibility, there are, in my judgment, four possible consequences.

First, public-sector interest arbitration laws may be amended to provide, as the Financial Emergency Act for the City of New York does,[40] that interest arbitrators must accord substantial weight to the employer's financial ability to pay when considering demands for increases in wages or fringe benefits and that this determination is subject to de novo judicial review.

Second, employers will increasingly favor granting public employees, including those in the uniformed services, the right to strike in lieu of compulsory arbitration.[41]

Third, there will be more efforts to seek judicial review of interest arbitration awards. While arbitrators can take some

---

[40]N.Y. Local Fin. Law, ch. 201 (Consol.) (Supp. 1978).

[41]Recently Detroit Mayor Coleman Young specifically advocated granting all public employees, including police and firefighters, the right to strike in lieu of compulsory arbitration. With respect to compulsory arbitration he noted that interest arbitrators in cases involving the City of Detroit had "ignored the factor that says 'The interest and welfare of the public and the financial ability of the unit of government to meet those costs.'" Address of Mayor Coleman A. Young to Legislative Forum on New Directions for Public Employee Labor Relations, Lansing, Mich., Dec. 4, 1979, at 10.

comfort from the New Jersey Supreme Court's decision in *Town of Irvington* in which the court confirmed the arbitrator's award, that same court in a companion decision issued on the same day in *Atlantic City* v. *Laezza*[42] strongly suggested that arbitration awards would be subject to invalidation if the hardships visited upon the public employer were "sufficiently severe."[43]

Fourth, compulsory arbitration laws may be repealed. This already happened in Massachusetts when the electorate adopted Proposition 2½ on November 4, 1980.

In many respects, the final verdict on compulsory arbitration in the public sector rests in the hands of interest arbitrators.[44] If they discharge their responsibilities in a balanced and reasoned way, taking into account and giving proper weight to an inability-to-pay argument where raised, the chances for its survival will be greatly enhanced.

---

[42]80 N.J. 255, 403 A.2d 465, 102 LRRM 2409 (1979).

[43]*Id.*, 102 LRRM at 2414.

[44]The following comments of Monroe Berkowitz are apropos: ". . . If arbitration of disputes is to be considered a success, it must not prevent strikes at the expense of contributing to the decline of the quality of life in the public sector. It must be alive to the importance of the effects of decisions on the economic survival of governments.

"If arbitrators cannot operate in such a fashion and make these decisions, either because they are too fundamentally political or because they are unwilling to assume the burden of moving into an unfamiliar economic world, then we must resort to alternatives." Berkowitz, *supra* note 13, at 173.

III. An Arbitrator's Viewpoint

William J. Fallon*

(with the assistance of Lawrence E. Katz**)

This paper will focus primarily on the six New England states with which I am most familiar. Although only one of those states, Massachusetts, now has a tax cap law, five have enacted legislation specifying the factors which are to be considered in interest arbitration proceedings. Moreover, the Commonwealth of Massachusetts has recently adopted legislation applicable to the Massachusetts Bay Transportation Authority, which represents probably the most extensive intervention in the collective bargaining/interest arbitration process which now exists in this country.

Within New England, New Hampshire is the only state without statutory public-sector interest arbitration. The remaining states provide for compulsory or voluntary, binding or nonbinding, interest arbitration for one or more categories of public employees, and in all such instances the legislation specifies the factors which are to be considered by the arbitrator or arbitration board. A summary of certain key factors are set out in Table 1.

At the risk of sounding heretical (at least to those legislators who drafted and adopted this "factor" legislation), I would suggest that none of these statutes (nor similar statutes which are found in other states) alters the substance of the interest arbitration process. Every one of the specific listed factors would legitimately be entitled to consideration under the "common law" (that is, case law) which has been developed over the years in public-sector interest arbitration. Indeed, four of the state legislatures have seen fit to recognize this body of case law by including the final, catchall factor which is typically phrased as:

> "Such other factors . . . which are normally or traditionally taken into consideration in the determination of wages, hours and conditions of employment through voluntary collective bargaining, mediation, fact-finding, arbitration or otherwise between parties, in the public service or in private employment."[1]

---

*Member, National Academy of Arbitrators, Boston, Mass.
**Full-time arbitrator associated with William J. Fallon.
[1]Mass. Stat. 1973, c.1078, §§4 & 4B.

TABLE 1

Factors Specified for Consideration in Public-Sector
Interest Arbitrations—New England States

	Conn.[a]	Maine[b]	Mass.[c]	MBTA[d]	R.I.[e]	Vt.[f]
1. Interest and welfare of public	x	x	x		x	x
2. Interest and welfare of employees	x					
3. Ability to pay	x	x	x	x		x
4. Comparable wages	x	x	x	x	x	x
5. Cost of living (CPI)	x	x	x	x		x
6. Comparable working conditions	x	x	x	x	x	x
7. Continuity and stability of employment		x		x		x
8. Other traditional factors		x	x	x		x

[a]The five factors noted in the table are found in Conn. Stats., §10-153f(c)(4) which provides for compulsory interest arbitration for teachers; a slightly narrower listing of factors, which excludes any reference to changes in the cost of living (CPI) is contained in §7-473(c)(2) and §7-474(j)(2), which, respectively, provide for voluntary and mandatory interest arbitration for municipal employees.

[b]The seven factors noted in the table are found in Maine Stats. 979-D.4.c., which provides for compulsory arbitration for state employees which is final and binding on all issues except salaries, pensions, and insurance. With respect to these latter items, the findings are merely advisory.

[c]The six factors noted in the table are found in Mass. Stats. of 1973, Ch. 1078 (as amended), §§4 and 4B, which, respectively, provided or provide for compulsory interest arbitration for municipal police and firefighters and for state and Metropolitan District Commission police. However, Section 4 was repealed by the so-called Proposition 2½, Stats. of 1980, Ch. 580, §10. Section 4B was not repealed; however, pursuant to Section 8A of c.1078, it expired on June 30, 1982.

Section 4A of c.1078 established a Joint Labor-Management Committee (the so-called "Dunlop Committee") which had the authority to refer municipal police and fire disputes to binding interest arbitration, pursuant to the now repealed provisions of Section 4. On February 10, 1981, in Opinion 80/81-12, the Attorney General ruled that the Committee retained its authority to order arbitration, but the repeal of Section 4 "has eliminated the binding effect of Committee awards on municipal legislative bodies." *Id.*, at 12.

[d]The six factors noted in the table are found in Mass. General Laws, c.161A, §19F, which was added by Stats. 1978, c.405, §2, and amended by Stats. 1980, c. 581, §9. This statute provides for compulsory, binding arbitration for MBTA employees.

[e]The three factors noted in the table are found in the somewhat differing provisions of R.I. General Laws, §§28-9.1-10, 28-9.2-10, 28-9.5-10, and 36-11-10, which, respectively, govern compulsory interest arbitration for firefighters, municipal police, state police, and state employees. With respect to the latter group only (state employees), the decision as to wages is advisory and not binding.

[f]The seven factors noted in the table are found in the Municipal Employee Relations Act, in Vt. Stats., Title 21, c.20, §1732(d), which is incorporated by reference into §1733(c), which provides for voluntary or compulsory interest arbitration.

Surely, in an interest arbitration proceeding, changes in the cost of living would be one relevant piece of evidence, regardless of whether that factor is mandated by statute. The fact that it is required by legislation in four New England states is essentially meaningless; so too is the fact that Rhode Island failed to recognize that factor explicitly, since the statutory listing does not purport to be all-inclusive; hence, the omission of this factor does not prohibit it being given appropriate consideration.

To say that "factor" legislation has not changed the substance of the interest arbitration process is not to say that it has not changed the procedure. It certainly has, particularly when the statute places an affirmative obligation on the arbitrator or board of arbitration to make detailed findings of fact which consider each of the enumerated factors. Such provisions are now common,[2] and they may become more so, because the existence of detailed findings as to statutory factors has played a major role in judicial decisions—for example, sustaining interest arbitration statutes against constitutional attacks, grounded on an improper delegation of legislative authority.[3]

"Factor" legislation, when coupled with "findings" legislation, requires more of the arbitrator or board than a lengthy and detailed decision. It also affects the course of the hearing itself. In the absence of "factor" legislation, the parties might feel free to omit evidence on a particular factor. In the absence of such evidence, the decision of the arbitrator or board would necessarily give no consideration to the omitted factor. When there is "factor" legislation, the parties seemingly must present evidence (or perhaps stipulations) on each specified factor, and if they fail to do so, the arbitrator or board may be obliged affirmatively to seek such evidence from them.

An illustration of this "procedural" point may be made with respect to the increasingly important factor of ability to pay. In the past, absent any "factor" legislation, if the employer failed

---

[2]*See, e.g.,* Conn. Stat. §10–153f(c)(4); Mass. Stat. 1973, c.1078, §4 (police and firefighter, now repealed) and §4B (state and MDC police); Mass. G.L. c.161A, §19G; N.J. Stat. §34:13A–16(f)(5) and 16(g); R.I. G.L. §§28–9.1–9 to 10, 28–9.2–9 to 10, 28–9.5–9 to 10, and 36-11-9 to 10; Vt. Stat. Title 21, c.20, §1733(c).

[3]*See, e.g., City of Detroit* v. *Detroit Police Officers Association,* 294 N.W.2d 68, 105 LRRM 3083 (Mich. 1980); *New Jersey State Policemen's Benevolent Assn., Local 29* (Irvington PBA) v. *Town of Irvington,* 80 N.J. 271, 403 A.2d 473, 102 LRRM 2169 (1979); *City of Richfield* v. *Local No. 1215, IAFF,* 276 N.W.2d 42 (Minn. 1979); *Town of Arlington* v. *Board of Conciliation and Arbitration,* 370 Mass. 769, 352 N.E.2d 914, 93 LRRM 2494 (1976); *City of Warwick* v. *Warwick Regular Firemen's Association,* 256 A.2d 205, 71 LRRM 3192 (R.I. 1969).

to present evidence of inability to pay, it would have been assumed that there was such an ability. And such an assumption probably made sense in an era of open-ended tax rates in which the ability to pay (as distinguished from the willingness to pay) always existed, in the sense that the power to levy the needed funds was there.

Now, with "factor" legislation, and particularly with the emergence of tax caps and other tax-limiting legislation, a union acts at its own peril if it fails to present evidence that the employer is able to fund the contractual demands that the union has made.

All of which now brings us more directly to the central topic of the day, which is the effect of tax caps and other tax-limiting legislation on the interest arbitration process. For starters, we are left largely to reasoned conjecture, since there is little real history to go on. Although California voters enacted Proposition 13 in June 1978, the state's large surplus was distributed as local aid, which has enabled the impact of Proposition 13 to be deferred until the upcoming fiscal year, commencing July 1, 1981 (by which time the state surplus will have been exhausted).

While the possible effects of Proposition 13 may have been considered in many fact-finding or interest arbitration cases, I have been able to find only one reported case on the issue, *County of Humboldt,*[4] in which a three-member fact-finding panel found that the union's economic demands were arguably justified, but recommended against them because the employer was *"not* in a position to finance the economic request. . . ."[5] The decision does not read easily because it involves a large amount of governmental accounting, which is apparently needed to make the crucial determination on ability to pay. If this detailed accounting analysis is to be the wave of the future, the Massachusetts legislature may well have been right in requiring that interest arbitrators for the MBTA "shall be experienced in state and local finance"[6]—although the American Arbitration Association, which has been given the responsibility of certifying the qualifications of the potential arbitrators,[7] may find it difficult to determine whether particular arbitrators meet the vague and general requirement of the statute.

Speaking of Massachusetts, although our Proposition 2½ is

---

[4]72 LA 63 (1978).
[5]72 LA at 66.
[6]Mass. G.L., c.161A, §19E.
[7]*Id.,* §19D

"brand new," having been approved by the electorate on November 4, 1980, we will not be able to blunt or defer its impact through increased state aid (as in California) because Massachusetts simply does not have a state surplus to fall back on. This means that Proposition 2½ began having a limited impact as of January 1, 1981, through a 62-percent reduction in automobile excise taxes (which are collected by cities and towns), and that it will have a far more devastating impact as of July 1, 1981, when local property taxes are reduced (in most communities) to the mandated 2½-percent ceiling, based on full and fair market value. To soften the blow, taxes are to reach the new level by reductions of a maximum of 15 percent per year, for those cities and towns, such as Boston, where taxes are so much higher than the new ceiling that a one-year adjustment would impose too great a hardship.

At this early point one might engage in informed speculation as to the effects of Proposition 2½ on the interest arbitration process. But in one sense there is little left to speculate about because the proponents of that proposition, apparently regarding interest arbitration as producing settlements that were too high, also eliminated the major form of binding interest arbitration in the public sector—involving local police and firefighters. However, these cases may still be submitted to interest arbitration in either of two ways. Governmental employers and public-sector unions (not limited to police and firefighters) may submit to voluntary interest arbitration in lieu of mandatory fact-finding.[8] Also, police and firefighter cases may still be considered by the joint labor-management ("Dunlop") committee and brought to arbitration, although the results of any such arbitration are not binding on the municipal legislative body, since the original arbitration statute has been repealed.[9]

Although it seems likely that this legislative limitation on the ability of municipalities to raise revenues would have had pro-

---

[8]Mass. G.L., c.150E, §9, par. 5. Although this paragraph contains a cross reference to §4 of c.1078 of the Acts of 1973, which was repealed by Proposition 2½, it would still appear that such a voluntary arbitration would be binding on the appropriate legislative body, in light of the provisions of the sixth paragraph of §9, which explicitly provides to that effect. This is in contrast to arbitration conducted under the authority of the joint labor-management committee, since the legislation authorizing such arbitration does not provide for such a binding effect, but relies exclusively upon the cross reference to §4 of c.1078. *See* note c to Table 1.

[9]*See* note c to Table 1. Mr. Dunlop might well be persuasive enough to surmount the nonbinding quality of arbitration under §4A by getting the parties to agree to "voluntary" arbitration under §9, which, as noted *supra* note 8, would be binding.

found effects upon the interest arbitration process, the legislature apparently had so little confidence in that process, even after "loading the deck" in favor of the municipalities, that it was not willing to allow the newly dealt hand to be played out at the arbitration table.

Police and firefighters are prohibited from striking and are unable to attempt to resolve their contractual impasses with their employers on that basis. Interest arbitration provided an alternative means of resolving such impasses. By removing arbitration as an option, the proponents of Proposition 2½ seem to be saying that the method of impasse resolution that they prefer is the unilateral determination of wages and conditions of employment by the employer. That this is a major step backward is unquestionable. That it will be perceived as a step backward by the police and firefighter unions is also unquestionable, and since they are being put in a no-win position of having to accept the unilateral determinations of the employer, they may well see themselves as having nothing to lose by engaging in unlawful strikes.

It is widely recognized in the private sector that a mandatory grievance arbitration clause and a no-strike clause are the quid pro quo for one another. The proponents of Proposition 2½ apparently do not realize that in public-sector bargaining, interest arbitration legislation is also the quid pro quo for no-strike legislation, and unions are not likely to sit back and quietly allow such one-sided interference in the impasse resolution process.

With the elimination of police and firefighter arbitration, the only public-sector bargaining units where the effects of Proposition 2½ may be played out in binding interest arbitration are those for state and metropolitan district police and employees of the MBTA.[10] Yet, ironically, none of the employing units in these three instances is a municipality and, therefore, none is affected by Proposition 2½ as directly as an individual municipality would be. Indeed, Proposition 2½ does not limit the state's sources of revenue (consisting largely of the proceeds from the state income tax). Hence, Proposition 2½ should have little effect on interest arbitration for state police.

On the other hand, the Metropolitan District Commission (MDC) and MBTA provide services to groups of cities and

---

[10]*Id.* In addition, pursuant to contract but not statute, interest arbitration is provided for the Massachusetts Turnpike Authority and Teamsters Local 127.

towns, upon which assessments are levied. The reduction in local revenues mandated by Proposition 2½ would therefore tend to have a greater effect upon these bargaining units than upon those within the state. However, just to make certain that the new policies of fiscal restraint are felt in these bargaining units, additional legislation has been passed under which both the MDC and the MBTA are now subject to a 4 percent "cap" on increases in the assessments which they levy upon their component cities and towns,[11] and under which the MBTA is also subject to a 104 percent budget cap, which may be overridden only by a two-thirds vote of its advisory board.[12]

The situation with respect to interest arbitration at the MBTA is rendered more complex by additional legislation which will be discussed later. At this point it would be appropriate to consider interest arbitration within the MDC police bargaining unit, in which the effects of Proposition 2½ will be more similar to those upon cities and towns (which could have been considered more directly were it not for the repeal of interest arbitration in the municipal sector).

Obviously, the impact of the new legislation will be felt first in the area of economic proposals. Wages will bear the direct brunt of the tax-limit or expenditure-limit legislation, but there will also be a concurrent effect upon other fringe-benefit economic issues. Also, and perhaps more importantly, since wages and other direct economic benefits will become fixed costs once they are set (unless there are COLA provisions), the employers will be forced to make economies in other areas in order to comply with the legislation, which may mean a reduction in bargaining-unit work through reductions in force, reductions in overtime, and increases in productivity. Thus, interest arbitrators will likely be faced with these kinds of issues far more frequently, as well as related issues such as job security, subcontracting, manning, and civilianization of the workforce (in the uniformed services).

Ability to pay and its effects upon wages will be of paramount importance. In the *Irvington PBA* case,[13] the New Jersey Su-

---

[11]Mass. G.L. c.59, §20A (added by Proposition 2½, St. 1980, c.580, §12) which applies directly to the MBTA, and which has also been made applicable to the MBTA by virtue of St. 1980, c.581, §21, beginning with calendar year 1981.

[12]Mass. St. 1979, c.151, §§8A–8B (added by St. 1980, c.581, §13). This 104-percent budget cap is similar to that imposed upon cities and towns by other sections of c.151— which, while still extant, has been effectively superseded by Proposition 2½.

[13]*Supra* note 3.

preme Court aptly pointed out the dilemma faced by a governmental employer, which is not dissimilar to that faced by an interest arbitrator:

> "In a world plagued by double-digit inflation, some group will likely suffer if municipal appropriations can increase each year by at most 5%. Non-payroll costs, such as utilities and insurance, will generally rise by more than 5%. As a result, payroll expenditures must increase by less than 5% if the municipality is to remain within permissible Cap Law limits. If the municipality desires to maintain its current level of services, it will therefore be forced to grant pay raises which are outstripped by the rate of inflation. In such a case, the real income of public employees will diminish with time.
>
> "If a municipality does not wish to or, as in the present case, cannot prevent salary levels from rising above a 5% figure, it will be forced to effect further genuine economies and thus cut back the services which it had theretofore provided its residents. In such a case, the burden ensuing from the Cap Law will be borne by those residents as well as by the employees whose jobs are eliminated on account of the town's fiscal situation."[14]

In the *Irvington* case, which involved last-best-offer arbitration, the arbitrator recommended the union's proposal which called for a wage increase in excess of 5 percent (seemingly in the vicinity of 7–8 percent). The town presented an inability-to-pay argument, maintaining that the maximum budgetary increment permitted under the 5 percent Cap Law was $536,000, and that all but $11,000 of this allowable increment was already accounted for (or "eaten up") by other unavoidable cost increases, such as previously negotiated pay increases for other employees, utilities, and insurance. The employer's argument was not dissimilar to that presented in the *County of Humboldt* case which was mentioned earlier.[15]

If similar arguments are presented in Massachusetts, as I assume they will be, their effect will be even more drastic because, at best, we are talking about a 4-percent cap on MDC and MBTA assessments, a 4-percent budget cap on the MBTA (rather than the 5-percent cap in *Irvington*), and budget reductions of as much as 15 percent per year in many of our municipalities.

I would characterize the "inability-to-pay" arguments presented by these employers as the "last-in-line" argument; that is, after money has been allotted to all the other creditors of the governmental unit involved—including whatever increases that

---

[14]403 A.2d at 486.
[15]*Supra* note 4.

have been allowed—whatever is left may be applied to the employees in the bargaining unit, and if that is not enough to fund an increase in wages, which would otherwise be justifiable when judged by all the traditional criteria, that is just too bad. The shortfall lands at the employees' doorstep.

Although this kind of "last-in-line" argument appears to have been accepted in the *Humboldt County* case, I believe that the New Jersey Supreme Court acted quite wisely and quite realistically in firmly rejecting such an approach in the *Irvington* case. There is no logical reason why an oil company should be granted a 25-percent increase, or an insurance company a 10-percent increase, simply because they sent their bills first.

Or, even if you accept the payment of these other bills as a given, that does not mean that the wages of employees should be determined by the amount of funding that remains. The employer may opt to reduce other services, and the attendant expenditures. Or, if the employer still concludes that the overall payroll for the particular group of employees must be limited or reduced, that may be accomplished by giving an appropriate wage increase and reducing the number of employees.

What the New Jersey Supreme Court was saying (and with which I am in full agreement) is that funding limitations must be shared fairly, to the extent that is possible, by the providers of public services who are paid by the employer (whether they be employees or other suppliers—although I recognize that the employer may not be in a position to bargain fully with some suppliers, such as oil companies) and by the recipients of those services, that is, the general public, who must expect a reduction or limitation in the services that they receive.

Also, within the group of employee providers, unless those employees "voluntarily" agree to provide the same level of services by accepting decreases or smaller increases in their wages, it seems unfair to force them to do so, because they are then being singled out as the only group which is paying the price of the tax-limit legislation; they are, in effect, subsidizing the municipality by providing full services previously provided at less than a fair rate of pay. (No doubt the employers would receive an interesting response if they should try to get their oil suppliers to reduce their prices or limit their increases.)

Of course, if the employees decline to subsidize municipal services in such a manner, layoffs will be one alternative method of achieving the needed cost reductions. While this is "fair" in the sense that the public is receiving less service (and therefore sharing the burden), it may be unfair, and unduly burdensome, to the particular employees who are laid off.

Because of the disproportionate burdens which layoffs impose on the laid-off employees, some unions may accept an employer's suggestion that wages be suppressed—if that will avoid layoffs. Such an approach was recently accepted by police in Belmont, Massachusetts, while being rejected by their firefighter brethren. Yet it is my feeling that, absent a willingness on the part of the employees to subsidize government in this manner, the arbitrator must grant an otherwise reasonable wage increase, notwithstanding the impact on employees who may be laid off, because the public is not entitled to get more services from its employees for less money. If the public has less money to spend on public employees, the logical consequence (excluding the possible effects of increased efficiency) is a reduction in services.

Having suggested that the "ability-to-pay" criterion does not require public employees to bear a disproportionate share of governmental belt-tightening, I am pleased to conclude this presentation with a fuller examination of statutory interest arbitration at the MBTA.

The changes in arbitration at the MBTA results from two pieces of legislation enacted in 1978 (c.405) and in 1980 (c.581). The 1978 legislation delineated the qualifications of the interest arbitrator (Massachusetts resident experienced in state and local finance[16]) and substantive factors which must be considered in rendering an award (as summarized in Table 1). In addition, the "scope of arbitration" was defined as being limited to ". . . wages, hours, and conditions of employment and shall not include any provisions for any cost of living adjustments which are based on changes in the Consumer Price Index *after* the expiration of the contract period covered by the Award."[17] This arbitrator, then sitting as the contractually designated umpire, sustained a grievance of the Carmen's Union (ATU Local Division 589) challenging the above limitations as in conflict with the collective bargaining agreement and Section 13(c) of the Urban Mass Transit Act, which the authority had agreed to abide by as a condition of receiving federal aid, and which precluded a dimi-

---

[16]G.L. c.161A, §19E, added by St. 1978, c.405, §2.
[17]G.L. c.161A, §19G, added by St. 1978, c.405, §2.

nution in employee benefits over the term of the agreement.[18] Since my ruling, the question has been tangled up in various court proceedings, bouncing from the federal system to the state system and back again without yet having been finally resolved.

Then, in the midst of the year-end MBTA fiscal crisis, during which the trains and buses actually stopped running for one day during the height of the December 1980 holiday shopping season, the legislature enacted further legislation (c.581) which provided emergency funding and which also imposed further limitations on the authority of management. These limitations on management's authority have a direct impact on the interest arbitration process since the interest arbitrator is permitted to consider only those factors "which are not precluded from bargaining" under the remainder of the legislation.[19]

The remainder of that legislation spells out the MBTA's authority to engage in collective bargaining, with numerous subjects being placed off limits, of which the most noteworthy, from the standpoint of an interest arbitrator, would be: (1) COLA clauses (this expands the limitation previously placed on the interest arbitrator by the 1978 legislation); (2) the use of overtime earnings as part of any pension benefit calculation; (3) the hiring of part-time employees; (4) the assignment and apportioning of overtime; (5) the subcontracting of services or goods; (6) levels of staffing and training; (7) hiring and promotion; (8) work assignments and productivity standards.[20]

As one who is reasonably familiar with the history of bargaining at the MBTA, I can understand "where the legislature was coming from" when it enacted c.581. The public perception is that past bargaining management "gave away the store" and that unions (primarily the Carmen's Union) are running the MBTA, being overpaid in the process, and resisting any changes that would improve the efficiency of the operation. While I disagree with this analysis, one may understand how people holding such views could legislate this unprecedented interference in the bargaining process.

Although the enumerated substantive limitations on the parties and the interest arbitrator are serious and unlikely to survive

[18]*MBTA and Local Division 589, Amalgamated Transportation Union,* arbitration award dated August 13, 1979.
[19]G.L. c.161A, §19F.8, as amended by St. 1980, c.581, §9.
[20]G.L. c.161A, §19, as amended by St. 1980, c.581, §8.

court challenges to them if a recent United States district court decision prevails, there still remains some discretion on important basic issues. For example, the legislature did not rule out wage increases or afix the lowest priority to them. Although a COLA is prohibited, and while inability to pay must be considered in light of the 4-percent budget as well as the fiscal plight of the component cities and towns under Proposition 2½, there is still room for reasonable increases although, as noted in the prior analysis, this may mean layoffs and attendant reductions in service on a public transit system at a time when fare increases may have to be imposed. All of this will necessitate an acrobatic interest arbitrator to perform the required balancing act.

On March 17, 1981, the United States District Court, District of Massachusetts, Walter Jay Skinner, United States District Judge, issued a decision in preliminary injunction matters between *Local Division 589, Amalgamated Transit Union, AFL-CIO and another* v. *The Commonwealth of Massachusetts, and others,*[21] which treated with the recently enacted statutes c.405 (1978) and c.581 (1980).

The court held:

> "a. The MBTA and the Transit Union are obliged forthwith to institute interest arbitration by three arbitrators chosen in accordance with the Articles of Agreement dated January 1, 1973, but otherwise subject to the qualifications and considerations contained in c. 405 of the Acts of 1978.
> "b. Chapter 581 of the Acts of 1980 is invalid to restrict the scope of collective bargaining contained in the unions' existing collective bargaining agreement, because said chapter constitutes an impairment of contract in violation of Article 1, Section 10, of the Constitution of the United States."

The court reasoned that the power of the state to alter existing contractual arrangements is subject to constitutional limitation even when the contracting party is a public body. A state may impair an obligation of a public body only with respect to some aspect of the contract which was not central to the reasonable expectations of the contracting parties, and then only if the impairment is reasonable and necessary in the furtherance of a valid state policy.

The court ruled that c.405 of the Acts of 1978 was effective to amend and add to the agreement of the parties, except to the central mutual consideration of the agreement and the core of the parties' reasonable expectations, which it found to be tripar-

---

[21]511 F.Supp. 312 (D.Mass. 1981).

tite interest arbitration with the neutral arbitrator being "experienced in transportation."

So much of c.405 as imposed arbitration by a single arbitrator was found to be invalid, but the c.405 requirements that the neutral arbitrator be a legal resident of the Commonwealth of Massachusetts and experienced in state and local finance were not in conflict with nor an impairment of the contract and were reasonable and valid provisions.

Where the contractual agreement to proceed to interest arbitration did not specify the standards to be applied by arbitrators, the court found no conflict or impairment of contract in the c.405 provision requiring arbitrators to rely primarily on eight factors in determining the award.

It was the court's finding that the c.405 prohibition of an award with a rollover COLA provision (with adjustment continuing for the period between the expiration of the old contract and the effective date of the new contract) was a limitation on the prior powers of the arbitrators, but it ruled that this was within the power of a state to control the affairs of a public corporation.

The court noted that c.405 granted two powers to arbitrators which they did not have before. The first was that the award of the arbitrator may be enforced against the appropriate legislative or appropriating body. The second was that they can now inquire into the financial capacity of the authority. The court stated: "The arbitrators are not limited to the specific considerations of tax burdens under this provision, but under the generality of the paragraph can presumably inquire as to other opportunities for savings or for the raising of fares."

It was the court's finding that the same legal criteria applied to the constitutional question about the effect of c.581 of the Acts of 1980 on the contract provisions. It further found that the obligation to continue to bargain collectively was a central consideration of the agreement in force when c.581 of the Acts of 1980 was passed, and to the extent that c.581 withdraws questions of substance from collective bargaining, it is in violation of Article 1, Section 10 of the Constitution of the United States.

The court ordered the parties to proceed to tripartite interest arbitration before a neutral arbitrator experienced in transportation and state and local finance who was also a resident of the Commonwealth, the arbitrators to rely on the eight factors cited in c.405.

The parties filed a joint affidavit with the court affirming that they had begun the process of arbitration as set forth in the court's order of March 17, 1981, but reserving their rights to appeal that order or any other order or to pursue relief pending appeal or pursue any other rights in this or other litigation.

It is difficult to predict what will happen with MBTA interest arbitration in the future, but at the moment management can seek in arbitration the rights it thought it had obtained in c.581. If this is done, the arbitrators will have much greater flexibility than would have been the case had they been confronting a wage question with most other major collective bargaining concerns having been ceded to management via statute.

Conclusion

It is hoped that the MBTA legislative history is an exception, but we certainly can expect to see legislative inroads on public-sector bargaining and interest arbitration for the foreseeable future. There is a pervasive atmosphere of fiscal restraint which is required by the times, and this must be respected by the parties and by interest arbitrators. At the same time we cannot permit our legitimate concern with fiscal restraint to obscure or obliterate our obligation to assure elemental and reasoned fairness in our interest arbitration awards.

Where interest arbitrators have been guided by the traditional "common-law" criteria in the past, it comes as no burden or hardship to respect and apply the recently enacted statutory criteria, and to do so in conformity to the spirit of equitable treatment of employees expressed or implied in most statutory limitations.

Chapter 8

TRIPARTITE INTEREST AND GRIEVANCE ARBITRATION

I. Tripartite Panels: Asset or Hindrance in Dispute Settlement?

Arnold M. Zack*

When I first set out to write a paper for this session, my assignment was to play the devil's advocate on the subject of tripartitism. I gleefully trotted out a whole chamber of horrors to demonstrate that tripartite arbitration was so susceptible to abuse by the parties that it contained the seeds for the destruction of the entire arbitration process.

But as I wrote, I began to recognize the assistance I'd received from some partisan arbitrators in difficult cases, and to appreciate the fact that I had been fortunate to work in a number of tripartite systems where my prophecies of doom bore not the slightest resemblance to reality. The fact that I had been "captivated" by my own literary license came home to me one day in the fall when I told one of my favorite wingpersons of my plans for the paper and was greeted with a dismayed, "How can you *do* that?"

When Bill Weinberg announced that he'd be unable to sit with us, I was forced to rewrite, with an opportunity to recant some of my dire forebodings. So now I am before you, purged of my devil's advocate responsibilities. I'm not ready to extoll tripartite arbitration as the cure for all labor-management ills, but I am satisfied that the system works for some parties, as it has on many occasions for me and for other arbitrators. However, I still harbor some skepticism about the ways in which it can be manipulated by the unscrupulous, to a far greater extent than can the single-arbitrator system.

With this new perspective, I'd like to examine and critique chronologically the operation of the tripartite system to point out some of its aspects that both please and trouble me.

---

*Member, National Academy of Arbitrators, Boston, Mass.

A brief look at the evolution of tripartitism will show that the procedure was intended to provide the neutral chairman with expert assistance in fulfilling his decision-making responsibilities. The passage of the Railway Labor Act in 1926 established the first system of grievance arbitration with provision for each of the parties to have a representative—a partisan arbitrator—to guide the neutral who was assumed to be a layman lacking the experience of a judge in the conduct of hearings and in the preparation of the decision.

Such naiveté, it followed, *required* the neutral to be guided in the proceedings by experts more intimately associated with the pending dispute—namely, arbitrators appointed by the parties themselves. In those days there was no question that the "experts" were the advocates. The neutral arbitrators were occasional, nonprofessional, and inexperienced in industrial problems. The vital national interests that were the basis for arbitration under the Railway Labor Act legitimized the provision of "wingmen" to prevent decisions by solo neutrals that would be harmful to both parties and the country.

The opportunity to have a representative on the panel to guide the neutral at the hearing and thereafter in the decision-making process made the tripartite system very appealing to the disputing parties by providing access to the neutral during the posthearing period. The parties could use this time to educate the neutral who didn't fully understand the uniqueness of their industry, their problem, and their specific dispute. The neutral, as an outsider not familiar with the parties' problems, was not fully trusted. It was not until the War Labor Board, also employing a tripartite structure, that the idea of a professional neutral arbitrator became acceptable. Yet the tripartite format continued.

Thus, when the use of arbitration expanded beyond the railroad industry and into airlines, public utilities, transit systems, and elsewhere, so did tripartitism, with the parties retaining that posthearing access to the neutral, whatever his expertise in their industry. This extra access and a lurking distrust of the neutral's having free rein over the parties' dispute, I suggest, has also contributed to the spread of tripartitism in the public sector, particularly in those jurisdictions that lack the tradition of private, industrial-sector, single-neutral arbitration.

Reflecting this background, tripartitism has now expanded into interest disputes, initially in fact-finding, and then into interest arbitration, culminating most recently in final-offer selection. Although this paper is directed primarily to tripartitism in grievance arbitration, the underlying rationale of party protection is obviously applicable to the problems of tripartitism in interest disputes, particularly in the postmediation step.

In 1968, in the 21st Proceedings of the NAA, Harold Davey concluded, in the most thorough analysis of the "Uses and Misuses of Tripartite Boards of Arbitration" that I've come across, that the future prospects were not bright for increased use of tripartite boards in grievance arbitration. But the fact that they have remained as prevalent as they are today dictates a reexamination of their benefits and risks, and their impact on the neutral's decision-making responsibilities.

Let us walk then through the case, examining the ideal and reality of tripartite panels in their three most crucial stages: the hearing, the posthearing period, and the executive session.

The Hearing

The textbook description of partisan arbitrators has them seated on either side of the neutral chairman, taking notes and permitting the chairman to rule on procedural and evidentiary questions without challenge. They may ask an occasional question of a witness, perhaps to clarify a point, and they join the neutral at lunch and recesses. No wave-making in that scenario!

The textbook description, I suspect, would have no great problem either with the partisans' occasionally caucusing with their respective teams, or caucusing with the neutral prior to rulings on important procedural or evidentiary issues, particularly if the privacy of the latter caucus is respected, with no reporting back to the teams. Most of the partisans I have worked with adhere to that restrained pattern. Indeed, when we recognize that they *are* partisans, there's little concern over their passing notes to their team or even leaning over to whisper something to them.

What does cause me concern is behavior that impacts on my role as a neutral—behavior which, but for the existence of the partisans, would not occur in a single-arbitrator format. Certain elemental standards of due process are accepted as necessary for fair hearing, even in arbitration hearings. That due process is corrupted by partisans who, acting within their authority as arbitrators, interrupt and disrupt counsel for the other side during cross examination of witnesses. It is corrupted by the partisan who interrupts the advocate for his own side and then asks the witness leading questions inappropriate in direct examination. It is corrupted when counsel for one side sits in the partisan arbitrator's seat and conducts his case from that location. It is also, I suggest, corrupted when a party calls its partisan arbitrator as a witness to testify about negotiating history—or when all other witnesses are sequestered. Is that partisan then expected to join the chairman in assessing his own credibility?

Although it could reasonably be argued that the partisans are, in reality, mere appendages of the parties who designated them, and thus subject to the procedural rulings of the neutral arbitrator, there are many parties who ignore the real roles of the partisans and insist that they are members of the arbitration panel and thus free from the chairman's scrutiny and rule. Even when they are excoriated by the neutral, the harm is often done, the opposition's presentation undermined, and the grievant's faith in the integrity of the process eroded.

Another gambit used by many parties, which I suggest is also unjust, is the substitution of the partisan arbitrator at the conclusion of the hearing. The person who heard the case for one side, who might have participated in caucuses of the board during the proceedings (and has perhaps divulged their content or the inclinations of the arbitrator to his team) is replaced for the executive session by the party's spokesperson. In at least one case, I have had as a substitute a higher ranking official of one side who was not even present at the hearing. With such tactics, the appearance of tripartite justice, as well as the form, is diminished.

Posthearing Period

After the close of the hearing, the tripartite panel usually holds a meeting, commonly referred to as the executive session. Since tripartitism appears to have bred increased reliance on transcripts and posthearing briefs, the session immediately following the hearing usually focuses on setting a time and place for the executive session. In cases where the argument has been oral, the panel may be in a position to commence its discussion on the merits. If the conventional wisdom were operant, the partisans would emphasize the best argument raised by counsel in the hearing, while the neutral chairman listened attentively to verify that he understood the positions of the advocates and had full comprehension of the case. But, unarmed with a draft decision, and absent the opportunity to have even reviewed his notes or a transcript, the neutral is usually wary and noncommittal during such a session.

It is in this session that the neutral must be alert to the efforts of one or both partisans to steer his decision away from the course logically followed by a single arbitrator. Most blatant is the request for an informed award, or an award that would treat the grievant in a different manner than would the solo arbitrator. In the single-neutral format, such an approach would result in resignation, or at least a revelation to the other side. But in tripartite arbitration, the suggestion of impropriety comes not from the parties, but from the so-called fellow arbitrators. I suggest that the response in tripartite arbitration should be no different from that in solo arbitration, although the form of the approach may be so sophisticated that the proposal of an informed award is not readily apparent. The neutral's problem arises from the requirement of a concurring vote for the majority award, or from the fact that integrity dictates a dissent from an award agreed to by the partisan arbitrators. Here, too, resignation is a palatable option.

A frustration of a different type arises from the posthearing meeting when there is discussion on matters such as credibility, with the neutral virtually baring his hand in respect to the future award. In one case recently, in a session immediately following the hearing, having expressed to the partisans my tendency to believe that a disciplinary penalty was excessive, with back pay probably appropriate, I was surprised to learn a week later that the case was settled: Reinstatement without back pay.

My chagrin arose, not due to lost writing time, but rather from the fact that the settlement reached by the parties was substantially different from what I would have awarded as a neutral. My annoyance was vitiated only after repeated reminders to myself that the process was the parties' and that settlement, rather than arbitrator's edict, is the goal of that process.

One other aspect of the session immediately following the hearing troubles me; that is the mandate from the partisans to "just write the opinion and send it to us for signature, with concurrence or dissent." Certainly I endorse the precept that the process is the parties' and the ideology that we lend ourselves to that process to facilitate the dispute-settlement machinery. But I guess I still covet some of the idealism of the textbook tripartite panel. If the opinion and decision bears three signatures, I like to assume that the two partisan arbitrators played a role in the decision-making process. I suspect my basic reaction is resentment, on the one hand, of the partisans' unwillingness to participate in the process called for in their agreement, and, on the other hand, of their continuation of the vestigial tripartite arbitration format with its appearance of joint decision-making, rather than deleting it in favor of single-person arbitration.

The credibility of the arbitration system, single or tripartite, dictates that the procedure called for in the parties' agreement be utilized, not fabricated. As long as the parties themselves have not amended their agreement to exclude the tripartite system, they and their partisan arbitrators are obligated to adhere fully to that process.

Preparing for the Executive Session

Here, too, arbitrators have had a wide variety of experiences. As noted by Syl Garrett in his Presidential Address to the Academy in 1964 (17th Proceedings), some arbitrators prepare completed drafts prior to the executive session, while others prepare partial drafts. Some arbitrators prepare simple memoranda for discussion purposes, and some present alternate drafts, suggesting opposite conclusions. Some, I suspect, do none of the above, approaching the executive session as a tabula rasa.

From the purist's viewpoint, these documents, whether in draft or final form, are the neutral's best judgment on resolving the dispute. If the format were for a single arbitrator, their judgment would prevail and the dispute would be resolved. To the extent that the partisans undertake to vary those draft decisions, they are diluting and politicizing the arbitration process by forcing, persuading, or, as Garrett uses the term, *mesmerizing* the neutral away from his or her best position, toward one that is affected by the parties.

The Executive Session

In the idealized tripartite arbitration, the executive session provides abundant opportunities to facilitate a more equitable decision than would obtain in the solo-arbitrator system. The conventional wisdom in favor of tripartitism is as follows:

First, it provides the parties with a positive assurance that the neutral fully understands the issue or issues before him. Only in the confines of the executive session can the partisans freely ask, "Do you understand?" or challenge the affirmative answer to that question if they feel the arbitrator does not. While deplored as a second bite at the apple, the conviction that the partisans have gotten their arguments across to the arbitrator is most easily attainable through the give and take of the off-the-record executive session. This opportunity to assure that the issues are understood is of particular importance in technical issues such as time study and bumping sequence.

Second, from the neutral's point of view, such easy access to the partisans is often a helpful tool for clarifying technical issues, or those on which the arbitrator acknowledges his uncertainty or fuzziness or on which he did not focus until receipt of the posthearing briefs. An unfortunate consequence of the trend toward increased legalism and posthearing briefs in arbitration is the abandonment of closing oral arguments which enlighten the arbitrator and increase the prospect that the parties will respond to each other's issues in their briefs. To that extent the executive session may provide a helpful safety net for the arbitrator who missed some point because he was tired, bored, or even somnolent. Certainly the same result can be achieved by a single arbitrator's calling in the advocates for a posthearing discussion or requesting reply briefs. But arbitrators rarely admit that they didn't completely understand the case as they left the hearing room.

Third, tripartite panels can better assure both the parties and the neutral that the language of the opinion does not create greater problems than existed before the arbitration. The luxury of language review is denied the solo arbitrator as well as the advocates in single-arbitrator cases. Only in the tripartite format do parties and arbitrators have the opportunity to steer the opinion away from rocky shores and so protect themselves from ancillary grievances or legal challenges. Only through such joint review can the arbitrator assure himself that his opinion expressed fully and clearly his thoughts and intent. Such sessions also tend to protect the arbitrator against hastily written as well as overwritten opinions and decisions.

Fourth, tripartite panels provide the ideal format for the mediated decision. Perhaps in the hands of a George Taylor the philosophy or reasoning together in an executive session to achieve a consensus decision was readily attainable. But I suspect that neutrals with his talent are rare and that the population of like-minded partisans is thinning. Settlements during executive sessions don't occur often.

Admittedly, in interest arbitration the subject matter of the dispute is broader, the number of issues greater, the tools for mediation more convenient, and thus the prospect of a mediated arbitration decision greater, but in grievance arbitration, with less gray area between the parties' positions, that approach has less applicability. Nonetheless it is clear that such opportunity is more readily available in the tripartite format than in single neutral arbitration. Many grievance disputes are mediable, and the executive session is an acceptable mode for attempting such resolution even to the point of settlement to avoid the arbitration decision.

Fifth, even if a complete settlement of the issue is not achieved through the mediation of the chairman, the tripartite forum provides an otherwise missing opportunity to narrow the area of dispute between the parties and thus fashion an opinion and decision that is more palatable to the parties and strengthens their faith in the dispute-settlement process. Such an approach is most useful in interest disputes where it has been described as med-arb. There, the acceptability of an award or the terms of a new contract, even though the award is to be binding, may hinge on a decision which falls within the range of the parties' expectations.

Sixth, and perhaps most hopefully for neutrals, adept handling of the hearing and particularly the executive session offers the arbitrator a forum for exhibiting his skill, his articulateness, his mediating ability. Such a demonstration may persuade the partisans that he may be valuable for a future dispute. But then again, such exposure may be the last thing the frequently eccentric arbitrator should be willing to risk. The lamentable consequence could be avoidance rather than the guarantee of future cases.

Despite the foregoing ideals of the tripartite system, the practitioners frequently have a different goal—to win cases. Thus, the idealized tool is only as good as the craftsmen who employ it.

Tripartite arbitration in the hands of mere mortals who are

saddled with representative responsibilities thus tends to evolve as merely another forum for achieving victory. The added complexity inherent in the tripartite system—the three-man panel, posthearing access to the neutral, the executive session, and the right to share in signing the decision—offers additional opportunities to influence and alter the neutral's decision-making process.

I am greatly concerned about partisan conduct which insidiously and adversely impacts on the independent judgment and decision-making role of the neutral and which can only raise questions as to the integrity of the arbitration process as a whole. Let's look at these problem areas.

First, the partisan arbitrators are often frustratingly unequal in competence. On one side is the competent, articulate partisan who has careful and complete notes and total recall of the testimony. On the other side is a second- or third-string player who sat and doodled through the hearing and who is virtually mum throughout the executive session. While such obvious imbalance may be unusual, and while it may not have any impact on the neutral's already-made-up mind, it can have an insidious impact on the marginal case where the articulate partisan arbitrator can swing the balance in his favor in the absence of effective opposition. Even worse is the undecided or marginal case where the silence or minimal contribution on the part of the incompetent partisan arbitrator may be interpreted as acquiescence to a decision in favor of the other side.

Second, there is a frightening and all-too-common tendency on the part of partisan arbitrators to confide in the neutral, during the executive session, the "real facts" behind a grievance. While most arbitrators seek to squelch the offering of such tidbits and nip such improper revelations in the bud, many do not or cannot do so before the unsought information is blurted out. This is not merely a matter of one partisan's providing information which the other may not have been privy to, it is a problem of providing assertions to the neutral which have not been subject to the truth-finding exercises of cross-examination or rebuttal and which may constitute a serious deprivation of the grievant's right to confront his accuser. The resulting impact on the neutral of such "private insights" is hard to gauge. It may be that they are accepted as gospel. It may be that they are resented as an underhanded effort to influence the neutral. Whichever reaction prevails, there is no question that it introduces into the decision-making process one more element that is precluded from the single-arbitrator format, providing the innuendo which forces a reweighing of the neutral's individual "best judgment," perhaps even to the point of changing the decision.

Third, there is too frequently the requirement of a majority award. While the problems of a majority decision may be avoided by the issuance of the chairman's opinion, this does not lessen the problems of securing agreement of the majority of the board of arbitrators on the decision. In most cases it is not a problem, since one party prevails and that partisan arbitrator signs the decision. But there are many cases where the neutral's decision does not endorse fully the position of one party or the other, as well as many instances where the partisans refuse to concur in part to the portion from which the other partisan(s) dissented. I have had one such deadlock case where I reinstated a discharged employee without back pay and both partisans dissented. In such a case the neutral may find himself in the awkward position of having to negotiate with one of the parties against the position he deems appropriate in order to secure a concurring signature and, thus, a majority opinion.

Fourth, attendant on the additional delays of tripartitism is the inequity of reinstatement which is held up that much longer. When viewed in the light of the frequency with which such reinstatement is made without back pay, it places the total cost of the delay on the shoulders of the grievant who can least afford it and who would have been more rapidly returned to work and to breadwinner status under the single-arbitrator format.

Conclusion

I would like to have concluded this paper by proclaiming that my arguments in support of the merits of tripartite arbitration swept me off my feet. But I must admit that despite a series of very pleasant, positive, and helpful relationships that I have enjoyed under tripartite arrangements, I am frankly unpersuaded that decisions emanating from tripartite arbitration systems are any better than those resulting from the solo-arbitrator system. My skepticism as to the supremacy of tripartitism is compounded by my own observations of the abuse of the tripartite system as well as its potential impact on the integrity of the neutral and on the arbitration system as a whole.

Arbitration is increasingly challenged because of delays and costs. With the delays necessitated by the need for an executive session, let alone transcripts and briefs, and with costs escalated by the use of partisan arbitrators with their lost work opportunities and expenses on top of the fees and expenses of the neutral, it is clear that tripartitism is a greater offender in the area of costs and delays than solo arbitration.

Moreover, if the suspicions are valid that tripartite arbitration is only a traveling road show existing solely to "cut the deal," then I suggest the institution and its participants are in jeopardy.

It is up to the partisans to recognize the consequences of their improprieties and to institute reform. It is up to the neutrals to be forceful in curbing these improprieties and to assert their unwillingness to continue in a procedure that they view as improperly influencing their independent judgment.

For the time being the jury—or should I say the "panel"—is still out on the question of whether tripartite arbitration has become an asset or a hindrance to the dispute-settlement process.

II. TRIPARTITE ARBITRATION:
OLD STRENGTHS AND NEW WEAKNESSES

CHARLES M. REHMUS[*]

One way of approaching the subject of tripartite arbitration is to examine the history of the way this subject has been treated at previous meetings of the Academy. I was the editor of the volume of *Proceedings* of the 21st Annual Meeting which took place in 1968. At that meeting the subject of tripartite arbitration boards was examined more thoroughly than at any Academy meeting before or since. Not only did Hal Davey present a thorough and thoughtful paper on the subject, but four panel sessions, each of them tripartite, discussed tripartitism in arbitration and reported on their conclusions. My recollection of editing the reports of those panel workshops was that, in general, the partisans expressed far greater support for and confidence in tripartite boards than did the arbitrators who participated. I thought then, and continue to believe now, that this fact alone should give our members pause. Apparently our general confidence in our competence and expertise is not uniformly shared, or shared to the same degree, by those who retain us. If those parties are willing to accept the delays and higher costs that are usually associated with genuine tripartitism in return for the greater confidence it gives them in both the process and the outcome, then there is obviously no reason to argue they should not do so. More importantly, perhaps we should be less quick to keep harping on the weaknesses of the process.

That was my thought a dozen years ago. Since then I have found my arbitration practice increasingly in industries that rely on tripartite boards. As a result I find myself in complete sympathy with Workshop D of 1968, which was composed entirely of practitioners from and arbitrators with experience in the airline industry. This group, alone among the four workshops, expressed itself as overwhelmingly in favor of the tripartite boards almost universally used in the airline industry. It is, of course, true that this evolution resulted from the Railway Labor Act's system board precedents. But does the statutory background in

---

[*]Member, National Academy of Arbitrators; Dean, New York State School of Industrial and Labor Relations, Cornell University, Ithaca, N.Y.

any real way explain these parties' preference? Surely such sophisticated practitioners could waive executive sessions and the like if they did not think them useful, even if they felt the Act constrained them to include the facade of a tripartite procedure in their contracts. The answer seems clearly to be that they, and some of us, find the tripartite procedure useful.

One of my early pilot experiences illustrates why. In a particular case, I genuinely awaited the posthearing executive session, not to understand the dispute itself, but rather the intensity of emotion that seemed to underlie it. Early in the executive session, I therefore asked the ALPA pilot board member, "Tell me, why do the pilots seem to feel so strongly about this work practice?" Before he could respond, a company member, also a pilot, jumped in: "Because the damn practice just isn't as safe as the alternatives!" Not only did I realize this was a situation where two pilots could and should outvote three others, I also began to appreciate the real values of tripartite boards, at least where they are manned, or womanned, by partisans of integrity.

Similarly, my friends from the flight attendants' side of the industry have often helped me to understand not simply the facts, but also the underlying stakes involved in some of their grievances—issues that had I been working alone I might have misunderstood or weighed inadequately. Most arbitrators, even if they have a few kind words to say about the tripartite board members, nevertheless conclude that the practice is wrong if it changes their bottom line—who wins or loses the award. In his paper, Arnold Zack expresses frustration about a case where parties, having received a hint in executive session as to which way he was leaning, proceeded to settle the grievance on a basis much different than he would have awarded. Again, why?

Every day in North America parties settle grievances on terms much different than I would have, but I have never wrapped myself in a mantle of omniscience and concluded they were wrong. Returning to the airline industry, I have gone to more than several executive sessions with my mind tentatively made up, only to find that the discussion led me to a wholly different award. And it goes both ways. Occasionally an employee I have thought hopeless is deemed by both company and union representatives to be potentially salvageable and worthy of another chance. At other times I have been very concerned by the apparent inequity of what happened to the grievant under the contract, only to discover that both parties conceded that that was what they bargained for, even if they did not foresee all the consequences. I cannot conclude that my resultant award, which might have been different without the further understanding I gained at the executive session, was somehow corrupted because the parties, even without knowing it, persuaded me to change the bottom line.

In summary, my experience with tripartitism among skilled and quasi-neutral board members is that it ranges from neutral to positive in terms of its value to the process—neutral in many cases because my board members genuinely cannot agree or because this industry, like any, has its share of five-and-dime grievances where the tripartite procedure contributed nothing to my understanding or the wisdom of my conclusion, but positive, often, for the reasons I have expressed.

Let me turn for a moment to tripartite boards in interest arbitration, particularly those in the public sector. At the 1974 Annual Meeting I gave a paper pointing out that if you combine final-offer arbitration with somewhat flexible procedures, the process becomes known as med-arb, where no award need ordinarily be rendered and even those that are necessary are often consent awards. I would simply repeat today that tripartitism is almost essential to this process. Moreover, med-arb has seemed a valuable enough tool that several states have deliberately sought by legislation to adopt med-arb procedures that we in Michigan happened on by accident.

Nor have I lost my confidence in such procedures. An interest arbitrator is a legislator, not a judge. We have not taken to legislating by philosopher-kings, either in Plato's time or now, and I don't think we should in labor-management relations. We who are occasionally asked to legislate in the public sector will almost invariably do so more wisely if we find our decisions informed and molded by the ideas and pressures of others' opinions, or even by their prejudices. This is the essence of the legislative process.

Having said that, let me add that I am not as enthused about some developments in the *practice,* as opposed to the *theory,* of public-sector arbitration as I was some seven or eight years ago. In practice, I have found that the wise legislative process of which I spoke increasingly breaks down, for several reasons.

First, as we have opted for public-sector interest arbitration in more and more states and as its use is therefore more common, the relationships between the parties and between the members of tripartite panels are often immature. Those who think or behave childishly cannot by definition do a wise job of accommodating, compromising, and creative problem-solving the process requires. Moreover, I cannot absolve my arbitrator colleagues from blame in this area. Since I gave my 1974 paper, I spent four years as chief administrator of the Michigan arbitration statute. Upon occasion, the senior experienced arbitrators were simply unwilling to shoulder what Arvid Anderson has called the "heavy lifting" of interest arbitration. This leaves it to their younger and less experienced colleagues to fill the void. Thus, we have too often seen immature parties led by less experienced neutrals—hardly the best recipe for industrial creativity or a happily rising cake.

Another problem with public-sector interest arbitration that has appeared increasingly in recent years is that arbitration has been required to substitute for collective bargaining in relationships where, because of eroded tax bases, taxpayer rebellions, or both, the wages and fringe benefits of public employees have fallen well behind inflation and even to substandard levels. If you will go back to the 1973 Annual Meeting, you will find that Herman Sternstein cautioned us that interest arbitration cannot work, at least in the local transit industry, if wages and benefits are substandard. Without taking time to repeat his reasons for this conclusion, I would simply note that the caution expressed there is equally true of the public sector. Where arbitration panels are asked to work with genuine inability to pay, whatever its cause, the resulting awards have sometimes become a political football. The neutrals have too often been attacked by the politicians and even by judges because *we* have not been able painlessly to overcome *their* or *society's* deficiencies. It is not healthy for arbitration to become mixed with the political process. I decry such happenings, though I doubt that even the strongest and most experienced arbitration panels can do much to avoid it.

In final conclusion, while I believe that tripartite interest arbitration in the public sector is here to stay, I fear we are not doing all we can to make it work as well as it might. Where the parties and their relationships are not mature, where they put partisan representatives on panels who possess neither experience nor credibility with their constituents, and where they are led by a relatively inexperienced neutral, the potential for mischief is present. If the parties then use the award that ensues as a scapegoat for their own political failures, the mischief becomes a reality. No matter where the fault lies—and I would spread it rather broadly, even including some of us—the result does no credit to arbitration, either as a profession or as an institution.

Comment—

I. J. GROMFINE*

I received and read Arnold Zack's paper around Easter time, and as I went through his catalogue of actual and potential misconduct by partisan arbitrators in tripartite grievance arbitrations, my mind kept returning to my favorite Easter story. It is a very old one, dealing with the American priest whose origins were in that part of Ireland where a pronounced distaste for the British is a way of life. Every time this priest delivered a sermon, no matter what the subject, he found some occasion to blast England. Finally the Bishop called him in, lectured him on the fact that Catholicism is a religion and not a political institution, and ordered that henceforth his sermons be confined strictly to theological matters and not involve any castigation of England or the British people. For a full year the priest complied with the injunction, though his heart was not in it at all. Finally, after a year of suppressing the only subject he had any interest in, he could stand it no longer. It was Easter, and he rose in the pulpit and said: "My friends, the gospels tell us that at the Last Supper the Lord Jesus rose, and he said to his disciples, 'Before the cock crows in the morn, one of you will deny me thrice.' And there was one amongst the disciples whose name was Judas, and he rose and said, "I sy gov'ner; you aynt lookin' at me ar yu?' "

To all of the high crimes and misdemeanors that Arnold has listed, I plead not guilty.

A very large proportion of the grievance arbitrations, and almost all of the interest arbitrations, handled by my office involve cases in which we act as counsel and partisan arbitrators representing, in tripartite arbitrations, the Amalgamated Transit Union, which is the dominant union in America in the local and over-the-road passenger industry. From its inception in 1892, the Amalgamated has been wedded to the process of

---

*Gromfine, Sternstein, Rosen and Taylor, P.C., Washington, D. C.

arbitration both in grievance and interest disputes. So far as I know, it is the only union in America which, from its beginning, has had a provision in its constitution denying sanction to any strike over any issue (including the terms of a new agreement) unless the employer has been offered and has refused the opportunity to arbitrate the dispute, whether or not the contract or any law requires such arbitration.

What is more, from the beginning tripartite arbitration has been the dominant method followed by this union, and provided for in its labor agreements both for grievances and interest disputes. When Arnold Zack suggests, as he does, that tripartite grievance arbitration had its inception with the Adjustment Board provisions of the Railway Labor Act in 1926, he overlooks the transit industry. Transit agreements in Boston, Washington, Pittsburgh, Memphis, St. Louis, and many other cities provided for tripartite arbitration of all disputes many years prior to 1926.

So far as interest disputes are concerned, there never was any question as to the preferred form. I know of no local of the Amalgamated that has ever willingly submitted a dispute over the terms of its contract to a single arbitrator or a board of neutrals. I will have more to say on that in a moment. But even as to grievances, the clear preference has been for the tripartite form, and that preference originally developed not alone—or even primarily—in the need to provide guidance to the early corps of nonprofessional arbitrators on the conduct of hearings or the preparation of decisions, or to provide assistance in the understanding of technical matters peculiar to the industry, as Arnold suggests was the case in the railroad industry. Those were factors that influenced the original decision to opt for tripartite arbitration in transit, but there was an even more fundamental consideration, at least from the union's point of view. And that is the simple notion that collective bargaining, which is the underpinning of any form of arbitration, implies that the union will have a meaningful voice in the grievance process from the moment the grievance is filed to the time when a decision on the dispute is issued. Win, lose, or draw—the union feels more secure, and is better able to live with the result (even when the result is a loss), if it knows that its representative has had an opportunity not only to present the facts and argue the merits, but to participate in the process by which a decision was reached.

That opportunity to participate in the decision-making process need not take any specific form, and techniques can be, and have been, developed which avoid many of the problems, particularly the problems during the hearing, that Arnold referred to. In the transit industry, for example, we typically employ in grievance arbitrations one person who serves both as the counsel for his party at the hearing and as the arbitrator for that party. On matters of procedure and evidence at the hearing, the neutral rules as if he were the sole arbitrator. After the hearing, the neutral studies the record and briefs (if any) and submits a proposed award to the two partisans. Either partisan then has 10 days in which to request an executive session of the board, failing which the proposed award becomes final.

In many of the cases no executive session is requested. The winner is happy with the result and the reasoning by which that result was reached. The loser is unhappy with the result, but is satisfied that the neutral chairman has given full consideration to all of his evidence and argument. But even when no executive session is held, I believe the tripartite system serves an important function. I recognize that, in cases where there is a single arbitrator with no executive session available, *most* professional arbitrators will still try their best to come up with a result that does justice to all of the evidence and arguments presented. Yet I must say that in my experience with tripartite arbitration, the fact that the neutral knows that his proposed award may have to be fully defended and explained in a face-to-face meeting of the board provides an added incentive that often makes the difference between a fair, well-reasoned decision and one that is not.

Sometimes when the decision is not clear, or where the neutral arbitrator may have ventured into areas not necessary to his decision that may cause more problems in the future, an executive session is requested, and such executive sessions are most frequently handled by a conference telephone call.

Sometimes, however, the problem with the proposed award is more serious. The losing party in the proposed award feels that the neutral has ignored or misconstrued some critical evidence or has overlooked or misunderstood an important argument. In those cases a meeting of the board is convened, and it is there that the tripartite form and the opportunity it provides for participation in the decision-making process takes on real meaning. In his listing of the elements of what he calls an "idealized tripartite arbitration," Arnold Zack mentions the fact that only in the confines of an executive session of a tripartite board are the partisans free to ask, and insist on an acceptable answer to, the question put to the neutral: "Do you understand?" In my judgment, that simple element, in and of itself, justifies the use of tripartite arbitration. Even when performed by the same individual who acted as counsel at the hearing, the advocacy in an executive session is a different kind of advocacy than is possible or appropriate at the hearing. When properly performed, it is no mere reargument of the case. It is a probing into the stated and unstated thought processes by which the neutral reached his proposed decision, in an effort to understand the decision even if it is not possible to change it. Even when I have not succeeded in changing the result, I have almost always come away from an executive session with a better understanding of why the neutral reached the result he did, and I have been in a better position to explain it to my client.

There have been times when the entire proposed decision was reversed. I remember a case in which a very eminent past president of this Academy reversed his proposed decision to sustain a discharge when, as a result of the discussion in the executive session, he discovered that he had totally ignored a very critical piece of evidence. There have been many other times in my experience when, even though the ultimate result was not changed, the neutral was able to strengthen the reasoning by which that result was reached on the basis of discussion by the partisan supporting that result in the executive session. There have been other times in appropriate cases when the executive session provided a forum for a mediated award that may have differed from what the neutral would have done on his own, but which provided a greater measure of acceptability to what would otherwise have been the losing party. Arnold suggests that it takes a George Taylor to pull that off and there are not many of his mold around, and that, in any event, it involves a kind of compromising of his judgment that many arbitrators may find distasteful. I believe that there are many arbitrators today who are equal to the task of achieving a mediated result in an appropriate case (and not all are), and if doing so compromises the neutral, so be it. It is the parties who have to live with each other long after the arbitrator has left the scene.

I recognize that there are many arbitrators who have no feel for the tripartite process, let alone participation in mediated awards. I remember one case in which I had requested an executive session after the neutral had issued a proposed award in which his decision turned entirely upon a finding of fact for which I could find not a scintilla of support in the record. When I arrived at the executive session, I was greeted with these words from the neutral: "Mr. Gromfine, you are of course free to make any statements or comments about my proposed award you may deem appropriate, but I am duty bound to tell you that once I have written a decision, I never change it."

Fortunately for those of us in the business of *interest* arbitration, such neutrals rarely make their way into interest cases, and it is about tripartite arbitration in interest cases that I want to direct my remaining comments.

The subject matter assigned to this panel does not, of course, go to the question of the merits of interest arbitration as an alternative to the strike or other means of resolving disputes over the terms of a contract. For the purposes of this discussion we assume that, for one reason or another, the terms of the contract are to be determined in arbitration, and we consider only the limited question of whether tripartite arbitration or arbitration before a single arbitrator or a multineutral panel is the most appropriate. On that question I do not believe there is any contest. Indeed, in my opinion, anyone who does not accept the compelling necessity for tripartite arbitration in interest cases does not really understand what interest arbitration is all about.

In such cases, typically, the stakes are very high—much higher by far than is true in the normal grievance case—and both sides have a vital interest in participating to the fullest degree in every aspect of the process by which a decision is made as to the terms of the contract under which they both must live in the year or years ahead. It is not enough to describe the difference between grievance and interest arbitration, as it commonly is by the scholars, in terms of the difference between the judicial and the legislative process. The executive session in an interest case is, in a very real sense, an extension, at a sophisticated level, of the process of collective bargaining. The union's capacity at the bargaining table to threaten a strike, and the employer's capacity at the bargaining table to fold its arms, say "no," and take its chances on a strike, are both removed. Left only is the opportunity, on both sides, to persuade the neutral, on the basis of evidence in the record before him or her.

Persuade the neutral to do what? If winning the day was all that counted, the persuading could be done by counsel at the hearing and the matter left to the neutral. Winning is *not* all that counts. Interest arbitration in the transit industry has survived for almost a century because, while there have been occasional catastrophies for one side or the other, over the long run it has produced results, fashioned in the give and take of tripartite executive sessions, which have achieved a reasonable measure of *acceptability* by both parties.

Only in an executive session do the partisans have an opportunity to do the kind of probing of the neutral I mentioned earlier (except that here it is so much more important than in grievance cases) to ascertain to what extent the neutral really understands the message in the typically voluminous economic evidence that will have been placed before him, and to correct him when he appears to be going astray. Only in an executive session (meeting jointly and individually with the partisan members of the board) can the neutral ascertain the depth of commitment each party has with respect to particular issues, and the real priorities each side assigns to the various issues before the board. Only in an executive session is there an opportunity for the neutral to fashion a mediated award (which is the ideal in an interest case), or, if not that, then at least an award that comes closer than the parties were able to do at the bargaining table to meeting the legitimate claims, justified by the evidence, of both parties.

The deep concern that the Amalgamated, at least, has in assuring that the tripartite process be maintained in interest cases evidences itself in some recent, and still pending, litigation in Massachusetts. The Amalgamated contract covering the employees of the MBTA (the transit system serving Boston and many other communities in the Boston area) has, since at least 1913, provided for tripartite interest arbitration, the only requirement as to the neutral being that he be experienced in transportation. In 1978 the state legislature enacted a law requiring among other things, that any future interest arbitrations involving the MBTA must be conducted before a single neutral who is a resident of the state and is experienced in state and local finance. With all due respect to the many fine arbitrators who are legal residents of Massachusetts, the union was offended at the insidious implications involved in restricting the selection of a neutral to local talent who the legislature obviously considered might be more susceptible to the less than impartial newspaper publicity that typically attends an arbitration involving the cost of providing a public service. But, while the union might be able to live with that burden and rest in the hope that a professional Massachusetts arbitrator will tune out the *Boston Globe,* it could not live with the concept of interest arbitration before a single neutral, for that, the union believed, would emasculate the process.

So far the union's position has been sustained. A federal district court has very recently adjudicated that the enactment by the Massachusetts legislature of the requirement that the MBTA interest cases be heard and determined by a single neutral arbitrator represented an unconstitutional impairment of the obligation of contract. The case is now on appeal to the First Circuit. The basic case and the appeal by both sides involve many other issues with a great deal of "lex appeal," but they are not germane to the question we are discussing this morning. I mention the case really to underscore the fact that, for the Amalgamated, the notion that interest arbitrations must be conducted before a tripartite board, with a full opportunity for both sides to participate in the decision-making process, is a fighting issue.

The techniques by which neutral arbitrators in transit interest cases have made the executive session perform the kinds of essential functions I have described are enormously varied. I could not possibly begin to describe the variations in the time allotted to me. Most neutrals do a lot of listening until they have reached at least some tentative conclusions on the major economic issues, leaving most of the debate initially to the partisans who must, if the process is to work, know what they are doing, have integrity, and be clothed with the authority to do something more than parrot arguments already made at the hearing. After a lot of listening, the neutral may then announce his tentative conclusions, usually to the great dismay of one or both partisans, modifying them in some respects on the basis of continuing discussions, or he may suggest alternative possible conclusions he would be willing to reach either on specific issues or on a total package, in the expectation that one or the other partisans will draw closer to one or the other alternatives.

I am obviously oversimplifying the matter, and as a very partisan partisan, it is not fitting for me to run a class in how neutrals do, or should, make tripartite interest arbitration work. This much, however, I can say—it is not a job for every arbitrator, regardless of how skilled and experienced he may be in grievance matters. In his discussion of interest arbitration in transit during the 1973 meetings of this Academy, my associate, Herman Sternstein, outlined what we regard as the essential qualifications of a neutral in a tripartite interest case: open-mindedness (that is, a willingness to plow new ground); experience and basic competence in the handling of economic and statistical material; diligence in reviewing the record and the arguments of the parties; and a combination of the kind of flexibility that will enable him to move from a position he may have been inclined to before the sessions began and the kind of toughness that will enable him to do battle for his position once he has reached a position he is satisfied is justified in the light of all he has heard in the hearings and in the executive session.

It is not by accident that 22 of the 31 past presidents of the National Academy of Arbitrators have served (several of them on a number of occasions) as neutral arbitrators in tripartite transit interest cases, and you may be interested in knowing that we now have several agreements in the industry that require that the panel of arbitrators from which the neutral is selected be members of this Academy.

Let me close these comments with this summary observation. Given my background and how I make my living, I would prefer *two-man* arbitrations—a neutral and a union representative. But until I can convince some management to go along with that notion, I will opt for tripartite arbitration for both grievance and interest cases every time.

Comment—

Roger H. Schnapp*

My comments today will be limited to tripartite *grievance* arbitration. I have no personal experience with tripartite interest arbitration and will, therefore, leave that subject to those members of this panel who do have such experience.

I am an enthusiastic proponent of tripartite grievance arbitration. My experience with it has been in the airline industry. At American Airlines, I frequently functioned both as a member of system boards of adjustment and as an advocate before those system boards. At Trans World Airlines, my role has been lim-

*Parker, Milliken, Clark & O'Hara, Los Angeles, Calif. (formerly Counsel-Industrial Relations, Trans World Airlines, Inc., New York, N.Y.).

ited to that of advocate. I also have had experience as an advocate, outside the airline industry, with sole-arbitrator arbitration. As a result of both experiences, I believe that the parties and the arbitration process are best served by tripartite grievance arbitration.

Arnold Zack has been critical of a number of practices that can and do occur under a tripartite system. I do not disagree with him concerning the undesirability of most of the practices that he has criticized. I would, however, place the blame differently. From my perspective, when tripartite grievance arbitration does not work properly, it is generally the fault of the arbitrator, not the parties. Like all generalizations, it is certainly not true in every instance. However, I respectfully submit that it is true in the great majority of situations.

In support of this proposition, I would like to relate to you two of my experiences with tripartite grievance arbitration. The first, I believe, is an example of the process at its best. The second is an example of the process at its worst.

For my example of the process at its best, let me describe an American Airlines case where I was the company-appointed member of the system board of adjustment. The case involved American's ground employees, and the issue was one of contract interpretation. At the hearing the company advocate did an outstanding job of supporting the denial of the grievance. Subsequent to the hearing, the union system board member and I had occasion to be together on another matter, and he took the opportunity to discuss the grievance with me. In essence, he agreed that the grievance was without merit and explained that the union had taken it to arbitration for essentially political reasons. Therefore, he had no trouble concurring in a decision denying the grievance. However, he was concerned about the *opinion* as opposed to the award. He shared my view that the company advocate had done an outstanding job of presenting the company's position and, as a result, his concern was that the arbitrator might go too far in denying the grievance. By "too far," he meant that the arbitrator might have found the advocate's arguments so persuasive that he would read the language as even more favorable to the company than the parties had intended. The union system board member and I were in complete agreement concerning the intent of the language and its proper interpretation. Similarly, we both agreed that the grievance should be denied in its entirety. As a result of our discussion, we also agreed that the opinion that was ultimately handed down by the system board of adjustment should be consistent with our joint understanding of what the language meant.

When we subsequently met with the arbitrator, the worst fears of my union counterpart were realized. The arbitrator was prepared to accept the arguments of the company's advocate and issue an opinion that was far more favorable to the company than the parties had intended when they negotiated the agreement. However, after the arbitrator had heard the arguments of his two "wingpersons," he agreed to modify his opinion so that it would be consistent with our joint understanding of what the language meant. In this instance, I believe that the tripartite process provided a result far superior to that which would have occurred in a sole-arbitrator situation. The company and union system board members were able to contribute something to the arbitrator's deliberations that would otherwise have been absent.

Contrast this case with the next one I will describe—which, in my experience, is an example of tripartite arbitration at its worst. This case involved an indefinite suspension of a flight attendant for health reasons. I was neither the company system board member nor the company advocate, but was functioning in my role as TWA's chief in-house industrial relations attorney. The grievant was an epileptic who had been suspended for medical reasons after having an epileptic seizure while working on board an aircraft. While TWA had a consistent policy, of long standing, of not permitting epileptics to work as flight attendants, a new area medical director permitted this flight attendant to return to duty after having been assured by the flight attendant's physician that there was no reason to expect a recurrence of the problem. On the attendant's first flight after returning to duty, a second seizure occurred, early in the flight. It not only incapacitated the flight attendant in question, but required another attendant to take care of him. Thus, as a practical matter, there were two less working flight attendants than there should have been. The flight attendant was suspended indefinitely for medical reasons. Two issues were submitted to the arbitrator: (1) Should the flight attendant have been suspended (as of the date of his suspension)? (2) Should the flight attendant have been continued on suspension (as of the date of the hearing)? The arbitrator answered both questions in the affirmative. He agreed that the flight attendant should have been suspended and should have been kept on suspension at least until the date of the hearing. However, he went on to indicate that he did not agree with the company's policy of not permitting epileptics to work as flight attendants. In the executive session, the company board members (it was a five-person system board) reminded the arbitrator that he had been asked only two questions—by either the company or the union—and that his gratuitous comments concerning the company's policy exceeded his authority. The arbitrator, demonstrating what I considered to be an egregious lack of integrity, withdrew that portion of his opinion and award which dealt with the company policy and *reversed* his position on the second question. Thus, his ultimate decision was that it was proper to suspend the grievant (at the time of the suspension), but that the grievant had to be reinstated. Regrettably, the arbitrator in question, while a member of the Academy, is not present today. Since he is, therefore, not able to defend himself, I have decided not to mention his name. That decision, however, represents the nadir of tripartite arbitration in my own experience.

Before closing, I would like to discuss briefly some questions that arise in tripartite arbitration and give you the benefit of my own thoughts on them. I should first indicate that the views that I am about to express are my own and do not always represent the view of my clients—the labor relations and personnel departments of TWA.

When I have served as a system board member, I have intentionally and studiously avoided acquiring any knowledge of the case prior to the hearing—other than that which is in the submission to the arbitrator. My reason for this is that I want to be in the same position as the neutral when the case is presented. Too often a company system board member does not recognize that the record is inadequate because his or her own knowledge—having been supplemented by a briefing prior to the hearing—is not similarly inadequate. By avoiding such a briefing, I attempt to insure that any inadequacy in the company's presentation will be as obvious to me as it is to the arbitrator. Often this results in my raising questions during the hearing—addressed to both parties—when I feel the need for clarification. Hopefully, my own need for clarification simply reflects a similar need by the neutral. My own experience has been that this "planned ignorance" has served me well as a company system board member.

A related, but somewhat different, problem occurs when a member of the system board has had previous contact with the case. For example, there are certain individuals who are routinely consulted concerning disciplinary matters by operating management. While they are not the ones who make the disciplinary decisions, they advise the supervisors who do. It is not uncommon for the same individuals to be selected as system board members. When this occurs, these individuals are, to some extent, reviewing their own advice. There have been a number of court decisions upholding the right of a party to select an individual as its system board member even though that individual has had prior contact with the case. TWA is now being sued by a former pilot who is alleging that the Air Line Pilots Association violated its duty of fair representation. One of the elements of this pilot's case is that ALPA did not challenge a TWA system board member who had previously been involved in discussions of the discharge decision. At United Airlines, company board members have been challenged, on the basis of their prior contact with the grievance, and it is my understanding that they have voluntarily disqualified themselves. This appears to be a subject that will receive increased attention in the future.

Arnold has indicated that he is troubled when the partisan system board members tell him to "just write the opinion and send it to us for signature, for concurrence or dissent." I am troubled by the mirror image of this situation. What disturbs me is the number of arbitrators who prepare a written decision—for all intents and purposes in final form—and bring it to the first executive session of the system board. By doing so, these neutrals destroy the essence of a system *board* of adjustment. The parties may as well have specified a sole-arbitrator system. While it is true that there will be the occasional situation where *neither* partisan system board member is willing to concur with the neutral's opinion and award, this is the exception and not the rule. Most often, the neutral can achieve concurrence by one or the other of the partisan system board members. To borrow a colorful phrase from the National Labor Relations Board, such conduct by a neutral has a "chilling effect" on the proper functioning of tripartite arbitration. I feel very strongly that a neutral should defer writing an opinion and award, or even becoming fixed in his position, until he has had an opportunity to discuss the case with the other members of the system board of adjustment. I do not believe it to be undesirable for the neutral to be affected by the arguments of his fellow system board members. The fact that this may result in a different decision than would have been achieved with sole-arbitrator arbitration only means that the parties are getting just what they bargained for—a tripartite award and opinion, with all of the benefits that result from that system.

A problem that is of growing concern to me is the increased tendency of neutrals to treat a request for arbitration as if it were a request for a management consultant. This occurs when the arbitrator says to the company system board member: "I believe that the company interpreted the contract properly, but it is bad employee relations to insist upon this interpretation. Therefore, even though the company is right, I believe it is to the company's advantage to have me rule (at least in part) in favor of the union." This is outrageous. My counterparts in management and I are paid to make decisions of this type. By the time a case reaches a neutral, we have already decided that we are willing to accept any adverse employee relations impacts that may result from our insisting upon the correct interpretation of the contract. Right or wrong, we have exercised the judgment and discretion for which we are paid. For a neutral to attempt to substitute his judgment for ours is highly inappropriate. The neutral in tripartite arbitration is not being asked to give either party the benefit of his opinion on how it should conduct itself; he or she is being asked to determine which party is properly interpreting the labor agreement. If the company's interpretation of the agreement is the right one, it is irrelevant if the neutral believes that it is otherwise to the company's advantage not to insist upon the benefit of its bargain. This is one area where I believe that strong partisan board members can play a major role in deterring a neutral from exceeding his authority. I would recommend that all partisan system board members follow the same procedure that I do—that is, to remind the neutral of his role and ask that he restrict himself to it.

Arnold has expressed concern about disparity in the competence of partisan system board members. To me, this problem is no different from the unequal competence of advocates. The *parties* must deal with it. Both management and labor must insure that only competent people are placed on system boards of adjustment and that these people are properly prepared for executive sessions. If one or the other fails to do this, it is not inappropriate for them to reap as they have sown. A neutral should not concern himself with this fact of life. As in the selection of advocates, a party gets just what it deserves when it selects an incompetent system board member.

In closing, let me join Iz Gromfine in noting that I am not now and never have been guilty of any of the sins of which Arnold complained in his presentation.

Rejoinder—

Arnold M. Zack

I have sat here patiently through these vituperative comments made by allegedly informed experts on the subject of tripartite panels. I can take it no longer. I am at the end of my wits' rope. The clearly blind adherence to the concept of tripartitism leaves me speechless. I must therefore renounce anything favorable I might have said about tripartitism and revert to extolling the conventional wisdom of the single neutral. After a detailed and cursory examination of the literature, I can find no better recitation of the benefits thereof than in Chapter IV, pages 18 and 19, of the 1694 volume, *Arbitrium Redivivum or the Law of Arbitration:*

> The arbitrator's "power is larger than the power of any ordinary or other extraordinary judge; for an Arbitrator hath power to judge according to the compromife or fubmiffion after his own mind, as well of the Fact as of the Law, but the other Judges are tyed to a prefcript form, limited to them by the Law of Magiftrate.
>
> "And fince his power is so great and incontrolable, Men ought to be cautious how they make choice of Arbitrators; therefore it is thought fit that fuch perfons be Elected as are fufficient and indifferent.
>
> "That they have fufficient skills of the matter fubmitted to them, and have neither legal nor natural impediments. That they be not infants who by reafon of their few years may want difcretion and knowledge.
>
> "That they be neither Mad nor Ideots, for fuch are void of underftanding.
>
> "That they be neither Deaf, Dumb or Blind, for thereby their principal fenfes necessary for the apprehenfion of the Matter may be impaired.
>
> "As for indifferency, That they be void of Malice and Favour to either of the parties, that they be not notorious by Outlawry, Excommunicated, Irreligious, nor Covetous. . . ."[1]

---

[1] See note 2 in John Kagel's paper, Chapter 5, *supra.*

CHAPTER 9

THE INTERNATIONAL LABOR SCENE: IMPLICATIONS FOR THE DECADE OF THE 1980s "THE WAY THE WIND IS BLOWING"

JOHN N. GENTRY*

As I was flying out here yesterday, busily attempting to redo the notes for today, the beauty of the day prompted me to think back many years ago when I was a child and every Monday (weather permitting) was very special in our home. It was wash day. This meant dragging out the Maytag washer (complete with hand wringer), filling innumerable tubs with hot water, cleaning off the old metal clothesline, and rounding up all dirty clothing, bedding, towels, and the like, for participation in an arduous exercise that took up most of the day.

Once the wash was done and hung out to dry, my fascination often turned to looking at the assorted collection of household and personal articles to determine whether there was a wind blowing and, if so, in which direction. It was just good lazy fun to sit and watch and to speculate on which piece would get the jump on the others, if and when a breeze developed.

As we look at the clothesline of the international labor scene today, we quickly conclude that there are so many crosscurrents at play that it is impossible to determine which area will have primary significance in the foreseeable future. Moreover, in our brief time today, it would be impossible to examine in depth any single development. So, perhaps my assignment would be discharged best by highlighting what appear to be emerging developments in which we all have a vested interest.

I think you are aware of the background of the International Labor Organization. It is the only truly tripartite international body—composed of representatives of government, employers, and workers representing, today, more than 140 nations. The ILO was established in 1919 and is the sole survivor of a collec-

---

*Washington, D. C.

tion of international organizations started under the auspices of the abortive League of Nations.

Since its inception, the ILO has had one primary mission: the establishment of a body of labor standards that will be observed by nations throughout the world. And over the 60 plus years of its existence, the ILO has adopted a variety of Conventions and Recommendations covering almost every aspect of human rights and labor relations as we know them here in the United States. Some of these instruments seek to guarantee basic human rights, such as freedom of association, freedom of labor, and equality of opportunity and treatment in employment. Others have been concerned with employment policy and employment services, industrial relations, labor administration, general conditions of employment, the employment of women and children, industrial safety, health, and welfare, social security, migrant workers, work on plantations, and the treatment of indigenous populations (the polite international phrase for the examination of apartheid).

The establishment of labor standards through the ILO process has had a profound effect on countries throughout the world—regardless of their state of economic development or of their political and ideological roots. However, the role of the ILO does not stop even after the laborious and time-consuming process of establishing a labor standard. The organization has developed an elaborate mechanism for the ratification of Conventions by member nations, together with continuing supervision by the ILO staff and oversight committees of the extent to which such members abide by the standards. Complaint procedures and special investigations by the ILO are utilized to call to the attention of the world any countries that are failing to abide by what the international body considers to be minimal acceptable labor standards. Special reports are utilized to highlight—and publicize—flagrant violations.

Since 1919, the International Labor Organization has adopted more than 300 Conventions and Recommendations which cover the spectrum of employer-worker rights and obligations. And without question, they have advanced the lot of working people throughout the world.

In addition, and almost since its inception, the ILO has played a principal role in providing technical assistance and vocational education and training, particularly to developing nations. Each year extensive training sessions are held in all parts of the world to provide government, employers, and workers with expert assistance in modifying and improving their labor laws, and also to equip today's managers and workers with the know-how to adapt to changing technology. The ILO maintains a permanent vocational education institute in Turin, Italy, which is supported both through general funds of the ILO and by individual contributions from member nations.

The United States has been a leading member of the ILO since its inception. Indeed, for many years the joint efforts of the United States government and its employer and worker delegations led the fight for the improvement of worker or labor standards on an international basis.

All of this, however, came to a screeching halt four years ago. In 1977 the United States formally withdrew from membership in the ILO. The circumstances surrounding this exit are detailed and complex, but they can be laid essentially to two factors: first, an increasing resentment of the blatant disregard of ILO standards by Eastern bloc countries, and, second, in more recent times the emergence into the membership of the International Labor Organization of a large number of Third World nations, many of whom felt compelled to use the forum of the ILO for overt political purposes. For example, recent debates of the Annual Assembly of the ILO have been heavily laced with virulent attacks upon the State of Israel.

The U.S. position in 1977 was that tripartitism could not survive if it was applied to one segment of the world and not to another. It was the position of the United States and a number of other ILO members that ILO standards are universal and open to only one universal interpretation. Moreover, the U.S. urged that the ILO return to its traditional role as a technical-human rights body and reverse the trend toward being a political forum.

The withdrawal of the United States from the ILO was a severe setback for the international organization. The U.S. had always made sizable financial contributions to the body, and the loss of this support required the ILO to cut back substantially on a variety of activities. Moreover, the historic leadership that the U.S. provided to the ILO was sorely missed.

During the intervening two and a half years, informal entreaties were made by a number of countries for the United States to reassess its position. Eventually, in the interest of the overall goals of the organization as well as in our own self-interest, and with some private assurances that procedures would be developed to make the organization a more democratic body, the United States rejoined the ILO last year.

In light of this background, one might appropriately ask whether the ILO serves a useful purpose. My answer, of course, is a resounding YES. Is it so important that the United States be a member of this body? And what are the long-range implications for the work of the ILO, particularly as they relate to U.S. interests? The answers to these questions can best be encapsulated in an assessment of the future of the ILO as it would appear today.

First, it seems obvious that the ILO will continue its traditional role of setting international labor standards, and despite the resistance or noncompliance from Eastern bloc nations, this should remain the paramount role of the organization.

Second, even with the swirling change of political and economic circumstances throughout the world, it is conceivable that the ILO will be able to carry out its primary mission and, at the same time, avoid some of the political posturing that has so frustrated the activities of the United Nations.

Third, from the point of view of the United States, the ILO represents the most significant international forum for the introduction of fair and humane working conditions for the people of all countries.

Fourth, with the growth of multinational corporations, the role and influence of the ILO will be of even greater significance.

This last point poses a problem of particular interest to United States corporations. Years ago it was relatively easy for U.S. employers to advocate improved international working conditions and standards for workers since, unquestionably, the U.S. enjoyed one of the most progressive labor standards programs in the world. So, it made sense for U.S. corporations, on humane grounds as well as competitive ones, to suggest that all other nations should live up to the same types of standards that were enjoyed here in the States.

Today the situation is somewhat different. U.S. corporations now have extensive facilities in many countries that only a few years ago were regarded as totally undeveloped. In this context, it will be interesting to see the posture that U.S. corporations take at the ILO with respect to labor standards in developing nations, and, particularly, if the ILO and other international organizations go, as they seem inclined to, in the direction of examining various aspects of multinational operations—including the possible usefulness and feasibility of establishing principles and guidelines governing the social policy of such enterprises. Undoubtedly there will be times when very difficult questions will arise in terms of the direction the U.S. employer community should pursue on the international labor front. Yet I remain confident that U.S. employers are going to continue to maintain that it is in their best interests, irrespective of their multinational character, to assure that advanced labor standards prevail in every region of the world. Although the U.S. employer and worker delegations might disagree on technical matters or the extent and timing of the introduction of a new standard, in the long run they will be much closer together than employer and worker delegations from a number of other countries.

The decade ahead is going to be a particularly significant one for U.S. employers on a variety of fronts, and of equal interest and concern to American trade unions and the United States government. As I mentioned a moment ago, the role of multinational corporations will undergo serious scrutiny over the next ten years.

By the same token, the question of international trade will inevitably loom larger and larger in the eyes of American interests. Take the current automobile situation alone. Where should we, as private citizens or the government, come out in terms of the current controversy over auto imports? Informed, intelligent sources, including employers and union leaders in the auto industry, see no easy answer. There seems to be general agreement that the imposition by legislation or executive order of import restrictions is undesirable. But how far does one go using only moral suasion, particularly when dealing in an international environment? Reactions to recent reports of a Japanese government decision to limit auto exports to the U.S. highlight the proliferation of divergent views on this subject—particularly in Japan.

The implications of anything done here are suggested by a cartoon I saw recently in the *Wall Street Journal.* An American couple were in an auto showroom full of shiny new U.S. cars. They were standing in front of a large TV set, with an eager auto salesman right behind them. The husband turned to the wife and said, "What do you think, dear? They promised that if we would buy an American-made car they would give us a Japanese-made TV set." As Charlie Wilson would *not* have said it, "What is good for General Motors is not necessarily good for General Electric."

Turning briefly to one final subject:

As we look at the international labor front today—and at the direction the winds are blowing—the most significant development of this decade, if not of our generation, is what has happened in Poland over the last year. And then I would quickly add that over and above the heroic efforts of the Polish workers, the ILO played a more significant part in those developments than might be apparent to the casual observer—and certainly if your source of information is limited to the U.S. media.

Solidarity and the rise of Lech Walesa did not come about in Poland overnight. The concerns of Polish workers have been developing for years and particularly since the unrest and repressions of 1970 and 1976. The strike in Gdansk of May 1980 represented only the culmination of increasing worker frustrations that have built up over a number of years.

So you may ask me, what does all this have to do with the ILO?

The fact of the matter is that for the past ten years officials of the ILO have had a series of discussions with the Polish government and also with Polish workers concerning two basic Conventions of the ILO. The first is Convention No. 87, enacted in 1948 and entitled "Freedom of Association and Protection of the Right to Organize." The second, Convention No. 98, was adopted in 1949 and is entitled "Right to Organize and Collective Bargaining." For the past six or seven years the ILO Committee of Experts on the Application of Conventions and Recommendations, chaired by our mutual distinguished friend, Frank McCulloch, has had a continuing dialogue with the Polish government on Convention No. 87. During this time the Committee of Experts repeatedly pointed out the inadequacies of the Polish law. The response from the Polish government over the same period was merely that the law was under review.

In 1978 the International Confederation of Free Trade Unions filed a complaint with the Freedom of Association Committee of the ILO governing board concerning the total disregard of the Polish government of Convention No. 87. Similar reports were filed by the ICFTU in May 1979 and November 1979. In May 1980 the ILO persuaded the Polish government to permit a senior ILO official, Nicholas Valticos, Assistant Director General for International Labor Standards, to meet with the Polish government and discuss with them the problems associated with continuing noncompliance with Convention No. 87. During 1980, Valticos had a number of discussions with Polish officials, leading eventually to the implementation of the spirit of the Convention on Freedom of Association. Indeed, Point No. 1 of the historic Gdansk agreement of August 31, 1980, signed by the duly appointed governmental commission and the Solidarity leadership, relies upon ILO Convention No. 87 as the basis for establishing trade unions in Poland free and independent of the Communist Party.

It is unquestionably in the minds of knowledgeable observers that the implications of the government's continuing refusal to abide by these ILO Conventions inspired the Polish workers to feel that they were on the right side of the issue. Indeed, the noncompliance by the government with these Conventions became the central issue in the ultimate judicial test leading to the establishment of Solidarity as an independent union representing the workers of Poland. In that case the Supreme Court of Poland, overruling a lower court decision, cited as decisive ILO Convention No. 87 and the Gdansk agreement. The courage of the Polish workers has been continually reinforced by their conviction that they were abiding by international law.

Although time does not permit full treatment, a parallel history surrounded the recent successful efforts of Polish farm workers to form their own union independent of the Communist Party. There the workers relied on ILO Conventions No. 11 (1921) and No. 141 (1975), both relating to freedom of association and right to organize for agricultural workers.

All of this is not to take away for a moment from the unbelievable courage that has been demonstrated by the leaders of Solidarity and the Polish workers themselves. It is almost inconceivable that in a Communist Bloc country a movement could be developed so effectively that in a relatively short period of time the vast majority of a nation's workers are organized within the same labor organization. In my judgment, the quiet, effective, and continual prodding of the ILO had a great deal to do with bringing about the recent events in Poland.

I wish I could say the same in terms of constructive input from the United States. On this score I am afraid our record has not been particularly impressive. I remind you that in the fall of last year the United States government criticized the American labor movement for publicly pledging financial support to Solidarity.

As recently as a month ago—but, fortunately, with decreasing intensity—the United States government repeatedly informed the world of the ominous threat of a Soviet invasion of Poland.

Yet, my grievance in this connection does not go so much to the United States government as it does to the media. I recently read a brief but very incisive report written by a member of the staff of the International Metalworkers Federation who spent two weeks in December 1980 touring nine large industrial cities in Poland. This individual interviewed more than 100 workers, members of the Solidarity leadership and others. As one reads the document, the persistent theme that comes through—from community after community throughout Poland—is that the workers and the government might be able to work out their own problems if the Americans would *please* stop insisting that Russia was going to invade at any moment. The Polish workers' point was that they had a strong and unified movement, that the government had developed a measure of trust and respect for its leadership, and so long as they could keep their own people in line, they felt that they could work out their differences with the Polish government. But each and every day of that conflict—not only on radio and television in the United States, but through various means of international communications— the constant U.S. media thrust was the imminence of a Russian invasion.

Where was the American press in the 1930s when the present-day United States industrial labor movement was getting off the ground? It certainly was not extolling the virtues of workers' rights or freedom of association. If we had had television in the 1930s, can you name one network anchor-person who would have given so much time and attention to the legitimate rights of American workers as to the violence and bloodshed that ensued?

But back to Poland only briefly: I have shared with you my feelings in terms of the significant developments in Poland over the past year. But do these developments have broader implications?

Let us revisit ILO Convention Nos. 87 and 98. The Russian government is not concerned about Poland only because it is a satellite country whose leadership potentially is losing a firm grip on its internal political situation. The Russians have to fear the fact that they and other satellite countries are legally bound by those same ILO Conventions. Can you imagine the consequences if a significant number of workers in Rumania or Bulgaria or Hungary or *Russia* decided to assert the same rights that are being exercised by their Polish brethren? Wishful thinking? The application of a theory until it reaches practical absurdity? Perhaps—but only perhaps. And what would be the international economic and political implications of such a development?

Yes, the winds on the international labor front are blowing. Currents and crosscurrents for change are affecting every part of the world, but often in very different forms. International labor matters will play a dominant role in the decade ahead—and beyond—in shaping social, economic, and, indeed, political changes that will have worldwide implications.

While neither you nor I know where these winds are going, we are all well-advised to keep an eye on their direction.

NATIONAL ACADEMY OF ARBITRATORS
OFFICERS AND COMMITTEES, 1981–1982

I. *Officers*

Edgar A. Jones, Jr., President
Alfred C. Dybeck, Vice President
John Phillip Linn, Vice President
Martin Wagner, Vice President
Arnold M. Zack, Vice President
Richard I. Bloch, Secretary-Treasurer
Byron R. Abernethy, President-Elect

II. *Board of Governors*

Martin A. Cohen
David E. Feller
Walter J. Gershenfeld
Marcia Greenbaum
James M. Harkless
Dallas L. Jones
John Kagel
Edward E. McDaniel
Charles J. Morris
Francis X. Quinn
Milton Rubin
James J. Sherman
Eva Robins (ex officio)

III. *Past Presidents*

Ralph T. Seward, 1947–49
William E. Simkin, 1950
David L. Cole, 1951
David A. Wolff, 1952
Edgar L. Warren, 1953

Saul Wallen, 1954
Aaron Horvitz, 1955
John Day Larkin, 1956
Paul N. Guthrie, 1957
Harry H. Platt, 1958

G. Allan Dash, Jr., 1959	Jean T. McKelvey, 1970
Leo C. Brown, S.J., 1960	Lewis M. Gill, 1971
Gabriel N. Alexander, 1961	Gerald A. Barrett, 1972
Benjamin Aaron, 1962	Eli Rock, 1973
Sylvester Garrett, 1963	David P. Miller, 1974
Peter M. Kelliher, 1964	Rolf Valtin, 1975
Russell A. Smith, 1965	H.D. Woods 1976
Robben W. Fleming, 1966	Arthur Stark, 1977
Bert L. Luskin, 1967	Richard Mittenthal, 1978
Charles C. Killingsworth, 1968	Clare B. McDermott, 1979
James C. Hill, 1969	Eva Robins, 1980

IV. *Appointments and Committee Rosters*

(a) *1981 Annual Meeting*

Program Committee

Theodore J. St. Antoine, Chairman

Reginald Alleyne	Raymond Goetz
Gabriel Alexander	Ronald Haughton
Arvid Anderson	Dallas L. Jones
Michael Beck	Robert B. Moberly
Merton Bernstein	Cornelius J. Peck
Raymond Britton	Charles M. Rehmus
Barbara Doering	Ivan C. Rutledge
William Dorsey	Anthony V. Sinicropi
James Duff	James L. Stern
Dana Eischen	Edwin R. Teple
Gerry Fellman	Martin Wagner

Arnold M. Zack

*Arrangements Committee for the
Thirty-Fifth Annual Meeting—1982*

Nicholas H. Zumas, Chairman

Robert J. Ables	James M. Harkless
Leon B. Applewhaite	George S. Ives
Howard G. Gamser	Thomas T. Roberts

Ted T. Tsukiyama

(b) *The Standing Committees*

Executive Committee

Edgar A. Jones, Jr., President

Richard I. Bloch
Byron A. Abernethy

Milton Rubin
Eva Robins

Membership Committee

Mark L. Kahn, Chairman

Arvid Anderson
Frances Bairstow
William J. Fallon
Joseph F. Gentile
J.B. Gillingham

Edward B. Krinsky
J. Joseph Loewenberg
William E. Rentfro
John C. Shearer
Marian Kincaid Warns

Committee on Professional Responsibility and Grievances

Howard A. Cole, Chairman

Gerald A. Barrett
John E. Dunsford
William J. Fallon
Robert W. Foster
Bert L. Luskin
Thomas J. McDermott
Richard Mittenthal

Eli Rock
Ralph T. Seward
Arthur Stark
Francis R. Walsh
John F.W. Weatherill
Sol M. Yarowsky
Dallas M. Young

Committee on Research and Education

Cornelius J. Peck, Chairman

Stephen B. Goldberg
Wayne E. Howard
Dallas L. Jones
Robert F. Korctz

Charles H. Livengood, Jr.
Marlyn E. Lugar
Charles A. Myers
Earl E. Palmer

Committee on
the Development of Arbitrators

Anthony V. Sinicropi, Chairman

Planning Section

Anthony V. Sinicropi, Chairman
Charles L. Mullin, Jr.   Eva Robins
Arnold M. Zack

Intern and Training Liaison Section

Charles L. Mullin, Jr., Chairman
John H. Abernathy   J.D. Dunn
Donald A. Anderson   B.M. Goldstein
Arnold O. Anderson   Malcolm G. House
Mario Bognanno   Paul D. Jackson
Sanford Cohen   Howard F. LeBaron
Eaton H. Conant   Harold H. Leeper
Earl M. Curry, Jr.   Edward V. Ott
Tia Schneider Denenberg   Henry L. Sisk
James C. Duff   Carlton J. Snow

Committee on
Future Meeting Arrangements

Thomas T. Roberts, Chairman
Alfred C. Dybeck   Clare B. McDermott
William J. Fallon   Anthony V. Sinicropi
Mark L. Kahn   Rolf Valtin
John Phillip Linn   John F.W. Weatherill

Committee on
Legal Representation

James M. Harkless, Chairman
Gabriel N. Alexander   Robert G. Meiners
Alex Elson   Milton Rubin
Nathan Lipson   Howard M. Teaf, Jr.

Editorial Committee

James L. Stern, Chairman

Tia Schneider Denenberg   John Kagel
Dana Eischen   Charles M. Rehmus

James J. Sherman

Future Directions Committee

William P. Murphy, Chairman (1981–82)
John E. Dunsford, Chairman (1982–83)

Byron R. Abernethy	Lewis M. Gill
Frances Bairstow	Edward McDaniel
Richard I. Bloch	Jean McKelvey
Howard Block	Thomas T. Roberts
Mario Bognanno	Eva Robins
Howard D. Brown	James J. Sherman
Martin A. Cohen	Anthony J. Sinicropi
Tia Schneider Denenberg	Edwin R. Teple
Alex Elson	Rolf Valtin
Julius G. Getman	Arnold M. Zack

1981–1982 Regional Chairpersons

Edwin R. Teple, Coordinator of Regional Activities

Region 1, New England	Robert M. O'Brien
Region 2, New York City	Irving Haley
Region 3, Eastern Pennsylvania	William M. Weinberg
Region 4, District of Columbia	Robert J. Ables
Region 5, Southeast	James J. Sherman
Region 6, Upstate New York	Milton M. Goldberg
Region 7, Canada	Howard D. Brown
Region 8, Western Pennsylvania	Helen M. Witt
Region 9, Ohio	Fred E. Kindig
Region 10, Michigan	Nathan Lipson
Region 11, Illinois	Martin Wagner
Region 12, St. Louis	Gladys Gruenberg
Region 13, Southwest	Raymond L. Britton
Region 14, Rocky Mountain	Bennett S. Aisenberg
Region 15, Northern California	Emily Maloney
Region 16, Southern California	Gerry L. Fellman
Region 17, Pacific Northwest	J.B. Gillingham

SIGNIFICANT DEVELOPMENTS IN PUBLIC EMPLOYMENT DISPUTES SETTLEMENT DURING 1980*

PAUL PRASOW**

This report covers significant developments for 1980—including statutory, judicial, and related activity—in public-employment disputes settlement at federal, state, and local levels. It begins, in Section I, with a state-by-state summary of legislation enacted during the year. Section II includes a summary of the year's experience of the Federal Labor Relations Authority and the Federal Service Impasses Panel as well as some key court cases involving the Postal Service. Section III deals with public-sector dispute resolution in Canada, and the report concludes with Section IV, covering judicial and related developments.

As has been the trend in recent years, relatively few states enacted labor legislation affecting the public sector. Most new laws covered arbitration and impasse resolution procedures. New interest arbitration provisions were adopted in three states and the District of Columbia.

In a continuation of the "Proposition 13" movement to place taxing limits on government, voters in Massachusetts approved a referendum limiting property taxes to 2.5 percent of full market value, limiting tax increases to 2.5 percent, reducing excise taxes on automobiles, and permitting renters to deduct half

---

*Report of the Committee on Public Employment Disputes Settlement. Members of the committee are John B. Abernathy, Reginald H. Alleyne, Arvid Anderson, Leon B. Applewhaite, Armon Barsamian, David R. Bloodsworth, Frederick H. Bullen, Irwin J. Dean, Jr., John F. Drotning, Jonathan Dworkin, Milton T. Edelman, Philip Feldblum, Jerome G. Greene, Irving Halevy, Allan J. Harrison, John E. Higgins, Morris A. Horowitz, Robert G. Howlett, Myron L. Joseph, Irvine L. H. Kerrison, Edward B. Krinsky, Leonard E. Lindquist, Nathan Lipson, Walter A. Maggiolo, Samuel S. Perry, William B. Post, Thomas N. Rinaldo, Josef P. Sirefman, Henry L. Sisk, Herman Torosian, Fred Witney, Helen M. Witt, Sidney A. Wolff, and Paul Prasow, chairperson.

**Research Economist, Institute of Industrial Relations, and Senior Lecturer in Industrial Relations, Graduate School of Business, University of California, Los Angeles, Calif.

their rent from their state income tax. These provisions in themselves are bound to have a profound effect on public-sector labor relations through layoffs and reductions in service.

The year 1980 also saw voters in six states—Arizona, Oregon, Nevada, South Dakota, Utah, and Michigan—turn down proposals to reduce taxes. However, by most predictions the eighties are likely to be difficult for labor-management relations. Against a backdrop of proposed federal budget and tax cuts and continuing double-digit inflation, there will be increasing confrontations over how the smaller pie is to be divided.

I. State Labor Legislation Enacted in 1980[1]

The year was a light one for state labor legislation, with some legislatures not meeting at all or only for brief sessions.[2] Twelve states enacted new legislation or amended existing labor relations laws affecting public employees; most of this legislation was concerned with arbitration and impasse resolution procedures.

Minnesota adopted a law granting state, local, and teaching employees the right to strike on 60 days' notice in the absence of an agreement or an arbitration award. The right to strike is not extended to "essential employees"—police, firefighters, correctional institution guards, and nurses providing direct care. Hawaii expanded the definition of "strike" to include sympathy strikes by public employees in support of other striking employees.

Two states—California and New Jersey—enacted laws that permitted organizational security agreements that would require employees to join an organization that was the employees' exclusive representative or pay that organization a service fee. The New Jersey law also established procedures for the rebate of pro rata share expenditures to nonmember employees.

Nine states modified existing bargaining laws affecting teacher labor relations. Instead of making major revisions to narrow the provisions of such laws, most state legislatures concentrated on ways to enforce statutory strike penalties without

---

[1]Reprinted in part, by special permission, from Labor Relations Reporter, © copyright 1981 by The Bureau of National Affairs, Inc. *See also* 104 Monthly Labor Review 21–34 (January 1981).

[2]Legislatures in Arkansas, Montana, Nevada, North Dakota, and Texas did not meet, while Missouri, New Hampshire, New Mexico, and Utah had abbreviated sessions that enacted no significant labor legislation.

interfering with dispute settlement machinery. The Kansas bargaining law, for example, was revised to provide for mediation and fact-finding of issues at impasse and to allow fact-finders to recommend settlement terms independently rather than limiting them to the "last best offer." The number of items on which teacher associations may negotiate with local school boards also was expanded to include supplemental contracts.

Compulsory retirement based solely upon age, a subject that has received considerable legislative attention at both the federal and state levels in recent years, received less attention during 1980. The mandatory retirement age was raised to 70 for public employees in Mississippi and for state employees and teachers in Virginia. Arizona and Tennessee enacted laws banning age-based employment discrimination against persons ages 40 to 70, and Kentucky raised the retirement-age upper limit from 65 to 70.

In legislation that affected private-sector industrial relations primarily, Michigan, Ohio, and Wisconsin prohibited the awarding of state contracts to persons or firms found to be in violation of the National Labor Relations Act. Connecticut passed a similar law in 1979. In addition, the use of strike breakers was "barred" in Wisconsin; in Oklahoma, prison inmates on work-release programs are not to report for work if a strike occurs and may not be used to replace strikers.

No new states ratified the proposed Equal Rights Amendment to the U.S. Constitution during 1980. In order that it be adopted, three additional states must approve it by June 30, 1982.

Arizona

The legislature enacted a law extending the terms of office of Employment Relations Board members until July 1, 1982.

California

The number of members of the Public Employment Relations Board (PERB) was increased from three to five. The new law also specifies that a board member is not precluded from participating in any case pending before the Board, and it transfers the responsibility for appointing the PERB executive director from the chairperson to the Board. Another amendment empowers the governor to appoint, upon the Board's recommendation, a general counsel to the PERB, to serve at its pleasure. An amendment to the law on public school employer-employee relations directs the Board to respond within 10 days to any inquiry from a party who has petitioned for extraordinary relief. In its response the Board must explain why it had not sought court enforcement of its final decision or order. The Board must seek such enforcement upon request and must file in a court the records of the Board proceeding and evidence disclosing a party's failure to comply with the Board's decision and order.

A new statute permits union security agreements between classified employees in public schools and their employers. As a condition of employment, these employees are required either to join the organization that is the exclusive representative of the employees or to pay that organization a service fee. Governing boards of school districts are authorized to check off union dues from salaries of classified employees. Employees who are not union members may pay service fees directly to the exclusive representative union in lieu of the salary deductions. The law states that public school employees who are members of a religious body that objects to supporting employee organizations are not required to join, maintain membership in, or financially support any such organization as a condition of employment. An employee, however, may be required to pay amounts equal to the agency fee to a nonreligious, nonlabor organization's charitable fund exempt under federal income tax regulations. The new law also permits employee organizations to charge a public school employee for the costs incurred in the resolution of any grievance arising from representation where the resolution of that grievance is requested by the employee.

The public school Employer-Employee Relations Act was amended to permit parties at impasse after mediation to agree mutually upon a person who is to serve as chairperson of a fact-finding panel. Previously, the PERB selected the chairperson and bore his or her costs. Under the new law, fees and expenses for the chairperson's services are borne equally by the parties.

Another statute authorizes the board of directors of fire protection districts in counties where the district board is composed of the county board of supervisors to call a referendum on whether or not district boards may provide for a system of binding arbitration for the resolution of impasses in employee-employer relations.

Connecticut

Claims that an issue is not a proper subject for arbitration cannot be reviewed by an arbitration panel unless the party making a claim gives at least 10 days' written notice to the opposing party and to the arbitration panel chairperson. A claim may be heard, however, if there is reasonable cause as to why a notice was not given.

A new law provides that employment contracts of a teacher who has served continuously for four years may be terminated at any time if that position is filled by another teacher and if no other position exists to which he or she may be appointed. If qualified, this teacher shall be appointed to a position held by a teacher who has not completed three years of continuous employment. Determination of employment contract termination is made in accordance with a layoff procedure agreed upon by the local or regional board of education or, in the absence of an agreement, with the written policy of a local or regional board of education. The law, however, does not prohibit a local or regional board of education from entering into an agreement with an exclusive employee representative on matters involving teacher recall. The law also specifies that a board of education, prior to contract termination, is required to give an affected teacher a written notice of termination.

The Connecticut labor relations law was amended to prohibit employers, employees, their agents, and their representatives from recording a conversation or discussion pertaining to employment contract negotiations between the parties to those negotiations by means of any instrument, device, or equipment without the consent of both parties.

District of Columbia

New provisions covering most aspects of the management-labor relationship of the District of Columbia and its employees were incorporated into the D.C. Government Merit Personnel Act by a new law that went into effect on April 4, 1980. Under this law, the Board of Labor Relations is replaced by the Public Employee Relations Board (PERB), authorized to resolve unit-determination and representation issues, to certify and decertify bargaining representatives, to conduct elections, to determine and decide unfair labor practice allegations and order remedies, to determine and decide scope-of-bargaining disputes, and to resolve bargaining impasses through fact-finding, mediation, and binding arbitration. The law empowers the PERB to retain its own legal counsel and to order remedies of back pay, and it provides for judicial review and enforcement of PERB decisions. The new law includes compensation in the list of bargainable items and extends organization and negotiation rights to public school supervisors.

Florida

Several changes were made in the public employee collective bargaining law. Local commissions established pursuant to local-option collective bargaining provisions now include a representative of employers and a representative of employees or employee organizations. Any other appointees, including alternates, are to be persons who, in their previous vocation, employment, or affiliation, are not or have not been classified as representatives of employers, employees, or employee organizations. The chairperson and members of local commissions are appointed for four-year staggered terms and may not be employed by, or hold any commission with, any state governmental unit or any employee organization while serving on the commission.

Another amendment reversed procedures for impasse resolution. A special master now is required to transmit the recommended decision to the Public Employee Relations Commission (PERC) and to the representative of each party by registered mail within 15 days after the close of a hearing on a dispute. The recommendations are to be discussed by both parties. Each recommendation shall be deemed approved by both parties unless specifically rejected by either party by a written notice filed with the PERC within 20 calendar days after recommendations have been received. The notice must include a statement of the reason for each rejection.

Hawaii

An amendment to Hawaii's collective bargaining law focused on strikes. "Strike" was redefined to include sympathy strikes by public employees in support of other groups of striking public employees. The amended law also prohibits "essential employees" from striking. Under the law, an "essential employee" is one who is designated by a public employer to fill an "essential position." An "essential position" is defined as one designated by the Public Employment Relations Board (PERB) as necessary to avoid an imminent or present danger to public health or safety. The law also empowers public employers to petition the PERB for an investigation of a strike or threat of a strike. Upon a finding that a strike constitutes a present danger to public health or safety, the PERB now is directed to designate which employees are "essential," to establish requirements to eliminate the danger, and to require the essential employees to contact their public employers for work assignments. The new law grants the affected public employer the power to petition a state circuit court for relief where the violations of the strike prohibitions are confirmed by the PERB, but it prohibits jury trial for these violations.

Kansas

Several changes were made in the law governing collective bargaining for the professional employees of Kansas schools. The list of negotiable items was expanded to include supplemental contracts covering extracurricular activities, employee grievances, extended and sabbatical leaves, probationary periods, evaluation procedures, dues checkoff, use of school facilities for association meetings, use of a school mail service, and reasonable leaves for organizing activities.

The law, as revised, now includes impasse resolution procedures providing for mediation and fact-finding. The revisions eliminated the provision which had required fact-finders to choose between the "last best offer" made by a school board or by an employee organization and to recommend adoption of one offer or the other. The law now allows fact-finders to make independent recommendations on each of the issues at impasse. Another change in the law shortened the period for negotiating a new contract to two months, and the deadline for serving notice to negotiate new items or to amend an existing contract was changed from September 1 to February 1 of each year. The law now provides that if agreement on a new contract is not reached by June 1, an impasse is automatically declared and the machinery to resolve differences goes into effect without the need for a court to declare that an impasse exists. The responsibility for the determination and declaration of an impasse was transferred from the district courts to the secretary of human resources, as was the authority to rule on alleged commissions of prohibited practices by either party.

Kentucky

Terms of office for members of the Labor-Management Advisory Council were changed under a new law. Two labor and two management members now are to be appointed for terms of one to four years. Appointments are to be made by the governor 30 days after the expiration of the term of any member.

Louisiana

A concurrent resolution requested that the joint legislature committee study of public-sector employer-employee relations, begun in 1979, be extended. The committee is to study related issues, including collective bargaining and strikes, and report its findings and proposals to the legislature 30 days prior to the beginning of the 1981 regular session.

Massachusetts

Elected officers of the Professional Firefighters of Massachusetts, if on duty, are to be given leave by the municipal employer for regularly scheduled work hours spent on union business. The chairperson of the Board of Conciliation and Arbitration may now appoint a nonmember to act as a temporary neutral member of the board, or to act as the single arbitrator with full powers of the board in the arbitration of a grievance arising under a public or private collective bargaining agreement.

Michigan

A new statute permits compulsory arbitration of labor disputes involving state police troopers and sergeants and provides procedures for the selection of arbitration panel members, hearings, and the enforcement and review of arbitration panel orders.

Minnesota

The name of the Department of Personnel was changed to the Department of Employee Relations. The new department is organized into the Division of Personnel and the Division of Labor Relations, the latter being responsible for negotiating and administering state employee collective bargaining agreements.

Under provisions of the law amended in 1973, public employees could strike only if their employer either refused to submit a bargaining impasse to arbitration or refused to implement an arbitrator's award; in teacher disputes, only school boards could decide whether arbitration could be used. The new law expands the right to strike for all state, local, and teaching employees except for those designated as "essential"—police, firefighters, nurses providing direct patient care, and institution guards.

The right to strike is granted 60 days (including 30 days after contract expiration) after mediation if either party rejects arbitration or, if arbitration is not requested, after an additional 45 days so long as a further 10 days' notice is given and the contract has expired.

New Jersey

An amendment to the New Jersey Employer-Employee Relations Act permits public employers and their employees to negotiate agency shop agreements requiring nonmembers to pay the representative union a fee for services rendered in lieu of membership dues. Under the amended law, the agency shop fee cannot exceed 85 percent of regular membership dues, fees, and assessments paid by union members. Public employees who pay representation fees may demand and receive a return of any part of the fee paid that represented pro rata shares of expenditures by the union for partisan political or ideological activities or for causes only incidentally related to terms and conditions of employment, or that were applied toward costs of benefits available only to union members. Pro rata share refunds do not apply to lobbying costs incurred in promoting policy goals in collective negotiations and contract administration or in securing advantages in employees' wages, hours of work, and conditions of employment in addition to those secured through collective negotiations with the public employer. Negotiated agreements on payroll deduction of representation fees may be made only if membership in the majority representative organization is available equally to all employees in the unit.

The new law also established a three-member board comprised of a public employer representative, a public employee organization representative, and an impartial public member who serves as chairperson in hearing and deciding issues on pro rata share challenges. Representation fees are to be paid to the majority representative organization during the term of the negotiated collective agreement affecting nonmember employees.

Under the amendment, public employers or public employee organizations may not discriminate between nonmembers who pay representation fees and members who pay regular membership dues.

New York

Although there was no significant public-sector labor legislation enacted in New York State, 13 amendments to the New York City Collective Bargaining Law were passed by the New York City Council and signed by the Mayor in 1980. These include a provision adding agency-shop deductions to the list of matters constituting mandatory subjects of bargaining, a provision defining more precisely the period of negotiation during which the parties are prohibited from taking any unilateral actions which would disturb the status quo or otherwise disrupt the bargaining process, and a provision to clarify the nature and effect of an impasse panel report which is accepted by the parties or rejected by either or both parties but not timely appealed. The latter amendment also redefines the scope of review by the Board of Collective Bargaining of impasse panel reports to provide explicitly for consideration of the conformity of such reports with applicable laws and regulations.

Rhode Island

Casual and seasonal state employees are excluded from coverage under the law giving state employees the right to organize and bargain collectively. Another revision of the Rhode Island Labor Relations Act requires that notice of a motion to vacate, modify, or correct an arbitration award be served upon an adverse party or his attorney within one month, rather than three months, after the award is filed or delivered and before the award is confirmed.

South Carolina

The South Carolina legislature approved a law directing the Commission on Higher Education to establish grievance procedures for employees and faculty members of state-funded post-secondary educational institutions. Procedures must provide a hearing process for an aggrieved employee which allows him or her the right to representation by counsel. Grievance procedures must also include the right to appeal decisions to the institution's governing board or a committee designated by the board. Issues subject to the grievance procedure include discrimination in compensation, promotion, and work assignment. Dismissal of tenured or other permanent employees and dismissal prior to the end of an employment contract shall be only for cause and are to be considered by the grievance procedure.

Vermont

Revised rules governing grievances, promotions, transfers, internal affairs, and disciplinary procedures are to be established by the Commissioner of Public Safety under legislature-established guidelines. A State Police Advisory Commission was established to review the rules and to act as an adviser to the Commissioner.

Virgin Islands

A Public Employee Labor Relations Law was enacted, granting public employees the right to form and join unions and to bargain collectively. The law defines unfair labor practices and provides for binding arbitration and a limited right to strike. An Office of Collective Bargaining was created in the Office of the Governor, with responsibility to represent the executive branch and negotiate on its behalf.

Wisconsin

Public- and private-sector employees have the right to inspect and make corrections in their personnel files and medical records at least twice a year, or as provided in a collective bargaining agreement. An employee may also authorize a union representative to inspect the records when a grievance is pending. Certain records are excluded, such as letters of reference, records relating to a criminal investigation, management planning records, and portions of test documents.

II. Federal-Sector Developments

New Legislation

A significant major development in the federal labor-management relations sector for 1980 was the passage of the Foreign Service Act of 1980 (Public Law 96-445). Chapter 10 of this act supersedes Executive Order 11636 which had governed labor-management relations in most of the Foreign Service since 1971. The act now governs the labor-management relations for approximately 14,500 Foreign Service employees at the Department of State, the International Communications Agency, the U.S. International Development Cooperation Agency, the Department of Agriculture, and the Department of Commerce.

The new Foreign Service Labor Relations Board was established to administer the provisions of Chapter 10 of the act. The chairman of the Federal Labor Relations Authority also serves as chairman of the Board pursuant to the act. Similarly, the general counsel of the Authority also serves as general counsel of the Board.

The Board's functions include supervising or conducting representation elections; resolving unfair labor practice complaints; resolving issues related to the obligation to bargain in good faith; resolving certain disputes concerning the effect, interpretation, or a claim of breach of a collective bargaining agreement; and taking other actions necessary to administer the act effectively.

Another significant development in the federal labor-management relations sector was the passage of the General Accounting Office Personnel Act of 1980 (Public Law 96-191) which resulted in the establishment of the General Accounting Office Personnel Appeals Board. This board was created by Congress to give the Government Accounting Office (GAO) full control over its internal personnel and labor relations systems.

The GAO, a legislative branch agency, serves as Congress's "watchdog" to see that executive agencies are spending appropriated funds in the manner intended by Congress. The GAO personnel legislation removes GAO from the jurisdiction of the Merit Systems Protection Board, the Office of Personnel Management, and other agencies which regulate personnel and labor relations matters in the executive branch.

The Comptroller General of the United States has appointed the five members of the board. Matters to be considered and decided by the board include adverse action appeals, prohibited personnel practices, Hatch Act questions, determinations of bargaining units, oversight of representation elections, unfair labor practice charges, and equal employment opportunity matters. The general counsel of the board will investigate allegations of prohibited personnel practices and political activities and all matters under the jurisdiction of the board, if so requested. The act further provides for judicial review of board decisions.

As part of the Panama Canal Act of 1979, Title VII of the Civil Service Reform Act was made applicable to employees of the Panama Canal Commission. Therefore, there still remains American jurisdiction over foreign nationals working and residing outside of the United States.

Federal Labor Relations Authority[3]

The Federal Labor Relations Authority is concerned with four major substantive areas: representation and certification of bargaining units, determination of scope of bargaining questions, unfair labor practice determinations, and review of arbitration awards.

During 1980, 5,570 cases were filed in the regional offices of the Authority. Of these, 4,955 were unfair labor practice charges and 615 were representation petitions. Approximately 700 cases were filed or appealed to the Authority for final disposition during 1980. Of particular interest, new filings of exceptions to arbitrators' awards climbed to 102 cases from fiscal 1979's 44 cases. The Office of Administrative Law Judges received 1,093 cases in 1980, more than four and one-half times the 238 cases reaching the office in fiscal year 1979.

---

[3]For a more complete discussion of the functions of the Federal Labor Relations Authority and the Federal Service Impasses Panel, see the 1978 and 1979 reports of the Committee on Public Employment Disputes Settlement, Walter J. Gershenfeld, Chairperson.

The rest of this discussion will focus on the Authority's role in reviewing arbitration awards. In the federal sector, the use of arbitration has expanded greatly and will continue to do so in the future. Section 7121 of the statute provides that every collective bargaining agreement must have a grievance procedure which terminates in final and binding arbitration. Under certain conditions the Authority can review exceptions to arbitrators' awards. This review is restricted and does not call for a retrial on the merits.

In reviewing exceptions to an arbitrator's award, the Authority considers two basic statutory guidelines. The first of these is that the award is not contrary to laws, rules, or regulations. When considering laws, rules, and regulations, the Authority will seek interpretation of the rules and regulations from the issuing agency where appropriate.

The agency's interpretation, however, is not uniformly utilized. In one case an employee who was denied a promotion filed a grievance claiming a violation of the collective bargaining agreement. The arbitrator held that a violation had occurred and awarded a promotion retroactively with back pay. In considering the agency's exceptions, the Authority interpreted the rules and regulations without referral to the agency and sustained the award by ruling that it was not contrary to the Federal Personnel Manual and the Back Pay Act.[4]

On the other hand, in another decision the Authority requested an advisory opinion from the Office of Personnel Management concerning its interpretation of the Federal Personnel Manual provisions regarding an arbitrator's award.[5] The Authority determines what action to take on a case-by-case basis.

The second area for Authority consideration of arbitration exceptions is Section 7122(a)(2) which states that the Authority, upon review, may find an award deficient on grounds similar to those applied by federal courts in private-sector labor-management relations. By interpretation and case law, this would involve situations where an arbitrator exceeds his or her authority, or issues an award that does not draw its essence from the collective bargaining agreement, or is based on a nonfact. In several decisions the Authority has applied this doctrine. For example, in the decision of *Overseas Education Association and Office*

---

[4]*Veterans Administration Hospital and AFGE Local 2201,* 4 FLRA 57 (1980).
[5]*U.S. Department of Commerce, National Bureau of Standards, Washington, D.C. and AFGE Local 2186,* 3 FLRA 98 (1980).

of Dependent Schools, Dept. of Defense,[6] the Authority overturned the arbitrator's award as not drawing its essence from the collective bargaining agreement.

In another case the arbitrator stated that since Section 7106(a), the management rights provision, pertained to the assignment of work, it was under the substantive jurisdiction of management and was not a procedural situation subject to grievance. The Authority remanded the case, stating that the merits are reachable but the clause could impact on the remedies available.[7]

The statutory provisions appear to bar direct appellate court review of the Authority determinations in arbitration cases except where the basis of the dispute involved could have been an unfair labor practice. The one decision which was taken to the appellate courts dealt with a situation in which the agency had disciplined an employee who was also a union activist. The arbitrator sustained the discipline for five incidents of misconduct under the "just cause" language of the bargaining agreement, even though the agency's action taken against the grievant was, in part, because of union activity.[8] Since the genesis of this case is an unfair labor practice, judicial review is authorized under Section 7123(a)(1).

Federal Service Impasses Panel

Cases

Requests Received and Cases Closed. At the start of the fiscal year, 44 cases were pending before the Federal Service Impasses Panel. It received 123 requests for assistance during the year, a rate of filing essentially unchanged from the previous reporting period. The number of filings represents a very small proportion (15 percent) of the approximately 800 sets of negotiations which take place in the federal sector each year.

A record 132 cases were closed during the year. Most of these disputes occurred at the end of the contract, but a few arose during the term of the agreement as the result of reopener provisions of employer-proposed changes in working conditions.

---

[6] 4 FLRA 17 (1980).

[7] *The Marine Corps Logistics Support Base, Pacific, Barstow, Calif. and AFGE Local 1482,* 3 FLRA 61 (1980).

[8] *Federal Correctional Institution and AFGE Local 1286,* 3 FLRA 111 (1980).

The Panel declined to assert jurisdiction in 27 percent of closed cases. In most instances the parties had failed to devote sufficient time and effort to negotiations and were directed to resume bargaining with mediation assistance, as necessary. In other cases jurisdiction was not asserted mainly because an agency had raised a question concerning its obligation to bargain with respect to union proposals. Such questions may be referred to the Authority for resolution.

Twenty-five percent of the requests for assistance were withdrawn. In most instances, the parties either reached agreement after assistance was sought or agreed to resume negotiations. In some cases—often at the urging of the Panel's staff—the agency and labor organization arranged for assistance from higher level persons within their organizations or from an FMCS representative.

Twelve percent of the closed cases were settled by the parties, often with the assistance of a fact-finder, prior to the issuance of formal recommendations or a decision. This represents a slight decline from the previous year. The percentage of settlements based upon post-fact-finding recommendations, however, was essentially unchanged (4 percent).

The number of *Decisions and Orders* issued by the Panel represents 27 percent of the cases closed during the year. Although this figure is small, whether considered in isolation or in the context of the potential number of impasses in the federal sector, it is a sizable increase over fiscal year 1979 when the figure was only 13 percent. This may be explained by the rising number and complexity of issues in cases brought to the Panel and the interest of the parties and the Panel in quick resolution of some disputes. In addition, budgetary constraints on the Panel often precluded the use of fact-finding hearings and associated opportunities for informal settlements, necessitating decisions based solely on written submissions from the parties. There was a related increase in the use of final-offer selection procedures, either on an issue-by-issue or package basis.

For the first time in its history, the Panel ordered the parties in one dispute to use an outside arbitrator for a final and binding decision. A similar procedure was recommended in two other cases. The parties in two impasses adopted such a procedure after their request for the Panel's approval was granted.

Examples of Different Procedures Utilized. The Panel continued to use a wide variety of dispute-resolution techniques. Consistent with its broad statutory mandate, it based the selection on such factors as sound collective bargaining principles, the complexity of the dispute, the preferences of the parties, and its budget. An underlying consideration, however, was the Panel's determination to remain flexible and unpredictable in the implementation of these procedures. The panel directed that a fact-finding hearing be conducted in 21 disputes, to be followed by whatever action the Panel deemed appropriate. The same kind of uncertainty was present in 15 cases where written submissions were received. In another 15 cases written submissions were to be followed by a final-offer selection procedure. Some examples of a few of these procedures follow:

Decline to assert jurisdiction: The Panel may decline to assert jurisdiction if the parties have not exhausted voluntary efforts to reach agreement or for other good cause such as the existence of a threshold question concerning a party's obligation to bargain over a proposal. In *Naval Air Engineer Center,* Panel Release No. 155, the employer filed a request for assistance, listing nine issues at impasse. The Panel's investigation revealed that two issues were pending before the Authority as negotiability appeals and that the parties had resumed bargaining after the filing of the request. The Panel declined to assert jurisdiction.

Panel recommendations following fact-finding: In *Federal Energy Regulatory Commission,* Panel Release No. 135, the parties were deadlocked over the employer's proposal to exclude EEO complaints from the grievance and arbitration procedures. After a fact-finding hearing and receipt of the fact-finder's report, the Panel issued a *Report and Recommendation* in which it concluded in the circumstances of this case that employees should have the option of choosing either the negotiated grievance procedure or the statutory system for the resolution of EEO complaints. Additionally, the Panel found that further negotiations were necessary for the parties to reach agreement on a procedure encompassing adequate time for the investigation and informal resolution of EEO complaints prior to the institution of formal procedures. Both parties accepted the recommendation.

Decision and Order based upon written submissions: In *Federal Trade Commission,* Panel Release No. 152, the union, which represented approximately 30 persons in the employer's Boston regional office, filed a request for assistance on 14 issues, including the status of nonveteran attorneys. This request was consolidated with a second union request to resolve an impasse concerning the impact and implementation of performance standards. After receipt of the parties' written submissions, the

Panel ordered the employer to grant both veteran and nonveteran attorneys access to the grievance and arbitration procedures on the same basis as other members of the bargaining unit. Since the parties agreed that this was the key issue, they were directed to resume bargaining on the other issues and notify the Panel of the results within 30 days. The parties subsequently notified the Panel that an agreement had been consummated.

Final-offer selection based upon written submissions: The union, representing some 70,000 employees, requested the Panel to break a deadlock over the composition of the ranking panel for the Management/Technical Intern Program in *Air Force Logistics Command,* Panel Release No. 151. The union proposed to designate one nonvoting observer to participate in panel discussions and file written comments, whereas the employer proposed that only management officials of GS-14 or equivalent grade be panel participants. Using a final-offer selection procedure, the Panel ordered the parties to adopt the union's proposal.

Approval of arbitration: Negotiating a new contract for approximately 6,500 employees, the parties in *Department of Labor,* Panel Release No. 150, were unable to reach agreement on 23 issues, including performance evaluation, disciplinary action, and adverse action. They jointly requested the Panel to authorize use of outside arbitration to resolve the dispute. The Panel's inquiry revealed that the parties had exhausted voluntary efforts for settlement and had otherwise met the conditions established by the Panel for the authorization of this procedure. Accordingly, the request was granted. Thereafter, the Panel was advised that the dispute had been resolved voluntarily through mediation assistance provided by the arbitrator at the parties' request.

Issues

Approximately one-half of the cases received by the Panel during the year contained only a single issue. The others typically involved less than five disputed items, although one impasse had more than 30 issues. The dominant issue was hours of work and overtime, which includes the subjects of flex-time and compressed workweek. Promotions and denials, and official time for union representation followed in frequency. The latter category includes official time requested by unions for the preparation for negotiations as well as the actual negotiations and administration of an agreement. The grievance and arbitration issues often centered on the scope of the procedure.

Compliance With Panel Decisions

The statute provides in Section 7116(a)(6) and (b)(6) that it is an unfair labor practice for either party to "fail or refuse to cooperate in impasse procedures and impasse decisions." In a number of cases involving the wearing of the military uniform, however, National Guard activities have sought direct review of Panel decisions in other forums.

In *Nevada National Guard* v. *United States,* [9] the U.S. Court of Appeals for the Ninth Circuit dismissed the employer's petition for review of an order of the Panel for lack of jurisdiction. The court stated that if judicial review were sought pursuant to Executive Order 11491, as amended, the court lacked original jurisdiction. Alternatively, if judicial review were sought under the statute, the court found that the Panel's decision was not a final order of the Authority reviewable under 5 U.S.C. 7123.

The California National Guard[10] and the New York National Guard[11] petitioned the Authority to review directly and overturn Panel decisions involving the wearing of the military uniform. In each instance the Authority denied the petition, noting that the legislative history of the statute states that final action of the Panel is not subject to appeal. The Authority further concluded that Congress intended to establish the unfair labor practice procedure as the exclusive means of obtaining such review by the Authority.

Unfair labor practice complaints involving these and five other National Guard components, based in part on an alleged refusal to comply with *Decisions and Orders* of the Panel, were pending before the Authority on September 30, 1980.

Postal Service

In 1980 four federal court decisions dealt with the United States Postal Service (USPS) and the proper role of grievance arbitration under various circumstances.

The U.S. Court of Appeals for the Fifth Circuit held that a

---

[9] No. 79-7235 (9th Cir., Dec. 14, 1980).
[10] 2 FLRA 21 and 2 FLRA 22.
[11] 2 FLRA 20.

postal employee is bound by an arbitrator's decision upholding her dismissal.[12] The court was "not unsympathetic" to a former employee's complaint that she received "disparate if not inequitable" treatment as a result of her use of the negotiated grievance procedure instead of the civil service appeal as the forum in which to contest her removal from the U.S. Postal Service. However, the fact that the employee herself consented to arbitration means that she accepted the final and binding nature of the arbitrator's award. This is so even though another employee tried for the same reason as the plaintiff was reinstated after appealing his removal through the civil service procedure as authorized by the Veterans Preference Act and the collective bargaining agreement.

In a second case, the U.S. Court of Appeals for the Fourth Circuit held that a lower court improperly enjoined the Columbia, South Carolina, post office from making certain shift changes until a union grievance could be arbitrated.[13] The court said that since the collective bargaining agreement provides for mandatory grievance-arbitration procedures, the federal courts should not intrude at the behest of either management or labor into disputes over arbitral issues unless intrusion by injunction is necessary to protect the arbitral process itself. In this case, since employees did not lose their jobs as a result of the management action, no irreparable injury resulted and the arbitrator could easily restore the status quo ante by his award.

On the other hand, the U.S. District Court for New Jersey held that a discharged postal employee need not exhaust his remedies under the collective bargaining agreement before filing suit alleging that the U.S. Postal Service breached that agreement.[14] According to the court, exhaustion is not required where the suit alleges that employer behavior effectively repudiated the grievance procedures contained in the contract.

In this case an employee was fired after having been charged with a criminal offense. The president of his local union told the employee that he (the president) would get an agreement from management to hold the grievance procedure in abeyance until the criminal case was resolved. Two years later the charges were

---

[12]*Smith* v. *Daws, Postmaster,* USCA 5, No. 79-1581, 859 GERR 7 (1980).
[13]*Columbia Local, American Postal Workers Union, AFL-CIO* v. *Bolger,* USCA 4, No. 79-1123, 863 GERR 8 (1980).
[14]*Riley* v. *Letter Carriers Local 380, et al.,* USDC NJ, Civil Action No. 78-1414, 867 GERR 9 (1980).

dropped, but when the former employee sought, through the union, to reinstate the grievance, USPS said it was untimely. He then sued the union for breach of the duty of fair representation and USPS for breach of the collective bargaining agreement.

The judge dismissed the suit against the union, but refused to do so for the Postal Service. Judge Debevoise reasoned that the special arrangement to hold the grievance in abeyance pending the outcome of the criminal matter amounted to a modification of the contract's grievance procedure, and he said that relief for alleged breaches of that modified procedure could be sought in court.

The Postal Service requested reconsideration based on the requirement stated by the Supreme Court in *Vaca* v. *Sipes* [15] that a plaintiff prove a violation of the union's duty of fair representation as a threshold matter before suing the employer for breach of a collective bargaining agreement. The court held, however, that *Vaca* does specifically provide, as in the present case, that the individual employee may resort to the courts before the grievance procedures have been fully exhausted when the conduct of the employer amounts to a repudiation of those contractual procedures.

Finally, in a decision currently under appeal to the U.S. Court of Appeals for the Ninth Circuit, a federal court in California ruled that once an arbitrator has made a threshold determination that an employee has participated in a strike against the federal government, no mitigation of the discharge penalty is possible.[16] The decision reasons that because it is unlawful for a person who has participated in a strike against the government to hold a federal job, an award of reinstatement would be unenforceable because it would compel the performance of an illegal act.

The arbitrator had ruled that the grievant did participate in a strike; however, the arbitrator had reinstated him with back pay based on mitigating circumstances. In setting aside the arbitration award, the federal court dealt a blow to efforts to win amnesty for several hundred strikers who took part in an abortive postal strike in 1978. Moreover, if the decision stands, it presumably would affect all federal agencies, not just the Postal Service.

---

[15]386 U.S. 171, 64 LRRM 2369 (1967).

[16]*American Postal Workers Union, AFL-CIO* v. *U.S. Postal Service, San Francisco Bulk Mail Center, Richmond, Calif.,* USDC Cal. No. C-80-0748-WWS, 872 GERR 5 (1980).

III. Dispute Resolution in Canada

Collective bargaining for federal and provincial public employees in Canada, like the United States, is a relatively recent development. Each of the provinces has adopted its own legislation to grant and regulate collective efforts by public employees. In 1967 the federal government enacted legislation establishing formal collective bargaining procedures, including binding arbitration to resolve disputes. This analysis will report, briefly, on relatively recent developments in the province of Ontario[17] and on legislation covering federal public employees.

Ontario

In 1975 Bill 100 was passed covering the negotiation of collective agreements between school boards and teachers. The act is administered by the Education Relations Commission consisting of five members, one of whom is designated as the chairperson and another as the vice-chairperson. Members of the Commission are experienced labor relations specialists. The Commission's authority resembles that of similar agencies in the United States administering collective bargaining statutes.

Section 29 of the act provides that the parties may refer matters in dispute to a binding voluntary interest arbitration board or to a single arbitrator. The parties themselves may name the arbitrator or request the Commission to appoint one. The parties may each select a person to a board of arbitration.

As an alternative, the parties may elect to submit unresolved negotiation matters to a "selector." Again, the parties may agree to the name of the selector or, if they are unable to agree, the Commission will appoint one. In essence, the parties submit their final offers to the selector who then makes a selection in writing of all of one of the party's final offers. Under certain circumstances teachers may legally strike.

The future of public-sector grievance arbitration in Ontario is somewhat in doubt, clouded by recent legislation in the private sector. Bill 25 was introduced in Ontario as an amendment to the Labour Relations Act. The bill provides that either party may request referral of a grievance to a single arbitrator not chosen by the parties, but rather appointed by the Minister of

---

[17]Legislation in other provinces is similar to that of Ontario.

Labour. The bill did not apply to collective agreements in effect on the date the bill came into force. Since several multiyear agreements are in existence, the full effect of the bill is not yet known. Although the bill applies only to the private sector, it is reasonable to believe that it may have a spillover effect into the public sector.

Other public employees in Ontario are likewise statutorily regulated. Employees of general hospitals are prohibited from striking; yet in early 1981 employees struck even though an arbitration process existed. Firefighters have the right to strike, but have traditionally refrained from doing so. Police are forbidden from striking, instead using interest arbitration to resolve their disputes.

Federal Sector

The Public Service Staff Relations Act of 1967 provided for collective bargaining for Canadian federal civil servants. One unique feature of the legislation is the choice of procedures for impasses. When first introduced, the legislation banned strikes and provided for binding arbitration. While the bill was being acted on, postal workers engaged in an illegal strike. Partly as a result of that strike, the legislation, as finally enacted, provides for an election of procedures. Prior to the start of bargaining, the union specifies whether, if agreement is not reached, the matters in dispute will be referred to arbitration or there will be a work stoppage. The choice cannot be altered during that bargaining round. It should be stressed that the choice is made by the union and is binding on the employer. The legislation provides that before either arbitration or a work stoppage, specified conciliation steps must be followed. The law also provides that certain employees designated as essential by the Public Service Staff Relations Board must continue working. Evidence indicates that the vast majority of bargaining units have chosen the arbitration route of impasse resolution. The legislation provides for a permanent arbitration tribunal which consists of a chairperson, an alternate chairperson, and three employer and three union partisan members. When arbitration is appropriate, a tribunal is formed consisting of the chairperson (or an alternate) and one union and one employer representative. The arbitration award is binding.

IV. Judicial and Related Developments

Constitutionality of Collective Bargaining Laws and Practices

California's Statute. A key case challenging the constitutionality of a collective bargaining statute came in California. Since the advent of collective bargaining in public employment, civil service and collective bargaining systems seem to have been on a collision course. Both systems now permeate all levels of government employment in California, including the state civil service where a constitutionally created State Personnel Board (SPB) administered the civil service system and a legislatively created Public Employment Relations Board (PERB) administers public employment relations acts.

In California abstract questions concerning the purported incompatibility of civil service and collective bargaining systems became a concrete case in *Pacific Legal Foundation* v. *Brown.* [18] On March 25, 1980, the California Court of Appeal held that the State Employer-Employee Relations Act (SEERA) conflicted with certain civil service provisions in the California constitution. Having found such a conflict between the two systems, the court resolved the matter in favor of the civil service system and declared SEERA unconstitutional.[19]

On May 22, 1980, the California Supreme Court agreed to review the Court of Appeal decision, and on March 12, 1981, the 4-2 decision, written by Justice Matthew Tobriner, was handed down.[20] It held that SEERA is constitutional and that the language in the statute does not conflict on its face with the constitutional powers of the State Personnel Board.

The ruling went further than some had anticipated. It was generally assumed that the court would find no inherent conflict between a collective bargaining system and a merit system, or between setting wages and the SPB's authority to classify jobs. However, the court surprised some by also determining that there is no facial conflict between PERB's jurisdiction over un-

[18]103 Cal.App.3d 801, 103 LRRM 3131 (1980).

[19]These introductory remarks have been drawn from a perceptive article written by UCLA Law Professor Reginald Alleyne in which he challenged the appellate court's findings and anticipated the basic reasoning used by the California Supreme Court in ultimately upholding the constitutionality of SEERA. Alleyne, *A Comment on the Constitutionality of SEERA,* 46 Cal. Pub. Emp. Rels. 2 (September 1980).

[20]*Pacific Legal Foundation* v. *Brown, et al., supra* note 18; *California State Employees Assn., et al., Interveners,* Sup. Ct. No. S.F. 24168, March 12, 1981.

fair practices involving state employees and the SPB's exclusive constitutional jurisdiction to review disciplinary actions involving state employees.

Leaving the door open for further constitutional litigation, the court made it clear that the case did not involve any specific action under SEERA which conflicted with the constitutional authority of the SPB. Rather, the question brought to the court was whether the act *on its face* inevitably poses such a total and fatal conflict with the constitution that it must be struck down. Although such an inevitable, fatal conflict was not found, as the act is implemented, disputes could arise over specific application of the statute—such as whether the terms of a collective bargaining agreement conflicted with the SPB's constitutional powers or whether a PERB action in an unfair practice case in fact encroaches on SPB's disciplinary jurisdiction. In such instances, the court stated that the conflicts may be resolved by litigation, by administrative accommodation, or by legislative action.[21]

Fair-Share Agreements. In recent years the issue of the proper amount of dues collectible under a fair-share provision has been the subject of much litigation. In February 1981 the Wisconsin Employment Relations Commission issued a decision of national importance on this subject.[22] Wisconsin's Municipal Employment Relations Act defines a "fair share agreement" as an agreement under which all employees are required to "pay their proportionate share of the cost of the collective bargaining process and contract administration. . . ."

Plaintiffs argued that the term "collective bargaining process" includes only those functions of the local union (as opposed to affiliated state and international unions and other affiliates) relating to the negotiation of collective bargaining agreements, to the contract administration, and to the resolution of grievances arising under such agreements.

The Commission rejected the narrow interpretation of the plaintiffs. In adopting a broad interpretation, the Commission stated:

"We deem that a union, which is the collective bargaining representative of employees in a collective bargaining unit, is pursuing its

---

[21]For a more complete discussion from which these remarks are drawn, *see* Bogue, *Supreme Court Upholds SEERA,* 48 Cal. Publ. Emp. Rels. Supp. 16 (March 1981).
[22]*Browne, et al.,* No. 18408 (February 1981).

representative interest by expending sums of money, either directly or by payments to others, for activities other than those found to be impermissible herein, relating to improving the wages, hours, and working conditions of the employees in the bargaining unit involved, as well as the wages, hours, and working conditions of other employees represented by said unions and its affiliates, and that therefore such expenditures are properly included in the amount of fair share payments by unit employees who are not members of said union."

Accordingly, a wide range of activities were found chargeable to fair-share payers, including lobbying for legislation or regulations affecting wages, hours, and working conditions of employees generally; per capita payments to affiliated organizations; advertising; union newspapers; litigation; payments for printed materials and technical personnel; conventions and meetings, depending on their purpose; and most impasse procedures. Not chargeable, however, are costs incurred in support of an illegal strike; support and contributions to political organizations and candidates for public office, to charitable organizations, to ideological causes, and for international affairs; and training in voter registration, get-out-the-vote, and campaign techniques.

Dues Checkoff. In Virginia an issue has arisen of the legality of dues checkoff absent a collective bargaining agreement or power to create one. Virginia does not have a statute authorizing collective bargaining for public employees. However, prior to 1977 some school boards and teacher organizations had reduced their agreement to writing. In that year the state supreme court declared public-employee collective bargaining illegal absent enabling legislation.[23] The decision expressly denied Virginia's public employees any implied power to bargain and rescinded contracts previously honored. Since 1977, proponents have tried unsuccessfully to secure express statutory authority for collective bargaining by public employers and employee organizations.

In 1980 it became apparent that seven Virginia cities and more than 100 school boards have permitted dues checkoff for members of employee organizations. A number of city managers or county councils, however, disclaimed knowledge of the checkoff.

---

[23]*Commonwealth of Virginia* v. *County Board of Arlington County,* Va. S. Ct., 232 S.E.2d 30, 94 LRRM 2291 (1977).

In May 1980, the Richmond city council adopted an ordinance authorizing payroll deduction of dues for police, firefighter, and teacher employee organizations which are not recognized as bargaining units. A suit filed in July 1980 in the Richmond circuit court will determine the legality of authorizing dues checkoff. Trial is scheduled for May 1981.

Significant Developments in Interest Arbitration During 1980

Court Decisions. On June 6, 1980, the Supreme Court of Michigan handed down the year's most significant interest arbitration decision when it upheld the constitutionality of the state's last-offer item-by-item interest arbitration statute for municipal police and firefighters.[24] Two issues that frequently arise in interest arbitration were treated in considerable detail: (1) whether the act was an unconstitutional delegation of legislative and political responsibility to politically unaccountable arbitrators, and (2) whether the arbitration panel's award was supported by the evidence.

In deciding the second issue, the court tackled the extremely important matter of the weight to be given to each of the eight factors which the law requires the arbitration panel to consider. The decision had been anxiously awaited since an arbitration panel issued its award on December 20, 1978, and since an evenly divided Michigan Supreme Court upheld the constitutionality of the law in 1975.[25]

On the accountability issue, the majority held that 1976 amendments changing the method of appointing the neutral chairperson of the arbitration panel removed any doubts regarding the panel's accountability that existed after the *Dearborn* decision. Chairpersons are now appointed by the Michigan Employment Relations Commission (MERC) from its permanent arbitration panel. The court reasoned that persons whose names appear on that panel will be concerned with the long-term impact of their decisions because they must be residents of Michigan and because they remain on the panel until removed by MERC. They serve in many disputes, so are not "hit and run arbitrators," a phrase used to describe the temporary nature of the arbitrator's role. As residents of the state, the arbitrators

---

[24]*City of Detroit* v. *Detroit Police Officers Assn.,* 294 N.W.2d 68, 105 LRRM 3083, 868 GERR 16 (1980).
[25]*Dearborn Firefighters* v. *City of Dearborn,* 231 N.W.2d 226, 90 LRRM 2002 (1975).

cannot escape to another jurisdiction, thus avoiding the impact of their decision. By serving an indeterminate term, the arbitrators acquire a degree of tenure. Furthermore, as appointees of MERC the arbitrators acquire a kind of political accountability they would not have if appointed by the partisan members of the arbitration panel.

The court may be stretching a bit to find arbitrators politically accountable, but the judges acknowledged that the statute struck a balance between political accountability and independence. Greater political accountability was not desirable, the court noted, because it would erode the independence of the arbitrator. A concurring justice pointed out that a politically accountable legislature had enacted the statute so arbitrators need not be as politically accountable as legislators. The majority believed that the "tension" between independence and political accountability was balanced by the act's standards to guide the arbitration panel, by the public atmosphere in which the act operates, and by the act's provision for judicial review.

Judicial review can rest on one of three bases: that the panel exceeded its jurisdiction, that its order was not supported by the evidence, or that the order was procured by unlawful means such as fraud. Only the second—weight of the evidence—had any applicability to this case. It constitutes the second major issue considered by the court.

The statute instructs the panel to be guided by eight factors, all of which are familiar to those who have worked in the field of interest arbitration. They include the lawful authority of the employing public jurisdiction, stipulations of the parties, financial ability of the employing unit along with the interest and welfare of the public, comparisons of wages and other conditions of employment with public and private employers, changes in consumer prices, overall compensation of the affected employees, and a general "catch-all" provision which covers all other factors not specifically listed but that are normally used in arbitration.

The panel must consider all eight factors, but is not told how to weight them. The court held that the legislature mandated the arbitration panel to weight the factors and that such was a constitutional delegation of authority. The panel may not ignore any factor, but is to decide which factors are of greater and which are of lesser importance.

By upholding the panel's authority to weight these factors, the court recognized that the economic, social, and political climate is instrumental in determining which factors are most important in any given case. Listing the factors may be necessary before courts will uphold the constitutionality of interest arbitration statutes, but the weight to be given each factor must be determined on a case-by-case basis before a decision can be reached.

Other 1980 court decisions upheld interest arbitration statutes; none was struck down. The Connecticut Supreme Court in a unanimous ruling overturned a 1978 decision of the Hartford superior court and upheld the constitutionality of the state's Municipal Employee Relations Act, which includes compulsory, binding, final-offer arbitration.[26] The lower court had ruled that the statute clothes arbitrators with too much authority. Not so, said the supreme court. Towns are "creatures of the state," so the state legislature may require them to submit disputes to binding arbitration. An unusual provision of the Connecticut statute requires that the appropriating authority provide the money necessary to implement an arbitration award although a party is permitted to file a motion to vacate the award.

The Pennsylvania Supreme Court ordered the Franklin County Prison Board to abide by an arbitration award dealing with salaries of prison guards.[27] The prison board refused to implement the award on the grounds that it required legislative enactment and, thus, under the statute the award was advisory only. The court held that the state legislature, not the county prison board, was the legislative body. The prison board was an administrative agency which received money from the legislature. The task of the prison board was to allocate that money. The award was advisory to the legislature, but binding on the prison board.

Another Pennsylvania decision dealt with the authority of arbitration panels to rule on particular issues. The Commonwealth Court of Pennsylvania upheld the authority of an arbitration panel to fix a five-day, 40-hour workweek for police under the statute governing collective bargaining for police and firefighters.[28] Hours of work is a proper subject for bargaining and, thus, is a proper subject for arbitral ruling, said the court.

---

[26] *Town of Berlin* v. *Frank Santaguida, et al.,* 870 GERR 11 (1980).
[27] *Franklin County Prison Board* v. *Pennsylvania Labor Relations Board,* 417 A.2d 1138, 103 LRRM 2461 (1980).
[28] *Arbitration between the Borough of Ambridge and the Police Department,* Pa. Cmwlth., 417 A.2d 29 (1980).

By contrast, the Massachusetts Appeals Court declared invalid that portion of an arbitration award which dealt with the authority of a chief of police to assign officers to shifts.[29] The Massachusetts statute limits the authority of arbitration panels in police matters by excluding certain managerial functions, among them the right to assign work. Assignment of shifts is a proper subject for bargaining, the court said, but the statute excludes that subject from arbitration.

In a noteworthy opinion, a New York supreme court held that certain amendments to the Taylor Law in 1977 were meant to provide for more stringent judicial review of public-interest arbitration awards.[30] Thus, judicial review of compulsory interest arbitration awards, while still concerned with consideration of whether the award, on the whole, is reasonably founded on the record, is now additionally focused by the statutory amendments on the reasonableness and rationality of *specific* findings which the arbitrators are required to make with respect to each and every statutory criterion placed in issue by the parties. The court vacated the arbitration award in this case on the ground that the panel majority had failed to specify the basis for most, if not all, of its findings, as required by the 1977 statutory amendments.

The Massachusetts Joint Labor-Management Committee for Municipal Police and Fire. In Massachusetts, the Joint Labor-Management Committee (JLMC) for police and fire was created effective January 1, 1978, in response to dissatisfaction—especially on the part of municipal governments—with last-best-offer arbitration. The committee, composed of six representatives from local government, three from the firefighters, three from police labor organizations, and an impartial chairperson and vice-chairperson, has oversight responsibility for all collective bargaining negotiations involving municipal police and firefighters.

The basic principle of the JLMC is to assist the parties to reach an agreement themselves, rather than to have an outsider make the decision through last-best-offer arbitration, which may leave the parties with an award that frequently results in unsatisfactory labor relations.

The JLMC has a wide range of options in the processing of a dispute brought to it by either party. Generally, the first step

---

[29]*City of Taunton* v. *Taunton Branch of Mass. Police Assn.*, Mass. App. Ct. Adv. Sh. 1359 (1980).

[30]*Buffalo Police Benevolent Assn.* v. *City of Buffalo*, 13 PERB 7539 (N.Y. 1980).

is to assign a staff mediator, who gathers the facts, identifies and seeks to narrow the issues, and engages in mediation. Subsequent steps would involve mediation efforts by senior staff members and then by labor and management representatives of the committee. If these steps do not resolve the dispute, a tripartite subcommittee of the JLMC may be assigned to meet with the parties for further mediation, which may include a formal mediation proposal. A formal fact-finding step may be used, with the chairperson, vice-chairperson, or an outsider as fact-finder. In those cases where informal procedures do not resolve the dispute, the committee may certify the issues in dispute and refer the matter to a form of final and binding arbitration before the chairperson, vice-chairperson, or an outside arbitrator. In a significant number of cases the parties reach settlement through the informal processes of the JLMC, but then request that the agreement be announced as a formal arbitration award to meet the political needs of either or both parties.

Prior to the establishment of the JLMC, there were 97 last-best-offer awards; since the establishment of the committee there have been only seven. The overall average time for all cases under the old procedures was 6.7 months, compared to an overall average of 3.6 months under the JLMC. Through fiscal 1980, the JLMC resolved about 68 percent of its cases through informal settlements; for fiscal 1980 alone, the disputes resolved by informal settlements rose to 80 percent.

The evidence is clear and convincing that during the past three years the procedures of the JLMC have enhanced the role of collective bargaining in the settlement of all disputes between communities and their public-safety unions, and by speeding up the settlement process the committee has eliminated considerable friction between the parties and substantially reduced the costs of the process to the parties.

The improved climate for responsible collective bargaining was subjected to a new set of uncertainties when, on November 4, 1980, the voters of Massachusetts approved a referendum item, Proposition 2½, an offspring of California's tax-cutting measure, Proposition 13. Although the JLMC rarely used the step of final arbitration, the threat of its use was always present. Now, however, one of the provisions of Proposition 2½ appears to have eliminated the final and binding aspects of arbitration awards upon the appropriate legislative body. The legality of the total proposition has been questioned and is now in the courts.

Also in the courts is the question of the authority of the JLMC. The number of cases coming to the committee has declined rather substantially since November 1980, with the parties apparently waiting the outcome of court cases as well as the potential drive to amend or drastically revise Proposition 2½.

Med-Arb in Wisconsin. The year 1980 was Wisconsin's third year of experience under its med-arb law which provides for final-offer arbitration by package for interest disputes involving municipal employees (except fire and law-enforcement personnel who are covered by a separate interest arbitration law). To date, the Wisconsin Employment Relations Commission has processed and closed 794 med-arb cases. Of the 794 closed cases, 175 have required an award. The remaining cases were resolved after a med-arb petition had been filed, but prior to an arbitrated award. Of the 175 awards, the union's offer was selected in 69 cases and the employer's in 58 cases; 48 awards were issued pursuant to a consent award.

The med-arb law was enacted with a sunset provision and, accordingly, is programmed to expire October 31, 1981. All indications at this time are that the law will be reenacted.

Significant Developments in Grievance Arbitration

Court Decisions

Grievance arbitration received considerable attention in two states, New York and Pennsylvania. As in the past, many court cases in 1980 dealt with the issue of arbitrability, while other decisions dealt with the individual's right to take a case to arbitration and the standards under which a court should review an arbitrator's award.

New York. The New York Court of Appeals rendered three decisions in 1980 which are further sequels to cases reported on last year which limited the doctrine enunciated in *Acting Superintendent of Schools of Liverpool Central School District* v. *United Liverpool Faculty Association.* [31] The decisions indicated a retreat from the restrictive view of public-sector arbitration announced in *Liverpool.*

In *Hannelore Lehnhoff* v. *Shepherd Nathan, et al.,* [32] the court of

---

[31] 42 N.Y.2d 509, 399 N.Y.S.2d 189 (1977).
[32] 48 N.Y.2d 990, 425 N.Y.S.2d 544 (1980).

appeals found that the parties' collective bargaining agreement, which permitted the employer to suspend petitioner from her position in a state psychiatric center without pay if he determined that there was probable cause to believe that her "continued presence on the job represents a potential danger to persons or property and would severely interfere with operations," contemplated that the issue of whether there had in fact been a probable-cause determination by the employer was to be submitted to arbitration. The court reversed a decision by the appellate division,[33] which held that the arbitration clause did not even come into play until the suspending authority had made a finding of probable cause. Thus, the court of appeals held, judicial resolution of the merits of the dispute over the propriety of petitioner's suspension was foreclosed.

In another case,[34] the court of appeals found the grievance of a probationary school teacher arbitrable within the meaning of the contract between the parties. Where the school district agreed to submit to arbitration all grievances involving "an alleged misinterpretation or misapplication of an express provision of [the] Agreement," it begs the question, said the court, to contend that the grievance is not arbitrable because it involves a dispute not unambiguously encompassed by an express substantive provision of the contract. The court distinguished *Liverpool* as requiring that arbitration be stayed only in cases where the parties' arbitration agreement did not unambiguously extend to the particular dispute. Here, however, the parties' agreement to arbitrate the dispute was clear and unequivocal. The ambiguity surrounded the coverage of the applicable substantive provision of the contract which is a matter of contract interpretation for an arbitrator.

In *Board of Education of Middle Island Central School Dist. No. 12* v. *Middle Island Teachers Association*,[35] the court of appeals held that a probationary teacher who was denied tenure for alleged professional incompetence in the performance of his nonclassroom duties had a right to arbitrate alleged breaches of contract evaluation procedures specifically referable to classroom performance. The court reversed a decision of the appellate divi-

---

[33]63 A.D.2d 694, 405 N.Y.S.2d 108 (2d Dept. 1978).
[34]*Board of Education of Lakeland Central School District of Shrub Oak* v. *Joseph Barni*, 49 N.Y.2d 311, 425 N.Y.S.2d 544, 103 LRRM 2903 (1980).
[35]50 N.Y.2d 426, 429 N.Y.S.2d 564 (1980).

sion[36] which had stayed arbitration on the ground that the school board had denied tenure for reasons unrelated to the teacher's classroom performance. Citing *Liverpool*, the court of appeals found that the subject matter of the dispute was encompassed by the broad arbitration clause in the parties' collective bargaining agreement. Since the school board is bound by an agreement which requires teacher evaluation procedures, failure to follow these procedures may form the basis for a grievance which may be submitted to arbitration. Even though the board had the right to deny tenure to a probationary teacher without an explanation, "the procedural aspect of the contract is discrete from the denial of tenure and should be so treated," said the court.

In a fourth New York case dealing with judicial review of arbitration awards,[37] the court of appeals held that it was an error for the appellate division to vacate an award merely because it believed the arbitrator had misconstrued the apparent, or even the obvious, meaning of the agreement. The court stated that "Parties who agree to refer contract disputes to arbitration must recognize that 'arbitrators may do justice' and the award may well reflect the spirit rather than the letter of the Agreement."

Pennsylvania. In Pennsylvania a continuing issue in the interpretation of Act 195 is the identification of those cases that are covered by the mandatory arbitration provision of the statute. In one case,[38] the commonwealth court upheld the common pleas decision that ruled that the school board lawfully refused to submit to arbitration a grievance alleging that teachers were denied professional advantage without "just cause" as a result of the board's decision to eliminate certain courses that they taught. There was no allegation that the teachers were suspended or reduced in rank, and the court concluded that the agreement's "just cause" provision did not provide for arbitration of disputes arising from the management decision to eliminate courses.

However, the commonwealth court ruled in another case[39] that the elimination of two academic positions was arbitrable

---

[36]68 A.D.2d 926, 414 N.Y.S.2d 373 (2d Dept. 1979).
[37]*Amalgamated Transit Union Local 1179* v. *Green Bus Lines*, 50 N.Y.2d 1007, 431 N.Y.S.2d 680, 409 N.E.2d 1354 (1980).
[38]*Greater Johnstown Area Vocational-Technical School*, 11 PPER 11061 (1980).
[39]*Greater Johnstown Area Vocational-Technical School*, 11 PPER 11044 (1980).

under the grievance/arbitration provisions in the collective bargaining agreement. In reversing a court of common pleas decision, the court found that the dispute did not involve the exercise of an inherent managerial function that would be unarbitrable under the act, but that the elimination of two positions presented an issue that deprived union members of work and, therefore, had an immediate and direct impact on their legitimate interests.

The commonwealth court rejected the argument that PERA gives a public employee the right to take a grievance to arbitration. In 1978 the court found that only the union and the employer, as parties to the collective bargaining agreement, could appeal an arbitrator's award. In the more recent case, the commonwealth and the union had entered into a memorandum of agreement under which individual employees could file grievances but could not appeal them to arbitration.[40] The court affirmed a PLRB finding that a state agency did not violate its duty to bargain in good faith by refusing to arbitrate a grievance when the union, but not the individual grievant, withdrew its request for arbitration. The court noted that the memorandum of agreement, which set forth the procedure for arbitration, referred to "the parties," and the court could not say that the PLRB's refusal to issue a complaint was a manifest and flagrant abuse of its discretion.

Although the court affirmed the principle that an individual employee does not have the right to take a grievance to arbitration, it ruled that the PLRB did not have the exclusive jurisdiction over allegations that fair representation was not being provided.[41] It held that the common pleas court had jurisdiction to decide whether a public employer discharged an employee without just cause, whether the union arbitrarily and in bad faith refused to demand arbitration on the employee's behalf, and whether the employer and union conspired and agreed to the discharge. The union had processed the grievance through the grievance procedure, but did not appeal it to arbitration. The commonwealth court rejected the argument that the grievant had not exhausted available remedies under the union's constitution and bylaws, noting that such remedies could not result in the employee's reinstatement with back pay. It also rejected the

---

[40]*Pennsylvania Dept. of Transportation,* 11 PPER 1103 (1980).
[41]*SEPTA,* 11 PPER 1161 (1980).

argument that the grievance procedure was the exclusive procedure for appealing the alleged wrongful discharge. The court
concluded that the alleged conspiracy made the case subject to
a principle established in 1960 that a member may sue the union
for breach of the duty of fair representation and may join the
employer as a co-defendant for participating in the union's
breach of its obligation. It found that the PLRB did not have
exclusive jurisdiction over the complaint because the breach of
the duty of fair representation in grievance proceedings was not
among the unfair labor practices described in Section 1201 of
PERA.

Grievance Arbitration and the Regulation of Public-Employee Life Style: The Image Offense

Since at least 1949, when our current Chief Executive, in a
somewhat less influential capacity, championed the right of a
small-town school mistress to enjoy off-duty hours at the beach
in a form-flattering swimsuit,[42] the fascination and the anxiety
of the public-at-large over the lifestyle of public employees has
been constant. In response to public anxiety, public employers
have sought to regulate the lifestyle of their workers into patterns acceptable to the conservative core of the community. It
may be stated as a general rule, applicable to public and private
sector alike, that an employer may regulate lifestyle to a degree,
that an employee must comport with whatever standards of
personal grooming and conduct his employer may choose to
promulgate, provided, however, that some demonstrable nexus
exists between the standards imposed and the legitimate
managerial concerns of the employer.[43]

It is sometimes stated in private-sector disputes that one is
constitutionally secured from too severe demands made by an
employer regarding comportment.[44] It is sometimes further
stated that the approach to be taken in determining the legiti-
macy of the employer's demands is to balance the employer's
needs against the employee's individual freedoms.[45] It would

---

[42]*The Girl from Jones Beach:* Ronald Reagan, Virginia Mayo; Warner Brothers Studios, 1949.
[43]*See generally, Changing Lifestyles and the Problems of Authority in the Plant,* in Labor Arbitration at the Quarter-Century Mark, Proceedings of the 25th Annual Meeting, National Academy of Arbitrators (Washington: BNA Books, 1972), 235 *et seq.*
[44]*Economy Super Mart,* 54 LA 816, 819 (Elson 1970).
[45]*Pepsi Cola General Bottlers, Inc.,* 55 LA 663 (Volz 1970).

seem that attributing a constitutional dimension to a private-sector dispute over employee lifestyle overstates the case. What is actually being examined in such cases is the enforceability of a code of grooming and conduct under the "just cause" provision of the collective bargaining agreement. In such cases, the issue is not whether the Constitution prohibits implementation of the code, but, simply, whether aspects of the code are so tenuously related to the legitimate managerial concerns of the employer that their violation could not provide just cause for discipline. We are not, or should not, in such cases be scouting for constitutionally protected activity; we should simply be determining whether the employer has an interest in proscribing the activity. There is little justification for conducting a constitutionally based inquiry in a private-sector extracurricular misconduct case.

By contrast, there are, minimally, three constitutional issues which inhere in most extracurricular misconduct cases involving public-sector workers. The issues arise, of course, from the presence of "state action," a factor lacking in the private sector. The issues are: (1) whether the safeguards of procedural due process have been observed in ordering discipline;[46] (2) whether a fundamental right to privacy has been violated;[47] and (3) whether an irrational classification has been imposed in violation of the equal protection clause.[48] It is not uncommon to encounter a spectrum of constitutional concerns in a single off-duty misconduct case. The focus of this discussion will not be on the full spectrum of claims available, but only on the right to privacy and to equal protection in relation to the regulation of one's lifestyle by one's employer.

In considering the situation of public employees, the courts have come to acknowledge such workers as a special category of individuals, a category with a less potent claim against state infringement upon lifestyle than the public-at-large.[49] The acknowledgement was made explicit most recently in *Fabio* v. *Philadelphia Civil Service Commission.* [50] In *Fabio,* the Pennsylvania Supreme Court allowed the discharge of a police officer who had

---

[46]*See, e.g., Skelly* v. *State Personnel Board,* 124 Cal.Rptr. 14, 539 P.2d 774 (1975).
[47]*Shuman* v. *City of Philadelphia,* 470 F.Supp. 449 (E.D.Pa. 1979); *Warren* v. *State Personnel Board,* 156 Cal. Rptr. 351, 94 Cal.App.3d 94 (1979).
[48]*Hollenbaugh* v. *Carnegie Free Library,* 436 F.Supp. 1328, *aff'd* 578 F.2d 1374, *cert. den.* 439 U.S. 1052, 99 S.Ct. 734 (1977).
[49]*Kelley* v. *Johnson,* 425 U.S. 238, 96 S.Ct. 1440 (1976).
[50]414 A.2d 82 (1980).

procured a fellow officer as a sexual partner for his wife, procured that fellow officer's girlfriend as a sexual partner for himself, and, subsequently, becoming dissatisfied, had instigated an affair with his wife's teenage sister. The stated basis for discharge was "conduct unbecoming an officer."

Officer Fabio alleged an impermissible infringement upon his penumbral First Amendment right to privacy. The plurality opinion, while conceding, perhaps erroneously,[51] that constitutionally protected activity was involved, rejected Fabio's claim. The court reasoned:

> "In Pennsylvania, individuals have the right to engage in extramarital sexual activities free from governmental interference. . . . However, in this case, we are concerned with the government's regulation of the conduct of its employees. This distinction is of considerable importance since a state has wider latitude and different interests in regulating the activities of its employees than in the behavioral pattern of the citizenry at large."[52]

Moreover, *Fabio* carried on the precept that the more visible a public employee is to the constituency, the more vulnerable that employee may be to employer attempts to curtail his or her lifestyle. Tribunals have upheld the dismissal of adulterous librarians in a small community,[53] of a public prosecutor who frequented a brothel,[54] and of an allegedly voyeuristic schoolteacher[55]—all without regard to the employee's efficiency on the job and with decided emphasis upon the public's impression of the employer.

Such cases involve "image offenses," extracurricular incidents which evidence a personality, demeanor, or attitude which is incompatible with the "image" of the public employer as a trustworthy repository of public esteem and traditional values and which, on that basis, is unacceptable to the employer. Employers have insisted that discipline be sustained for off-duty, off-premises conduct which tends to cloud the public's perception of the particular governmental entity, whether or not such conduct adversely affects the employee's actual ability to perform his or her tasks competently. In Pennsylvania it has been stated that no ascertainable link between an image-damaging

---

[51]*Ibid.*, Roberts, J., concurring; *Hollenbaugh, supra* note 48, at 1333–1334.
[52]*Fabio, supra* note 50, at 89.
[53]*Hollenbaugh, supra* note 48.
[54]*Moore* v. *Strickling*, 46 W.Va. 515, 33 S.E. 274 (1899).
[55]*Raymond* v. *Western Wayne School District*, Teacher Tenure Appeal No. 38-78 (Pa. 1980).

offense and a public employee's ability to perform on the job need be established to support disciplinary action.[56] There might be severe employment consequences of essentially private behavior ranging from transsexuality[57] to mildly aberrant Saturday-night pranks[58] as tribunals become receptive to a public agency's claims that its preferred image cannot endure the continued employment of a worker straying from the straight and narrow during off-hours.[59]

The relation of constitutionally oriented litigation over public-employee lifestyle to public-sector arbitration seems obvious. If the courts are prepared to acknowledge the special vulnerability of public employees to regulation of lifestyle and an interest by public employers in their own image that is so compelling that it overrides individual constitutional privileges, then it seems a public employer's authority to promulgate and enforce far-reaching rules of conduct under the management rights and just cause provisions of a collective bargaining agreement should be acknowledged in arbitration proceedings.

There is little problem with acknowledging the right to proscribe outside activity which threatens some tangible, immediate impact upon a public agency's operations.[60] The concept of an image offense, however, embraces conduct with no readily discernible effect upon operations. In *Lone Star Gas Co.*,[61] for instance, any real damage to the employer utility company seemed highly speculative, yet the arbitrator upheld the grievant's discharge, notwithstanding a satisfactory work record, because the grievant's arrest and conviction for incest contrasted with the "good public image" of the employer. *Lone Star* parallels remarkably the rationale expressed in court considerations of image-damaging conduct. The concern is not only for the smooth

[56]*Id.*, citing *Penn. Delco School District* v. *Urso*, 33 Pa. Cmwlth. 501, 382 A.2d 162 (1978).
[57]*Warren, supra* note 47; *DeTore* v. *Local 245, Jersey City Public Employees*, 3 Pa. L.J. 9.
[58]In an unpublished Pennsylvania arbitration case, the commonwealth sought to discharge a psychiatric aide on the premise that, *inter alia*, he had, while off duty, "mooned" police officers.
[59]It is not a universally occurring phenomenon that public employees are found to be properly disciplined for extracurricular behavior which damages the staid image of an employer but has no effect upon operations. The requirement of an appreciable effect of off-duty conduct on on-duty performance, apparently abandoned to a substantial degree by some courts and tribunals considering image offenses, remains in force in others. *See, e.g., Nightingale* v. *State Personnel Board*, 102 Cal.Rptr. 758, 7 Cal.3d 507 (1972); *Shuman, supra* note 47.
[60]*See, e.g., Baltimore Transit Line*, 47 LA 62 (Duff 1966), wherein community outrage at the grievant's open participation in the Ku Klux Klan was so extreme that violence, strikes, and boycotts against the public employer were imminent.
[61]56 LA 1221, 1223 (Johannes 1971).

running of day-to-day operations, but also for the preservation, for whatever intrinsic value it may have, of an unsullied reputation within the community. The concept of an image offense asks that an arbitrator accept reputation per se, not merely reputation as it affects morale or productivity, as a legitimate managerial interest of a public employer—an interest which may be protected by disciplining employees for off-duty, off-premises conduct which does not conform with a "good public image."

The special circumstance which permits a public, but not a private, employer to encroach so extensively upon the outside activity of its workers is that the public employer, as an extension of government, acts, by definition, as a spokesman and representative of the public-at-large. A school board cannot, for instance, retain an intemperate, licentious, or morally unrestrained school administrator without granting, or appearing to grant, imprimatur to his lifestyle on behalf of the community. A public employer is charged not only with the obligation of ensuring quality service but also with the obligation of accurately reflecting community morals; it is within the legitimate interest of a public employer to avoid giving the appearance of tacit approval to communally disapproved lifestyles.[62]

Perhaps the most compelling aspect of an image-offense dispute is the compassion that it invites for the grievant/plaintiff. Although Officer Fabio may have obviously overstepped the bounds of propriety in establishing his adulterous menage and a California Highway Patrol officer may have obviously risked disciplinary action when he succumbed to the solicitation of homosexual prostitutes,[63] there are other employees whose conduct less obviously offends community standards, who are caught in a swirl of altering lifestyles, and who, understandably, have no firm grasp of approved behavior. It is ironic that students may assert a stronger equal-protection right to lifestyle than do "role model" public employees.[64] The behavior of public employees is strictly policed in order to foster an approved public image, but in an environment where private citizens freely indulge their preferences and do so with constitutional

---

[62]*Hollenbaugh, supra* note 48; *Warren, supra* note 47.
[63]*Warren, supra* note 47.
[64]*Stull* v. *School Board of Western Beaver Junior High School,* 459 F.2d 339 (1972); *Hollenbaugh, supra* note 48.

sanction, who can cite with clarity what is approved and what is expected from public employees?

Once one accepts the concept of an image offense, the more difficult question is whether the public employer is seeking to preserve an outmoded image. The public employer may have a legitimate managerial interest in presenting a good public image and protecting its reputation per se, but the image and reputation must be that expected by the community, not that which is more puritanical or reminiscent of more restrained times.

Spielberg-Collyer in the States

We start with a brief review of the *Spielberg-Collyer* doctrine as developed in the private sector and then show how it is being applied by the states in the public sector.

The National Labor Relations Board decision in *Spielberg Manufacturing Co.* [65] involved a complaint of an unfair labor practice by an employer who had failed to reinstate strikers following alleged picket-line misconduct. The issue had been arbitrated, the arbitrator holding that the employer was not obligated to reinstate the employees. The NLRB held that, while it is not bound as a matter of law by an arbitrator's award, it will defer to an arbitrator's award if specified conditions have been met.

In *Dubo Manufacturing Corp.,* [66] the NLRB withheld action on a complaint because a U.S. district court, after the issuance of the complaint, had issued an order directing arbitration.

In 1971, in *Collyer Insulated Wire Co.,* [67] the NLRB, in a 3-2 decision, extended the deferral doctrine to include deferral to contract arbitration prior to hearing an unfair labor practice case on the merits. The NLRB retained jurisdiction to determine whether the standards enunciated in its opinion were met by the arbitrator.

In *Collyer,* the respondent was charged with violation of Sections 8(a)(1) and (5) of the National Labor Relations Act. In the other cases, the Board included Sections 8(a)(3) and 8(a)(4) in its deferral doctrine.

Three cases decided by the NLRB in 1977 generally limited

---

[65] 112 NLRB 1080, 36 LRRM 1152 (1955).
[66] 142 NLRB 431, 53 LRRM 1070 (1963).
[67] 192 NLRB 837, 77 LRRM 1931 (1971).

the scope of deferral to issues involving the rights and obligations of the parties under a collective bargaining agreement as distinguished from cases involving the rights of an individual employee.[68]

Later, in a *Spielberg* case, the NLRB deferred to arbitration where an 8(a)(3) violation, as well as an 8(a)(5) violation, had been charged[69] and where an employer was charged with violating Section 8(a)(1).[70]

The Board has deferred in *Collyer* cases where (1) the unfair labor practice dispute is cognizable under the parties' collective bargaining agreement and the issue was presented to and considered by the arbitral tribunal; (2) the arbitral proceedings were fair and regular; (3) all parties to the arbitral proceedings agreed to be bound thereby; and (4) the decision of the arbitral tribunal was not repugnant to the purposes and policies of the NLRA.[71]

Changes in the NLRB's approach are due in large part to changes in Board membership.

Several state agencies which have jurisdiction in the public sector have applied the *Spielberg* and *Collyer* doctrines with some variations. The discussion that follows is a report of various state agencies. The committee has summarized briefly the results of our inquiry and an examination of state agency decisions.[72] We start with a state supreme court decision of considerable significance.

Michigan. In 1980, the Michigan Supreme Court, in a 4-3 decision, held that the Michigan Employment Relations Commission (MERC) does not have the power to defer unfair labor practice charges until an arbitration proceeding under the par-

---

[68]*Filmation Associates, Inc.,* 227 NLRB 237, 94 LRRM 1470 (1977); *Roy Robinson, Inc., d/b/a Roy Robinson Chevrolet,* 228 NLRB 828, 94 LRRM 1474 (1977); *General American Transportation Corp.,* 228 NLRB 808, 94 LRRM 1483 (1977).

[69]*Kansas City Star Co.,* 236 NLRB 119, 98 LRRM 1320 (1978).

[70]*United States Postal Service,* 241 NLRB 192, 101 LRRM 1074 (1979).

[71]A report on *State Labor Board Deferral to Arbitration* is included in the Selected Proceedings of the 25th Conference of the Association of Labor Relations Agencies (July 22–27, 1979), Madison, Wisconsin, published by Labor Relations Press. The paper was presented by Joan G. Dolan, member of the Massachusetts Labor Relations Commission, following the receipt of questionnaires sent to the states which are ALRA members. Commissioner Dolan's paper is well worth reading by persons interested in *Spielberg/ Collyer* as applied by the states.

[72]It is regrettable that space limitations necessitated deleting much of Mr. Howlett's excellent contribution. Thus, in the interest of brevity, not all cases have been cited and several states for which he provided a more detailed discussion have been relegated to a summary at the end of this report.

ties' collective bargaining agreement has been completed.[73] The case ended the *"Collyer"* policy adopted by MERC one year before the NLRB did so.[74]

The MERC deferred in *City of Flint* and later cases under the following conditions: (1) there is a stable bargaining relationship between the parties; (2) the respondent is willing to exhaust the grievance procedure, which culminates in binding arbitration; and (3) the underlying dispute centers on the interpretation or application of the contract.

Ten years after *City of Flint,* the Michigan Supreme Court held that the Public Employment Relations Act (PERA) does not authorize MERC to defer to arbitration in a *Collyer* situation. The four-member majority distinguished the NLRA and the PERA on the ground that:

1. The Michigan legislature did not intend that MERC would have authority to defer to private arbitration, because the PERA requires that MERC comply with the State Administrative Procedures Act; there is no such requirement in a proceeding before an arbitrator.

2. The Michigan PERA does not include a policy statement of preferences for the private resolution of contractual labor disputes through private arbitration.[75]

3. The PERA and related state statutes manifest "a clear legislative intent that, once a party to a public sector employment collective bargaining relationship invokes MERC's jurisdiction under PERA, that party's complaint should be resolved by MERC in accordance with the statutory processes."[76]

4. The PERA prohibits public employee strikes, in contrast to the private sector where a union is normally willing to give up the legal right to strike in exchange for an employer's agreement to acceptable methods of grievance resolution.[77]

California. California has adopted *Spielberg* and *Collyer* under

---

[73]*Detroit Fire Fighters Assn.* v. *City of Detroit,* 408 Mich. 663, 293 N.W.2d 278, 105 LRRM 3386 (1980).

[74]*City of Flint,* 1970 MERC Lab. Op. 367.

[75]The majority opinion noted that the Michigan Labor Mediation Act, applicable to the private sector, does, like the NLRA, include as one purpose "the . . . arbitration of labor disputes."

[76]*Detroit Fire Fighters, supra* note 73, at 685.

[77]The majority opinion does not address itself to *Spielberg,* although the language appears to be broad enough to cover it. However, the dissenting opinion of Mr. Justice Williams states that the court does not entertain "the statutory or constitutional efficacy of post-arbitration award, or *Spielberg*-type deferral." *Id.,* at 686.

the statutes applicable to public-school employees and state employees.

The State Employer-Employee Relations Act provides that the California Public Employment Relations Board (PERB) shall not issue a complaint on a charge of an unfair labor practice "against conduct also prohibited by the provisions of the agreement between the parties until the grievance machinery of the agreement, if it . . . covers the matter at issue, has been exhausted, either by settlement or binding arbitration." If appeal to the contract grievance procedure would be futile, exhaustion is not necessary. The PERB has power to review the settlement or arbitration award to determine whether it is repugnant to the purposes of the act. If it finds so, a complaint shall be issued.[78]

The Higher Education Employer-Employee Relations Act does not contain comparable language, but provides that the PERB shall not issue a complaint on any charge based on alleged violation of an agreement that would not also constitute an unfair labor practice under the act.[79]

The PERB has held an arbitrator's award deficient and repugnant to the public school statute.[80] A hearing officer held that an employer seeking deferral must waive all procedural defenses.[81]

Massachusetts. Massachusetts has adopted *Spielberg* and *Collyer.* The Massachusetts Labor Relations Commission (MLRC) first deferred to arbitration in a *Collyer* situation in *Cohasset School Committee and Cohasset Teachers' Association.*[82]

A union filed both an unfair labor practice charge and sought arbitration on the transfer of employees from one division to another. The arbitrator's award was issued before the completion of the MLRC hearing. The MLRC dismissed the unfair labor practice complaint, "[s]ince we find no violation of procedural safeguards and do not find the award to be repugnant to the purposes of the Law or the policies of the Commission, we decline to reconsider the matters herein and therefore adopt the arbitrator's award."[83]

The MLRC deferred where the issue was whether an administrative assistant position in the city's police department was

---

[78]Sections 3514.5, 3541.5, California Statutes.
[79]Section 3563.2
[80]*Drycreek Joint Elementary School District,* 2 NPER 05-11141 (1980).
[81]*Oakland Unified School District,* 2 NPER 05-11143 (1980).
[82]MUP 419 (1973).
[83]*City of Boston and Boston Police Patrolmen's Assn., Inc.,* 5 MLC 1155 (1978).

includable in a unit comprised of all nonprofessional employees of the city. The MLRC held that the arbitrator would, in all probability, resolve the status of the disputed position, so that the current litigation before the MLRC would serve no public service.[84] Patently, this case could have been decided as a unit clarification issue, if the MLRC had such a policy.

In a *Spielberg* case, the MLRC refused to decide an issue of transfer of work from one classification to another.[85] An MLRC hearing officer held that the MLRC will not defer where (1) neither party filed for arbitration, (2) arbitration proceedings would not resolve all issues, and (3) the issue is not a bona fide contract dispute.[86]

Commissioner Joan G. Dolan of the Massachusetts Labor Relations Commission advises that the commissioners are "debating the issue of whether or not we should defer (a)(1) or (a)(3) cases," and that a decision on an (a)(1) case will be issued soon. The MLRC has "been firm in deferring (a)(5) cases."

New York. New York State has adopted *Spielberg* and *Collyer*. The New York Public Employment Relations Board (PERB) adopted *Spielberg* in *New York City Transit Authority.* [87] *Collyer* was also adopted in 1971.[88]

In 1978 the Taylor Law was amended to provide:

"[T]he Board shall not have authority to enforce an agreement between an employer and an employee organization and shall not exercise jurisdiction over an alleged violation of such an agreement that would not otherwise constitute an improper employer or employee organization practice."

Thus, where a charge alleges a unilateral change by an employer and the employer claims a contractual basis for its action, the board dismisses the charge on jurisdictional grounds instead of deferring.[89]

Wisconsin. Wisconsin has adopted *Spielberg* (and *Dubo*), but not *Collyer*.

The Wisconsin Employment Relations statutes, applicable to both the public and private sectors, provide that the violation of a collective bargaining agreement is an unfair labor practice.

[84]*Boston Police Department,* 2 NPER 22-11132 (1980).
[85]*Winchester School Committee and Winchester School Secretaries Assn.,* 5 MLC 1047 (1979).
[86]*Burlington School Committee,* 2 NPER 22-11046 (1980).
[87]4 PERB 3031 (1971).
[88]*Board of Education of the City of Buffalo,* 4 PERB 3090 (1971).
[89]*City of Oneida,* 1 NPER 33-14615 (1979).

The Wisconsin Employment Relations Commission (WERC) enforces the provisions of a collective bargaining agreement which provides that grievances may be submitted to arbitration. In such cases, the WERC refuses to assert its jurisdiction. It does not consider this to be a "deferral" to arbitration, but gives effect to the collective bargaining contract; that is, contracts are enforceable through arbitration and not through court or administrative proceedings.

The first such WERC action involved the private-sector statute.[90] In language that sounds like *Collyer*, the WERC directed the employer to cease and desist from refusing to submit a dispute to arbitration and to comply with the arbitration provisions of the collective bargaining contract. However, action was based on the commission's power to require compliance with a contract, not on the principle of deferral.

Thus, the WERC has not adopted the *Collyer* policy of requiring a charging party to arbitrate, except in the context of breach of a collective bargaining contract. Query: Is this not what all agencies that apply *Collyer* do? WERC members are reluctant to adopt *Collyer* because:

"1. The Commission does not investigate or prosecute unfair labor practices, thus making the *Collyer* procedure difficult to administer and of limited administrative economy;
"2. The Commission has generally pursued a policy of allowing charging parties to assert statutory rights notwithstanding the mere existence of possible parallel contractual rights."[91]

The fact that it does not investigate or prosecute unfair labor practices did not deter the Michigan Employment Relations Commission from applying the *Collyer* doctrine.

It should be noted that the WERC provides arbitration by staff members for employers and unions who request it. The WERC holds:

"There are sound labor law principles to support [its] deferral policies . . . which are designed to discourage a charging party from proceeding simultaneously in two forums and thus 'taking two bites from the apple' and to insure that agreements to arbitrate contract interpretation questions are enforced."[92]

---

[90]*Int'l Union of Operating Engineers Local No. 311* v. *Milwaukee Lodge No. 46 of the Benevolent and Protective Order of Elks of the United States of America,* Case III, No. 10889, Ce-1096, Decision No. 7753 (1966).
[91]Letter dated June 30, 1980 from WERC general counsel in reply to inquiry from MERC chairman, dated June 18, 1980.
[92]*Milwaukee District Council 48 AFSCME* v. *Milwaukee Board of School Directors,* Decision No. 10663-A, Case XXXVI, No. 15096 MP-100 (1972).

Because of the foregoing, "[t]he possibility of parallel proceedings in two separate forums on the same facts is particularly repugnant to the statutory purpose . . . of the Municipal Employment Relations Act providing peaceful settlement through the processes of collective bargaining agreements."[93]

Milwaukee Board of School Directors[94] is a *Dubo* case. The WERC withheld action pending arbitration. The arbitrator found that the action of a principal (the individual charged) constituted coercion and discrimination within the meaning of the provisions of the contract, that the grievance had been resolved to the satisfaction of both parties, and that "clean hands" did not exist on either side of the case. He issued an award dismissing the grievance. The union urged before the WERC that the arbitrator had erred in his award by taking equity considerations into account. The WERC noted that it does not apply a "clean hands" doctrine, but found that further proceedings "would be redundant." The WERC noted that the arbitrator made it clear from his opinion that the principal's conduct was improper, and his discussion provides guidelines for future conduct.

Other States. Based on information from those states which responded to the committee's inquiry or those for which state agency cases were found, the following summarizes the positions in the states not discussed above:

These states have adopted both the *Collyer* and *Spielberg* doctrines either under statutory, judicial, or administrative auspices: Connecticut, Florida, Maine, New Jersey, Oregon, and Pennsylvania. The New York City Office of Collective Bargaining and the New York Port Authority also have adopted both doctrines.

The following states have adopted *Collyer*, all or in part, but have not adopted or, in some instances, have not been confronted with *Spielberg:* Delaware, Hawaii, Indiana, Vermont, and Washington.

Nebraska has adopted neither *Spielberg* nor *Collyer.*

Acknowledgements

The Chairperson deeply appreciates the scholarly contributions of the following committee members: Reginald Alleyne, on the constitutionality of SEERA; Arvid Anderson, on develop-

---

[93] *Id.*
[94] *Id.*

ments in New York City and State; Leon B. Applewhaite, on the
Federal Labor Relations Authority and new federal legislation;
Frederick H. Bullen, on developments in the U.S.; Irwin J. Dean,
Jr., assisted by Richard Dissen, on arbitration and employee
lifestyle; Milton Edelman, assisted by Elaine Edelman, on inter-
est arbitration; Philip Feldblum, on developments in New York
State; Morris A. Horowitz, on police and firefighters in Massa-
chusetts; Robert G. Howlett, on *Spielberg/Collyer* in the States;
Myron Joseph, on developments in Pennsylvania and West Vir-
ginia; Thomas N. Rinaldo, assisted by Donald P. Goodman, on
dispute resolution in Canada; Josef P. Sirefman, on the Federal
Service Impasses Panel; Henry L. Sisk, on developments in
Texas; Howard W. Solomon, on the Federal Services Impasses
Panel; Herman Torosian, on developments in Wisconsin; Helen
M. Witt, on developments in Delaware, Maryland, and Virginia.

The Chairperson also wishes to thank Barbra L. Davis, Research Assistant, Institute of Industrial Relations, UCLA, for her
assistance in the preparation of this report.

CUMULATIVE AUTHOR INDEX*
1973–1981

A

Aaron, Benjamin
Labor-Management Relations in a Controlled and Rationed Economy (comment on); 1974   171
Should Arbitrators Be Licensed or "Professionalized"?; 1976   152

Adair, J. Leon
Arbitration of Discrimination Grievances (comment on); 1980   295

Adair, Thomas S.
Arbitration of Wage and Manning Disputes in the Newspaper Industry; 1973   31

Adams, Walter L.
Judicial Review of Labor Arbitration Awards: A Second Look at Enterprise Wheel *and Its Progeny* (comment on); 1977   52

Aksen, Gerald
Post-Gardner-Denver Developments in Arbitration Law; 1975   24

Alleyne, Reginald
Courts, Arbitrators, and the NLRB: The Nature of the Deferral Beast; 1980   240

Anderson, Arvid
Lessons From Interest Arbitration in the Public Sector: The Experience of Four Jurisdictions; 1974   59
Outer Limits of Interest Arbitration: Australian, Canadian, and United States Experiences: III. The U.S. Experience; 1981   94

Significant Developments in Public Employment Disputes Settlement During 1973 (Report of the Committee on Public Employment Disputes Settlement); 1974   291
Significant Developments in Public Employment Disputes Settlement During 1974 (Report of the Committee on Public Employment Disputes Settlement); 1975   297
Significant Developments in Public Employment Disputes Settlement During 1975 (Report of the Committee on Public Employment Disputes Settlement); 1976   287
Significant Developments in Public Employment Disputes Settlement During 1976 (Report of the Committee on Public Employment Disputes Settlement); 1977   311

Arthurs, Harry W.
Future Directions for Labor Arbitration and for the Academy: I. Arbitration: Process or Profession?; 1977   222

Ashe, Bernard F.
Due Process and Fair Representation in Grievance Handling in the Public Sector (comment on); 1977   147

Asher, Lester
The Individual Employee's Rights Under the Collective Agreement: What Constitutes Fair Representation (comment on); 1974   31

---

*For the Cumulative Author Index covering the period 1948 through 1972, refer to Labor Arbitration at the Quarter-Century Mark, Proceedings of the 25th Annual Meeting of the National Academy of Arbitrators, eds. Barbara D. Dennis and Gerald G. Somers (Washington: BNA Books, 1973), 355 *et seq.*

TOPICAL INDEX

377